CHINESE-ENGLISH COLLECTION OF REGULATIONS FOR PUDONG NEW AREA AND MANAGEMENT MEASURES (2021—2023)

浦东新区法规和管理措施（2021—2023）汇编

（中英对照）

浦东新区法规和管理措施汇编编委会 编译

法律出版社 LAW PRESS · CHINA

北京

图书在版编目（CIP）数据

浦东新区法规和管理措施（2021-2023）汇编：汉英对照/浦东新区法规和管理措施汇编编委会编译.
北京：法律出版社，2024. -- ISBN 978-7-5197-9857-4

Ⅰ. D927.513.09

中国国家版本馆CIP数据核字第2024GP8924号

浦东新区法规和管理措施（2021—2023）汇编
（中英对照）
PUDONG XINQU FAGUI HE GUANLI CUOSHI (2021-2023) HUIBIAN (ZHONG-YING DUIZHAO)

浦东新区法规和管理措施汇编编委会　编译

策划编辑 朱　峰
责任编辑 韩泓宇
装帧设计 贾丹丹

出版发行 法律出版社
编辑统筹 辞书·融出版编辑部　法律翻译与出版研发中心
责任校对 马秋婧
责任印制 吕亚莉
经　　销 新华书店

开本 787毫米×1092毫米　1/16
印张 34.25　**字数** 798千
版本 2024年12月第1版
印次 2024年12月第1次印刷
印刷 北京虎彩文化传播有限公司

地址：北京市丰台区莲花池西里7号（100073）
网址：www.lawpress.com.cn
投稿邮箱：info@lawpress.com.cn
举报盗版邮箱：jbwq@lawpress.com.cn

销售电话：010-83938349
客服电话：010-83938350
咨询电话：010-63939796

书号：ISBN 978-7-5197-9857-4
定价：208.00元

凡购买本社图书，如有印装错误，我社负责退换。电话：010-83938349

序　言

以习近平同志为核心的党中央对上海市浦东新区（以下简称浦东）发展一直高度重视并寄予厚望。2020 年 11 月，时逢浦东开发开放 30 周年，习近平总书记亲临浦东，勉励浦东勇于挑最重的担子、啃最硬的骨头，努力成为更高水平改革开放的开路先锋、全面建设社会主义现代化国家的排头兵和彰显“四个自信”的实践范例。2021 年 4 月，中共中央、国务院印发《关于支持浦东新区高水平改革开放打造社会主义现代化建设引领区的意见》（以下简称《引领区意见》），标志着浦东立足新发展阶段，肩负起新使命，踏上更高水平改革开放的新征程。

新征程的行稳致远离不开法治固根本、稳预期、利长远的强有力保障。《引领区意见》明确授权上海市人民代表大会及其常务委员会（以下简称上海市人大及其常委会）立足浦东改革创新实践需要，遵循宪法规定以及法律和行政法规基本原则，制定法规，可以对法律、行政法规、部门规章等作变通规定，在浦东实施；对暂无法律法规或明确规定的领域，支持浦东先行制定相关管理措施。2021 年 6 月，全国人民代表大会常务委员会作出授权上海市人大及其常委会制定浦东新区法规的决定；上海市人民代表大会常务委员会作出加强浦东新区高水平改革开放法治保障，制定浦东新区法规的决定。授权制定浦东新区法规和管理措施，为浦东“大胆试、大胆闯、自主改”提供了坚实的法治支撑。

获得授权以后，上海市和浦东新区建立健全法治保障相关体制机制，全力推动浦东新区法规和管理措施制定工作。截至 2023 年 12 月，形成了包括 18 部浦东新区法规和 21 部管理措施的法治保障成果。2024 年 3 月，上海市人民代表大会常务委员会法制工作委员会、上海市浦东新区人民代表大会法制委员会、上海市浦东新区司法局组建浦东新区法规和管理措施汇编编委会对上述成果进行汇编。汇编成果的出版是浦东法治保障成果的一次全面展示，纳入汇编的浦东新区法规和管理措施，以问题为导向，以创新为特色，聚焦浦东改革发展瓶颈问题，深化制度集成创新，主题涉及优化营商环境、推动新质生产力发展、推进城市建设和治理转型升级、加强生态文明建设等方面，具有鲜明的“小快灵”特色。

此外，本书还提供了制度文本的相应英译本。以书为媒，这是向世界展示浦东法治形象的一个窗口，将进一步提升浦东在国内外的知名度和影响力。事实上，本书所蕴含的国际化元素，不仅是制度文本的翻译，更重要的是制度创新内容吸收接轨国际，包括主动对标世界银行营商环境评估体系，对接国际高标准经贸规则，尊重国际商事惯例原则等，这也有助于浦东稳步扩大制度型开放，加快形成更具国际竞争力的治理能力和制度体系。

习近平总书记强调：“法律的生命力在于实施，法律的权威也在于实施。”从已出台浦东新区法规和管理措施成效评估及执法检查情况看，浦东新区法规和管理措施的引领示范效应、改革牵引效应、创新带动效应已初步彰显。透过本书，读者可以感受到浦东奋力推进中国式现代化的坚实步伐。

作为浦东法治保障的新形式，浦东新区法规和管理措施从诞生伊始就备受关注。浦东立法工作的每一步成长、每一点成果，都离不开中央部门的大力支持、上海市相关部门的全力配合，也少不了对民意的吸纳、对民智的汇集。在此，我们对长期以来关注、关心和支持立法工作的社会各界表示衷心的感谢！

我们也要感谢汇编成果翻译团队每一位成员的辛勤付出。浙江大学求是特聘教授屈文生，是一位在法律翻译领域深耕多年的优秀中青年学者，其带领团队完成了本书汇编成果的英译工作。其中，初译由华东政法大学副教授万立、讲师詹继续、研究生林海斌完成。屈文生、Adrian Dunbar（李安谆）、万立、詹继续、林海斌负责译文审校定稿工作。他们以严谨的态度和专业的技能，确保了翻译的高质量和高标准。我们还要感谢法律出版社法律翻译与出版研发中心朱峰女士和韩泓宇先生对本书顺利出版作出的贡献。

展望未来，我们将踔厉奋发、笃行不怠，以高质量立法为浦东高质量发展提供强有力的法治保障。我们也会定期组织开展浦东新区法规和管理措施翻译工作，以满足日益增长的国际交流需求，助力营造市场化、法治化、国际化一流营商环境，在浦东新区高水平改革开放、打造社会主义现代化建设引领区的新征程上不断贡献法治力量。

浦东新区法规和管理措施汇编编委会

2024年12月

Preface

The Central Committee of the Communist Party of China (CPC), with Comrade Xi Jinping at its core, has consistently placed great importance on and set high expectations for Shanghai Pudong New Area (hereinafter referred to as "Pudong")'s development. In November 2020, on the 30th anniversary of Pudong's establishment, General Secretary Xi Jinping visited Pudong, encouraging it to shoulder the most significant responsibilities and overcome the toughest challenges. He called on Pudong to become a pioneer in higher-level reform and opening-up, a trailblazer in building a modern socialist country, and a model showcasing the "Four-sphere Confidence". In April 2021, the Central Committee of CPC and the State Council issued the Opinions on Supporting the High-level Reform and Opening-up to Establish a Pilot Area for Modern Socialism in the Pudong New Area (hereinafter referred to as the "Opinions"), marking Pudong's entry into a new development phase with a new mission and a journey toward higher-level reform and opening-up.

This new journey requires robust legal guarantees to lay a solid foundation, stabilize expectations, and ensure long-term benefits. The Opinions explicitly authorized the Shanghai Municipal People's Congress and its Standing Committee to make Local Regulations based on Pudong's reform and innovation needs, adhering to the Constitution of the People's Republic of China and the basic principles of the Laws and Administrative Regulations. Such Local Regulations to be implemented in Pudong allow for adaptive provisions to Laws, Administrative Regulations, and Ministerial Rules. Moreover, for fields where there are currently no Laws, Regulations, or clear provisions, Pudong is authorized to take the lead in formulating relevant Management Measures. In June 2021, the Standing Committee of the National People's Congress passed an authorization decision granting the Shanghai Municipal People's Congress and its Standing Committee to formulate Regulations for Pudong New Area. Subsequently, the Standing Committee of the Shanghai Municipal People's Congress issued a decision to strengthen legal guarantees for Pudong's high-level reform and opening-up by formulating Regulations for

Pudong New Area. Such decisions provided a solid legal foundation for Pudong to experiment boldly, innovate boldly, and reform independently.

Following this authorization, Shanghai and Pudong established and improved related legal assurance systems and mechanisms, fully promoting the formulation of Regulations for Pudong New Area and Management Measures. By December 2023, these efforts had resulted in a legal framework comprising 18 Regulations for Pudong New Area and 21 Management Measures. In March 2024, the Compilation Committee was established, comprising the Legislative Affairs Committee of the Standing Committee of the Shanghai Municipal People's Congress, the Legislative Affairs Committee of the Pudong New Area People's Congress, and the Pudong New Area Department of Justice, to oversee the compilation of these legal achievements. With a focus on problem-solving and a commitment to innovation, these Regulations for Pudong New Area and Management Measures aim to address bottlenecks in Pudong's reform and development. They emphasize deepening institutional integration and innovation, tackling key areas such as optimizing the business environment, fostering new productive capacities, advancing urban development and governance, and promoting ecological sustainability. Notably, they stand out for their distinctive characteristics of being "targeted, agile, and adaptable".

This Chinese-English bilingual compilation serves as a platform to showcase Pudong's legal framework to a global audience, enhancing its recognition and influence both domestically and internationally. Beyond translating the legal texts, the compilation reflects an international outlook by incorporating institutional innovations aligned with global standards. These include adopting benchmarks from the World Bank's business environment assessment system, aligning with high-standard international economic and trade rules, and adhering to principles of international commercial practice. These efforts contribute to Pudong's progressive institutional openness, accelerating the development of globally competitive governance capabilities and institutional systems.

General Secretary Xi Jinping once emphasized that "the vitality of the law lies in its implementation, and its authority stems from effective enforcement." Evaluations of the effectiveness of the Regulations for Pudong New Area and Management Measures, along with law enforcement inspections, have highlighted their role in driving leadership, reform, and innovation. This book offers readers a glimpse into the significant progress Pudong is making toward advancing Chinese path to modernization.

As a pioneering approach to legal assurance, these Regulations for Pudong New Area and

Management Measures have garnered significant attention since their inception. Every milestone and achievement in Pudong's legislative journey has been made possible through the strong support of central authorities, the close collaboration of relevant municipal departments, and the valuable input and insights from the public. We sincerely thank all those who have shown care, provided support, and contributed to our legislative efforts over the years.

We extend our heartfelt gratitude to the translation team for their tireless efforts. Professor Qu Wensheng, a Qiushi Distinguished Professor at Zhejiang University, a renowned scholar with extensive experience in legal translation, has led the team in producing the English version of this compilation. The translation was completed by Zhan Jixu, Wan Li, and Lin Haibin from East China University of Political Science and Law. With the help of Adrian Dunbar, they conducted a thorough review and revision process, ensuring the highest standards of quality and accuracy. We also extend our thanks to Ms. Zhu Feng and Mr. Han Hongyu from the Legal Translation and Publication Center of Law Press·China for their valuable contributions to the publication of this book.

Looking to the future, we remain committed to diligent and steadfast efforts, ensuring strong legal support for Pudong's high-quality development through high-quality legislation. We will also continue to organize regular translations of the Regulations for Pudong New Area and Management Measures to meet the growing need for international collaboration. These initiatives aim to cultivate a world-class business environment that is market-driven, law-based, and globally oriented, providing legal momentum for Pudong's journey as a pilot area of high-level reform and opening-up for socialist modernization.

The Compilation Committee

December 2024

目　录

第一编　浦东新区法规
Part Ⅰ　Regulations for Pudong New Area

第二编 管理措施

Part Ⅱ Management Measures

第一编　浦东新区法规

Part Ⅰ　Regulations for Pudong New Area

上海市浦东新区深化“一业一证”改革规定

Provisions for the Pudong New Area of Shanghai Municipality on Advancing the Consolidated Business License Reform

上海市浦东新区深化“一业一证”改革规定

（2021年9月28日上海市第十五届人民代表大会常务委员会第三十五次会议通过）

第一条　为了持续深化“一业一证”改革，推动政府审批服务向以市场主体需求为中心转变，优化营商环境，根据有关法律、行政法规的基本原则，结合浦东新区实际，制定本规定。

第二条　本规定适用于浦东新区在市场主体注册登记后深化“一业一证”改革的相关管理服务活动。

本规定所称的“一业一证”改革，是指通过优化审批流程和集中审批程序，将市场主体进入特定行业涉及的多张许可证整合为一张行业综合许可证的改革举措。

第三条　浦东新区深化“一业一证”改革，应当坚持需求导向，再造审批管理服务流程，创新制度供给；坚持系统集成，建立市场主体全生命周期集成服务机制，落实放管结合；坚持重点突破，激发市场主体发展活力，助力产业发展。

第四条　浦东新区人民政府应当加强深化“一业一证”改革的组织领导，建立健全深化改革的统筹推进工作机制。

浦东新区审批制度改革部门负责组织协调“一业一证”改革工作，开展改革满意度社会评价，总结提炼改革创新举措。

Provisions for the Pudong New Area of Shanghai Municipality on Advancing the Consolidated Business License Reform

(Adopted at the 35th Session of the 15th Shanghai Municipal People's Congress Standing Committee on September 28, 2021)

Section 1 The Provisions for the Pudong New Area of Shanghai Municipality on Advancing the Consolidated Business License Reform (these "Provisions") are formulated to continue the One Integrated License reform, promote the transfer of government approval into market-oriented service and optimize the business environment, pursuant to the basic principles of applicable laws and administrative regulations, and in light of the actual circumstances in the Pudong New Area.

Section 2 These Provisions shall apply to the administration of services provided as part of the initiative to advance the Consolidated Business License reform for market entities registered in the Pudong New Area.

"Consolidated Business License reform" in these Provisions refers to the refinements made to the reform that will consolidate multiple industry-specific licenses into one Consolidated Business License through streamlined and centralized approval processes.

Section 3 The Consolidated Business License reform in the Pudong New Area shall be demand-driven. The review service process is to be reorganized, with the aim of innovating the institutional supply and a focus on system integration, establishing integrated lifecycle service processes, and enforcing requirements for simplified administrative procedures, as well as breakthroughs in key areas to enhance the vitality of market entities and drive industrial development.

Section 4 The Pudong New Area People's Government shall improve organization and coordination to advance the Consolidated Business License reform and establish effective coordination work systems for its ongoing enhancement.

The Pudong New Area review reform department takes charge of organizing and coordinating Consolidated Business License reform activities, conducting public satisfaction surveys, and reflecting on potential innovative reforms.

浦东新区有关审批部门依据职权或者接受委托，负责具体有关行政许可的受理、审查、决定以及相应的事中事后监管等工作。

浦东新区行政审批局负责行业综合许可证的具体办理工作。

第五条 浦东新区应当根据国家和本市改革部署，编制“一业一证”改革行业清单。

对纳入“一业一证”改革的行业，浦东新区人民政府应当确定牵头管理部门和协同管理部门。牵头管理部门负责协调指导该行业“一业一证”改革中的审批、监管、服务等工作，组织制定统一适用于该行业的综合许可细则，建立健全行业综合许可全流程管理和综合监管制度。

第六条 浦东新区应当深入推进政务服务“一网通办”，开设“一业一证”线上专栏和线下专窗。申请人可以通过“一网通办”平台，查询“一业一证”改革行业，获取集成该行业全部准入条件的告知单和申请表，并进行线上办理。

申请人的申请由浦东新区行政审批局统一收件后，各有关审批部门应当并联审批、限时办结，并由行政审批局统一制作、送达行业综合许可证等文书。

第七条 行业综合许可证是“一业一证”改革行业经营活动涉及的多项行政许可的效力集成，是确认市场主体取得相关行政许可、获得行业准营资格的证明。

各有关国家机关应当对行业综合许可证的效力予以认可，对有关行业准入涉及的单项行政许可不再单独受理、发证；在相关管理服务活动中，不得要求市场主体提供单项行政许可证件。

The appropriate review department in the Pudong New Area, *motu proprio* or upon being commissioned, takes charge of accepting, reviewing, and deciding on applications for specific business licenses and managing the regulation during and after licensing.

The Pudong New Area administrative review agency takes charge of the administration of the Consolidated Business License process.

Section 5 An industry list for the Consolidated Business License reform shall be prepared for the Pudong New Area based on national and municipal reform policies.

The Pudong New Area People's Government shall designate the lead and support departments for the industries covered by the reform. The lead department takes charge of guiding the review, regulation, and services, and organizes the creation of consolidated licensing rules for the industry and the development of stable, integrated, and full-process administration and regulation systems.

Section 6 The Pudong New Area integrated online government service platform shall be expanded to include an online Consolidated Business License section, together with offline service counters. Applicants may check which industries are covered by the reform, obtain the notice on the consolidation of access conditions for a particular industry and the corresponding application form, and complete application procedures online.

Applications shall be collected by the Pudong New Area administrative review agency and subject to parallel processing by the appropriate departments within specified timelines. The administrative review agency shall prepare and issue the consolidated licenses and other documentation.

Section 7 A Consolidated Business License validates the recognition of the several administrative licenses required to operate in any of the industries covered by the reform and asserts the market entity's compliance with appropriate administrative and industry access requirements.

Appropriate national agencies shall recognize the Consolidated Business License and may no longer accept applications or issue licenses for single, industry-specific administrative matters; they shall not require market entities to provide individual specific business licenses for the associated administrative activities or services.

第八条 对纳入“一业一证”改革的行业，浦东新区应当建立行业综合许可证统一有效期制度。单项行政许可设定的有效期，整合为行业综合许可证后可以取消或者延长。

行业综合许可证所整合的单项行政许可变更或者失效的，相关行政审批部门应当同步调整该行业综合许可证的相应信息。

第九条 对纳入“一业一证”改革的行业涉及的场所、设备、人员、资金、管理制度等审批条件，可以实行告知承诺制，允许申请人以告知承诺书替代证明符合相关审批条件的材料，但是直接涉及国家安全、国家秘密、意识形态安全、公共安全、金融业审慎监管、生态环境保护、人身健康、生命财产安全的除外。

支持浦东新区探索实行基于“一业一证”改革的市场准营承诺即入制。

第十条 对纳入“一业一证”改革的行业，应当依托“一网统管”平台，通过“双告知、双反馈、双跟踪”证照衔接机制和“双随机、双评估、双公示”协同监管机制，实行对市场主体全生命周期的动态监管、风险监管、信用监管和分类监管。

行业监管部门与市场监督管理部门应当做好业务系统对接和工作衔接，方便市场主体在公示信息时一并填报经营活动的有关信息。

第十一条 浦东新区应当建立深化“一业一证”改革长效机制，针对行业综合许可单轨制、行业综合许可证统一有效期制度、市场准营承诺即入制等改革举措，结合改革创新实践编制改革举措清单，及时动态调整，并向社会公布。

Section 8 A centralized system shall be created to manage validity periods for Consolidated Business Licenses to operate in the industries included in the reform. The validity period of any specific business license may be canceled or extended upon its consolidation into the Consolidated Business License.

Should any specific business license consolidated into the Consolidated Business License be modified or expire, the appropriate administrative review agency shall update the information in the Consolidated Business License.

Section 9 Applicants may submit a declaration of compliance in lieu of documentation for matters subject to review, such as premises, equipment, staff, financial resources, and management systems, for industries covered by the Consolidated Business License reform that do not affect national security, state secrets, ideological security, public safety, prudential regulation for financial industry, ecological and environmental protection, and the health and safety of individuals and property.

The Pudong New Area receives support to pilot the implementation of the market access commitment system based on the Consolidated Business License reform.

Section 10 Market entities in industries included in the Consolidated Business License reform shall be subject to full dynamic lifecycle regulation covering risks, credits, and categories through the integrated online platform that includes synchronized notifications, reports, and tracking, and systems for dual sampling, evaluation, and public disclosures.

The industrial and market regulatory departments shall integrate their service systems to facilitate the public disclosure of market entity operational information.

Section 11 The Pudong New Area shall establish a long-term mechanism on advancing the Consolidated Business License reform, dynamically prepare the list of innovative reform measures on the single administrative license, unified validity period of consolidated license, and market access commitment system, and make the list known to the public.

第十二条　本市建立与“一业一证”改革相适应的政务信息共享机制。对纳入“一业一证”改革的行业，有关部门和单位应当将市场主体的许可、年报、处罚、信用、电子证照等信息，及时、准确共享至浦东新区有关部门，不得要求市场主体重复填报。

涉及“一业一证”改革的市级相关部门，应当优化完善相关业务应用系统，及时与浦东新区“一业一证”申办系统对接，建立数据交换机制，保障“一业一证”改革的深化实施。

第十三条　市人民政府及其有关部门应当积极争取国家有关部门对浦东新区深化“一业一证”改革的支持，加大赋权力度，帮助解决改革中的问题，及时总结推广改革经验。

第十四条　纳入“一业一证”改革的行业，不改变该行业行政许可实施的法律关系。浦东新区行政审批局应当建立行政复议和行政诉讼咨询服务机制，将行政复议被申请人和行政诉讼被告告知相关当事人。

第十五条　本规定自 2021 年 10 月 1 日起施行。

Section 12 This Municipality creates a government information-sharing system appropriate for the Consolidated Business License reform. Appropriate departments shall share information on licenses, annual reports, penalties, credit statuses, and electronic certificates with municipal departments in a prompt and accurate manner, eliminating the need for multiple information submissions.

The municipal departments involved in the Consolidated Business License reform shall improve their service systems to ensure prompt integration with the Consolidated Business License application system for the Pudong New Area, create a data exchange process, and ensure the continued implementation of the reform.

Section 13 The Municipal People's Government shall, together with the appropriate departments, proactively seek national support for the Consolidated Business License reform in the Pudong New Area, improve the delegation of authority, address issues arising during reform, and document and disclose reform experiences for broader application.

Section 14 The legal relationships governed by administrative licensing for industries subject to the Consolidated Business License reform shall remain unchanged. The Pudong New Area administrative review agency shall set up the service process for administrative reconsideration and litigation inquiries, and notify all parties involved about respondents in administrative reconsiderations and defendants in administrative lawsuits.

Section 15 These Provisions shall take effect from October 1, 2021.

上海市浦东新区市场主体退出若干规定

Several Provisions for the Pudong New Area of Shanghai Municipality on Market Entity Exit

上海市浦东新区市场主体退出若干规定

（2021 年 9 月 28 日上海市第十五届人民代表大会常务委员会第三十五次会议通过）

第一条 为了深化“放管服”改革，畅通市场主体退出渠道，完善优胜劣汰的市场机制，优化营商环境，根据有关法律、行政法规的基本原则，结合浦东新区实际，制定本规定。

第二条 本规定适用于在浦东新区的市场监督管理部门（以下称“登记机关”）注册登记的有限责任公司、非公司企业法人、合伙企业和个人独资企业等市场主体退出及相关管理活动。

本规定所称的市场主体退出，包括简易注销、承诺制注销，以及登记机关依职权作出的强制除名和强制注销。

第三条 市场主体未发生债权债务、已将债权债务清偿完结或者具有国家规定的其他情形的，可以适用简易注销程序。

市场主体申请简易注销登记的，应当通过国家企业信用信息公示系统（以下称“公示系统”）或者政府网站公示拟申请简易注销登记以及全体投资人承诺等信息，公示期为十日。

市场主体注销依法须经批准或者市场主体存在股权（财产份额）被冻结、出质，有正在被立案调查或者采取行政强制、司法协助以及国家规定的其他情形的，不适用简易注销程序。

Several Provisions for the Pudong New Area of Shanghai Municipality on Market Entity Exit

(Adopted at the 35th Session of the 15th Shanghai Municipal People's Congress Standing Committee on September 28, 2021)

Section 1 The Several Provisions for the Pudong New Area of Shanghai Municipality on Market Entity Exit (these "Provisions") is formulated to advance reform initiatives in the delegation of authority, streamlining administration, optimizing government services, simplifying market entity exit process, improving market competition, and improving the business environment, pursuant to the basic principles of the applicable laws and administrative regulations, and in light of the actual circumstances in the Pudong New Area.

Section 2 These Provisions shall apply to the exit of market entities, including limited liability companies, unincorporated entities with juristic personality, partnerships, and sole proprietorships, registered with market regulation departments in the Pudong New Area (the "registration office") and the associated administrative activities.

"Market entity exit" in these Provisions includes summary deregistration and deregistration by commitment, as well as involuntary removal and involuntary deregistration enforced by the registration office *motu proprio*.

Section 3 Where market entities have no existing claims or debts, have fully settled their claims or debts, or have other circumstances provided by the state, they may pursue a summary deregistration procedure.

A market entity applying for summary deregistration procedure shall disclose its proposed application and commitment from all investors on the National Enterprise Credit Information Publicity System (the "Publicity System") or the government website. The publicity period is ten days.

Those market entities legally required to obtain approval for the deregistration, having their equity interests frozen or pledged, subject to investigation or administrative enforcement, judicial assistance, or other circumstances provided by the state shall be ineligible for summary deregistration procedure.

第四条　市场主体决议解散后无法完成清算，具备下列条件的，可以适用承诺制注销：

（一）非公司企业法人主管部门（出资人）、合伙企业全体合伙人等承诺对市场主体的所有债务依法承担责任，并对因市场主体未清算造成的损害承担连带责任；

（二）市场主体的债务有担保的，担保人承诺继续承担责任。

市场主体有本规定第三条第三款所列情形的，不适用承诺制注销。

第五条　市场主体拟申请承诺制注销的，应当通知债权人，并通过公示系统或者政府网站公示承诺事项，公示期为四十五日。登记机关应当同时将市场主体拟申请承诺制注销的相关信息推送至同级税务、人力资源社会保障等部门。

有关利害关系人及相关政府部门在公示期内未向登记机关提出异议的，市场主体可以提出承诺制注销申请。登记机关应当对申请材料进行形式审查。申请材料齐全、符合法定形式的应当当场作出准予注销登记的决定；不能当场作出的，应当在三个工作日内作出决定；情形复杂的，经登记机关负责人批准，可以再延长三个工作日。

第六条　市场主体被吊销营业执照、责令关闭或者撤销的，清算义务人应当依法组织清算；满六个月未办理清算组公告或者申请注销登记的，登记机关可以作出强制除名决定。

强制除名决定应当向市场主体的住所地或者先行确认的送达地送达，并可以通过公示系统或者政府网站公告送达，公告期为六十日。

第七条　强制除名决定生效后，产生以下法律后果：

Section 4 A market entity opting to dissolve but unable to complete liquidation may apply for the deregistration by commitment if:

(1) the controlling shareholders (investors) of an unincorporated entity or all partners in a partnership agree to assume liability for all the entity's debts and to be held jointly and severally liable for damages resulting from the failure to complete the liquidation; and

(2) guarantors of secured debts agree to assume liability.

Market entities falling under Paragraph 3 of Section 3 of these Provisions shall be ineligible for the deregistration by commitment.

Section 5 A market entity purposing to apply for the deregistration by commitment shall notify creditors and disclose its commitment through the Publicity System or government website. The publicity period is forty-five days. The registration office shall forward the details of the entity's proposed deregistration to similar agencies involved, including tax and human resources and social security departments.

The market entity may then file an application for the deregistration by commitment if no objections from interested parties or administrative departments are raised during the publicity period. The registration office shall conduct a formal evaluation of the application documents. If the documents are complete and meet legal requirements, deregistration shall be approved on the spot. Otherwise, the registration office shall issue the decision within three business days. The review period may be extended for an additional three business days for complex matters, with the approval of the registration office director.

Section 6 If a market entity has its business license revoked, is ordered to close business, or has its business registration revoked, the liquidator shall complete liquidation lawfully. If no notice to form a liquidation committee or deregistration application is submitted within six months, the registration office may proceed with the involuntary removal of such entity.

The decision on such involuntary removal shall be sent to the market entity's registered address or previously provided postal address, and may be announced on the Publicity System or government website. The publicity period is sixty days.

Section 7 The following legal consequences occur when a decision to effect an involuntary removal is made:

（一）市场主体的营业执照（正本、副本）作废；

（二）以统一社会信用代码（注册号）代替市场主体的名称；

（三）除统一社会信用代码（注册号）、被强制除名时间和原因等信息外，市场主体的其他信息不再向社会公示；

（四）不再作为市场主体统计基数；

（五）市场主体状态作相应标记。

第八条　强制除名决定生效届满六个月，市场主体仍未办理清算组公告或者申请注销登记的，登记机关应当通过公示系统或者政府网站催告，并启动强制注销程序。

登记机关应当通过登记系统查询市场主体是否存在股权（财产份额）被冻结、出质以及投资设立其他市场主体的情况，并向同级人民法院、人力资源社会保障、税务部门和自然资源确权登记部门征询市场主体是否涉及审理、办理或者执行中的案件、拖欠职工工资、欠缴社会保险、欠缴税款及未结涉税事项等情形以及不动产权利登记情况。相关部门收到征询意见函后应当于十五个工作日内书面答复。

第九条　市场主体不存在本规定第八条第二款所列情形或者相关部门收到征询意见函后未作答复的，登记机关应当通过公示系统或者政府网站发布拟作出强制注销决定的公告。公告应当载明市场主体名称（统一社会信用代码）、债权人等利害关系人提出异议的方式、强制注销的后果等，公告期为六十日。

公告期满，登记机关应当作出强制注销决定，并向社会公布，但是公告期内有下列情形之一的除外：

(1) the market entity's business license (duplicate original and counterpart original) is to be invalidated;

(2) the market entity's name is to be replaced by its unified social credit code (registration number);

(3) other than details such as the unified social credit code and the time and cause for the involuntary deregistration, details of the market entity are no longer be publicly available;

(4) the market entity is to be excluded from the statistical base for market entities; and

(5) the status of the market entity is to be updated accordingly.

Section 8 If the market entity has not issued a liquidation committee notice or applied for deregistration within six months since the effect of the decision for the involuntary removal, the registration office shall issue a reminder through the Publicity System or government website, and effect the involuntary deregistration.

The registration office shall review the business entity registration system for any freezes, pledges on equity (property shares), or investments in the formation of other market entities and consult with people's courts, human resources and social security departments and taxation, and natural resource registration departments at the same level on whether the market entity is implicated in any trial, handling or ongoing enforcement, owes wages, social insurance contributions, or taxes, has unresolved tax issues, or property registrations. The appropriate departments shall provide a written response within fifteen business days of receiving the inquiry letter.

Section 9 If a market entity does not meet the conditions prescribed in Paragraph 2 of Section 8 of these Provisions, or if the appropriate departments fail to respond after receiving the inquiry letter, the registration office shall announce the proposed involuntary deregistration decision through the Publicity System or government website. The notice shall list the market entity's name (unified social credit code), methods for creditors and other interested parties to object, and consequences of involuntary deregistration. The publicity period is sixty days.

If no objections are raised during this period, the registration office shall proceed with the involuntary deregistration and announce the decision, unless any of the following circumstances arise during the said period:

（一）市场主体办理清算组公告或者申请注销登记的；

（二）利害关系人或者相关政府部门提出异议的。

强制注销决定可以通过公示系统或者政府网站公告送达，公告期为六十日。

第十条 强制注销决定生效后，市场主体资格终止。除因登记机关违反本规定的条件和程序作出决定外，强制注销决定不予撤销。

登记机关应当同步向同级人民法院、人力资源社会保障、税务和自然资源确权登记部门推送市场主体强制注销的信息。人力资源社会保障、税务等有关部门应当根据登记机关的推送信息，及时更新社会保险和税务登记等信息。

第十一条 因市场主体已经注销导致其分支机构或者其出资的市场主体无法办理注销等相关登记的，可以由该已经注销市场主体的继受主体或者投资人代为办理。

因市场主体之外的其他主体已经撤销或者注销导致其管理或者出资的市场主体无法办理注销等相关登记的，可以由该已经撤销或者注销主体的继受主体或者上级主管单位代为办理。

第十二条 市场主体在简易注销、承诺制注销程序中提交虚假材料或者采取其他欺诈手段隐瞒重要事实的，登记机关应当根据情形作出撤销注销登记等处理，并依法追究相应的法律责任。

市场主体未经清算被依法注销的，其清算义务人承担的组织清算义务不变。有关利害关系人认为其合法权益受到侵害的，有权通过民事诉讼向市场主体的投资人或者清算义务人等追究民事责任；构成犯罪的，依法追究刑事责任。

(1) the market entity has either issued a notice for liquidation or applied for deregistration; or

(2) interested parties or government departments object to the deregistration.

The involuntary deregistration decision may be published on the Publicity System or government website. The publicity period is sixty days.

Section 10 Upon the effectiveness of the involuntary deregistration decision, the qualification of the market entity shall be terminated. The involuntary deregistration decision shall not be revoked, unless the decision is made by the registration office in violation of the conditions and procedures provided for in these Provisions.

The registration office shall forward details of the involuntary deregistration to other agencies at the same level, including people's courts, human resources and social security departments, taxation, and natural resources registration departments. Departments such as human resources and social security and taxation shall promptly update the information based on the details received from the registration office.

Section 11 If a market entity's branch office or an entity in which it has invested is unable to complete deregistration or other relevant registration procedures due to the deregistration of the said market entity, the successor entity or investor of the deregistered market entity may handle the procedures on its behalf.

If the revocation of business registration or deregistration of an entity other than the market entity impacts another market entity's ability to manage deregistration procedures, the successor of such an entity or a superior competent authority may complete these procedures on its behalf.

Section 12 If a market entity submits fraudulent documents or intentionally conceals key details during the summary deregistration or deregistration by commitment, the registration office shall revoke the deregistration and hold such entities liable based on the circumstances.

A liquidator's obligation to manage the liquidation shall persist if a market entity is deregistered lawfully without prior liquidation. If interested parties believe their lawful rights and interests have been infringed, they may bring a civil suit against and hold the investors or the liquidator liable. Any market entity that is guilty of an offense shall be criminally liable.

第十三条 市市场监督管理部门负责组织协调全市市场主体退出改革推进工作，加强对浦东新区市场主体退出工作的支持。

浦东新区的市场监督管理部门负责实施优化市场主体退出登记程序，通过“一网通办”平台，推动市场主体退出全程线上办理。人力资源社会保障、税务、自然资源确权登记、大数据管理等相关部门应当落实信息共享、程序对接和协同办理等工作。

人民法院作出终结强制清算程序或者终结破产程序的裁定的，登记机关应当依据申请办理注销登记。

第十四条 本规定自2021年11月1日起施行。

Section 13 The municipal market regulation department shall organize and coordinate city-wide reforms for the market entity exit, and enhance support for the market entity exit in the Pudong New Area.

The competent market regulation department in the Pudong New Area shall implement optimized procedures for the market entity exit, ensuring the entire process can be completed online via the integrated online government service platform. Other competent departments, such as the human resources and social security, taxation, natural resources easement, and big data management, shall collaborate on information sharing and procedural integration.

Where the people's courts issue a ruling to terminate involuntary liquidation or bankruptcy proceedings, the registration office shall process the deregistration based on the application.

Section 14 These Provisions shall take effect from November 1, 2021.

上海市浦东新区建立高水平知识产权保护制度若干规定

Several Provisions for the Pudong New Area of Shanghai Municipality on Developing a High-level Intellectual Property Protection System

上海市浦东新区建立高水平知识产权保护制度若干规定

（2021 年 10 月 28 日上海市第十五届人民代表大会常务委员会第三十六次会议通过）

第一条　为了贯彻落实在浦东新区建立高水平知识产权保护制度的要求，强化知识产权全链条保护，率先构建制度完备、体系健全、环境优越的国际知识产权保护高地，根据法律、行政法规的基本原则，结合浦东新区实际，制定本规定。

第二条　浦东新区人民政府应当加强对知识产权保护工作的领导，统筹协调推进知识产权保护工作中的重大事项，整合优化知识产权保护工作资源，完善知识产权统一管理的体制机制和综合服务平台建设，全面推进知识产权领域综合执法，加强知识产权保护的教育宣传和经费保障。

浦东新区知识产权部门负责知识产权保护工作的统筹协调和组织实施，开展国家知识产权部门相关业务在浦东新区的综合受理，依据职权或者接受委托综合行使相关部门在知识产权领域的行政执法权，配合国家知识产权部门开展集成电路布图设计行政执法。

浦东新区知识产权保护中心建立健全知识产权事务“一站式”保护机制，对接国家知识产权保护平台，推动国家知识产权事务在浦东新区“一网通办”，并可以依托“一网统管”平台协助开展前款规定的相关行政执法工作。

Several Provisions for the Pudong New Area of Shanghai Municipality on Developing a High-level Intellectual Property Protection System

(Adopted at the 36th Session of the 15th Shanghai Municipal People's Congress Standing Committee on October 28, 2021)

Section 1 The Several Provisions for the Pudong New Area of Shanghai Municipality on Developing a High-level Intellectual Property Protection System (these "Provisions") are formulated to establish a comprehensive intellectual property protection system, enhance comprehensive intellectual property protection, and position the Pudong New Area as a global leader in intellectual property protection by creating a robust and supportive environment, pursuant to the basic principles of applicable laws and administrative regulations, and in light of the actual circumstances in the Pudong New Area.

Section 2 The Pudong New Area People's Government shall promote the leadership of intellectual property protection initiatives, enhance coordination, solve key issues, integrate resources, develop a unified management and comprehensive service system, advance comprehensive enforcement, as well as improve education, public awareness, and financial support for intellectual property protection.

The Pudong New Area intellectual property administration takes charges of coordinating and implementing intellectual property protection initiatives, managing service requests from the national intellectual property administration, exercising administrative enforcement authority, and cooperating with the national intellectual property administration on law enforcement of integrated circuit layout designs.

The Pudong New Area Intellectual Property Protection Center develops and enhances a comprehensive intellectual property protection system linked to the national intellectual property protection platform to facilitate comprehensive processing of intellectual property matters in the Pudong New Area, and uses the integrated online platform to support the administrative enforcement work described in the preceding paragraph.

第三条 浦东新区知识产权部门应当对生物医药、高端装备制造、新一代信息技术等领域拟报请加快审查的专利申请，根据国家知识产权部门的规定提供预审服务。

浦东新区知识产权部门应当配合国家知识产权部门开展专利复审无效案件优先审查、专利无效案件远程视频审理等快速确权服务，推进专利确权案件与行政裁决案件联合审理。

第四条 单位和个人在实施专利、进入国外市场前或者拟上市等阶段，委托专业机构对产品或者技术是否侵犯他人专利权进行专利实施调查并获取专利实施调查报告的，可以作为判断是否故意侵权的参考依据。

第五条 在涉及公共利益的著作权侵权行政执法程序中，被投诉人主张其不承担侵权责任的，应当提供证据证明已经取得权利人的许可，或者具有法律规定的不经权利人许可而可以使用的情形。被投诉人不能提供或者提供的证据不足以推翻投诉人提供的侵权证据的，可以认定被投诉人的行为构成侵犯著作权。

第六条 单位和个人恶意申请商标注册的，应当对申请人给予警告，有违法所得的，可以并处违法所得五倍最高不超过五万元的罚款；没有违法所得的，可以并处三万元以下的罚款。

第七条 禁止任何单位和个人实施下列违反地理标志保护规定的行为:

（一）通过使用地理标志产品名称或者产品描述，使公众误认为该产品来自获得保护的地理标志产地范围的；

（二）在产地范围之外的相同或者类似产品上使用获得保护的地理标志产品名称或其意译、音译、字译，或者同时使用“类”、“型”、“式”、“仿”等表述的；

Section 3 The Pudong New Area intellectual property administration shall offer pre-application services for patent applications in fields such as biopharmacy, advanced equipment manufacturing, and cutting-edge information technology, to ensure expedited examination pursuant to national intellectual property administration's guidelines.

The Pudong New Area intellectual property administration shall work with the national intellectual property administration to prioritize and expedite patent services, such as reexamination of patent invalidations, remote video hearings for patent invalidation cases, and facilitate coordinated administrative adjudication for patent ownership cases.

Section 4 Entities or individuals shall entrust professional agencies to carry out patent clearance searches when commercializing patents, entering international markets, or launching new products to identify any potential patent infringements. Search reports may then be used as a reference when determining whether a patent infringement is deliberate.

Section 5 During administrative enforcement for copyright infringement involving the public interest, respondents who deny such infringement allegation shall prove their right to use the disputed work either through licensing from the rightsholder or as permitted by law to use such work. Failure to provide adequate proof of such rights shall imply copyright infringement.

Section 6 Entities or individuals submitting trademark applications in bad faith shall be issued a warning, and may be subject to fines of up to five times the amount of any illegal proceeds generated, with a maximum of RMB 50,000. A fine of up to RMB 30,000 may be imposed if no illegal proceeds are generated.

Section 7 The following actions are prohibited:

(1) misleading the public with names or descriptions that suggest a product originates from a protected destination of origin when it does not;

(2) using the name of a protected geographical indication product name, or its direct translation, phonetic transcription, or transliteration, on identical or similar products originating outside the protected area, or describing such goods by appending terms like "class," "type," or "imitation" to the geographical indication product name;

（三）未经批准擅自在产品上使用地理标志专用标志的；

（四）在产品上使用与地理标志专用标志相似的标志，使公众误认为是地理标志专用标志的；

（五）销售上述产品的。

违反前款规定的，责令立即停止违法行为，没收、销毁违法生产、销售的产品和伪造地理标志专用标志的工具；违法经营额五万元以上的，可以处违法经营额五倍以下的罚款，没有违法经营额、违法经营额难以计算或者违法经营额不足五万元的，可以处二十五万元以下的罚款。销售不知道是违反前款规定的产品，能够证明该产品是自己合法取得并说明提供者的，责令停止销售。

第八条　在商业秘密行政执法程序中，商业秘密权利人提供初步证据，证明其已经对所主张的商业秘密采取保密措施，且合理表明商业秘密被侵犯，涉嫌侵权人应当证明权利人所主张的不属于商业秘密或者其不存在侵犯商业秘密的行为。

对于侵犯商业秘密的行为，除依据《中华人民共和国反不正当竞争法》的规定处理外，还应当责令侵权人返还或者销毁载有商业秘密的图纸、软件或者其他有关载体，不得继续披露、使用或者允许他人使用商业秘密。侵权人利用权利人的商业秘密生产的产品，尚未销售的，应当监督侵权人销毁，但是权利人同意收购或者同意侵权人继续销售的除外。

权利人向人民法院请求返还或者销毁载有商业秘密的图纸、软件或者其他有关载体，清除其控制的商业秘密信息的，人民法院应予支持。

第九条　会展活动举办单位不得允许未提交知识产权合规承诺或者相关知识产权权属证明的参展方参加展会。

(3) unauthorized use of protected destination of origin labels on products;

(4) using labels similar to those for protected destinations of origin in a manner that misleads the public into believing that the products originate from a protected destination of origin; and

(5) sales of any above-mentioned products.

Violators of the preceding paragraph shall be ordered to immediately stop all illegal activities, and any illegally produced or sold products, along with tools used to counterfeit geographic indication, shall be confiscated and destroyed. Violators shall be subject to fines of up to five times the illegal proceeds generated if illegal proceeds exceed RMB 50,000, or up to RMB 250,000 if illegal proceeds are not quantifiable or are less than RMB 50,000. Sellers who unknowingly violate these rules shall be ordered to immediately cease sales of such products, provided they prove that the products are obtained legally and disclose the name of the supplier.

Section 8 In administrative enforcement proceedings involving alleged trade secret infringement, the alleged infringer shall demonstrate that the alleged information is not a trade secret or that no infringement occurred, when the rightsholder has presented *prima facie* evidence of adopting confidentiality precautions for the trade secret, and reasonably indicates the infringement.

Infringements of trade secrets shall result in mandatory destruction or return of all carriers containing the secrets such as the drawings and software, a prohibition on their use, disclosure or granting others to use the secrets. The infringer shall be supervised to destroy all the unsold products derived from such secrets, unless the rightsholder agrees to purchase or grant the infringer for sale. These actions are in addition to those specified in the Anti-Unfair Competition Law of the People's Republic of China.

Any rightsholder's request to the people's court to return or destroy drawings, software, or other media containing trade secrets, or to delete any trade secret information obtained shall be granted.

Section 9 Trade fair organizers shall ensure all participants submit declarations of compliance or proof of intellectual property ownership.

参展项目被权利人投诉侵权的，会展活动举办单位应当立即要求参展方在限定时间内提供未侵权证明；参展方无法提供的，会展活动举办单位应当立即采取遮盖、下架展品或者取消参展资格等措施。

会展活动举办单位违反本条第一款、第二款规定的，给予警告，并可以处三万元以上十万元以下的罚款。

第十条 故意侵犯知识产权，情节严重的，人民法院可以根据规定按照权利人因被侵权所受到的实际损失、侵权人因侵权所获得的利益、许可使用费或者权利使用费倍数的一倍以上五倍以下确定赔偿数额；情节特别严重的，人民法院可以按照权利人因被侵权所受到的实际损失、侵权人因侵权所获得的利益、许可使用费或者权利使用费倍数的五倍以上十倍以下确定赔偿数额。权利人的实际损失、侵权人因侵权所获得的利益、许可使用费或者权利使用费难以计算的，由人民法院根据侵权行为的情节，判决给予一千万元以下的赔偿。

专利侵权纠纷司法判决、行政裁决生效后，再次侵犯同一专利权的，没收违法所得，并处违法经营额一倍以上五倍以下的罚款；没有违法经营额、违法经营额难以计算或者违法经营额不足五万元的，处五万元以上二十五万元以下的罚款。

因侵犯商业秘密被司法判决或者行政处罚，自司法判决、行政处罚决定生效之日起二年内再次侵犯商业秘密的，可以对侵权人从重处罚。

第十一条 浦东新区知识产权部门在知识产权纠纷立案前或者立案后，可以自行、委托或者移交相关组织进行调解，但是涉嫌犯罪的案件除外。

知识产权行政案件立案前达成调解协议并履行完毕的，可以不予立案。立案后达成调解协议并履行完毕的，可以从轻或者减轻处罚；没有损害第三人合法权益和公共利益的，可以免除处罚。

Trade fair organizers shall immediately require any participants alleged of infringement by rightsholders to submit proof disproving such allegation within a specific deadline, and organizers shall immediately take action against any participants unable to disprove the infringement, including but not limited to covering or removing displays, or removing participants from the trade fair.

Any organizer in violation of Paragraphs 1 and 2 of this Section shall be subject to warnings and a potential fine ranging from RMB 30,000 to RMB 100,000.

Section 10 For serious and intentional intellectual property infringements, the damages determined by the people's court may range from one to five times the actual losses suffered by the rightsholder due to the infringement, the value of the illegal proceeds, licensing fees, or royalties and may range from five to ten times in serious cases. If it is not possible to assess the actual losses, illegal proceeds, licensing fees or royalties, compensation capped at RMB 10 million may be awarded by the people's court based on the infringement's nature.

Repeat infringements of the same patent since the effect of the judgment or administrative decision shall result in the forfeiture of illegal proceeds and a fine ranging from one to five times the illegal proceeds shall be imposed. A fine ranging from RMB 50,000 to RMB 250,000 is to be imposed if the illegal proceeds are difficult to quantify or under RMB 50,000.

Any violator who is subject to prior punishment for trade secret infringements reoffends within two years since the execution of a prior judgment or administrative punishment shall be subject to a heavier punishment.

Section 11 The Pudong New Area intellectual property administration may independently mediate, outsource mediation, or refer disputes to designated organizations before or after initiating an intellectual property dispute, other than those implicated in criminal offenses.

Disputes may be exempted from filing the administrative proceedings if a mediation agreement is reached and executed prior to the initiation of administrative proceedings. Penalties may be extenuated or mitigated if a mediation agreement is reached and executed after the initiation of the proceeding, and penalties may be waived if no third-party rights or public interests are infringed.

第十二条 浦东新区人民法院应当明确相关审判组织统一审理管辖范围内的知识产权民事、行政和刑事案件。

高等院校、科研机构、知识产权服务机构等单位具有专门知识的人，经遴选可以担任知识产权案件的专家陪审员。

支持浦东新区人民法院在知识产权案件办理中探索书状先行模式。

第十三条 浦东新区人民检察院应当明确相关检察办案部门统一履行知识产权刑事、民事、行政和公益诉讼检察职能。

支持浦东新区人民检察院在地理标志、集体商标、药品专利等涉及公共利益的知识产权领域探索开展公益诉讼。

第十四条 支持浦东新区设立科创板拟上市企业知识产权服务站，依法为全国拟上市企业提供知识产权问询辅导、知识产权评估评价等服务。

第十五条 鼓励金融机构优化知识产权质押融资模式，建立融资担保风险分担机制，加大对中小企业、科技创新企业、文化创意企业的增信服务力度。

鼓励企业以高价值知识产权组合为基础构建底层知识产权资产，在能产生稳定现金流的前提下探索知识产权证券化模式。

第十六条 本规定自 2021 年 12 月 1 日起施行。

Section 12 The Pudong New Area People's Court shall designate specific court divisions to adjudicate all intellectual property litigations within their jurisdictions, including civil, administrative, and criminal proceedings.

Experts from higher education institutions, research institutes, intellectual property organizations, or intellectual property service fields may serve as expert witnesses in legal proceedings after selection.

The Pudong New Area People's Court shall receive support to research and prioritize document review processes for more effective handling of intellectual property litigation.

Section 13 The Pudong New Area People's Procuratorate shall designate specific prosecution divisions to standardize the prosecution of intellectual property criminal, civil, administrative, and public interest litigation.

The Pudong New Area People's Procuratorate is encouraged to research and prosecute public interest litigation in intellectual property areas such as collective trademarks, geographical indications, and pharmaceutical patents.

Section 14 Authorized intellectual property service centers assist firms seeking listing on the STAR Market of the Shanghai Stock Exchange in the Pudong New Area by lawfully providing nationwide intellectual property consultations, assessments, and evaluations.

Section 15 Financial institutions are encouraged to refine intellectual property pledge models, create a financial guarantee system for risk sharing, and increase credit facilities, particularly for small and medium-sized enterprises and those in technology innovation and culturally creative sectors.

Businesses generating stable cash flows are encouraged to develop intellectual property asset foundations for securitization using valuable intellectual property portfolios.

Section 16 These Provisions shall take effect from December 1, 2021.

上海市浦东新区城市管理领域非现场执法规定

Provisions for the Pudong New Area of Shanghai Municipality on Remote Law Enforcement in Urban Management

上海市浦东新区城市管理领域非现场执法规定

（2021 年 10 月 28 日上海市第十五届人民代表大会常务委员会第三十六次会议通过）

第一条 为了规范城市管理领域非现场执法工作，提高城市管理科学化、精细化、智能化水平，提升城市治理能力和治理成效，根据法律、行政法规的基本原则，结合浦东新区实际，制定本规定。

第二条 本规定适用于浦东新区城管执法部门运用非现场执法方式对违法行为进行查处的相关工作。

本规定所称的非现场执法，是指运用现代信息技术手段收集、固定违法事实，采用信息化等方式进行违法行为告知、调查取证、文书送达、罚款收缴等的执法方式。

第三条 浦东新区人民政府负责统筹协调有关部门推进非现场执法工作。

浦东新区城管执法部门负责非现场执法具体推进以及业务指导和监督，依托“一网统管”平台推动非现场执法工作。浦东新区发展改革、科技经济、公安、财政、人力资源社会保障、规划自然资源、市场监管等部门在各自职责范围内履行相关职能，为非现场执法工作提供协助与保障。

浦东新区街道办事处、镇人民政府负责完善本辖区社会各方共同参与的共建共治共享基层治理格局，开展城市管理领域非现场执法工作。

Provisions for the Pudong New Area of Shanghai Municipality on Remote Law Enforcement in Urban Management

(Adopted at the 36th Session of the 15th Shanghai Municipal People's Congress Standing Committee on October 28, 2021)

Section 1 The Provisions for the Pudong New Area of Shanghai Municipality on Remote Law Enforcement in Urban Management (these "Provisions") are formulated to regulate the work on remote law enforcement in urban management, and improve the effectiveness and efficiency of remote law enforcement in urban management through advanced, precise, and intelligent methods, pursuant to the basic principles of applicable laws and administrative regulations, and in light of the actual circumstances in the Pudong New Area.

Section 2 These Provisions shall apply to all activities of the Pudong New Area urban management and law enforcement department when investigating and addressing violations remotely.

"Remote law enforcement" in these Provisions refers to an enforcement approach utilizing modern information technology to identify and record violations, which involves using electronic means to notify offenders, conduct investigations, compile evidence, serve legal documents, and administer fines.

Section 3 The Pudong New Area People's Government takes charge of coordinating appropriate departments to support remote law enforcement activities.

The Pudong New Area urban management and law enforcement department takes charge of the comprehensive implementation, guidance, and monitoring of remote law enforcement activities via the integrated online platform. Various supporting departments, including development and reform, technology and economy, public security, finance, human resources and social security, planning and resources, and market regulation departments, shall each collaborate and support these remote law enforcement activities to the extent of their duties.

Pudong New Area sub-district offices and township governments take charge of improving community management with multi-party involvement to support remote urban management enforcement activities.

第四条　浦东新区城管执法部门查处城市管理领域多发易发、直观可见且依托信息化设备设施能够辨别、易于判断的违法行为，可以实施非现场执法。

浦东新区人民政府应当编制非现场执法事项清单，在政府网站公布，并及时动态调整。

第五条　浦东新区城管执法部门开展非现场执法工作应当依法行政，规范执法流程，坚持公平公正，做到高效与便民相一致、处罚与教育相结合、法律效果与社会效果相统一。

第六条　浦东新区城管执法部门开展非现场执法工作应当为当事人政策查询、陈述申辩、权利救济、责任履行等活动提供便利，充分保护当事人的合法权益。

第七条　浦东新区城管执法部门可以在道路、广场等公共场所以及具备条件的社区公共区域，利用电子技术监控设备收集、固定违法事实。

电子技术监控设备的安装使用应当经过法制审核和技术审核，确保电子技术监控设备符合国家标准或者行业标准。电子技术监控设备应当定期维护、保养、检测，保持功能完好。

电子技术监控设备分为固定式和移动式。固定电子技术监控设备设置的地点应当有明显可见的标识标志，并向社会公布。移动电子技术监控设备应当安装在统一标识的车辆上，监控区域应当向社会公布。

第八条　浦东新区城管执法部门应当建立相关信息数据库和信息平台，与新区公安、市场监管、民政、住房管理等部门建立信息互通共享机制。

浦东新区城管执法部门应当依据必要合理原则，依法规范采集行政相对人的相关主体身份信息，并对采集的个人信息按照有关法律、法规进行处理。

Section 4 The Pudong New Area urban management and law enforcement department may implement remote law enforcement in cases of repeat violations that can easily be detected electronically.

The Pudong New Area People's Government shall maintain and periodically update a public list of violations subject to remote law enforcement on its official website.

Section 5 Remote law enforcement by the Pudong New Area urban management and law enforcement department shall be conducted based on law, in strict compliance with procedural guidelines, fairness, justice, and ensure efficiency and convenience for the public, integrating corrective actions with educational initiatives, and aligning legal actions with social effects.

Section 6 The Pudong New Area urban management and law enforcement department shall provide convenience for parties concerned in policy inquiry, statements and defenses, remedies, and performance of responsibilities and others, and fully protect legitimate rights and interests of parties concerned.

Section 7 The Pudong New Area urban management and law enforcement department may use electronic monitoring devices in designated public areas and community spaces with specified criteria when collecting evidence of violations.

All electronic monitoring devices shall be subject to strict legal and technical reviews to ensure national and industry standard compliance. All electronic monitoring devices shall be regularly maintained, serviced, and tested for operational integrity.

The electronic monitoring device includes both fixed and mobile monitoring devices. Fixed monitoring devices shall be clearly marked and mapped publicly, while mobile monitoring devices be installed on distinctly marked vehicles, with the areas being monitored known to the public.

Section 8 The Pudong New Area urban management and law enforcement department shall cooperate with government departments in other sectors like public safety, market regulation, civil affairs, and housing administration to develop critical databases and sharing platforms to optimize information usage.

The collection of personal information of regulated entities by the Pudong New Area urban management and law enforcement department shall follow the principles of necessity and appropriateness, and such information shall be processed pursuant to applicable laws and regulations.

浦东新区街道办事处、镇人民政府应当发挥基层治理机制作用，协助城管执法部门落实基层信息规范采集和依法按需共享制度。

第九条 浦东新区城管执法部门可以通过视频、音频等方式开展询问调查。视频、音频询问时，应当表明执法人员身份，告知被询问人相关权利和义务。

视频、音频资料可以替代书面询问笔录。必要时，浦东新区城管执法部门应当对视频、音频资料的形成时间和关键内容等作文字说明。

第十条 浦东新区城管执法部门应当审核视听资料、电子数据记录的内容是否符合真实、清晰、完整、准确的要求。未经审核或者经审核不符合要求的，不得作为行政处罚的证据。

第十一条 浦东新区城管执法部门依据审核确认的证据，拟作出行政处罚的，可以采用电子邮件、短信、互联网应用程序、“一网通办”平台等信息化方式将违法事实、拟处罚内容、陈述申辩途径等告知当事人，要求其在指定时间内接受处理。

第十二条 浦东新区城管执法部门应当设置指定处理窗口，并采取信息化等方式为当事人陈述、申辩提供便利。

浦东新区城管执法部门应当及时对当事人提出的事实、理由和证据进行复核。当事人提出的事实、理由或者证据成立的，应当予以采纳，不得因当事人陈述、申辩而给予更重的行政处罚。

第十三条 浦东新区城管执法部门在非现场执法案件中制作的法律文书，可以使用电子公章和电子签名。

经当事人同意并签订确认书的，浦东新区城管执法部门可以采用电子邮件、短信、互联网应用程序等信息化方式送达行政处罚决定书等相关法律文书。

Sub-district offices and township governments shall work at the community level to regularize information gathering and share information as needed, enhancing local governance practices.

Section 9 The Pudong New Area urban management and law enforcement department may use video and audio tools for investigative purposes, with an obligation to disclose their identity and inform individuals of their rights and obligations during such interactions.

Recordings may replace written documents in investigation records, with essential details such as timestamps and content summaries provided by the Pudong New Area urban management and law enforcement department as necessary.

Section 10 The Pudong New Area urban management and law enforcement department shall confirm the integrity and accuracy of all audiovisual and digital evidence that cannot be used in administrative proceedings if they have not been reviewed or do not meet the required standards after review.

Section 11 If administrative penalties are warranted based on substantive evidence, the Pudong New Area urban management and law enforcement department may notify the implicated parties of their violations, potential penalties, and options for response through digital channels including emails, SMS, applications, the integrated online government service platform, providing a deadline for replies.

Section 12 The Pudong New Area urban management and law enforcement department shall set up designated service counters and leverage technology to help individuals present their cases and defenses more effectively.

Submissions by parties shall be promptly reviewed by the Pudong New Area urban management and law enforcement department, and credible facts, reasons, or evidence shall be accepted without imposing heavier punishment because of their statement or defense.

Section 13 The Pudong New Area urban management and law enforcement department may use electronic signatures and seals for legal documents related to remote law enforcement.

With a confirmation letter signed by the implicated parties, the Pudong New Area urban management and law enforcement department is authorized to electronically serve legal documents, such as administrative penalties, to implicated parties.

第十四条 当事人可以通过电子支付系统缴纳罚款。浦东新区城管执法部门应当开通电子支付系统缴纳罚款的途径，并出具财政部门统一制发的专用电子票据。

第十五条 对当事人的违法行为，浦东新区城管执法部门应当通过短信告知或者语音电话等方式进行劝阻教育，责令及时改正；当事人及时改正且违法行为轻微的，不予处罚。

第十六条 浦东新区城管执法部门应当制定信息数据保护规范，建立信息数据安全管理机制和信息数据查询制度，明确本单位工作人员的查询权限和查询程序，加强信息数据安全保护。

对于履行职责中知悉的当事人的个人信息、隐私或者商业秘密，浦东新区城管执法部门及其工作人员应当严格保密，不得泄露、出售或者非法向他人提供。

违反前款规定的，责令改正，并对直接负责的主管人员和其他直接责任人员依法给予处分。

第十七条 市城管执法部门应当加强对浦东新区城市管理领域非现场执法工作的监督和支持，制定处罚裁量基准，开展业务指导和执法监督。

浦东新区城管执法部门应当加强与相关部门的协同联动，完善前端管理、普法教育、街区包干、行业自治、小区自我管理等多元化治理机制，充分发挥基层组织、社区、物业服务企业等的积极作用，提升城市管理效能。

浦东新区城管执法部门应当加强非现场执法工作的宣传，增强市民自觉遵守城市管理规定的意识，共同维护城市管理秩序。

第十八条 本规定自 2021 年 12 月 1 日起施行。

Section 14 Fines may be paid using the digital payment system. The Pudong New Area urban management and law enforcement department shall provide channels for the payment of fines through electronic payment systems and issue special electronic receipts uniformly produced by the finance department.

Section 15 In cases of violations, the Pudong New Area urban management and law enforcement department shall contact violators via text or voice call to request immediate correction; parties who promptly address minor violations may be exempt from penalties.

Section 16 The Pudong New Area urban management and law enforcement department shall establish information and data protection standards, create a secure management system for information and data access and inquiries, and specify data access permissions and processes for their employees to improve information and data security.

Employees of the Pudong New Area urban management and law enforcement department shall keep any personal information, privacy or trade secrets acquired during their work strictly confidential, and the unauthorized disclose, sale, or transfer such information to third parties is strictly prohibited.

Employees in violation of the above shall be ordered to correct their violation, and their individuals directly responsible and others with direct responsibilities shall be subject to disciplinary actions lawfully.

Section 17 The municipal urban management and law enforcement department shall intensify support and oversight for remote law enforcement by establishing criteria for discretionary penalties and maintaining continuous operational guidance.

The Pudong New Area urban management and law enforcement department shall improve cooperation among government departments, and promote an integrated approach to urban management that includes early intervention, community education, localized accountability, and community-driven management.

The Pudong New Area urban management and law enforcement department shall improve citizens' awareness of urban management regulations and encourage compliance to help maintain urban management order.

Section 18 These Provisions shall take effect from December 1, 2021.

上海市浦东新区完善市场化法治化企业破产制度若干规定

Several Provisions for the Pudong New Area of Shanghai Municipality on Improving the Market-based and Law-based Enterprise Bankruptcy System

上海市浦东新区完善市场化法治化企业破产制度若干规定

（2021 年 11 月 25 日上海市第十五届人民代表大会常务委员会第三十七次会议通过）

第一条 为了进一步加强企业破产工作，完善市场化、法治化的企业破产制度，促进企业优胜劣汰和市场资源高效配置，持续优化营商环境，根据有关法律、行政法规的基本原则，结合浦东新区实际，制定本规定。

第二条 本规定适用于在浦东新区办理企业破产以及相关的管理、保障活动。

浦东新区人民法院设立破产审判内设机构，集中管辖市高级人民法院指定的破产与强制清算案件。

第三条 浦东新区应当建立区人民政府和区人民法院共同牵头、相关部门参加的企业破产工作府院协调机制，统筹推进企业破产相关工作，加强企业破产信息共享，协同研究解决企业破产办理的重大问题。

浦东新区人民政府应当切实发挥在企业破产工作中的公共管理和服务职能，保障破产工作所需相关经费，完善破产企业财产快速处置和职工合法权益保障等机制，并指定相关部门承担企业破产府院协调机制的日常工作。浦东新区发展改革、建设交通、市场监管、公安、商务、税务、金融工作、人力资源社会保障、规划资源、司法行政等部门应当按照各自职责，建立破产信息平台和查询中心，健全破产案件财产处置联动机制，保障破产管理人依法规范履职，协同做好企业破产办理相关行政事务。

Several Provisions for the Pudong New Area of Shanghai Municipality on Improving the Market-based and Law-based Enterprise Bankruptcy System

(Adopted at the 37th Session of the 15th Shanghai Municipal People's Congress Standing Committee on November 25, 2021)

Section 1 The Several Provisions for the Pudong New Area of Shanghai Municipality on Improving the Market-based and Law-based Enterprise Bankruptcy System (these "Provisions") are formulated to strengthen enterprise bankruptcy administration, enhance the market-based and law-based enterprise bankruptcy system, develop business competitiveness, improve resource efficiency, and continuously refine the business environment, pursuant to the basic principles of applicable laws and administrative regulations, and in light of the actual circumstances in the Pudong New Area.

Section 2 These Provisions shall apply to enterprise bankruptcy proceedings and associated administrative and assurance activities in the Pudong New Area.

The Pudong New Area People's Court is to establish a dedicated bankruptcy adjudication division to manage bankruptcy and involuntary liquidation cases assigned by the municipal high people's court.

Section 3 The Pudong New Area shall establish a government-court coordination mechanism for enterprise bankruptcy, jointly led by the District People's Government and the District People's Court, with participation from relevant departments, to promote information exchange, and address key issues in bankruptcy proceedings.

The Pudong New Area People's Government shall actively provide management and enterprise bankruptcy services, secure the necessary funding, create systems for expedited asset disposal and employee rights protection, and direct the appropriate department to regularly carry out the government-court coordination mechanism. Departments of development and reform, construction and transportation, market regulation, public security, commerce, taxation, financial regulation, human resources and social security, planning and resources, and judicial administration shall develop a bankruptcy information platform and inquiry center, improve asset disposal coordination systems, ensure compliance by the bankruptcy administrator, and facilitate administrative tasks associated with enterprise bankruptcy.

浦东新区人民法院应当推进破产审判专业化建设，完善支持企业庭外重组、预重整等破产拯救机制，完善破产案件繁简分流、简易程序快速审理等破产审判机制，提高破产案件办理的质量和效率。

第四条 企业董事、高级管理人员知道或者应当知道本企业出现《中华人民共和国企业破产法》第二条情形的，应当及时采取启动重组、向债权人披露经营信息、提请企业申请预重整或者破产重整、和解、清算等合理措施，避免企业状况继续恶化和财产减损。

企业董事、高级管理人员因故意或者重大过失违反前款规定造成企业财产损失，管理人或者债权人主张其在造成损失范围内向企业承担赔偿责任的，人民法院应当予以支持。

第五条 鼓励和引导企业在向人民法院申请破产重整前通过与债权人、出资人等利害关系人进行谈判协商，拟定重组方案。重整程序启动后，可以以重组方案为依据拟定重整计划草案提交人民法院依法审查批准。

对于具有挽救价值，且在短期内有实现重组可能的债务人，经债务人或者主要债权人申请，人民法院可以决定对企业进行预重整。申请人可以请求人民法院给予法律指导和监督，并协调政府有关部门依法给予必要的支持。

预重整中债务人与部分债权人已经达成的有关协议，与重整程序中拟定的重整计划草案内容一致的，该部分债权人对协议的同意视为对重整计划草案表决的同意。

第六条 在企业破产重整程序中，债权人未在人民法院确定的期限内申报债权的，不得在重整计划执行期间及重整保护期内行使权利。重整保护期为重整计划执行完毕后的一年期间。

The Pudong New Area People's Court shall promote professionalism in managing bankruptcy proceedings, refine out-of-court restructuring and pre-reorganization systems, streamline the resolution of complex and summary proceedings, and expedite summary procedures to improve case handling quality and efficiency.

Section 4 Directors or executives who are or ought to have been aware of their company circumstances meeting the conditions for bankruptcy under Section 2 of the Enterprise Bankruptcy Law of the People's Republic of China shall promptly initiate restructuring, disclose business information to creditors, apply for pre-reorganization, reorganization, settlement, and dissolution to mitigate financial decline and asset losses.

If directors or executives, through intent or gross negligence, fail to comply and cause asset losses, the people's court shall uphold claims for indemnification for losses filed by the bankruptcy administrator or creditors.

Section 5 Enterprises are encouraged to negotiate and draft a reorganization plan with creditors and other stakeholders before seeking reorganization approval from the people's court. Draft plans submitted prior to the people's court reviews may serve as the basis for the formal court-reviewed request following the initiation of reorganization proceedings.

Debtors with salvageable assets and potential for quick restructuring may have pre-reorganization proceedings initiated by the people's court at the request of the debtor or primary creditors. Enterprises applying for pre-reorganization may request court guidance and coordinated government support.

If the agreements between the debtor and some creditors reached during pre-reorganization align with the drafted reorganization plan, creditors' agreement to such preliminary arrangements shall be deemed as consent to the draft plan.

Section 6 Creditors who fail to file claims during bankruptcy proceedings within the timeframe designated by the people's court shall forfeit their rights during the execution of the reorganization plan. The protection period shall be one year after the completion of the reorganization plan.

破产重整案件的已知债权人收到债权申报书面通知和失权后果告知后，无正当理由未在人民法院确定的期限内申报债权的，视为放弃债权，债务人不再向该债权人承担清偿责任。

第七条 破产案件事实清楚、债权债务关系明确、财产状况清晰且具备下列情形之一的，应当先行适用简易破产程序：

（一）债务人账面资产为一千万元以下；

（二）已知债权人为三十人以下；

（三）已知债务总额为一百万元以下。

第八条 破产重整案件符合本规定第七条情形的，应当适用简易破产重整程序，债务人可以在管理人的监督下自行管理财产和营业事务。

债务人或者管理人应当自人民法院裁定债务人重整之日起三个月内，同时向人民法院和债权人会议提交重整计划草案。人民法院应当自收到重整计划草案之日起十五日内召开债权人会议对重整计划草案进行表决。债权人会议可以采用非现场方式召开。

第九条 破产衍生诉讼案件登记立案前，人民法院可以先行委派特邀调解组织或者特邀调解员进行调解。委派调解达成协议的，当事人可以依法申请司法确认。

当事人明确拒绝调解的，人民法院应当依法登记立案。登记立案后或者在审理过程中，人民法院认为破产衍生诉讼案件适宜调解，经当事人同意，可以委托特邀调解组织、特邀调解员或者由人民法院专职调解员进行调解。委托调解达成协议的，经审查后依法出具调解书。

第十条 破产案件受理后，管理人可以申请通过人民法院执行网络查控系统查询、控制债务人的存款、车辆、不动产、证券、对外投资等财产，人民法院应当于收到结果反馈之日起二日内将财产查控情况告知管理人。

Creditors in reorganization proceedings who neglect to file their claims by the timeframe designated by the people's court, after receiving written notice, and with no valid reason, shall be deemed to have waived their claims, and the debtor is released from repayment obligations.

Section 7 Summary bankruptcy proceedings may be used for straightforward bankruptcy cases where creditor-debtor relationships and property statuses are clear and any one of the following conditions is met:

(1) the debtor's total assets are less than RMB 10 million;

(2) there are fewer than 30 known creditors; or

(3) the total known debt is less than RMB 1 million.

Section 8 Summary restructuring proceedings shall be carried out if a company reorganization meets the criteria in Section 7. The debtor may be permitted to carry on management of the assets and business operations under the oversight of the bankruptcy administrator.

The debtor or bankruptcy administrator shall submit a draft reorganization plan to the people's court and the creditors' meeting within three months from the date on which the people's court issues the ruling to accept the reorganization application. The people's court shall then convene a creditors' meeting within fifteen days to vote on the plan, which may be conducted remotely.

Section 9 The people's court may appoint mediators to conduct mediation prior to the registration and filing of bankruptcy proceedings. Parties successfully reaching an agreement through mediation may then request judicial confirmation according to law.

If the parties involved in the proceedings explicitly refuse mediation, the people's court shall proceed with registration lawfully. If the people's court deems mediation appropriate during registration or the proceedings, it may, with the consent of all parties involved, entrust a specially invited mediation organization, a specially invited mediator, or a full-time mediator of the people's court to conduct mediation. If an agreement is reached through entrusted mediation, the people's court shall issue a mediation statement after examination in accordance with the law.

Section 10 Upon accepting a bankruptcy case, the bankruptcy administrator may apply to monitor the debtor's assets, including but not limited to deposits, vehicles, real estate, securities, and investments through the people's court's enforcement network. The people's court shall inform the administrator of the inquiry and control within two days of receiving system feedback.

需要采取保全措施的，人民法院应当于收到申请之日起五日内作出裁定并执行，情况紧急的应立即开始执行。

第十一条 人民法院受理破产申请后，应当向已对债务人财产采取保全措施的有关单位发出解除通知，并附破产受理裁定书及指定管理人决定书。有关单位收到通知或者知悉破产申请受理后七日内未解除的，财产处置方案经债权人会议同意和人民法院审核后，管理人可以先行处置被查封债务人财产，处置后依据人民法院出具的法律文书办理解封和资产过户、移交手续。

第十二条 处置破产财产时，经债权人会议同意可以直接变价处理，不适用拍卖程序。确需进行拍卖的，由债权人会议自行确定或者授权管理人确定起拍价，并优先通过网上拍卖平台进行。拍卖应在规定的最短期限内完成。法律法规对特定财产处置方式有特别规定的，从其规定。

第十三条 处置破产财产时，破产企业的在建建筑工程符合竣工验收条件，但因材料缺失、相关单位不配合等原因导致无法办理竣工验收手续的，管理人可以委托有资质的专业机构鉴定。鉴定意见认为符合建筑工程质量标准的，视为完成竣工验收，并由管理人办理竣工验收备案手续。

破产企业的机动车交通违法的罚款作为破产债权在破产程序中依法处理，累计记分予以核销。

第十四条 企业被人民法院宣告破产后，管理人应当依法组织清算并拟定破产财产分配方案，财产分配方案经人民法院裁定认可后予以执行。

企业应当清算而未及时清算的，主管机关或者利害关系人可以申请人民法院指定有关人员组成清算组强制清算。强制清算执行本规定有关破产办理的规定。强制清算过程中，清算组发现企业财产不足以清偿债务，但企业具有挽救价值和重整可能的，应当注重维护企业运营价值，及时申请破产重整。

If preservation actions are necessary, the people's court shall issue and enforce a ruling within five days upon receiving the application, with immediate enforcement in emergencies.

Section 11 Upon accepting a bankruptcy application, the people's court shall notify any entities with preservation actions on the debtor's assets and issue bankruptcy acceptance and bankruptcy administrator appointment rulings. If these entities fail to release the assets within seven days upon receipt of the notification or aware of the bankruptcy application, the administrator may, after the creditors' meeting and the people's court approve the disposal plan, dispose of the assets and handle the release, transfer, and handover process pursuant to the legal instruments issued by the people's court.

Section 12 Assets subject to disposal may be directly sold with creditor approval and without auction. If an auction is deemed necessary, the creditors' meeting may independently or authorize the bankruptcy administrator to determine the auction price, and online auction platforms shall be prioritized to complete the auction in the shortest specified timeframe. Any specialized laws and regulations on the disposal of specific assets shall govern.

Section 13 The bankruptcy administrator may appoint a certified evaluator if a bankrupt company's construction project meets final inspection standards but lacks essential documentation or stakeholders refuse to cooperate. Projects that meet quality standards shall be deemed completed, and the administrator shall file the acceptance records.

Traffic fines on vehicles of the bankrupt company are to be treated and processed as bankruptcy claims lawfully and any accumulated demerit points are to be written off.

Section 14 After an enterprise is declared bankrupt by the people's court, the bankruptcy administrator shall coordinate liquidation lawfully and draft an asset distribution plan, which shall be implemented after being approved by the people's court.

If an enterprise is required to undergo liquidation but delays occur, competent authorities or interested parties may request the people's court to appoint a team for involuntary liquidation, as governed by these Provisions. If the team determines that the company's assets are insufficient but that the enterprise is salvageable and possible for reorganization, they shall prioritize preserving operational value and promptly file for reorganization.

第十五条 浦东新区建立完善破产信息共享和破产状态公示机制。浦东新区人民法院应当将企业破产、强制清算程序中的下列重要信息及时与浦东新区社会信用主管部门共享，并由浦东新区社会信用主管部门按照规定向社会公示：

（一）企业破产、强制清算程序的受理、办理、终结的相关基本信息；

（二）管理人的名称、指定程序、履职情况等信息；

（三）企业董事、监事、高级管理人员违反忠实义务和勤勉义务，承担相关法律责任等信息；

（四）其他重要信息。

第十六条 浦东新区建立完善破产重整企业信用修复机制。浦东新区人民法院裁定批准重整计划或者认可破产和解协议后，管理人可以通过“一网通办”平台或者直接向原失信信息提供单位申请信用修复。

重整计划执行期间及执行完毕后，不得因破产重整直接排除其参与招投标、融资等市场行为的资格，不得限制其参与评优评先以及在政府审批、公共服务中享受容缺受理、证明替代等便利措施，法律、行政法规另有规定的除外。

第十七条 破产案件管理人由人民法院指定。债权人或者债务人提出破产申请的，可以向人民法院书面提名一名管理人人选。被提名人选符合任职条件并事先作出相关书面承诺的，人民法院应当指定其担任破产案件管理人。

数名申请人同时提出破产申请且提名的管理人人选不一致的，人民法院应当组织全体申请人协商，协商一致的，人民法院应当指定其担任破产案件管理人；协商不成的，人民法院应当直接指定管理人。

Section 15 The Pudong New Area is to develop and enhance the process for sharing and disclosing bankruptcy information. The Pudong New Area People's Court shall share critical information from enterprise bankruptcy and involuntary liquidation proceedings with the social credit regulatory administration, which shall publicly disclose the following details as required:

(1) key details on the acceptance, management, and conclusion of company bankruptcy and involuntary liquidation proceedings;

(2) information including the bankruptcy administrator's name, appointment, and performance;

(3) reports on breaches of loyalty and due diligence duties by company directors, supervisors, and executives, and their legal obligations; and

(4) other important information.

Section 16 The Pudong New Area is to develop and improve the credit restoration process for reorganized enterprises. Upon approval of the reorganization plan or bankruptcy settlement by the Pudong New Area People's Court, the bankruptcy administrator may apply for credit restoration through the integrated online government service platform or directly to the initial credit reporter.

During and following the reorganization, an enterprise's eligibility to bid, finance, and engage in other market activities shall not be automatically invalidated due to its past bankruptcy. The enterprise shall retain full access to recognition and acceptance with missing documents and certificate substitution in government approval and public services, unless otherwise specified by laws and administrative regulations.

Section 17 Bankruptcy administrators shall be appointed by the people's court, and creditors or debtors may nominate an administrator in writing during a bankruptcy filing. The people's court may appoint eligible nominees who sign a written commitment in advance as bankruptcy administrators.

If multiple applicants file bankruptcy applications with different candidates, the people's court shall organize negotiations among all applicants. If negotiations succeed, the agreed-upon candidate shall be appointed by the people's court as the bankruptcy administrator. If negotiations fail, the people's court shall appoint an administrator directly.

第十八条 债权人会议可以作出更换管理人的决议，并由人民法院指定新的管理人。

人民法院召集第一次债权人会议时，可以组织债权人就是否更换管理人进行讨论和表决。债权人会议确定了符合任职条件的管理人人选的，人民法院应当指定其担任破产案件管理人。债权人会议确定的人选不符合任职条件或者未确定新的人选的，人民法院可以直接指定新的管理人。

第十九条 浦东新区司法行政部门在市主管部门指导下会同有关部门支持破产管理人协会在浦东新区开展活动，推行管理人职业规范、履职评价、投诉处理、行业信用等常态化的行业监管制度。

浦东新区人民法院应当建立管理人履职情况的个案监督和指导机制。债权人会议和债权人委员会应当督促管理人勤勉履职。人民法院、债权人会议和债权人委员会对管理人的个案履职评价信息及时向社会公布。

发现虚假破产、妨碍清算、侵占公司财物或者虚假诉讼的犯罪线索的，管理人可以依法向有关机关控告或者举报。有关机关对管理人的控告、举报应当依法处理。

第二十条 本规定自 2022 年 1 月 1 日起施行。

Section 18 The creditors' meeting may resolve to change the bankruptcy administrator, and the people's court shall initiate the appointment of a new bankruptcy administrator.

Creditors may vote on replacing bankruptcy administrator at the first creditors' meeting convened by the people's court. If the creditors' meeting selects an eligible administrator candidate, the people's court shall appoint that candidate as the bankruptcy administrator. If the selected candidate does not meet the requirements or no new candidate is chosen, the people's court may appoint a new administrator directly.

Section 19 The judicial administration of the Pudong New Area, under municipal guidance and in cooperation with appropriate departments supports the bankruptcy administrator association's activities, ensuring standardized industry regulation, including best practices, performance evaluations, complaint processes, and credit systems.

The Pudong New Area People's Court shall issue specific guidelines for overseeing the bankruptcy administrator's performance. The creditors' meeting and creditors' committee shall ensure that the administrator performs their duties diligently. The people's court, creditors' meeting, and creditors' committee shall promptly disclose the administrator's performance evaluation case by case.

If the bankruptcy administrator identifies potential crimes, such as fraudulent bankruptcy filings, obstruction of liquidation proceedings, misappropriation of assets, or malicious prosecution, they shall report these to the appropriate departments, who are obliged to process these complaints according to law.

Section 20 These Provisions shall take effect from January 1, 2022.

上海市浦东新区促进张江生物医药产业创新高地建设规定

Provisions for the Pudong New Area of Shanghai Municipality on Improving the Development of the Zhangjiang Biopharmaceutical Industrial Innovation Hub

上海市浦东新区促进张江生物医药产业创新高地建设规定

（2021 年 12 月 29 日上海市第十五届人民代表大会常务委员会第三十八次会议通过）

第一条 为发挥以张江为引领的生物医药科创策源和产业生态优势，实施国家战略要求，促进浦东新区生物医药产业高质量发展，推动浦东新区形成世界级生物医药产业集群，更好地满足人民群众对健康生活的需求，根据有关法律、行政法规的基本原则，结合浦东新区实际，制定本规定。

第二条 本规定适用于在浦东新区行政区域内从事生物医药研发、生产、经营、使用以及相关促进保障活动。

第三条 本市坚持制度引领、改革创新、以人为本、开放合作、风险预防、科学规范的原则，推进浦东新区生物医药产业高质量发展。

第四条 市人民政府应当加强对浦东新区生物医药产业发展工作的领导，建立和完善促进生物医药产业发展议事协调机制，深化与国家有关部门的协作，统筹协调浦东新区生物医药产业发展中的重大事项。

浦东新区人民政府应当建立浦东新区生物医药产业发展促进工作机制，加强以张江为引领的生物医药产业发展工作，推动浦东新区生物医药产业创新发展。

Provisions for the Pudong New Area of Shanghai Municipality on Improving the Development of the Zhangjiang Biopharmaceutical Industrial Innovation Hub

(Adopted at the 38th Session of the 15th Shanghai Municipal People's Congress Standing Committee on December 29, 2021)

Section 1 The Provisions for the Pudong New Area of Shanghai Municipality on Improving the Development of the Zhangjiang Biopharmaceutical Industrial Innovation Hub (these "Provisions") are formulated to leverage sci-tech innovation and industrial ecosystem within the biopharmaceutical industry led by Zhangjiang, fulfill national strategic goals, enhance the quality of industrial development, establish a world-class biopharmaceutical hub, and better meet public health demands, pursuant to the basic principles of applicable laws and administrative regulations, and in light of the actual circumstances in the Pudong New Area.

Section 2 These Provisions shall apply to all biopharmaceutical research, development, production, operations, utilization, and pertinent promotion activities within the Pudong New Area.

Section 3 This Municipality commits to the principles of leadership in governance, innovative reform, a people-centered approach, openness, collaboration, risk management, and rigorous, systematic administration to advance biopharmaceutical development in the Pudong New Area.

Section 4 The Municipal People's Government shall increase its leadership over biopharmaceutical development, create and refine coordination processes, deepen collaboration with appropriate government authorities, and address key developmental issues in the sector.

The Pudong New Area People's Government shall implement systems to enhance biopharmaceutical development, step up efforts to develop biopharmaceuticals led by Zhangjiang, and facilitate innovation in the Pudong New Area.

浦东新区相关镇人民政府、街道办事处、园区管理机构应当在职责范围内做好生物医药产业发展的促进保障工作。

第五条 市经济信息化部门负责统筹本市生物医药产业发展，协调推进浦东新区生物医药产业创新高地建设。

市和浦东新区发展改革、科技、商务、卫生健康、药品监管、医疗保障、财政、规划资源、生态环境、人力资源社会保障、地方金融监管、绿化市容等部门以及海关等单位根据各自职责和本规定，负责浦东新区生物医药产业促进工作。

第六条 浦东新区人民政府设立浦东新区生物医药产业发展专家委员会。专家委员会负责对浦东新区生物医药产业发展、项目规划、重点布局等事项开展科学论证，提出意见建议。专家委员会的意见建议作为生物医药产业发展决策的重要参考。

第七条 市、浦东新区人民政府应当将促进人体细胞和基因产业发展纳入生物医药产业发展协调促进机制，在风险可控的前提下，支持符合条件的多元化投资主体开展人体细胞、基因技术研发和推进产业化进程。

市和浦东新区科技、卫生健康等部门应当强化对浦东新区生物医药企业开展人体细胞、基因技术开发和应用的监管，加强风险管控。

第八条 对于国家有关部门准许范围内的浦东新区生物医药企业，探索对其开展跨境研发所需的货物（含材料、耗材、试剂等）实施保税监管。

按照监管部门信息共享、风险可控的要求，浦东新区相关重点生物医药企业可以根据国家规定开展高附加值、高技术含量、符合环保要求的医疗器械保税维修业务；浦东新区特定区域内的相关企业可以根据国家规定开展出口高端医疗设备的返境维修。维修后的医疗器械，应当根据其来源复运至境外。

Township governments, sub-district offices, and industrial parks administrations shall encourage and improve biopharmaceutical development within their jurisdictions.

Section 5 The municipal economy and technology department takes charge of coordinating the development of the biopharmaceutical industry in this Municipality and advancing the development of the Zhangjiang biopharmaceutical industrial innovation hub.

The municipal and Pudong New Area departments, including development and reform, science and technology, commerce, health, medical products regulation, healthcare security, finance, planning and resources, ecology and environment, human resources and social security, local financial supervision, landscaping and city appearance, and customs, contribute to the development of the biopharmaceutical sector under these Provisions to the fullest extent of their authority.

Section 6 The Pudong New Area People's Government is to establish an advisory committee to assess scientific developments and offer opinions and recommendations on biopharmaceutical industry strategy, project planning, and organization, which are to guide decision-making for biopharmaceutical industry development initiatives.

Section 7 The municipal and Pudong New Area people's governments shall integrate the advancement of human cell and gene industries into biopharmaceutical management policies, supporting eligible investors in their research and ensuring manageable risks to facilitate the industrialization process.

The municipal and Pudong New Area departments, including the science and technology and health administrations, shall improve regulation and risk controls in the development and application of human cell and gene technologies by biopharmaceutical firms in the Pudong New Area.

Section 8 Eligible biopharmaceutical companies licensed by the appropriate government authorities in the Pudong New Area may participate in a pilot project on bonded regulation for cross-border research and development materials (including raw materials, consumables, and reagents).

Pursuant to national regulations, leading biopharmaceutical companies may offer bonded repair services for high-tech medical devices that conform to environmental standards; designated enterprises may conduct domestic repairs on previously exported high-quality medical devices, which shall be returned overseas under the same conditions as their original export.

第九条 浦东新区具备药品商业化规模生产条件并且符合药品生产质量管理规范的生物医药企业，药物临床试验阶段申请药品生产许可的，在承诺临床样品的生产条件与申请上市许可阶段的生产条件一致的情况下，市药品监管部门可以核发《药品生产许可证》。

第十条 浦东新区药品上市许可持有人可以自行生产药品，也可以依法委托药品生产企业生产。经国家药品监管部门核准后，浦东新区药品上市许可持有人可以委托本市范围内一家以上符合条件的药品生产企业生产。市药品监管部门应当做好指导、服务，并配合国家药品监管部门开展相关审查工作。

血液制品、麻醉药品、精神药品、医疗用毒性药品、药品类易制毒化学品不得委托生产，但国家药品监管部门另有规定的除外。

第十一条 对国内尚无同品种产品上市的体外诊断试剂，浦东新区符合条件的医疗机构根据临床需要，可以自行研制，在执业医师指导下在本单位内使用。具体办法由市药品监管部门会同市卫生健康部门制定。

第十二条 市人民政府在国家授权范围内，可以批准浦东新区符合条件的医疗机构进口少量临床急需的药品和医疗器械。进口的药品和医疗器械应当在指定医疗机构用于特定医疗目的。

鼓励符合条件的生物医药企业对临床急需进口的少量药品和医疗器械开展临床真实世界数据应用研究，探索将临床真实世界数据用于药品和医疗器械注册，推动药品和医疗器械加快上市。

第十三条 本市按照国家有关授权，在相关区域内试点推动符合条件的浦东新区药品和医疗器械交易平台开展跨境电子商务零售进口部分药品和医疗器械业务。

Section 9 Biopharmaceutical enterprises with commercial-scale production capabilities that meet Good Manufacturing Practice standards during clinical trials may receive a Drug Manufacturing License from the municipal drug regulatory administration, subject to a declaration that clinical production conditions conform to those required for marketing authorization.

Section 10 Drug marketing authorization holders in the Pudong New Area may independently produce medicines or entrust production to approved manufacturers. Upon approval by the national drug regulatory administration, the drug marketing authorization holder may entrust production to one or more eligible enterprises in this Municipality. The municipal drug regulatory administration shall guide and support the process, and cooperate with the national drug regulatory administration during reviews.

Outsourcing production for blood products, narcotics, psychotropic substances, certain toxic medications, and precursor chemicals shall be prohibited unless specifically authorized by the national drug regulatory administration.

Section 11 Eligible healthcare institutions in the Pudong New Area may develop and use in-vitro diagnostic reagents for internal needs under physician guidance. The Municipal drug regulatory and health administrations are to issue specific guidelines on such processes.

Section 12 The Municipal People's Government may authorize eligible healthcare institutions in the Pudong New Area to import limited amounts of critical medicines and medical devices for specific medical use under national authorization.

Biopharmaceutical enterprises are encouraged to conduct research on critical medicines and medical devices using real-world data to streamline registration and accelerate market availability.

Section 13 This Municipality encourages eligible drug and medical device platforms to engage in cross-border e-commerce to facilitate retail and import businesses under national authorization.

市药品监管部门应当结合浦东新区生物医药产业发展的实际需求，在保证经营质量安全可控的前提下，优化药品批发经营许可实施，满足药品现代物流需求。

第十四条 本市根据浦东新区生物医药企业的研发需求，规划布局和建设进境非人灵长类等实验动物隔离检疫场。

浦东新区鼓励社会资本依法投资开展与生物医药研发相关的非人灵长类等实验动物及相关产品的保种、繁育、生产、供应等活动，保障生物医药研发使用需求。需要生产和使用非人灵长类等实验动物的，应当经浦东新区科技经济部门和野生动物保护主管部门批准，依法取得实验动物生产、使用许可证。

浦东新区卫生健康部门会同农业农村部门负责浦东新区新建、改建或者扩建与人体健康相关的动物生物安全二级实验室的备案。

第十五条 本市建立微生物、人体组织、生物制品、血液及其制品等生物医药特殊物品出入境联合监管机制。浦东新区人民政府应当会同有关部门对生物医药企业及其出入境特殊物品开展综合评估，对通过评估的企业及物品出具相应生物安全控制能力的证明。上海海关凭证明和企业提交的其他材料，简化通关手续。

本市建立生物医药研发用物品进口试点联合推进机制。浦东新区人民政府应当会同有关部门对企业及进口研发用物品进行认定。通过认定的企业及物品在办理通关手续时不需提交进口药品通关单。

浦东新区建立企业研发进口微量耗材管理服务平台，在进口许可、通关便利、允许分销等方面予以支持。

The municipal drug regulatory administration shall, in light of the actual needs of the biopharmaceutical industry in the Pudong New Area, optimize the implementation of drug wholesale business licenses to meet the needs of modern pharmaceutical logistics while ensuring the safety and controllability of operational quality.

Section 14 In response to R&D needs, this Municipality constructs quarantine facilities for laboratory animals, including non-human primates.

Private sector investment in the conservation, breeding, production, and supply of laboratory animals to support biopharmaceutical research is encouraged in the Pudong New Area. Such activities shall require appropriate licensing from technology and economy and wildlife protection administrations of the Pudong New Area.

The Pudong New Area health and agriculture and rural development departments are to take charge of the registration of biosafety level 2 laboratories focused on human health concerns, regardless of whether the laboratories are newly built, renovated, or expanded.

Section 15 A joint regulatory system is to be established in this Municipality to monitor the import and export of sensitive biopharmaceutical products, including microorganisms, human tissues, biological products, blood, and blood products. The Pudong New Area People's Government shall assess biopharmaceutical enterprises and their import and export of specific products, issuing biosafety certificates in collaboration with other appropriate departments. Shanghai Customs shall facilitate streamlined customs procedures based on the certificates, in addition to the submission of additional documents by the enterprises.

A joint pilot project for biopharmaceutical research imports is to be developed in this Municipality, and the Pudong New Area People's Government shall collaborate with appropriate departments to identify enterprises and imports for biopharmaceutical research for exemption from certain drug import procedures during customs processes.

A management and service platform is to be established in the Pudong New Area to streamline the import of R&D consumables, providing support for import licensing, customs facilitation, and distribution.

第十六条 本市在浦东新区设立人类遗传资源管理服务机构，开展人类遗传资源咨询、服务、培训、研究等工作，协助国家和本市人类遗传资源管理机构开展人类遗传资源的事中事后监管等工作。

第十七条 浦东新区行政区域内的药品检验检测机构经国家药品监管部门指定，可以开展创新药品的注册检验工作。市药品监管部门、浦东新区人民政府应当为药品检验检测机构的检验检测能力提升提供政策支持和保障。

浦东新区应当加强生物医药产品注册指导服务工作站建设。对符合产业发展方向的药品和医疗器械，注册指导服务工作站应当及时跟踪、对接注册进度，开展药品和医疗器械注册工作的前期指导服务，推动药品和医疗器械加快上市。

第十八条 本市支持国家药品监管局药品审评检查长三角分中心、医疗器械技术审评检查长三角分中心建设，协助配置职业化专业化的审评员、检查员，建立科学高效专业的审评检查工作机制。

市和浦东新区有关部门应当依托国家药品监管局药品审评检查长三角分中心、医疗器械技术审评检查长三角分中心，为生物医药企业提供高效便捷的指导和服务，根据相关规定推动创新药品和医疗器械纳入优先审评审批通道，加快推进创新药品和医疗器械注册上市。

第十九条 本市支持创新药品和医疗器械进入医疗机构使用。市和浦东新区有关部门对浦东新区医疗机构采购和使用的创新药品和医疗器械不纳入药品（耗材）收入所占比例、药品品种规格总数、采购比例限制等考核。

Section 16 A genetic resource management institution is to be created in this Municipality to offer consultation, services, and training, and research on genetic resources, and to facilitate regulation by national and municipal genetic resource management institutions both during and after genetic resource activities.

Section 17 Pharmaceutical testing laboratories designated by the national drug regulatory administration are permitted to offer testing services for drug registration applications. The municipal drug regulatory administration and the Pudong New Area People's Government shall support and encourage these laboratories to improve their capabilities.

Guidance and service sites in the Pudong New Area shall be further developed to facilitate biopharmaceutical product registration, providing prompt tracking, registration progress updates, and early guidance, while supporting rapid market access for drugs and medical devices in line with industrial development.

Section 18 This Municipality encourages the establishment of branches of national drug regulatory administration evaluation centers for drugs and medical devices in the Yangtze River Delta, and provides expert reviewers and inspectors to build an effective assessment system.

The municipal and Pudong New Area departments shall leverage these centers to offer efficient support and guidance to biopharmaceutical enterprises, prioritize expedited assessments for innovative drugs and medical devices, and ensure rapid market access for such products.

Section 19 This Municipality encourages medical institutions to use innovative drugs and medical devices. The appropriate municipal and Pudong New Area departments shall exclude these innovative products from assessments of medicine revenue proportions (consumables), medicine variety and specifications, and procurement ratio limits.

第二十条 本市支持高校、科研院所、医疗机构与浦东新区生物医药企业开展合作，通过共建实验室、研究院等方式推动建设创新协作产业生态圈。本市支持国家级和市级医药临床研究中心建设，探索浦东新区研究型医院试点建设，推进科技成果与临床研究对接，推动产学研医深度融合。

浦东新区科技经济、卫生健康部门应当开展创新药品和医疗器械研发项目评估工作，依托本市医院企业协同临床试验加速平台，促进临床试验需求对接，提升产医融合质量效率。

第二十一条 鼓励各类医疗卫生机构推进健康医疗数据采集、存储，加强应用支撑和运维技术保障。加快建设和完善以居民电子健康档案、电子病历、电子处方等为核心的基础数据库。

市和浦东新区卫生健康部门应当依据相关法律法规建立健康医疗数据共享与开放机制，制订健康医疗数据开放分类分级标准，推动健康医疗数据有序开放，为本市生物医药创新研发提供数据支撑。

第二十二条 本市支持在浦东新区建设高标准、集约化的生物样本库。

市卫生健康部门和浦东新区人民政府应当建立有效的生物样本研究应用与共享机制，支持企业牵头或者参与制定样本库建设管理标准。市和浦东新区卫生健康部门应当加强生物样本及其信息数据的存储与管理的指导，保障生物样本采集、存储、使用、共享等符合生物安全管理规范。

医疗卫生机构的生物样本，可以委托有相关资质的第三方机构集中存储和管理。

Section 20 This Municipality encourages higher education institutions, research institutes, and medical institutions to partner with biopharmaceutical enterprises in the Pudong New Area to develop an innovation-driven industrial ecosystem supported by the creation of laboratories and research centers. This Municipality encourages the development of national and municipal clinical biopharmaceutical research centers, trial pilot research hospitals in the Pudong New Area, and promotes the integration of scientific achievements with clinical research to improve collaborations between industry, academia, research, and medicine.

The Pudong New Area technology and economy and health administrations shall evaluate and support drug and medical device R&D projects that align with clinical trial goals in order to advance developments in the integration of industrial and healthcare sectors.

Section 21 Medical and health institutions are encouraged to improve medical data collection and storage practices, and to improve application support and technical operations. Efforts are to focus on building and refining a central database with residents' electronic health records, medical records, and prescriptions.

The municipal and Pudong New Area health administrations shall develop a health data sharing and disclosure system pursuant to applicable laws and regulations, create tiered standards for health data access, and facilitate the streamlined disclosure of data to support biopharmaceutical innovation and R&D in this Municipality.

Section 22 This Municipality supports establishing high standards and centralized biorepositories in the Pudong New Area.

The municipal health administration and the Pudong New Area People's Government shall establish an effective process for researching and sharing biological samples to encourage companies to initiate or participate in standards setting for central database development and management. The municipal and Pudong health administrations shall improve guidance on the storage and management of biological samples and data to ensure the collection, storage, use, and sharing of biological samples comply with biosafety management standards

The centralized storage and management of the biological samples may be outsourced to certified third-party organizations.

第二十三条 本市支持建设张江综合性国家科学中心，推进大科学设施规划建设，完善设施使用保护，严格设施周边管理，为生物医药产业发展提供基础性研究和保障。

第二十四条 对符合条件的新型生物医药研发机构，市和浦东新区有关部门应当在其管理模式、成果转化、体制机制改革等方面给予指导和支持。

浦东新区人民政府应当支持具备条件的生物医药企业开放创新中心建设。对符合条件的创新中心，在建设运营、人才奖励、知识产权保护等方面给予支持。

第二十五条 本市鼓励各类市场主体建设众创空间、孵化器、加速器等生物医药共享公共服务平台，创新服务模式，针对创新企业不同发展阶段提供完善的基础设施、针对性的运营管理和专业的研发服务，强化产业园区、创新研发企业、研发生产服务企业之间的协同联动。

第二十六条 本市推进生物医药制造业创新链、产业链、人才链深度融合。鼓励生物医药产业链核心企业牵头带动产业链供应链持续向高级化、现代化发展，打造一批拥有关键核心技术的生物医药领军企业。

第二十七条 本市建立浦东新区生物医药项目信息数据库并动态更新，创新研发成果有序转化的利益分享机制，实现本市生物医药创新研发与生产制造协同发展。

第二十八条 对符合生物医药产业发展导向的重点项目，市和浦东新区有关部门可以按照规定对土地用途、容积率、建筑高度等予以优化。

Section 23 This Municipality supports the development of the Zhangjiang National Comprehensive Scientific Center by enhancing research facilities and securing the necessary protections for these assets, providing fundamental research and safeguards for biopharmaceutical industrial development.

Section 24 The municipal and Pudong New Area departments shall guide and support eligible biopharmaceutical R&D institutions with management, commercialization, and system optimization.

The Pudong New Area People's Government shall support eligible biopharmaceutical enterprises in developing innovation centers by providing operational guidance, professional incentives, and intellectual property protection.

Section 25 Public biopharmaceutical product-sharing platforms, along with emerging business platforms like maker spaces, incubators, and accelerators, are to be encouraged to develop and provide comprehensive facilities, specialized operations, and professional R&D services to biopharmaceutical enterprises throughout their development stages in order to enhance collaboration among industrial parks, R&D companies, and manufacturing service providers.

Section 26 This Municipality supports the integration of innovation, industrial supply chains, and professionals within the biopharmaceutical manufacturing sector, encourages leading biopharmaceutical enterprises to drive the industrial supply chain toward advanced and modern growth, and establishes themselves as industry leaders in key technologies.

Section 27 The Pudong New Area dynamic biopharmaceutical project database created by this Municipality is to facilitate the sharing of benefits gained through the commercialization of R&D results and integrate the sector's innovation and manufacturing activities.

Section 28 The appropriate municipal and Pudong New Area departments may adjust land use, plot ratio, and building height policies as necessary for supporting major biopharmaceutical projects in line with industrial development goals.

市和浦东新区规划资源部门应当深化产业用地“标准化”出让方式改革，增加混合产业用地供给。在符合产业功能导向和生物医药项目主导产业用途的前提下，对浦东新区生物医药产业用地试点允许受让人自主确定土地产业用途比例。

第二十九条 本市对符合规定的生物医药创新产品实行首购和订购制度。浦东新区健全优先使用生物医药创新产品的政府采购政策，加大生物医药创新产品政府采购力度，促进生物医药创新产品研发和示范应用。

第三十条 市地方金融监管部门、浦东新区人民政府应当创新生物医药产业金融服务模式，推动生物医药企业在科创板等资本市场上市；持续优化张江指数样本和权重，突出张江国家自主创新示范区生物医药等优势产业，引导资本市场支持张江生物医药产业发展。

市财政、地方金融监管部门应当加大对生物医药供应链金融的指导，重点支持金融机构围绕生物医药供应链核心企业开发适合产业发展需求的供应链金融产品，为生物医药产业链上下游中小企业融资提供服务。

本市发挥上海市中小微政策性融资担保基金作用，通过批次担保、联合担保、再担保等多种方式引导相关金融机构和融资担保机构，为浦东新区生物医药企业融资提供增信服务。

第三十一条 浦东新区生态环境部门可以会同科技经济部门按照生态保护红线、环境质量底线、资源利用上线和生态环境准入清单的生态环境分区管控要求，对抗体、疫苗、血液制品等生物制品领域建设项目，根据所在区域环境敏感程度、建设项目可能产生的环境影响和环境风险，制定细分行业的生态环境管理措施，实行差异化监管。

The municipal and Pudong New Area planning and resources departments shall deepen reforms of industrial land transfer strategies to increase mixed-use spaces. The transferees of the biopharmaceutical land use pilot projects in the Pudong New Area are authorized to determine appropriate industrial land use ratios, provided they align with industrial development and biopharmaceutical project needs.

Section 29 A priority purchasing system for compliant innovative biopharmaceutical products is to be implemented in this Municipality. Government procurement policies for the Pudong New Area are to be revised to prioritize the use of compliant innovative biopharmaceutical products, increase government procurement operations, and support the research, development and trial of innovative biopharmaceutical products.

Section 30 The municipal financial regulatory administration and the Pudong New Area People's Government shall innovate financial services specific to biopharmaceutical companies, facilitating access to capital markets, such as the Shanghai Stock Exchange STAR Market. They shall continuously optimize the constituents and weightings of the Zhangjiang Index to highlight leading industries, such as biopharmaceuticals, within the Zhangjiang National Independent Innovation Demonstration Zone, guiding capital markets to support the growth of the Zhangjiang biopharmaceutical industry.

The municipal fiscal and financial supervision administrations shall expand guidance on biopharmaceutical supply chain finance to support the creation of financial products that meet the needs of the biopharmaceutical sector, providing financial services for small and medium-sized enterprises throughout the supply chain.

The financial guarantee fund for micro, small and medium-sized enterprises is leveraged to provide credit enhancement services for biopharmaceutical enterprises in the Pudong New Area, utilizing various guarantee schemes including batch guarantees, joint guarantees, and re-guarantees to guide the financial institutions and organizations issuing the guarantees.

Section 31 The Pudong New Area ecology and environment protection department may, in collaboration with the technology and economy department, establish tailored ecological and environmental management processes and implement differentiated regulation for biological product development projects, such as those for antibodies, vaccines, and blood products. These processes shall be based on the ecological protection red line, environmental quality standards, resource utilization limits, and the ecological access list, taking into account the area's environmental sensitivity and the potential environmental impacts and risks of the project.

第三十二条 浦东新区生物医药研发机构、医疗机构可以将其依法取得的职务科技成果的知识产权或者知识产权的长期使用权给予成果完成人。

浦东新区组建生物医药专业职称评审委员会，对区域内非公领域生物医药产业专业技术人才开展职称评价；根据国家授权制定发布国际职业资格证书认可清单，研究国际职业资格与国内职称的衔接办法。

浦东新区生物医药研发机构、医疗机构的专业技术人员在其他企业、机构兼职或者利用与本人从事专业相关的科技创新成果在职创办企业的，相关权利义务由其所在单位规定，或者由其所在单位与专业技术人员约定。

第三十三条 本市贯彻落实国家生物安全战略，建立健全生物安全风险监测预警体系，健全完善生物安全科研攻关机制，推动本市生物安全技术及其产业化应用引领发展。

第三十四条 本规定自2022年1月1日起施行。

Section 32 Biopharmaceutical research or medical institutions are entitled to grant work for hire intellectual property rights or long-term license to inventors.

A professional title evaluation panel will be established in the Pudong New Area to recognize the certifications of biopharmaceutical professionals working for non-public sectors. The Pudong New Area also develops and discloses a list of recognized international certifications and explores how to link international certification and domestic professional titles as authorized by the state.

The rights and obligations of biopharmaceutical research and medical institutions professionals engaged in multiple roles or entrepreneurial ventures derived from their professional achievements shall be clearly defined by their primary employers or contractual agreements.

Section 33 This Municipality implements the national biosecurity strategy, establishing robust systems for risk monitoring and improving the research and use of biosecurity technologies.

Section 34 These Provisions shall take effect from January 1, 2022.

上海市浦东新区市场主体登记确认制若干规定

Several Provisions for the Pudong New Area of Shanghai Municipality on the Market Entity Registration System

上海市浦东新区市场主体登记确认制若干规定

（2022 年 2 月 18 日上海市第十五届人民代表大会常务委员会第三十九次会议通过）

第一条 为了推进市场主体登记确认制，深化“放管服”改革，维护良好市场秩序和市场主体合法权益，优化营商环境，根据有关法律、行政法规的基本原则，结合浦东新区实际，制定本规定。

第二条 本规定适用于浦东新区的市场监督管理部门（以下称“登记机关”）推进市场主体登记确认制改革及其相关的管理、服务活动。

本规定所称市场主体登记确认制，是指登记机关依据法定的权限和程序，对有限责任公司、非公司企业法人及其分支机构，个人独资企业、合伙企业及其分支机构（以下统称“市场主体”）的主体资格和登记事项予以认定并公示其法律效力的登记制度。

第三条 实施市场主体登记确认制，应当遵循尊重意思自治、贯彻形式审查、全程公开透明、智慧便捷高效的要求，赋予市场主体更大的经营自主权，降低制度性交易成本。

申请人应当实名申请登记，并对其提交材料的真实性、合法性和有效性负责。登记机关对申请材料进行形式审查，对申请材料齐全、符合法定形式的予以确认并登记。

Several Provisions for the Pudong New Area of Shanghai Municipality on the Market Entity Registration System

(Adopted at the 39th Session of the 15th Shanghai Municipal People's Congress Standing Committee on February 18, 2022)

Section 1 The Several Provisions for the Pudong New Area of Shanghai Municipality on the Market Entity Registration System (these "Provisions") are formulated to facilitate the market entity registration system, advance reform initiatives in the delegation of authority, streamlining administration, optimizing government services, ensure market order, protect market entities' lawful rights and interests, and improve the business environment in the Pudong New Area, pursuant to the basic principles of applicable laws and administrative regulations, and in light of the actual circumstances of the Pudong New Area.

Section 2 These Provisions shall apply to all initiatives to promote the market entity registration system reform and their associated administrative activities and services performed by the Pudong New Area market regulation agency (the "registration office").

"Market entity registration system" in these Provisions refers to the registration system used by the registration office to verify an entity's eligibilities and registration criteria, including for limited liability companies, unincorporated businesses with juristic personality and their branches, sole proprietorships, and partnerships and their branches, and to legally disclose such to the extent of their duties.

Section 3 The implementation of the market entity registration system shall respect businesses' autonomy, ensure thorough formal reviews, maintain transparency throughout, prioritize intelligent and efficient services, empower market entities, and minimize administrative costs.

Applicants shall apply using their real names and warrant the authenticity, legality, and validity of their submissions. The registration office conducts formal reviews and registers those applications that include all required documentation and meet legal requirements.

第四条 市场主体的设立登记实行行政确认。符合法律法规规定的设立条件的，由登记机关确认其主体资格，并分别登记为相应类型的市场主体，签发营业执照。取得营业执照的市场主体即可从事一般经营项目。

第五条 市场主体名称登记实行申报承诺制。申请人可以通过“一网通办”平台以自主申报、事先承诺的方式办理名称登记。

登记机关应当运用现代信息技术，对申请人申报的名称是否与他人相同或者近似等情形进行自动比对，实时导出比对结果，及时提示申请人可能存在的法律风险。

第六条 市场主体自主确定经营范围，并记载于章程（合伙协议）。

市场主体仅需将主营项目、许可项目以及涉及外商投资准入特别管理措施的项目申请登记。登记机关按照经营项目分类标准予以确认并登记。

市场主体超越登记的经营范围开展非许可类经营活动的，登记机关不予处罚；未经许可开展许可类经营活动的，由有关许可部门依法处理。

第七条 推进市场主体住所和经营场所分离改革。市场主体需要在住所以外开展经营活动的，可以备案多个符合条件的经营场所，也可以办理分支机构设立登记。

第八条 市场主体之间有控制关系、有共同投资方或者隶属于同一集团的，可以将同一地址作为住所登记。

符合住所托管要求的市场主体，可以将指定的场所登记为住所。

第九条 市场主体应当置备股东（合伙人、投资人）名册。股权（财产份额、出资额）转让的，应当书面通知市场主体。

Section 4 Market entity formation requires administrative confirmation. The registration office is to verify their eligibility, register them under the appropriate business type, and issue business licenses for general business activities.

Section 5 Market entity name registration shall use a declaration of compliance system. Applicants may independently process declarations through the integrated online government service platform.

The registration office shall perform an automatic electronic check and comparison of any proposed names against registered names and promptly disclose its findings and notify applicants of any potential legal issues.

Section 6 Market entities independently define their permitted business activities in their articles of incorporation (or partnership agreement)

Market entities are only required to register principal projects, regulated business activities, and activities subject to foreign investment access restrictions with the registration office, which will classify, review, and record such.

Market entities conducting non-regulated business activities beyond their registered activities shall not be subject to penalties from the registration office. Those engaging in regulated business activities without the required license shall be subject to lawful enforcement by the appropriate agencies.

Section 7 The reform to separate the domicile of market entities from their business addresses shall be supported. Market entities needing to operate outside their registered domicile shall be permitted to register multiple eligible business addresses or form local offices.

Section 8 Market entities sharing control, investors, or group affiliations may use a common domicile address for registration purposes.

Market entities eligible for domicile trusteeship may register a designated location as their official domicile.

Section 9 Market entities shall maintain an updated shareholder (or partners and investors) register, and shareholders are required to notify the market entity of any equity (or property shares or capital contributions) assignments in writing.

市场主体应当及时变更名册并申请变更登记，免于向登记机关提交转让协议等材料。

第十条　推进市场主体备案事项改为自主公示。市场主体应当在设立时或者下列事项变动之日起二十个工作日内通过国家企业信用信息公示系统、“一网通办”平台向社会公示：

（一）董事、监事、高级管理人员；

（二）市场主体登记联络员；

（三）外商投资企业法律文件送达接受人。

市场主体公示前款规定的材料和事项应当合法、准确、完整。公示虚假信息的，应当将其违法失信行为记入市场主体信用档案，依法实施失信惩戒；损害他人合法权益的，依法承担法律责任。

第十一条　按照分级分类监管原则，结合市场主体信用和风险状况，开展针对市场主体自主公示事项和留存文件的“双随机、一公开”抽查，并实施差异化监管措施。

对市场主体的登记事项和自主公示信息，利害关系人提出异议或者经抽查发现异常的，登记机关应当及时进行核查。核查期间，登记机关可以对市场主体的相关信息作出标注。

第十二条　发挥律师事务所、会计师事务所、税务师事务所等专业服务机构和有关行业协会等的共治功能，推进市场主体托管机制创新。

托管服务机构应当按照登记机关要求建立托管服务工作台账，配合协助有关部门开展对市场主体的监督管理，督促市场主体履行相关义务。

市场主体可以根据约定以托管服务机构的住所申请住所登记。市场主体在住所以外活动的，应当向托管服务机构提供相关信息。

Market entities shall regularly update their registers and file for necessary registration changes and be exempt from the requirement to submit assignment documentation to the registration office.

Section 10 Market entities are encouraged to voluntarily disclose registration details. Market entities shall publicly disclose specific details via the National Enterprise Credit Information Publicity System or the integrated online government service platform within twenty Market days of formation or the filing of any changes, including details of:

(1) directors, supervisors, and executives;

(2) market entity registration liaison persons; and

(3) recipients of legal documents for foreign investor businesses.

Materials disclosed pursuant to the previous paragraph shall be valid, accurate, and complete. Misrepresentation is to result in a record of dishonesty being added to the enterprise's credit profile and legally mandated penalties for dishonesty, and the enterprise shall be held liable for any infringement against third party's lawful rights and interests pursuant to law.

Section 11 Sampling and disclosures are to be conducted under differentiated regulatory approaches for any matters and documents disclosed by a market entity, following the principle of tiered and classified regulation and based on their credit and risk status.

If an interested party raises an objection or a discrepancy is noted during a sample review, the registration office shall promptly review the registered matters and self-disclosed information of the market entity, and may mark any relevant market entity information during the review period.

Section 12 In addition to industry associations, collaborations with professional service providers, such as law firms, accounting firms, and tax firms are encouraged to support the development of innovative agency services for market entities.

Professional services providers shall keep accurate service records as required by the registration office and cooperate with appropriate agencies to ensure compliance by all market entities.

Market entities may register their domicile using the address of a professional services provider based on their agreement. Market entities shall notify service providers if they operate outside their registered domicile.

第十三条 登记机关应当建立覆盖市场主体全生命周期的登记服务体系，实现登记工作的标准公开、服务公开和结果公开。

登记机关应当优化登记流程，推行材料清单标准化、办理流程电子化、登记服务智能化，便利市场主体通过“一网通办”平台全程线上办理登记。除登记法定代表人（执行事务合伙人）外，登记机关不再收取股东会决议、董事会决议、任免职文件等材料。

第十四条 推进以电子营业执照为载体，归集各类电子许可证信息，实现电子证照“一照通用”和市场主体营业执照记载项目精简化。营业执照记载项目包括市场主体的名称、法定代表人（执行事务合伙人、负责人或经营者）姓名、住所（主要经营场所）、注册资本（出资额）、登记机关等。

第十五条 市场主体违反本规定，未及时公示有关材料和事项或者公示的信息违法、虚假、遗漏的，责令限期改正；拒不改正的，可以处一万元以上十万元以下的罚款，列入经营异常名录；情节严重的，列入严重违法企业名单，实施信用惩戒。

托管服务机构违反本规定的，责令限期改正；拒不改正的，处一万元以上十万元以下的罚款。

提交虚假材料或者采取其他欺诈手段取得市场主体登记的，依法撤销登记。

第十六条 本市有关司法机关和行政机关应当支持市场主体登记确认制改革，建立与其相适应的评价、考核制度。

登记机关及其工作人员在实施确认登记中依据本规定和相关制度尽责履职、未牟取私利，但因现有科学技术、监管手段限制未能及时发现问题的，不予追究执法过错责任。

第十七条 规定自 2022 年 3 月 15 日起施行。

Section 13 The registration office shall develop a comprehensive registration service system covering the entire lifecycle of market entities to ensure the disclosure of registration standards, service processes, and results.

The registration office shall facilitate the registration process by standardizing material lists, digitizing procedures, and providing intelligent services, enabling market entities to complete all registration procedures through the integrated online government service platform. Submission of documents such as shareholder meeting resolutions, board decisions, and appointment and removal to the registration office shall be phased out, excluding registrations of representatives by operation of law (or managing partners).

Section 14 The introduction of electronic business licenses is to consolidate various electronic permits or licenses into a single integrated license format, consolidating the number of activities recorded on a market entity business license. These records include the business name, the name of the representative by operation of law (or managing partner, responsible person, or operator), domicile (primary business address), registered capital (or capital contributions), and the registration office.

Section 15 Market entities failing to disclose the required information promptly pursuant to these Provisions or those that provide false, illegal, or incomplete information shall correct their entries within a specified deadline. Non-compliance may result in fines ranging from RMB 10,000 to RMB 100,000, enrolled into the list of enterprises with irregular operations, or, in case of material non-compliance, enrolled into the list of enterprises with serious violations, along with any associated credit penalties.

Professional service providers in violation of these Provisions shall be ordered to make corrections within a set deadline. Continued non-compliance shall incur fines ranging from RMB 10,000 to RMB 100,000.

The falsification of any information disclosed during the application process or employing any other fraudulent methods to obtain business registration shall result in the registration being revoked lawfully.

Section 16 The municipal judicial and administrative authorities shall support business entity registration system reforms and create appropriate evaluation and assessment systems.

The registration office and its staff shall not be held liable for any failure to promptly identify issues due to technological or procedural limitations, provided they strictly comply with these Provisions and associated protocols and do not seek personal gains.

Section 17 These Provisions shall take effect from March 15, 2022.

上海市浦东新区绿色金融发展若干规定

Several Provisions for the Pudong New Area of Shanghai Municipality on Sustainable Finance Development

上海市浦东新区绿色金融发展若干规定

（2022 年 6 月 22 日上海市第十五届人民代表大会常务委员会第四十一次会议通过）

第一条 为了提升浦东新区绿色金融服务水平，促进绿色金融和普惠金融、科创金融的融合发展，推进上海国际金融中心核心区建设，打造上海国际绿色金融枢纽，加快经济社会发展全面绿色转型，促进生态文明建设，根据有关法律、行政法规的基本原则，结合浦东新区实际，制定本规定。

第二条 本规定适用于浦东新区行政区域内开展绿色金融活动及相关促进保障工作。

本规定所称绿色金融，是指为支持改善生态环境、应对气候变化、资源节约高效利用等经济社会活动所提供的金融服务。

第三条 市人民政府应当加强对浦东新区绿色金融工作的领导，深化与国家金融管理、发展改革、生态环境、财政等部门协作，推动绿色金融改革创新，加强绿色转型风险管理，协调解决绿色金融发展中的重大问题。

浦东新区人民政府应当建立绿色金融发展工作协调机制，健全与国家金融管理部门在沪机构联系机制，将绿色低碳转型纳入国民经济和社会发展规划，推动气候投融资等绿色金融改革创新试点，统筹各项支持政策，提升重点产业绿色能级，促进经济社会绿色发展。

Several Provisions for the Pudong New Area of Shanghai Municipality on Sustainable Finance Development

(Adopted at the 41st Session of the 15th Shanghai Municipal People's Congress Standing Committee on June 22, 2022)

Section 1 The Several Provisions for the Pudong New Area of Shanghai Municipality on Sustainable Finance Development (these "Provisions") are formulated to enhance sustainable finance services, integrate sustainable financing with inclusive and technology-driven financing, further advance the Shanghai International Financial Center, develop Shanghai as a global hub for sustainable financing, accelerate socioeconomic green reforms, and support a higher-quality environment, pursuant to the basic principles of applicable laws and administrative regulations, and in light of the actual circumstances of the Pudong New Area.

Section 2 These Provisions shall apply to all sustainable finance initiatives and their related support activities within the Pudong New Area.

"Sustainable finance" in these Provisions refers to financial services facilitating economic and social activities that improve the ecological environment, mitigate climate change, and improve resource conservation.

Section 3 The Municipal People's Government shall lead in enhancing sustainable finance in the Pudong New Area in cooperation with national financial regulation, development and reform, ecology and environment, and fiscal departments, facilitating innovation in sustainable financial innovation, improving risk management in ecological transformations, and addressing critical challenges in sustainable finance development.

The Pudong New Area People's Government shall develop a coordination process for sustainable finance, improve communications with national financial regulators, integrate green and low-carbon strategies into national economic and social development plans, support pilot projects for innovative sustainable finance initiatives, consolidate support policies, improve sustainability in major industries, and promote sustainable economic growth.

第四条 市地方金融监管部门应当加强与国家金融管理部门在沪机构的沟通协调，指导浦东新区绿色金融改革创新和依法开展绿色金融监督管理相关工作。

市发展改革、生态环境、财政、经济信息化、科技、住房城乡建设管理、交通、市场监管、知识产权等部门应当按照各自职责，完善配套政策，支持浦东新区开展绿色金融改革创新。

市国有资产监督管理部门应当强化市属国有金融机构绿色金融业绩考核管理，推动市属国有金融机构落实国家金融管理部门绿色金融活动监督管理要求。

浦东新区金融工作部门应当做好本行政区域的绿色金融发展促进和服务保障等工作。浦东新区发展改革、生态环境、财政、科技经济信息化、建设交通、国有资产监督管理、市场监管、知识产权等部门应当按照各自职责支持开展绿色金融改革创新。

第五条 市人民政府应当统筹建立绿色企业评价要求、评价标准和绿色项目认定条件、认定标准工作机制。市发展改革、经济信息化、科技、生态环境、住房城乡建设管理、交通、市场监管等部门根据国家规定，研究制定行业绿色企业评价要求、评价标准和绿色项目认定条件、认定标准。

市生态环境部门会同市发展改革等部门，根据绿色企业评价要求、评价标准和绿色项目认定条件、认定标准，统筹市级各行业主管部门建立绿色项目库，引入第三方机构评估论证或者组织专家开展科学论证，将绿色企业、绿色项目、绿色技术等入库，并实行动态调整。

Section 4 The municipal financial regulatory department shall improve communications and coordination with national financial administrations to direct sustainable finance reforms and innovation in the Pudong New Area, and regulate and oversee sustainable finance activities lawfully.

Municipal departments, including development and reform, ecology and environment, finance, economy and information technology, science and technology, housing and urban-rural development, transportation, market regulation, and intellectual property administrations, shall refine policies to support sustainable finance innovation in the Pudong New Area to the extent of their duties.

The municipal state-owned assets regulatory administration shall improve sustainable finance evaluations and regulation in municipal state-owned financial institutions, ensuring compliance with national financial regulatory requirements for sustainable finance activities.

The Pudong New Area financial supervision administration shall lead efforts in facilitating and safeguarding sustainable finance, supported by the Pudong New Area reform and development, ecology and environment, finance, science and technology, economy and information technology, construction and transportation, state-owned asset regulation, market regulation, and intellectual property administrations to the extent of their duties.

Section 5 The Municipal People's Government shall create a work process to develop evaluation requirements and standards for eco-friendly organizations and sustainable projects. Municipal development and reform, economic informatization, science and technology, ecology and environment, housing and urban-rural development, and market regulation departments shall issue specific requirements and criteria for assessing eco-friendly organizations and evaluating sustainable projects pursuant to national regulations.

The municipal ecology and environment department cooperates with the municipal reform and development department to build a sustainable project database based on the eco-friendly organization and sustainable project assessment requirements and criteria, facilitating evaluations through third-party organizations or expert panels. The database shall be regularly updated to include new records for eco-friendly organizations, sustainable projects, and technologies

浦东新区人民政府应当会同国家金融管理部门在沪机构、市地方金融监管部门等，实施绿色金融国家标准和行业标准，组织制定国家绿色金融标准浦东新区配套制度或者补充性绿色金融地方标准，统一浦东新区绿色金融产品和项目评估、认定和分类标准。

第六条　市人民政府应当支持国家金融管理部门在沪机构在浦东新区建立改革试验机制，促进绿色金融等领域创新监管互动，支持金融机构等市场主体在有效控制风险的基础上开展产品业务创新。

市人民政府应当鼓励国家金融管理部门在沪机构开展金融科技创新监管工具实施工作，支持在浦东新区开展绿色金融活动的金融机构（以下统称浦东新区金融机构）利用金融科技手段，实现对绿色项目的识别、环境效益的测算。

第七条　市人民政府应当支持国家金融管理部门在沪机构通过完善绿色金融评价机制，引导浦东新区金融机构制定绿色金融发展规划，完善组织机制，建立绩效考核、激励约束和内部风险管理制度。

浦东新区人民政府及各部门在选择金融机构开展相关合作时，应当将其实施环境信息披露情况和绿色金融评价结果作为重要依据。

第八条　本市支持金融机构、金融基础设施机构、相关交易场所等为碳密集型、高环境风险的项目或者市场主体向低碳、零碳排放转型提供金融服务。

市人民政府应当支持国家金融管理部门在沪机构结合浦东新区产业实际和区域特征，制定补充性转型金融标准、分类和管理规则。

The Pudong New Area People's Government shall work with both national financial regulators in Shanghai and municipal financial regulators to enforce national and industrial sustainable finance standards and draft local regulations to support national sustainable finance standards, ensuring uniformity in assessing, recognizing, and classifying sustainable finance products and projects in the Pudong New Area.

Section 6 The Municipal People's Government shall encourage the creation of sustainable finance reforms and pilots as directed by national financial regulators in Shanghai, facilitate dynamic sustainable finance regulation, and encourage innovation in products and business models in market entities such as financial institutions based on effective risk management.

The Municipal People's Government shall encourage national financial regulators in Shanghai to implement fintech regulatory systems and encourage Pudong New Area sustainable financial institutions ("Pudong New Area financial institutions") to use financial technologies to identify sustainable projects and assess their environmental benefits.

Section 7 The Municipal People's Government shall provide support for improvements made for the sustainable finance evaluation framework for national financial regulators in Shanghai, guiding Pudong New Area financial institutions in drafting sustainable finance development plans, refining organizational structures, and establishing comprehensive systems for performance, incentives, constraints, and risk management.

When selecting financial institution partners, the Pudong New Area People's Government shall prioritize performance in environmental information disclosure and sustainable finance.

Section 8 This Municipality supports financial institutions, infrastructure institutions, and trading venues in providing financial services for carbon-intensive and high-environmental-risk projects or entities as they transition to low- or zero-carbon emissions.

The Municipal People's Government shall support national financial regulators in Shanghai in developing supplementary standards, classifications, and management rules for transition finance based on industry practices and regional conditions in the Pudong New Area.

第九条 本市支持符合条件的境内外机构发起设立为改善生态环境、应对气候变化、资源节约高效利用等经济社会活动提供金融服务的银行、证券、保险、基金、信托等金融机构。

本市支持世界银行、亚洲开发银行、亚洲基础设施投资银行等为绿色项目提供投融资和技术服务，发挥新开发银行总部效应，推动绿色金融国际合作项目在浦东新区落地。

本市发挥中国（上海）自由贸易试验区、中国（上海）自由贸易试验区临港新片区跨境资金流动先行先试优势，为绿色企业提供更便利的跨境投融资服务。

第十条 本市鼓励金融机构响应国际国内生物多样性金融相关倡议，利用国际绿色金融合作框架，参与生物多样性金融示范项目。

浦东新区人民政府鼓励金融机构创新业务模式，加强区域协作，参与生物多样性金融示范项目。

第十一条 浦东新区人民政府应当按照国家部署，开展气候投融资试点，探索差异化的投融资模式，以市场手段强化各类资金有序投入，创新激励约束机制，完善资金安排联动机制，抑制高碳投资。

支持浦东新区金融机构创新气候投融资产品和业务。

第十二条 国家金融管理部门在沪机构鼓励银行业金融机构改革内部资金转移定价机制，探索通过有关结构性货币政策工具、监管评价、提高绿色信贷不良率容忍度等方式，支持开展绿色信贷业务。

浦东新区银行业金融机构应当优化、创新绿色信贷产品和服务，扩大信贷规模，提供信贷便利，降低信贷成本，将环境、社会和治理要求纳入管理流程和全面风险管理体系。

Section 9 This Municipality encourages eligible domestic and foreign institutions to form banks, securities, insurance, funds, trusts, and other financial institutions to provide services for ecological improvement, climate change mitigation, resource conservation, and efficient utilization.

This Municipality encourages global institutions, such as the World Bank, the Asian Development Bank, and the Asian Infrastructure Investment Bank, to provide financial and technological services related to sustainable finance and to collaborate on sustainable finance projects, following the strategic position of the New Development Bank to enhance international collaborations.

This Municipality gives full play to the cross-border capital flow pilot advantages of the China (Shanghai) Pilot Free Trade Zone and its Lin-gang Special Area to facilitate cross-border investment and financing services for eco-friendly organizations.

Section 10 This Municipality encourages financial institutions to participate in both global and domestic biodiversity finance initiatives, utilizing international sustainable finance partner systems to participate in pilot projects.

The Pudong New Area People's Government encourages these institutions to innovate business models and enhance regional collaboration for biodiversity finance pilot projects.

Section 11 The Pudong New Area People's Government shall carry out climate investment and financing pilot programs as directed by national guidelines, experiment with diverse financing models, optimize fund allocation through market solutions, innovate incentive mechanisms and improve collaborative funding arrangement process to discourage high-carbon investments.

Pudong New Area financial institutions are to receive support to develop innovative climate investment financial products and services.

Section 12 National financial regulators in Shanghai encourage banking institutions to reform internal fund transfer pricing policies, explore structural monetary policies, carry out regulatory assessments, and increase tolerance for non-performing sustainable finance to support the development of sustainable finance services.

Pudong New Area banking institutions shall be encouraged to refine and innovate their sustainable finance products and services, broadening accessibility and convenience to credit, reducing costs, and incorporating environmental, social, and governance criteria within their operational and risk management frameworks.

第十三条 本市支持上海票据交易所为绿色票据发展提供技术支持，参与制定绿色票据标准，探索形成包括票据融资、应收账款融资、保理融资等供应链融资的绿色标准。

鼓励浦东新区金融机构依托上海票据交易所发展绿色票据业务，发挥绿色票据再贴现业务的定向支持作用，向绿色产业链上下游企业提供优质的支付融资方案。

第十四条 浦东新区人民政府探索将符合条件的重大清洁低碳能源项目等纳入地方政府专项债券支持范围，支持区域绿色项目建设。

浦东新区人民政府应当建立绿色债券项目储备，支持金融机构、地方金融组织、企业发行碳中和债券、可持续发展挂钩债券等各类债券，降低发债成本。

纳入绿色债券项目储备范围内的企业发行债券的，浦东新区人民政府鼓励区内融资担保机构提供担保支持，市中小微企业政策性融资担保基金按照规定提供再担保支持。

鼓励符合条件的第三方机构开展绿色债券信用评级，揭示绿色债券信用风险。

第十五条 中国外汇交易中心、上海证券交易所、上海清算所、跨境银行间支付清算公司、中国证券登记结算公司上海分公司、中央国债登记结算公司上海总部等金融基础设施机构应当为绿色债券的发行、登记、托管、交易、清算、结算等提供便利服务。鼓励金融机构承销绿色公司债券、绿色企业债券、绿色债务融资工具、绿色资产支持证券等。

国家金融管理部门在沪机构支持中国外汇交易中心、上海证券交易所等金融基础设施机构组织绿色债券做市，为金融机构开展绿色债券做市业务提供系统便利和支持。

Section 13 This Municipality supports the Shanghai Commercial Paper Exchange to develop sustainable financial instruments by providing technical support, participating in setting standards, and exploring sustainable practices for supply chain finance, including instrument financing, accounts receivable financing, and factoring.

Pudong New Area financial institutions are encouraged to explore sustainable financial instrument ventures through the Shanghai Commercial Paper Exchange, leveraging rediscounting services to offer comprehensive solutions for sustainable industry chains.

Section 14 The Pudong New Area People's Government is to consider incorporating major clean and low-carbon energy projects into the local government's specialized bond initiatives, facilitating regional sustainable projects.

The Pudong New Area People's Government shall create a reserve of green bond projects to aid financial institutions and organizations in issuing sustainable bonds including carbon neutrality bonds and sustainability-linked bonds, and reduce issuance costs.

The Pudong New Area People's Government encourages financial guarantee institutions to support bond-issuing organizations listed in the green bonds project reserve, with municipal micro, small and medium-sized enterprises ("MSME") financial guarantee funds providing additional support.

Eligible third-party institutions are encouraged to assess the creditworthiness of green bonds to disclose potential risks.

Section 15 Key financial infrastructure providers, including the China Foreign Exchange Trade System, Shanghai Stock Exchange, Shanghai Clearing House, Cross-border Interbank Payment System, Shanghai Branch of China Securities Depository and Clearing Corporation, and Shanghai Headquarters of China Central Depository & Clearing, shall support the issuance, registration, management, trading, and clearing and settlement of green bonds, to enhance the framework for green corporate bonds, debt financing instruments, and asset-backed securities.

National financial regulators in Shanghai are to support China Foreign Exchange Trade System, Shanghai Stock Exchange and other key financial infrastructure providers to facilitate market-making for green bonds, ensuring that financial institutions have the necessary system support to conduct market activities.

第十六条 本市支持上海保险交易所在浦东新区试点建立绿色保险产品登记、清算、结算服务平台。

登记注册在中国（上海）自由贸易试验区的保险公司分支机构，可以办理绿色再保险分入业务。

第十七条 浦东新区从事涉及重金属、危险废物、有毒有害物质等环境高风险企业，应当投保环境污染责任保险。浦东新区生态环境部门应当每年制定并公布应投保企业名录。

国家金融管理部门在沪机构建立环境污染责任保险产品和服务监管机制。上海保险交易所试点建立浦东新区环境污染责任保险信息管理平台。

第十八条 本市支持银行业金融机构加大对绿色融资租赁项目的资金支持。

支持登记注册在浦东新区的融资租赁公司探索开展绿色低碳相关技术专利等无形资产的融资租赁业务。

登记注册在浦东新区的融资租赁公司开展节能环保、清洁生产、清洁能源、生态环境、基础设施绿色升级以及绿色服务等领域融资租赁业务的，经国家金融管理部门授权，可以适当放宽租赁资产余额集中度与关联度的监管限制。

第十九条 本市支持浦东新区信托机构通过信托贷款、股权投资、债券投资、资产证券化、公益（慈善）信托等方式开展绿色信托业务。

以不动产设立信托的，可以向不动产登记机构申请记载为信托财产。中国信托登记公司可以在浦东新区试点信托财产登记，办理绿色信托产品登记、统计、流转等事项。

Section 16 This Municipality supports the Shanghai Insurance Exchange's new platform for green insurance products, promoting transparent registration, clearing, and settlement processes.

Insurance branches in the China (Shanghai) Pilot Free Trade Zone may manage green reinsurance inward initiatives.

Section 17 Pudong New Area enterprises engaged in environmentally risky operations, such as those involving heavy metals, hazardous waste, toxic and harmful substances, shall secure liability insurance against environmental pollution. The Pudong New Area ecology and environment department shall annually specify the enterprises obligated to purchase this insurance.

National financial regulators in Shanghai shall establish a regulatory system for environmental liability insurance products and services, with the Shanghai Insurance Exchange piloting a dedicated information management platform in the Pudong New Area.

Section 18 This Municipality supports banks in expanding their financial contributions to sustainable leasing projects.

Pudong New Area financial leasing enterprises are encouraged to delve into financial leasing for intangible assets like patented sustainable technology.

Subject to authorization from national financial regulators, Pudong New Area financial leasing enterprises may have fewer restrictions on the concentration and relatedness of leased asset balances for the enterprises involved in financial leasing for energy conservation, environmental protection, clean production, clean energy, ecological improvements, sustainable infrastructure upgrades, and sustainable services.

Section 19 This Municipality supports Pudong New Area trust institutions in conducting sustainable trust businesses through trust loans, equity investments, bond investments, asset securitization, and public welfare (charitable) trusts.

Applications for recording real estate as trust property during trust formation may be submitted to the real estate registration institution. China Trust Registration may pilot the registration of trust properties in the Pudong New Area, managing activities such as registration, statistics, and distribution of sustainable trusts.

第二十条 本市鼓励浦东新区金融机构遵循负责任投资原则，将环境、社会和治理因素纳入投资决策，督促被投资方改善环境绩效，减少环境风险，开展环境信息披露。

有关部门应当在绿色投资主题基金的市场主体登记、基金跨境投资审批等方面提供便利。

第二十一条 本市支持私募股权基金、创业投资基金等加大对绿色企业、绿色项目、绿色技术等的投资。

本市区域性股权市场运营机构组织建立私募股权与创业投资份额转让平台，开展私募股权和创业投资份额的托管、转让、质押登记等业务。国家对公司股权出质登记另有规定的，从其规定。

第二十二条 本市推动清洁低碳能源、生态环保等领域符合条件的项目纳入全国基础设施领域不动产投资信托基金试点项目库，并开展试点。

本市支持国家绿色发展基金等在沪各类绿色股权投资基金，聚焦浦东新区环境保护、污染防治、能源资源节约利用、绿色建筑、绿色交通、绿色制造等领域开展绿色投资。

浦东新区人民政府应当依托政府引导基金或者产业投资基金，通过政府和社会共同出资的方式，支持绿色产业发展。政府出资产生的投资超额收益部分可以按照一定比例，让利给社会出资人。

第二十三条 市、浦东新区相关部门应当按照规定对绿色低碳技术的创新开发给予支持。鼓励浦东新区金融机构对绿色低碳技术成果转化和应用开展投贷联动业务。

Section 20 This Municipality encourages Pudong New Area financial institutions to abide by responsible investment principles, incorporate environmental, social, and governance factors in their decisions, and encourage investees to improve environmental performance, reduce environmental risks, and disclose environmental data.

Appropriate departments shall streamline procedures for enterprise registrations for sustainable investment funds and cross-border investment reviews.

Section 21 This Municipality encourages private equity and venture capital funds to increase their investments in eco-friendly enterprises, sustainable projects and technologies.

Regional equity market operators in this Municipality shall create a share transfer platform for private equity and venture capital, handling custody, share transfers, and pledge registrations. Specific national regulations on equity pledge registration shall govern.

Section 22 This Municipality is to support the inclusion of eligible low-carbon source and ecological projects into the national pilot projects reserve for real estate investment trusts within the infrastructure sector.

This Municipality is to support sustainable equity investment funds in Shanghai, including the national sustainable development fund, to focus on investments in environmental protection, pollution control, energy conservation and use, sustainable buildings, transportation, and manufacturing in the Pudong New Area.

The Pudong New Area People's Government shall use government or industrial investment funds to promote sustainable industries through government and social investment, sharing excess investment returns with private investors based on a predetermined ratio.

Section 23 The appropriate municipal and Pudong New Area departments shall improve the advancement of innovative sustainable and low-carbon technologies. Pudong New Area financial institutions are encouraged to facilitate the transformation and application of these technologies by linking investments and loans.

第二十四条 市中小微企业政策性融资担保基金应当为开展绿色项目融资的中小微企业加大担保支持力度，提高绿色融资担保业务比重和担保额度，给予费率优惠。市人民政府相关部门应当完善资本金补充、风险补偿和绩效考核机制。

对于获得市中小微企业政策性融资担保基金担保的浦东新区中小微企业，浦东新区相关部门应当按照规定给予经费补助等支持。

第二十五条 本市支持金融机构开展环境权益担保融资、回购、拆借等业务，推动金融机构成为上海环境能源交易所的直接交易主体。

本市支持浦东新区金融基础设施机构和金融机构等依法合规开展天然气、电力、氢能等绿色相关衍生产品和业务，推动浦东新区金融基础设施机构和金融机构依法参与创设、交易碳衍生品等相关业务。

第二十六条 市场主体可以办理有关环境权益担保登记，并对登记内容的真实性、完整性和合法性负责。中国人民银行征信中心动产融资统一登记公示系统、上海环境能源交易所等机构不对担保登记内容进行实质审查。

设定担保的碳排放权价值发生较大幅度减少等情形的，担保权人可以按照法律规定或者合同约定，请求补足担保价值，压降借贷资金额度或者提前收回借贷资金并处置担保标的。

债务人未能按期履行债务或者发生约定实现担保权的情形，担保权人可以与担保人协议以碳排放权折价或者拍卖、变卖该碳排放权。通过上海环境能源交易所进行转让的，可以采取协议交易、单向竞价或者其他符合规定的方式。

Section 24 The municipal financial guarantee fund for MSMEs shall increase support for MSMEs involved in sustainable project financing by increasing the business proportion of sustainable finance guarantees issued and raising both guarantee limits and offering preferential rates. Appropriate municipal departments shall enhance capital support, risk compensation, and performance assessments.

Appropriate Pudong New Area departments shall provide necessary financial subsidies to MSMEs eligible for guarantees from the municipal financial guarantee fund for MSMEs.

Section 25 This Municipality is to encourage financial institutions to engage in environmental credit activities such as secured financing, repurchase transactions, and interbank lending, and encourage their direct trading through the Shanghai Environment and Energy Exchange.

This Municipality is to support financial infrastructure providers and financial institutions in the Pudong New Area to manage and offer sustainable financial derivative products according to law, including those in natural resources such as natural gas, electricity, and hydrogen, encouraging their participation in carbon derivatives and similar markets.

Section 26 Market entities may register environmental credits as collateral and ensure the registration's authenticity, completeness, and legality. The People's Bank of China Credit Reference Center's Unified Registration and Publicity System and the Shanghai Environment and Energy Exchange are not to perform in-depth reviews of these collateral registrations.

Should the value of carbon credits pledged as collateral substantially decrease, the secured party, pursuant to statutory or contractual terms, may require collateral replenishment, reduce the loan amount, or expedite loan recovery and collateral disposal.

If the debtor defaults or meets the criteria to liquidate security interests, the secured party may negotiate with the guarantor to either settle debts with carbon credits or to auction or sell them. Such transfers through the Shanghai Environment and Energy Exchange may be conducted through negotiated transactions, unidirectional bidding, or other lawful methods.

第二十七条　浦东新区内生产经营活动涉及温室气体重点排放、曾发生过环境事故的企业，从浦东新区金融机构或者地方金融组织获得绿色金融服务的，应当向资金融出方提供相关环境信息。

第二十八条　从浦东新区金融机构或者地方金融组织获得绿色金融服务的区内企业，发生下列情形之一的，应当在五个工作日内将相关信息告知资金融出方：

（一）与环境保护相关的行政许可事项发生变更的；

（二）发生突发生态环境事件的；

（三）发生对社会公众及投资者有重大影响的生态环境损害赔偿等事件的；

（四）因生态环境违法行为受到行政处罚或者被追究刑事责任的；

（五）资金融出方要求提供的其他环境信息。

第二十九条　浦东新区银行业金融机构法人应当按照中国人民银行发布的《金融机构环境信息披露指南》等标准要求，发布年度环境信息报告。鼓励浦东新区银行业金融机构法人开展环境信息临时披露，并增加披露频次和范围。

鼓励浦东新区内除银行业金融机构法人之外的金融机构发布年度环境信息报告，开展环境压力测试等环境风险量化分析，并将分析结果纳入信息披露范围。

第三十条　浦东新区人民政府应当依托市大数据资源平台建立绿色金融数据服务专题库，探索金融数据与公共数据的交互融合，与智慧能源双碳云平台、产业绿贷综合性融资服务平台等建立数据对接机制，依法推进信息的归集、整合、查询、共享。

Section 27 Pudong New Area enterprises involved in significant greenhouse gas emissions or past environmental incidents shall disclose pertinent environmental information to financiers when seeking sustainable finance from Pudong New Area financial or local financial institutions.

Section 28 Pudong New Area enterprises that secure sustainable finance shall notify the financier within five business days if any of the following occur:

(1) changes in environmental protection administrative approval;

(2) sudden ecological or environmental incidents;

(3) events warranting ecological or environmental damage compensation or other significant public or investor impacts;

(4) actions subject to administrative penalties or criminal liability for environmental violations; or

(5) other environmental information as requested by the financier.

Section 29 Banking financial institutions registered in the Pudong New Area shall disclose annual environmental information reports following the People's Bank of China's Environmental Information Disclosure Guidelines of Financial Institutions, and are encouraged to provide more frequent and extensive ad hoc environmental information disclosures.

Financial institutions in the Pudong New Area, excluding banking financial institutions, are encouraged to disclose annual environment information reports, conduct quantitative analysis of environmental risk including environmental stress tests, and incorporate the findings into their transparency reports.

Section 30 The Pudong New Area People's Government shall create a dedicated sustainable finance database on the municipal big data resource platform to facilitate the dynamic integration of financial and public data, establish data linking processes with platforms like the smart energy carbon cloud platform and the comprehensive financing service platform for industrial sustainable finance, while enhancing the collection, integration, searching and sharing of information lawfully.

浦东新区人民政府支持各类市场主体使用绿色金融数据服务专题库，推动金融资源精准服务绿色项目库中的企业或者项目等。

第三十一条 浦东新区人民政府应当依托绿色金融数据服务专题库，与各类第三方机构开展数字化协作，探索建立企业碳账户和自然人（常住人口）碳账户，将企业碳排放表现信息和个人绿色低碳活动信息等纳入碳账户、形成碳积分。

鼓励浦东新区金融机构为碳积分高的企业和自然人提供优惠的金融产品或者服务。

加强浦东新区企业碳账户和自然人碳账户与全市碳普惠相关平台的衔接。

第三十二条 市人民政府应当将绿色金融发展纳入上海金融创新奖评选范围，按照规定评选和奖励。

浦东新区人民政府应当将绿色金融发展纳入财政政策体系予以专项支持，通过相关领域财政专项资金对下列机构加大支持力度：

（一）符合财政支持条件的金融机构、金融基础设施机构、地方金融组织、企业、第三方机构等；

（二）金融机构在区内新设符合财政支持条件的绿色金融事业部（业务中心）或者绿色金融分支机构。

第三十三条 浦东新区人民政府应当为吸引绿色金融高层次、紧缺急需和优秀青年人才提供便利支持。对绿色金融创新项目获得上海金融创新奖具有突出贡献的个人，浦东新区人民政府可以按照规定引进落户。

浦东新区人民政府应当为外籍绿色金融人才在居留、出入境、办理工作许可等方面提供便利支持。

The Pudong New Area People's Government is to support the use of the sustainable finance database by market entities to precisely allocate financial resources to enterprises or projects in the sustainable project database.

Section 31 The Pudong New Area People's Government shall leverage the sustainable finance database to digitally collaborate with various third-party organizations to develop both corporate and individual (residential) carbon accounts, which include information on corporate carbon emissions and individuals' green activities, leading to the generation of carbon credits.

Financial institutions in the Pudong New Area are encouraged to offer preferential financial products or services to entities and individuals with high carbon credits.

The linkage between corporate and individual carbon accounts in the Pudong New Area with citywide carbon management platforms is to be improved.

Section 32 The Municipal People's Government shall integrate sustainable finance development into the criteria for the Shanghai financial innovation award and perform evaluations and recognitions as required.

The Pudong New Area People's Government shall specifically support sustainable finance development by integrating it within its fiscal policies and increasing support for the following entities in sectors that are eligible for fiscal support:

(1) financial institutions, financial infrastructure institutions, local financial organizations, enterprises, and third-party institutions; and

(2) financial institutions launching new sustainable finance divisions (service center) or branches within the Pudong New Area.

Section 33 The Pudong New Area People's Government shall provide support for attracting top-tier, in-demand, and outstanding young sustainable finance professionals. Professionals who have made significant contributions to awarded sustainable finance innovation pilot projects may receive support for residency and registration from the Pudong New Area People's Government.

The Pudong New Area People's Government shall facilitate residency, entry and exit, and work permit processes for international sustainable finance professionals.

浦东新区人民政府支持金融机构、高校、第三方机构等组织开展绿色金融相关专业技能培训。

第三十四条 本市各级人民法院、人民检察院应当充分发挥司法职能，为绿色金融创新发展提供司法保障。

支持人民法院、仲裁机构在审判、仲裁活动中尊重金融行业交易规则和习惯，发布绿色金融典型案例。支持上海金融法院探索金融市场案例测试机制，向金融市场提供规则指引，服务绿色金融创新。

第三十五条 本市支持提供绿色认证、环境咨询、资产评估、资信评级、数据服务、碳排放核算、环境信息披露报告核查等服务的第三方机构，依法开展专业化业务活动。

第三方机构应当勤勉尽责、恪尽职守，严格遵守数据安全和权益保护要求，对文件资料的真实性、准确性、完整性进行核查和验证。第三方机构制作、出具的文件有虚假记载、误导性陈述或者重大遗漏，给他人造成损失的，应当依法承担法律责任。

第三十六条 本规定所称环境权益，是指政府为解决外部性问题，对行为主体在自然资源和环境容量消耗数量方面设定许可、进行总量控制而产生的权益。

本规定所称碳排放权，是指分配给重点排放单位的规定时期内的碳排放额度。

第三十七条 本规定自2022年7月1日起施行。

The Pudong New Area People's Government is to encourage financial institutions, higher education institutions, and third-party organizations to provide professional training in sustainable finance.

Section 34 People's courts and people's procuratorates at all levels in this Municipality shall utilize their functions to provide legal protections for innovation in sustainable finance development.

People's courts and arbitration institutions are to be supported in complying with financial market trading norms and practices in their decisions and encouraged to share notable sustainable finance cases. The Shanghai Financial Court is encouraged to trial financial market case mechanism, provide regulations-based guidance to financial markets, and support sustainable finance innovation.

Section 35 This Municipality encourages third-party institutions that provide services like green certification, environmental consulting, asset valuation, credit rating, data services, carbon emission accounting, and verification of environmental information reports to conduct specialized business activities lawfully.

Third-party organizations shall responsibly perform their duties, strictly comply with data security and rights protection policies, and validate the authenticity, accuracy, and completeness of documents and materials. If documents produced or issued by third parties contain false records or misleading statements that result in losses, they shall assume legal liability as required by law.

Section 36 "Environmental credits" in these Provisions refers to the rights when the government sets license limits and manages the overall consumption of natural resources and environmental capacities by entities due to external factors.

"Carbon credits" in these Provisions refers to the assigned carbon emission allowance given to major emitters within a specified timeframe.

Section 37 These Provisions shall take effect from July 1, 2022.

上海市浦东新区推进市场准营承诺即入制改革若干规定

Several Provisions for the Pudong New Area of Shanghai Municipality on Advancing the Market Access Commitment System Reform

上海市浦东新区推进市场准营承诺即入制改革若干规定

（2022年6月22日上海市第十五届人民代表大会常务委员会第四十一次会议通过）

第一条 为了创新政府服务管理方式，推进市场准营承诺即入制改革，优化营商环境，根据有关法律、行政法规的基本原则，结合浦东新区实际，制定本规定。

第二条 本规定适用于浦东新区推进市场准营承诺即入制改革的相关管理服务活动。

本规定所称的市场准营承诺即入制，是指通过一次性告知市场主体从事特定行业许可经营项目须具备的全部条件和标准，由市场主体书面承诺其已经符合要求并提交必要材料，即可取得行政许可的改革举措。

第三条 浦东新区推进市场准营承诺即入制改革，应当以市场主体需求为导向，统筹行政审批制度和商事制度改革，注重政府职能转变和改革系统集成，不断激发市场主体活力。

第四条 浦东新区人民政府应当加强组织协调，建立健全深化市场准营承诺即入制改革的统筹推进工作机制。

浦东新区审批制度改革部门负责牵头推进市场准营承诺即入制改革工作。

浦东新区行政审批局负责市场准营承诺即入手续的具体办理工作。

Several Provisions for the Pudong New Area of Shanghai Municipality on Advancing the Market Access Commitment System Reform

(Adopted at the 41st Session of the 15th Shanghai Municipal People's Congress Standing Committee on June 22, 2022)

Section 1 The Several Provisions for the Pudong New Area of Shanghai Municipality on Advancing the Market Access Commitment System Reform (these "Provisions") are formulated to innovate governmental service and administration approaches, advance the reform of the market access commitment system, and improve the business environment, pursuant to the basic principles of applicable laws and administrative regulations, and in light of the actual circumstances in the Pudong New Area.

Section 2 These Provisions shall apply to market access commitment system reform management and service activities in the Pudong New Area.

"Market access commitment system" in these Provisions refers to a government reform initiative through which the government notifies market entities of all conditions and standards needed for permitted business activities within specific industries. Upon submitting a written declaration of compliance assuring that these conditions are met, along with the necessary documentation, the market entities are to be issued with administrative approvals.

Section 3 The Pudong New Area shall respond to the needs of market entities by coordinating reforms of the administrative review and business systems, transforming government functions, integrating reform systems, and supporting market entities to advance the market access commitment system reform.

Section 4 The Pudong New Area People's Government shall enhance organizational coordination, create and refine efficient workflows for advancing the market access commitment system reform.

The Pudong New Area administrative review reform department is to lead efforts to facilitate the market access commitment system reform.

The Pudong New Area administrative review department takes charge of handling specific market access commitment system procedures.

第五条 除涉及国家安全、社会稳定、生态环境安全、金融业审慎监管、重大公共利益的领域，浦东新区人民政府应当根据国家和本市改革部署，按照稳妥审慎、循序渐进、风险可控的要求，确定实行市场准营承诺即入制的行业及相应的事项，并向社会公布。

第六条 市场主体设立登记后，浦东新区行政审批局应当通过企业专属网页等途径推送通过承诺即入方式办理行业许可的线上链接和线下渠道。

市场主体选择承诺即入方式办理许可的，可以通过“一网通办”平台等在线办理，也可以线下办理。

在自然灾害、事故灾难、公共卫生和社会安全等突发事件应对处置期间，浦东新区行政审批局应当充分发挥“一网通办”平台作用，推进实现无接触服务、不见面办理。

第七条 浦东新区有关行政机关负责具体行业市场准营承诺即入制的推进以及相应市场主体的事中事后监管等工作。

对实行市场准营承诺即入制的行业，浦东新区有关行政机关应当按照场所、设备、人员、资金、管理制度等要素，对从事该行业经营活动涉及的法定许可条件进行标准化集成，对要求市场主体提交的材料整合精简，编制许可条件清单和材料清单，并向社会公开。

第八条 浦东新区行政审批局应当通过告知承诺书一次性告知市场主体从事特定行业经营活动涉及的行政许可事项、许可条件、法律法规依据以及所需材料目录、提交方式、提交期限等。

告知承诺书的告知内容应当全面、准确、易懂，可量化、可操作，不得模糊表述，不得含有兜底条款，不得在告知承诺书外另附许可审批条件。

Section 5 The Pudong New Area People's Government shall determine and publicly disclose which industries and matters shall be added to the market access commitment system based on national and municipal reform policies, other than fields involving national security, social stability, ecological and environmental safety, prudential regulation for financial industry, and major public interests. The determination shall follow principles that ensure prudent, gradual implementation and controlled risks.

Section 6 The Pudong New Area administrative review department shall, upon registration of a market entity, provide online and offline channels for obtaining industry licenses via the market access commitment system, facilitated through a dedicated enterprise webpage.

Market entities may apply for licenses through the market access commitment system either online using the integrated online government service platform or offline.

In emergencies such as natural disasters, accidents, public health, or social security incidents, the administrative review department shall use the integrated online government service platform to support seamless, contactless services and processing.

Section 7 Pudong New Area administrative departments are to oversee the implementation of the market access commitment system in specific industries, as well as the regulation of market entities during and after their operations.

These administrative departments shall standardize and integrate licensing requirements for industries adopting the market access commitment system, considering factors such as business address, devices, staff, funds, and management systems, simplifying and centralizing the documentation required from market entities, and compile and publicly disclose lists of these conditions and required materials.

Section 8 The Pudong New Area administrative review department shall issue a notice regarding the declaration of compliance to market entities, detailing the administrative approvals necessary for specific business activities, alongside the terms, legal basis, required documentation, submission methods, and submission deadlines.

The declaration of compliance shall be clear, accurate, understandable, measurable, and practicable; it shall not contain any ambiguous expressions or catch-all clauses, nor shall it attach additional conditions beyond the declaration of compliance.

第九条 市场主体按照承诺即入方式办理市场准营手续的，应当书面承诺其已经满足告知的条件、标准和技术等要求，并能够在约定的期限内提交相关材料。

第十条 浦东新区有关行政机关应当建立全流程指导和服务机制，通过线上线下多种渠道，为市场主体理解和履行承诺内容提供专业化、智能化的导航指引和咨询服务。

浦东新区行业牵头部门应当会同行政许可部门编制市场准营承诺即入制告知承诺书示范文本，并向社会公布。

对因承诺可以减省的材料，不再要求提供。对可以在行政许可后一定期限补交的材料，实行容缺办理、限期补交。

市场主体因突发事件影响超出提交材料期限的，按规定予以期限中止、顺延。

第十一条 市场主体从事许可经营项目应当符合许可条件和标准。市场主体向浦东新区行政审批局提交市场准营告知承诺书以及符合要求的有关材料后，即可取得行政许可。

第十二条 签署市场准营告知承诺书的市场主体及其承诺的内容由浦东新区行政机关向社会公开。

鼓励市场主体自行公开告知承诺书。

第十三条 市场主体告知承诺书的内容，构成行政机关实施事中事后监管的依据。

市场主体在告知承诺书约定的期限内未提交材料、提交的材料不符合要求的，浦东新区有关行政机关应当依法注销相关行政许可。

Section 9 Market entities seeking market access via the commitment system shall submit a declaration of compliance confirming they meet all specified conditions, standards, and technical requirements, and provide the necessary documentation by the specified deadline.

Section 10 Pudong New Area administrative departments shall create a support process to provide comprehensive professional and intelligent guidance and consultancy via various online and offline channels, assisting market entities in understanding and meeting compliance declaration requirements.

Pudong New Area lead industry departments shall cooperate with the administrative approval department to develop and publicly disclose a standard declaration of compliance template for the market access commitment system.

Certain documents may no longer be required due to the streamlined process. For other documents that are still necessary, market entities may submit incomplete initial applications upon administrative approval, provided the remaining documents are submitted by the specified deadline thereafter.

Submission deadlines may be postponed or extended as required if emergencies prevent a market entity from submitting the required documents on time.

Section 11 Market entities shall comply with all licensing requirements and standards when conducting regulated business activities. Upon submission of a declaration of compliance for market access and all required documentation, a market entity may receive its administrative approval from the Pudong New Area administrative review department.

Section 12 Pudong New Area administrative departments shall publicly disclose declarations of compliance signed by the market entities and their descriptions.

Market entities are encouraged to voluntarily disclose their declarations of compliance to the general public.

Section 13 The information within a market entity's declaration of compliance shall be the basis for regulation by administrative departments both during and after processing.

If a market entity fails to meet the submission deadline specified in the declaration of compliance or fails to meet documentation submission requirements, the administrative departments shall deregister the applicable administrative approvals lawfully.

浦东新区有关行政机关应当按照分级分类监管原则，结合市场主体信用和风险状况，根据“双随机、一公开”的要求，在作出行政许可后二个月内对市场主体的承诺内容开展检查。

第十四条 浦东新区有关行业管理部门应当结合市场主体及其主要投资人等信用信息及行业管理实际，确定可以适用市场准营承诺即入方式的市场主体范围。依法列入严重违法失信企业名单的市场主体，不得适用市场准营承诺即入方式。

浦东新区社会信用管理部门应当加强市场主体公共信用信息的归集、共享等工作，有关行业管理部门应当建立健全市场主体信用记录，依法归集至公共信用信息服务平台。

第十五条 市大数据管理部门应当加强推进市场准营承诺即入制改革的信息化保障，开发有关功能模块和数据接口，推动与浦东新区市场准营承诺即入制申办系统对接。市级有关部门应当优化完善相关业务系统，建立数据交换机制，确保市场准营承诺即入制全程线上办理。

浦东新区大数据管理部门应当为市场准营承诺即入制平台日常运行提供技术支撑。

第十六条 市人民政府及其行政审批制度改革等有关部门应当积极争取国家有关部门对浦东新区市场准营承诺即入制改革的支持，加大赋权力度，加强对浦东新区推进市场准营承诺即入制改革的指导、协调，帮助解决改革中的问题，及时总结推广改革经验。

第十七条 市场主体以不正当手段取得许可的，浦东新区相关行政机关应当依法给予行政处罚；开展相应经营活动的，适用未经许可从事经营活动的法律、法规处理。

第十八条 本规定自 2022 年 8 月 1 日起施行。

In line with principles of tiered and categorized regulation, Pudong New Area administrative departments shall review market entities based on their compliance, credit, and risk assessments within two months of granting the administrative approval, following a transparent sampling and disclosure process.

Section 14 Pudong New Area industrial administrative departments shall identify the market entities eligible for inclusion in the market access commitment system based on the entity's and primary investor's credit details and industry regulatory practices. Those listed as having engaged in significant illegality or dishonesty shall be ineligible for participation in the market access commitment system.

The Pudong New Area social credit regulatory department shall intensify efforts to gather and share the credit information of market entities. Industrial administrative departments shall create and maintain accurate credit records for market entities, incorporating into the public credit information service platform lawfully.

Section 15 The municipal big data management department shall enhance IT support for the market access commitment system reform by developing the necessary functional modules and data interfaces, and integrating them with services for commitment-based market commitment access applications. The appropriate municipal departments shall optimize and synchronize their systems to facilitate online processing of all market access commitment procedures.

The Pudong New Area big data management department shall provide ongoing technical assistance for the routine operation of the market access commitment system platform.

Section 16 The Municipal People's Government and the appropriate departments, including the administrative review reform department, shall actively seek support from the national departments to advance the market access commitment system reform in the Pudong New Area for increased authorization, proper guidance and coordination, address issues arising from the reform, and promptly summarizing and sharing the reform experiences.

Section 17 A market entity that improperly acquires a license shall be subject to administrative punishments imposed by Pudong New Area administrative departments according to law. If it conducts business activities without a proper license, it shall be subject to laws applicable to unlicensed business operations.

Section 18 These Provisions shall take effect from August 1, 2022.

上海市浦东新区化妆品产业创新发展若干规定

Several Provisions for the Pudong New Area of Shanghai Municipality on Innovative Development of the Cosmetics Industry

上海市浦东新区化妆品产业创新发展若干规定

（2022年7月21日上海市第十五届人民代表大会常务委员会第四十二次会议通过）

第一条 为了促进浦东新区化妆品产业创新发展，培育化妆品领域新模式新业态，助力上海国际消费中心城市建设，根据有关法律、行政法规的基本原则，结合浦东新区实际，制定本规定。

第二条 市人民政府应当加强对化妆品产业发展工作的领导，深化与国家有关部门的协作，承接国家创新试点，统筹协调浦东新区与其他区域化妆品产业发展中的重大事项。

浦东新区人民政府应当加强对区域化妆品产业创新发展工作的领导，整合优化资源，综合协调化妆品产业创新发展中的重大问题。

第三条 市药品监督管理部门应当支持和指导浦东新区化妆品产业创新发展，开展化妆品监督管理工作。

市经济信息化部门负责推进化妆品产业规划布局和产业发展。

市和浦东新区发展改革、科技、商务、市场监督管理、知识产权、人力资源社会保障等部门以及上海海关，根据各自职责和本规定，负责化妆品产业发展、消费促进、贸易便利等相关工作。

Several Provisions for the Pudong New Area of Shanghai Municipality on Innovative Development of the Cosmetics Industry

(Adopted at the 42nd Session of the 15th Shanghai Municipal People's Congress Standing Committee on July 21, 2022)

Section 1 The Several Provisions for the Pudong New Area of Shanghai Municipality on Innovative Development of the Cosmetics Industry (these "Provisions") are formulated to encourage innovative development in the cosmetics industry, develop new business models, and contribute to Shanghai's role as an international commerce hub, pursuant to the basic principles of applicable laws and administrative regulations, and in light of the actual circumstances in the Pudong New Area.

Section 2 The Municipal People's Government shall expand its leadership role in the cosmetics industry, expand cooperation with national agencies, organize national innovation pilot projects, and address significant challenges in the development of the cosmetics industry throughout the Pudong New Area and beyond.

The Pudong New Area People's Government shall take the leadership in encouraging innovation within the local cosmetics sector by integrating resources and coordinating key innovative development initiatives for the cosmetics industry.

Section 3 The municipal medical products administration shall provide support and guidance for cosmetics industry innovation in the Pudong New Area while overseeing and regulating the industry.

The municipal economy and information technology department takes charge of advancing strategic planning and development within the cosmetics industry.

Municipal and Pudong New Area departments, including development and reform, science and technology, commerce, market regulation, intellectual property, human resources and social security departments, along with Shanghai Customs, take charge of supporting the development of the cosmetics industry, enhancing consumption, facilitating trade, and conducting other associated tasks as provided by these Provisions to the extent of their duties.

第四条 本市建立浦东新区化妆品产业创新发展工作市、区两级会商机制。

市和浦东新区相关部门应当加强沟通协调，对浦东新区化妆品产业创新发展工作中跨部门、跨领域的事项共同协商研究。

第五条 市科技部门和浦东新区人民政府应当支持化妆品企业与高校、科研院所、医疗机构合作，促进产学研医深度融合，提升行业创新能力和新产品研发能力，推动化妆品领域科技成果转化。

市科技部门和浦东新区人民政府应当引导和支持化妆品企业加大研发投入，开展技术创新和专业人才培养，培育、发展高新技术企业，支持有条件的化妆品企业创建科技创新基地。

第六条 市和浦东新区鼓励化妆品生产企业数字化转型，推进化妆品领域工业互联网和消费互联网融合，构建生产全过程关键数据的实时采集与分析系统，提升质量安全风险管控能力。

第七条 市经济信息化、商务、药品监督管理等部门应当根据各自职责，推动化妆品企业加强品牌引领示范培育和建设。

浦东新区应当采取措施，推动建设化妆品品牌孵化基地，为品牌研发设计、宣传推广等提供服务。

第八条 市商务、经济信息化、药品监督管理等部门应当根据各自职责支持、培育化妆品消费领域新模式新业态。

市商务部门应当支持化妆品领域数字消费模式，建设化妆品智慧购物示范场景，培育化妆品经营电子商务标杆企业。

浦东新区应当采取措施，支持推进全球化妆品品牌集聚，鼓励和引导在综合商圈开展展示、推广、体验等活动，支持在免税店设立国产化妆品销售专区，助推国际消费中心城市建设。

Section 4 A new municipality and district consultation mechanism is to be developed for the innovative development of the cosmetics industry in the Pudong New Area.

Appropriate municipal and district departments shall increase communication and collaboration, and jointly address cross-department and interdisciplinary issues on the innovative development of cosmetics industry in the Pudong New Area.

Section 5 The municipal science and technology department shall cooperate with the Pudong New Area People's Government to support partnerships between cosmetics companies and academic or medical institutions, advance integrated projects spanning production, education, research, and healthcare, enhance industry innovation and new product R&D, and facilitate the application of scientific and technological advancements in cosmetics.

The municipal science and technology department and the Pudong New Area People's Government shall provide guidance for cosmetics enterprises to broaden R&D efforts, implement technological innovations, develop professional expertise, support high-tech organizations, and assist eligible enterprises to establish technological innovation centers.

Section 6 This Municipality and the Pudong New Area encourage cosmetics manufacturers to adopt digital technologies, integrate online commercial platforms with industrial systems, implement real-time data collection and analytics throughout production processes, and improve risk management practices for quality and safety.

Section 7 The municipal economy and information technology, commerce, and drug regulatory administrations shall, to the extent of their duties, encourage cosmetics enterprises to enhance their branding strategies, and support their growth and market presence.

The Pudong New Area shall implement initiatives to build incubation centers for cosmetics brands and shall provide support for R&D, design, marketing, and other associated activities.

Section 8 The municipal commerce, economy and information technology, and medical products administrations shall support the development of new business models and consumer formats in the cosmetics sector to the extent of their duties.

The municipal commerce department shall support digital consumer models, develop pilot use cases for intelligent cosmetics commerce, and support leading e-commerce cosmetics organizations.

The Pudong New Area shall encourage international cosmetics brands to expand their presence, encourage and facilitate promotional and experiential activities in comprehensive commercial districts, establish zones for domestic cosmetics in duty-free shops, and further develop the area as an international commerce hub.

第九条 本市鼓励化妆品企业提升匹配消费需求的能力，开展皮肤科学基础研究，探索小批量、多品种、高灵活度的生产模式，精准研发适合消费者个性化需求的化妆品。

精准研发的普通化妆品上市前，本市化妆品备案人应当根据产品特点进行安全评估和功效评价，按照国家规定提交备案资料。

第十条 本市化妆品备案人、境内责任人可以在浦东新区设立的经营场所，根据消费者的个性化需求，对其备案的普通化妆品（不含儿童化妆品、眼部护肤类化妆品、使用新原料的化妆品等）现场提供包装、分装服务，或者自行、委托本市化妆品生产企业生产。

现场提供包装、分装服务且涉及直接接触化妆品内容物的化妆品备案人、境内责任人应当对化妆品质量安全进行风险评估，并向浦东新区市场监督管理部门申请生产许可。符合条件的，核发化妆品生产许可证。化妆品备案人、境内责任人应当建立相应的化妆品生产质量管理体系，定期向浦东新区市场监督管理部门提交生产质量管理体系自查报告。

具体生产许可条件和管理要求由市药品监督管理部门制定。

第十一条 本市支持产业园区管理机构、第三方机构建立化妆品原料供应服务平台，为浦东新区化妆品注册人、备案人、受托生产企业提供原料供应和质量管理等服务。

提供化妆品原料供应服务的平台运营机构应当建立原料进货查验记录制度，加强原料的检验检测、贮存和运输管理，并做好原料采购、供应记录。

第十二条 本市支持相关企业依法开展进口化妆品的包装和贴标服务，促进贸易便利化。

Section 9 This Municipality encourages cosmetics enterprises to closely align with consumer needs, conduct foundational dermatological research, explore the production of small, diverse, and customizable batches of products, and develop cosmetics tailored to individual consumer preferences.

Before launching such products, cosmetics enterprises registered in the Municipality shall perform safety assessments and efficacy evaluations based on product features, and submit the necessary registration documentation pursuant to national regulations.

Section 10 Cosmetics enterprises registered in this Municipality or their domestic representative offices may offer on-site packaging and subpackaging services for registered general cosmetics (excluding children's cosmetics, eye care cosmetics, and cosmetics with new raw materials) products at their Pudong New Area facilities, tailored to consumer preferences, or produce these cosmetics themselves or by entrusted manufacturers in this Municipality.

Those offering packaging, subpackaging, and direct-contact cosmetic services shall conduct quality and safety risk assessments, apply for production licenses with the Pudong New Area market regulation administration upon meeting the set criteria, and create comprehensive quality management systems for cosmetics production, submitting regular reports on these systems to local market regulators.

The municipal medical products administration shall detail specific licensing conditions and management requirements.

Section 11 This Municipality supports the creation of service platforms for cosmetic raw materials by industrial park management organizations and third-party providers, ensuring supply and quality management for cosmetic registrants, manufacturers, and cosmetics companies registered in the Pudong New Area.

Operators of these platforms shall set up systems for inspecting and documenting incoming raw materials, and maintain strict standards for the inspection, testing, storage, and transportation of raw materials, keeping accurate procurement and supply records.

Section 12 This Municipality supports businesses lawfully providing packaging and labeling services for imported cosmetics to promote trade facilitation.

在进口化妆品直接接触内容物的包装已完成标注标签并可追溯的情况下，境外化妆品注册人、备案人或者其境内责任人可以在浦东新区符合相关监管要求的区域内自行或者委托其他企业，在直接接触内容物的包装上标注中文名称和使用期限，并按照国家化妆品标签的相关规定进行包装和加贴中文标签，但不得接触或者暴露化妆品内容物。

第十三条 对于通过浦东新区进口用于注册或者备案检验的化妆品样品，以及用于企业研发、非试用或者非销售的展览展示化妆品，符合相关要求的，可以免予提供进口特殊化妆品注册证或者进口普通化妆品备案信息，并免予进口检验。

第十四条 中国国际进口博览会和本市其他化妆品专业会展的参展商，经过海关等部门批准，可以在会展结束后将原进口化妆品转为浦东新区行政区域内的海关特殊监管区域的保税货物，举办消费促进等推广活动，符合条件的可以按照跨境电商方式销售。

第十五条 本市鼓励化妆品相关行业协会、企业、科研院所等参与化妆品新原料、新技术和新业态等创新领域相关标准的制定。

浦东新区知识产权部门应当运用专利快速审查服务机制，根据国家相关规定，为企业申请涉及化妆品的相关技术专利提供预审服务。

第十六条 本市鼓励专业院校为化妆品产业培养专业人才，加大引进海内外化妆品安全评估等专业领域高端人才。

市和浦东新区有关部门应当支持第三方检验检测机构、专业研发生产服务平台等建设，支持化妆品相关行业协会加强产业链信息沟通与合作，建立中国特色植物资源化妆品研究开发体系。

If the packaging of imported cosmetics directly in contact with the substances is labeled and traceable, foreign cosmetics registrants, enterprises registered in the Pudong New Area, or their domestic responsible individuals may label the Chinese name and shelf life on the packaging themselves or through other entrusted organizations within designated areas in the Pudong New Area that meet regulatory requirements. They may package and affix Chinese labels pursuant to national regulations, provided the cosmetic substances are not touched or exposed.

Section 13 Imported cosmetic samples for registration or review, as well as for enterprise R&D, non-trial use, or non-commercial exhibition products in the Pudong New Area that meet specified requirements may be exempt from specialized cosmetics licenses, mandatory filings for imported general cosmetics, or import inspections.

Section 14 Exhibitors authorized to participate in the China International Import Expo and cosmetics trade fairs held in this Municipality may reclassify imported products as bonded merchandise within specific customs regulatory zones in the Pudong New Area after the event, promoting them through consumer engagement activities and potentially selling them via cross-border e-commerce platforms under applicable conditions as authorized by departments such as customs.

Section 15 This Municipality encourages cosmetics industry associations, enterprises, and academia to help participate in the formulation of standards for new raw materials, technologies, and business practices within the cosmetics sector.

The Pudong New Area intellectual property administration shall use expedited patent review processes to provide pre-application services for enterprises filing cosmetic technology patents pursuant to national regulations.

Section 16 This Municipality encourages professional education institutions to develop expertise in the cosmetics field and attract both domestic and international high-quality professionals in specialized areas such as cosmetics safety assessments.

The appropriate municipal and Pudong New Area departments shall support the creation of independent testing labs and professional R&D and production platforms, facilitate communication and collaboration among cosmetics industry associations, and establish research programs that leverage unique Chinese botanical resources.

市药品监督管理部门、浦东新区市场监督管理部门可以委托第三方专业机构开展化妆品质量安全风险评估。

第十七条 本市建立健全与化妆品产业创新发展相适应的包容审慎监管机制。

市药品监督管理部门应当与浦东新区相关部门、上海海关等建立化妆品风险信息交换机制，实现化妆品风险信息的共享、预警和及时处置。

浦东新区市场监督管理部门应当加强对浦东新区化妆品注册人、备案人、受托生产企业、境内责任人的日常监管，可以结合浦东新区实际和产业创新发展要求依法制定监管规范。

第十八条 违反本规定第十条从事现场包装、分装服务且涉及直接接触化妆品内容物活动的，由负责药品监督管理的部门没收违法所得、违法生产经营的化妆品和专门用于违法生产经营的原料、包装材料、工具、设备等物品；违法生产经营的化妆品货值金额不足一万元的，并处一万元以上五万元以下的罚款；货值金额一万元以上的，并处货值金额五倍以上二十倍以下罚款；情节严重的，责令停产停业，依法取消备案或者吊销化妆品许可证件，并对违法单位的法定代表人或者主要负责人、直接负责的主管人员和其他直接责任人员依法处理。

违反本规定的其他行为，有关法律、行政法规已有处罚规定的，从其规定。

第十九条 本规定自 2022 年 8 月 1 日起施行。

The municipal medical products administration and the Pudong New Area market regulation administration may entrust third-party professionals to assess cosmetics safety and quality.

Section 17 This Municipality creates and refines an inclusive and prudent regulatory process suitable for the dynamic nature of the innovations in the cosmetics industry.

The municipal medical products administration shall create a cosmetics risk information sharing system with the appropriate Pudong New Area departments and Shanghai Customs to enable risk sharing, early warnings, and prompt action.

The Pudong New Area market regulation administration shall intensify routine regulation of cosmetics registrants, registered cosmetics entities, entrusted manufacturers, and domestic representatives, establishing regulatory standards that reflect the actual circumstances in the Pudong New Area and the industry innovation needs.

Section 18 Those who violate Section 10 of these Provisions by engaging in on-site packaging or subpackaging involving direct contact with cosmetic substances shall face the following penalties from the medical products administration: confiscation of illegal proceeds, unlawfully produced cosmetics, raw materials, packaging, tools, devices, and other items used for illegal production. If the illegal production and operation value is less than RMB 10,000, a fine of RMB 10,000 to RMB 50,000 is to be imposed. If the value is over RMB 10,000, the fine is to be five to twenty times the value. In serious cases, the entity may be ordered to cease operations, and its registration or cosmetics license is to be revoked, and representatives by operation of law, principally responsible individuals, or individuals directly responsible is to be punished lawfully.

Punishments for other violations of these Provisions shall be governed by the applicable laws and administrative regulations (if any).

Section 19 These Provisions shall take effect from August 1, 2022.

上海市浦东新区文物艺术品交易若干规定

Several Provisions for the Pudong New Area of Shanghai Municipality on Transactions of Cultural Artifacts and Artworks

上海市浦东新区文物艺术品交易若干规定

（2022年8月27日上海市第十五届人民代表大会常务委员会第四十三次会议通过）

第一条　为了规范与促进浦东新区文物艺术品交易，推动上海国际文物艺术品交易中心建设，提升城市软实力，根据有关法律、行政法规的基本原则，结合浦东新区实际，制定本规定。

第二条　本规定适用于在浦东新区开展的文物艺术品交易活动。

第三条　本市坚持守正创新、扩大开放、交流互鉴、科学监管的原则，推动文物艺术品市场高水平开放、高质量发展。

从事文物艺术品交易活动，应当遵守文物保护和艺术品经营有关法律、法规、规章的规定，不得交易国家禁止买卖的文物艺术品，不得将国家禁止出境的文物转让、出租、质押给外国人或外国组织。

第四条　市人民政府应当加强与国家有关部门的协作，建立健全本市促进文物艺术品市场发展的综合协调机制，统筹协调文物艺术品市场发展中的重大事项。

浦东新区人民政府应当建立促进文物艺术品市场发展的工作机制，制定配套政策，落实支持措施，依托区域制度基础、开放优势和资源条件，推动文物艺术品交易集聚化、规模化发展。

Several Provisions for the Pudong New Area of Shanghai Municipality on Transactions of Cultural Artifacts and Artworks

(Adopted at the 43rd Session of the 15th Shanghai Municipal People's Congress Standing Committee on August 27, 2022)

Section 1 The Several Provisions for the Pudong New Area of Shanghai Municipality on Transactions of Cultural Artifacts and Artworks (these "Provisions") are formulated to regulate and enhance transactions of cultural artifacts and artworks, facilitate the Shanghai International Trading Center for Cultural Artifacts and Artworks, and elevate the cultural status of this Municipality, pursuant to the basic principles of applicable laws and administrative regulations, and in light of the actual circumstances in the Pudong New Area.

Section 2 These Provisions shall apply to cultural artifacts and artworks transactions conducted in the Pudong New Area.

Section 3 This Municipality commits to preserving foundational values while innovating and expanding openness, promoting mutual learning, and applying evidence-based regulation to foster an advanced and thriving market for cultural artifacts and artworks.

All transactions involving cultural artifacts and artworks shall comply with applicable laws and guidelines regulating the protection of cultural artifacts and artwork business activities. It is prohibited to trade cultural artifacts and artworks that are nationally banned or to transfer, lease, or pledge cultural artifacts prohibited for export to foreign entities or individuals.

Section 4 The Municipal People's Government shall enhance collaboration with appropriate national agencies and develop and refine a comprehensive coordination process to support and address significant issues within the cultural artifacts and artworks market.

The Pudong New Area People's Government shall create a work process to bolster the market for cultural artifacts and artworks, develop support policies, implement actions, and leverage the area's institutional strengths, openness, and resource advantages to encourage concentrated and large-scale development of these transactions.

第五条 市文物行政管理部门负责统筹推进本市文物艺术品市场发展，依法实施相关监督管理工作。

浦东新区文物行政管理部门负责制定并实施本行政区域有关促进文物艺术品市场发展的制度、规划和标准，依法实施具体监督管理工作。

市和浦东新区文化旅游、商务、市场监管、经济信息化、公安、人力资源社会保障等部门以及海关、外汇管理部门按照各自职责，做好促进文物艺术品市场发展的相关服务保障与监督管理工作。

第六条 本市在浦东新区设立上海国际文物艺术品交易服务中心（以下简称服务中心），为文物拍卖经营活动和艺术品交易提供场所、设施、鉴定等服务。

服务中心依法取得文物拍卖许可证，接受市文物行政管理部门的监督管理，并依法承担相应的法律责任。

服务中心的管理办法由市文物行政管理部门另行制定。

第七条 具备相应的资金、人员、技术等条件的拍卖企业可以通过服务中心开展文物拍卖经营活动。

服务中心对拍卖企业实行名单制管理，配合相关行政管理部门对其进行监督管理。拟列入、移出的拍卖企业名单应当由服务中心报市文物行政管理部门审核同意。列入名单的拍卖企业通过服务中心以自己的名义开展文物拍卖经营活动。

通过服务中心开展文物拍卖经营活动的拍卖企业不得从事文物购销经营活动。服务中心不得允许文物商店通过其开展文物拍卖经营活动。

Section 5 The municipal cultural artifacts administration takes charge of thoroughly facilitating the development and lawfully overseeing the management of the cultural artifacts and artworks market.

The Pudong New Area cultural artifacts administration takes charge of designing and implementing systems, strategies, and standards that support the cultural artifacts and artworks market within its jurisdiction, ensuring compliance with legal oversight and management requirements.

Appropriate departments in this Municipality and the Pudong New Area, including but not limited to those involved in culture and tourism, commerce, market regulation, economy and information technology, public security, human resources and social security, customs, and foreign exchange management, support and oversee the development of the market for cultural artifacts and artworks to the extent of their duties.

Section 6 The Shanghai International Trading Center for Cultural Artifacts and Artworks (the "Trading Center") is to be created in the Pudong New Area to provide venues, devices, and appraisal services for auctioning and transacting cultural artifacts and artworks.

The Trading Center shall lawfully obtain an operational license for cultural artifacts auctions, comply with oversight and management from the municipal cultural artifacts administration, and assume their legal liability.

Regulatory protocols for the Trading Center shall be determined by the municipal cultural artifacts administration.

Section 7 Auction businesses with the requisite capital, staff, technology, and other resources are permitted to conduct cultural artifacts auctions through the Trading Center.

The Trading Center shall maintain a registry of auction businesses and collaborate with appropriate administrative departments to oversee and manage these organizations. Inclusion or removal of businesses from the registry requires submission to the municipal cultural artifacts administration for evaluation and approval. Registered businesses shall conduct auctions under their own names through the Trading Center.

Auction enterprises operating through the Trading Center shall be strictly prohibited from trading cultural artifacts. The Trading Center shall be prohibited from allowing cultural artifact dealers to participate in auctions.

服务中心应当履行下列管理责任：

（一）制定相关交易规则及管理规范，明确开展文物拍卖经营活动和艺术品交易的条件、范围与要求，以及各方的权利义务、违反相关规定的处理措施等；

（二）配合相关行政管理部门做好监督管理工作，建立内控内审机制，发现交易国家禁止买卖的文物艺术品以及其他违法经营行为的，应当立即制止并向相关行政管理部门报告；

（三）对在提供服务中获悉的个人信息、商业秘密等，应当依照法律法规和协议约定予以保密；

（四）其他应当履行的管理责任。

第八条 通过服务中心开展文物拍卖经营活动的拍卖企业应当在拍卖文物前，将拟拍卖标的报经服务中心内部审核通过后，由服务中心将拟拍卖标的整场报市文物行政管理部门审核，不得瞒报、漏报、替换标的，或者以其他方式逃避文物拍卖标的审核。未经市文物行政管理部门审核同意的，不得对文物拍卖标的进行宣传、预展和拍卖。

服务中心的报审材料应当包含服务中心文物拍卖专业人员签署的标的征集鉴定意见。服务中心和拍卖企业应当对报审材料的真实性、准确性和完整性负责。

第九条 市文物行政管理部门受理文物拍卖标的审核申请后，应当按照国家有关文物拍卖标的审核规定，严格组织开展实物审核，于二十个工作日内办理审核批复文件，并同时报国务院文物行政管理部门备案。

下列物品不得作为文物拍卖标的：

（一）依照法律应当上交国家的出土（水）文物，以出土（水）文物名义进行宣传的标的；

The Trading Center shall have the following management responsibilities:

(1) creating trading rules and management standards, defining the conditions, items, and requirements for conducting auctions and transactions, clarifying rights and obligations of all parties, and outlining regulatory actions for violation;

(2) collaborating with appropriate administrative departments to oversee and manage activities, develop internal control and audit systems, and immediately halt and report any transactions involving cultural artifacts and artworks prohibited by the state or any other illegal activities detected to the appropriate administrative departments;

(3) keeping confidential personal information and trade secrets acquired during service provision as specified by laws and agreements; and

(4) performing other necessary management obligations.

Section 8 Prior to auctioning cultural artifacts at the Trading Center, auction businesses shall submit items for internal review to the Trading Center. Upon approval, these items are to be forwarded to the municipal cultural artifacts administration for further evaluation. Auction businesses may not misrepresent, omit, alter items, or otherwise avoid scrutiny. No advertising, previewing, or auctioning of items is allowed without explicit approval by the municipal cultural artifacts administration.

Submissions for review shall include signed accredited appraisals from the Trading Center's cultural artifacts auction professionals. Both the Trading Center and auction businesses shall be accountable for the truthfulness, accuracy, and completeness of these submissions.

Section 9 Upon receiving a request to review cultural artifacts for auction, the municipal cultural artifacts administration shall conduct a thorough inspection in line with national regulations, complete the review and issue the decision within twenty business days, and report the findings to the State Council's cultural artifacts administration.

Items ineligible for auction include:

(1) cultural artifacts unearthed or retrieved from water that are legally required to be surrendered to the government;

（二）被盗窃、盗掘、走私的文物或者明确属于历史上被非法掠夺的中国文物；

（三）公安、海关、市场监管等执法部门和人民法院、人民检察院依法没收、追缴的文物，以及银行、冶炼厂、造纸厂、废旧物资回收单位拣选的文物；

（四）国有文物收藏单位及其他国家机关、部队和国有企业、事业单位等收藏、保管的文物，以及非国有博物馆馆藏文物；

（五）国有文物商店收存的珍贵文物；

（六）国有不可移动文物及其构件；

（七）涉嫌损害国家利益或者有可能产生不良社会影响的标的；

（八）其他法律法规规定不得流通的文物。

第十条 通过服务中心报审的文物拍卖活动结束后三十日内，服务中心应当将拍卖记录报市文物行政管理部门备案。市文物行政管理部门应当按照有关规定，将文物拍卖记录报国务院文物行政管理部门。

服务中心和拍卖企业应当对备案材料的真实性、准确性和完整性负责。

第十一条 文物临时进境，应当向海关申报，并报文物进出境审核机构审核、登记。除经海关和文物进出境审核机构批准外，临时进境文物在境内滞留时间不得超过六个月。

经国务院文物行政管理部门授权，中国（上海）自由贸易试验区保税区内的临时进境文物滞留时间满六个月，需要延长期限的，携运人应当在期限届满十个工作日前向国家文物进出境审核上海管理处书面申请延期复出境，每次延期不得超过六个月。滞留时间每累计满二年再次申请延期复出境的，携运人应当在期限届满十个工作日前向国家文物进出境审核上海管理处办理实物审核手续。

(2) cultural artifacts that are stolen, unlawfully excavated, smuggled, or historically identified as illicitly plundered;

(3) cultural artifacts recovered by people's courts, people's procuratorates, law enforcement authorities such as public security, customs, or market regulation, or selected by banks, smelters, paper mills, or material recycling organizations;

(4) cultural artifacts owned and kept by government agencies including the state-owned cultural artifact collection organizations, military units, state-owned enterprises, public institutions, and private museums;

(5) valuable artifacts in state-owned artifact shops;

(6) immovable state-owned artifacts and their components;

(7) items likely to harm national interests or cause adverse social effects; and

(8) other cultural artifacts restricted by law from circulation.

Section 10 Within thirty days of the submission of a request for the review of cultural artifacts for auction, the Trading Center shall submit a detailed record to the municipal cultural artifacts administration for documentation. The municipal cultural artifacts administration shall then report these records as legally required to the State Council's cultural artifacts administration.

The Trading Center and auction businesses shall be responsible for ensuring the documentation's authenticity, accuracy, and completeness.

Section 11 The temporary import of cultural artifacts shall be declared to customs and reported to the appropriate import and export control authorities for assessment and registration. Temporarily imported artifacts shall not remain in the country for more than six months without approval from both customs and the cultural artifacts import and export control authorities.

Carriers of temporarily imported cultural relics within the bonded area of the China (Shanghai) Pilot Free Trade Zone, whose stay exceeds six months and requires an extension, shall submit a written application for re-export extension to the Shanghai office of the national cultural artifacts import and export control administration authorized by the State Council administrative department for cultural artifacts at least ten business days before the expiration date. Each extension is limited to six months. For those staying a cumulative total of two years or more, carriers shall complete a physical review with the Shanghai office at least ten business days before the expiration date.

未按照规定申请延期复出境的临时进境文物，再次出境时，依照文物出境审核标准和程序进行审核。

第十二条 海关特殊监管区域内的企业可以按照国家和本市有关规定，在海关特殊监管区域外开展文物艺术品保税展示交易活动。

鼓励有条件的文物艺术品经营单位通过电子商务新业态、新模式，开展文物艺术品在线展示、交易、定制服务等活动。对依法开展的在线文物拍卖活动，市文物行政管理部门应当通过“一网通办”、告知承诺等方式简化拍卖标的审核流程，提高审核效率。

第十三条 本市加强文物鉴定等各类专业人才培养，支持文物经营单位的专业人员参加文物博物专业技术人员职称评定。本市社会文物行业协会应当定期举办文物鉴定专业技术培训，对考核合格的人员颁发合格证书。

申请文物商店设立许可或者文物拍卖许可证的，取得合格证书并达到相应专业技术能力的人员视同符合条件的文物博物专业技术人员。

文物鉴定专业技术人员培训、考核、惩戒的管理办法由市文物行政管理部门另行制定。

第十四条 浦东新区人民政府应当在文化领域专项资金中作出专门安排，用于促进文物艺术品市场发展。

浦东新区人民政府应当为符合相关条件的文物艺术品专业技术人员，落实有关支持和保障政策，提供便利服务。

浦东新区应当采取措施，鼓励各类金融机构为文物艺术品交易提供专项金融服务方案。

Temporarily imported cultural artifacts whose permits have not been properly extended are to be treated based on the standards and procedures for exporting cultural artifacts when they are re-exported.

Section 12 Enterprises within specific regulatory areas may conduct bonded display and transaction activities with cultural artifacts and artworks outside these areas pursuant to national and municipal provisions.

Entities that manage cultural artifacts and artworks are encouraged to adopt new e-commerce models for online display, transactions, and customized services. The municipal cultural artifacts administration shall streamline the review process and improve the review efficiency for online auction of cultural artifacts through the integrated online government service platform and declaration of compliance.

Section 13 The Municipality is to enhance training for cultural artifacts appraisers and other professionals, supporting staff in cultural artifacts management organizations in qualification assessments. Local cultural artifacts associations shall provide regular professional training and issue certificates to those who meet the assessment standards.

Professionals who obtain these certificates and demonstrate the requisite skills for operating cultural artifact shops or conducting auctions are recognized as qualified cultural artifacts and museum professionals.

Specific guidelines for the training, evaluation, and discipline of cultural artifacts appraisal professionals are to be developed by the municipal cultural artifacts administration.

Section 14 The Pudong New Area People's Government shall allocate ad hoc fund to support the growth of the cultural artifacts and artworks market.

The Pudong New Area People's Government shall provide targeted support and protective action to facilitate the work of cultural artifacts and artworks professionals who meet established criteria.

The Pudong New Area shall take action to encourage financial institutions to develop specialized financing programs tailored for the cultural artifacts and artworks transaction market.

第十五条 市文物行政管理部门应当建立文物市场信用监管平台，并与本市公共信用信息服务平台对接。市和浦东新区文物行政管理部门应当根据文物经营单位的许可、备案、日常监督检查结果、违法行为查处以及企业公共信用综合评价等情况，确定其信用等级，并作为实施差别化分类监管的依据。对信用等级较高的，建立相应的激励机制；对信用等级较低的，加强监督检查力度，依法实施警示、惩戒。

市和浦东新区文化旅游、文物行政管理部门应当开展日常巡查、随机抽查和专项检查，并会同商务、市场监管、经济信息化、公安、海关、外汇管理等部门建立联合监管机制，强化工作协同和信息共享，加强文物艺术品市场事中事后监管，确保文物安全和文物艺术品市场健康规范有序发展。

第十六条 有下列情形之一的，由相关主管部门依法处理；构成犯罪的，依法追究刑事责任：

（一）交易国家禁止买卖的文物艺术品，或者将禁止出境的文物转让、出租、质押给外国人或外国组织的；

（二）文物商店从事文物拍卖经营活动，或者经营文物拍卖的拍卖企业从事文物购销经营活动的；

（三）未按照国家有关规定进行文物拍卖标的审核或者文物交易记录备案的；

（四）其他违反有关法律、法规规定的行为。

Section 15 The municipal cultural artifacts administration shall develop a credit regulatory platform linked to the Municipality's public credit information service platform. The municipal administrative department, along with its Pudong New Area counterpart, shall assess the creditworthiness of cultural artifacts entities based on licensing, registration, routine inspection results, regulatory compliance, and overall business entity credit assessment to determine the credit ratings. These ratings are to guide regulatory actions, offering incentives to high-credit entities while imposing stricter oversight and possible disciplinary actions on lower-rated entities.

The municipal and Pudong New Area departments in charge of culture and tourism as well as cultural artifacts administration shall conduct regular, random, and targeted inspections, and collaborate with other appropriate departments including but not limited to commerce, market regulation, economy and information technology, public security, customs, and foreign exchange management to develop a regulatory system that enhances collaboration and information sharing to intensify regulation during and after cultural artifacts and artworks market events to ensure a safe, standardized, and orderly market environment.

Section 16 In any of the following circumstances, the relevant competent authorities shall handle the matter according to law; if a crime is constituted, criminal liability shall be pursued according to law:

(1) engaging in unauthorized transactions of protected cultural artifacts, or improper transferring, leasing, or pledging of such cultural artifacts to foreign entities or individuals;

(2) cultural artifact shops involved in unauthorized auctions, or auction houses buying and selling cultural artifacts;

(3) failure to adequately review auction artifacts or properly document transactions as mandated by law; or

(4) other violations of applicable laws and regulations.

第十七条 服务中心未履行本规定第七条规定的相关管理责任，或者允许文物商店通过其开展文物拍卖经营活动的，由市文物行政管理部门责令改正，可以处一万元以上十万元以下的罚款；情节严重的，处十万元以上五十万元以下的罚款，责令停业整顿或者吊销文物拍卖许可证。

第十八条 本规定自 2022 年 10 月 1 日起施行。

Section 17 If the Trading Center fails to meet the management responsibilities prescribed in Section 7 of these Provisions, or allows unauthorized auction activities by cultural artifact shops, the municipal cultural artifacts administration shall order corrective action be taken and may impose fines ranging from RMB 10,000 to RMB 100,000; in serious cases, fines shall range from RMB 100,000 to RMB 500,000, and either operations is to be suspended for rectification or licenses for cultural artifacts auction is to be revoked.

Section 18 These Provisions shall take effect from October 1, 2022.

上海市浦东新区推进住宅小区治理创新若干规定

Several Provisions for the Pudong New Area of Shanghai Municipality on Advancing Community Management Innovation

上海市浦东新区推进住宅小区治理创新若干规定

（2022年9月22日上海市第十五届人民代表大会常务委员会第四十四次会议通过）

第一条 为了推进浦东新区住宅小区治理创新，提高治理能力和水平，营造安全有序、美丽和谐的高品质生活环境，根据有关法律、行政法规的基本原则，结合浦东新区实际，制定本规定。

第二条 浦东新区推进住宅小区治理创新应当贯彻“人民城市人民建，人民城市为人民”的重要理念，完善党组织统一领导、政府依法履职、各类组织积极协同、群众广泛参与，自治、法治、德治、共治相结合的治理体系。

浦东新区建立健全基层党组织领导，居民委员会、业主委员会、物业服务企业和业主等共同参与的住宅小区治理模式。

第三条 浦东新区人民政府应当加强对住宅小区治理工作的领导，建立依据常住人口配置公共服务资源的制度，建立健全协调机制，推动执法力量、专业力量、服务力量下沉基层，统筹赋权、减负、增能相关政策，及时研究决定住宅小区治理的重大事项。

浦东新区房屋管理、城管执法、规划资源、建设交通、民政、公安、应急管理、卫生健康、财政、人力资源社会保障等部门应当按照各自职责履行职能，对住宅小区治理进行分类指导、协同管理。

Several Provisions for the Pudong New Area of Shanghai Municipality on Advancing Community Management Innovation

(Adopted at the 44th Session of the 15th Shanghai Municipal People's Congress Standing Committee on September 22, 2022)

Section 1 The Several Provisions for the Pudong New Area of Shanghai Municipality on Advancing Community Management Innovation (these "Provisions") are formulated to advance innovations in community management, and create a safe, orderly, beautiful, and harmonious high-quality living environment, pursuant to the basic principles of applicable laws and administrative regulations, and in light of the actual circumstances in the Pudong New Area.

Section 2 Community management in the Pudong New Area shall embody the principle of a city built by and for its people. This involves refining governance systems that incorporate self-governance, the rule of law, virtuous governance, and collaborative approaches, led by Party organizations and supported by lawful performance of duties by the government with comprehensive public and organizational participation.

The Pudong New Area shall further develop a community management model featuring primary-level Party organizations, residents' committees, homeowners' committees, property management companies, and homeowners.

Section 3 The Pudong New Area People's Government shall enhance its leadership in community management, creating a resource allocation system based on population, improving coordination processes, decentralizing enforcement and services to the grassroots, implementing policies that empower, reduce burdens, and enhance capabilities, while promptly addressing critical community management issues.

Key departments including housing management, urban management and law enforcement, planning and resources, construction and transportation, civil affairs, public security, emergency management, health, finance, and human resources and social security shall perform their roles and provide specialized guidance and collaborated management in community management.

第四条 浦东新区街道办事处、镇人民政府负责本辖区内住宅小区治理和综合执法工作，强化区域资源统筹，协调区人民政府相关部门及其派出机构等共同做好相关服务管理工作。

街道办事处、镇人民政府应当建立健全常态化联系基层工作机制，定期走访社区群众，倾听群众意见建议，协调解决突出矛盾问题。

第五条 浦东新区应当根据居民人口规模、居住状况、公共服务资源配置等因素，合理设置居民委员会。居民委员会应当以服务居民为宗旨，组织开展居民自治，指导和监督业主委员会工作，依法协助相关部门做好公共服务、公共管理、公共安全等工作。

浦东新区人民政府和街道办事处、镇人民政府应当按照管辖居民户数为居民委员会配备社区工作者。对于老龄社区、老旧小区等存在特殊情况的居民委员会，应当适当增加社区工作者。政府开发的社区公共管理、公共卫生、应急服务等公益性岗位，应当优先为居民委员会配备。

居民委员会应当以居民小组或者楼组为基本单元加强住宅小区管理。社区工作者负责日常巡查走访、社情民意收集、安全隐患排查等工作。

第六条 住宅小区业主（物业使用人）应当遵守国家和本市住宅物业管理、房屋使用安全、房屋租赁、环境绿化、消防安全、卫生防疫等规定，履行自治公约和管理规约，依法配合社区治理和综合执法工作。

物业服务企业应当按照法律法规规定和物业服务合同约定履行职责。街道办事处、镇人民政府结合物业服务情况对辖区内住宅小区物业服务企业提出评价意见，纳入本市物业服务企业综合评价体系。

Section 4 Sub-district offices and township governments in the Pudong New Area take charge of community management and comprehensive enforcement within their jurisdictions, and improve regional resource planning and coordinate services and management efforts with appropriate Pudong New Area departments and their dispatched offices.

Sub-district offices and township governments shall develop and enhance regular processes for engaging with residents, conduct routine visits to listen to their opinions and suggestions, and coordinate efforts to address major conflicts and issues.

Section 5 The Pudong New Area shall set up residents' committees based on factors such as population size, living conditions, and the distribution of public service resources. These committees shall serve residents by organizing self-governance, guiding and overseeing homeowners' committees, and assisting appropriate departments with public services, management, and safety.

The Pudong New Area People's Government, sub-district offices, and township governments shall allocate residential community workers to residents' committees based on household numbers. In communities with higher populations of elderly or aging and deteriorating residential communities, the number of workers shall be increased. These officers shall prioritize positions in community management, public health, and emergency services.

Residents' committees shall improve community management by organizing resident groups or building groups. Residential community workers conduct daily patrols, collect feedback, and address safety hazards.

Section 6 Homeowners (or property occupants) shall follow national and municipal regulations on residential property management, housing safety, leasing, environmental greening, fire safety, health and epidemic prevention, comply with self-governance agreements and management protocols, and lawfully follow community management and comprehensive law enforcement efforts.

Property management enterprises are obligated to perform their duties as mandated by laws and their service contracts. Sub-district offices and township governments shall assess these companies and incorporate their evaluations into the municipal assessment system for property management companies.

浦东新区人民政府相关部门、街道办事处、镇人民政府和居民委员会、物业服务企业等相关单位依法执行应急处置措施和其他管理措施时，业主（物业使用人）应当依法配合。

第七条 浦东新区应当加强居民自治能力建设，推进住宅小区建立基层党组织牵头，居民代表、业主委员会、物业服务企业以及相关企业事业单位共同参与的议事协商机制，对住宅小区的物业管理、房屋使用安全、房屋租赁、环境绿化、消防安全、卫生防疫等公共事务进行民主协商，形成自治公约、管理规约。

街道办事处、镇人民政府应当支持居民委员会以居民小组或者楼（组）为基本单元，引导居民通过建立互联网群组等线上或者线下方式有序开展邻里互助和协商自治。居民委员会应当加强与楼（组）长、互联网群组管理人的沟通联系，为楼组居民开展自我服务和协商自治提供指导、服务。

第八条 浦东新区街道办事处、镇人民政府应当指导居民委员会加强居民志愿服务队伍建设，将具备志愿服务条件、热心公益的各类人员吸纳进入社区居民志愿队伍，纳入社区统一调度和管理。有条件的居民委员会，可以建立公共卫生或者其他专业志愿服务队伍。

街道办事处、镇人民政府和居民委员会应当支持志愿服务队伍以楼组、片区或者住宅小区为单元开展互助性、服务性、公益性志愿服务活动，并根据所开展志愿服务活动的需要对志愿者进行相关培训，为志愿服务活动的开展提供必要场所和相应条件。

第九条 因业主委员会无法选举产生或者无法正常运作，可能引发公共安全事件、损害业主共同利益的，根据居民委员会的报告，住宅小区所在地街道办事处或者镇人民政府可以指定住宅小区所属居民委员会在一定期限内暂时代行业主委员会的相关职责，并在住宅小区内公告。

Homeowners (or property occupants) shall cooperate with the Pudong New Area People's Government, sub-district offices, township governments, residents' committees, and property management companies during the implementation of emergency responses and other management activities.

Section 7 The Pudong New Area shall enhance residents' self-governance capabilities, creating a deliberation and consultation framework involving primary-level Party organizations, residents' representatives, homeowners' committees, and property management companies. This framework is to facilitate democratic discussions on public affairs like property management, housing safety, leasing, environment greening, fire safety, and hygiene and epidemic prevention to create self-governance conventions and management regulations.

Sub-district offices and township governments shall support residents' committees in utilizing resident groups or building groups as fundamental units for neighborly assistance and deliberative governance through both online and offline platforms Residents' committees shall improve interactions with building (or group) leaders and online group managers to support community-led governance and deliberative self-governance.

Section 8 Sub-district offices and township governments in the Pudong New Area shall guide residents' committees in organizing volunteer service teams, composed of community members who are passionate about public welfare and under community coordination and management. These boards may also form specialized volunteer groups focused on areas such as public health if the circumstances permit.

Sub-district offices, township governments, and residents' committees shall support volunteer activities centered on assistance, service, and public welfare within building groups, neighborhoods, and residential communities. They shall provide necessary training, venues, and appropriate facilities to support these activities.

Section 9 If a homeowners' committee cannot be elected or fails to function effectively, jeopardizing public safety or homeowners' interests, the sub-district office or township government may, based on the residents' committee report, authorize the residents' committee to temporarily take over the responsibilities of the homeowners' committees for a designated period. This decision shall be announced within the residential community.

街道办事处或者镇人民政府应当就居民委员会暂时代行业主委员会相关职责的方案征询业主意愿，并由三分之二以上的业主参与征询，经参与征询的业主过半数同意。住宅小区管理规约另有约定的，从其约定。

居民委员会暂时代行业主委员会的，应当遵守业主委员会的工作规范，代行时限一般不超过一年。暂时代行业主委员会职责期间，街道办事处、镇人民政府应当尽快推动业主委员会组建或者改选。

第十条　浦东新区应当建立居民需求诉求响应机制。居民委员会应当及时了解居民实际需求和困难，并在区人民政府相关部门和街道办事处、镇人民政府的指导下，及时回应解决居民实际问题。

街道办事处、镇人民政府应当指导居民委员会及时排查独居高龄老人、困境儿童、孕产妇、重大疾病患者、残障人士以及困难群众等人员情况，动态编制人员和需求清单，开展精准关爱帮扶工作。

对于居民委员会反映的需要区人民政府相关部门协调解决的群众诉求，街道办事处、镇人民政府应当及时向该部门发起约请，被约请的部门应当明确专人负责沟通协调工作；对于涉及多个部门的综合性事项，区人民政府应当建立健全组团式服务协调机制，切实推动问题解决。

第十一条　浦东新区街道办事处、镇人民政府应当在住宅小区统筹设立联勤联动站（点），完善联勤联动机制，持续优化住宅小区内各类突发事件和违法行为的发现、应对、处置、反馈等工作流程，实现事件闭环高效处理。

浦东新区街道办事处、镇人民政府和承担住宅小区管理事务的区人民政府相关部门及其派出机构，应当充分利用住宅小区联勤联动站（点），实现多方联动、共建共治。

Homeowners shall be consulted about the temporary assignment of duties to the residents' committee by the sub-district offices or township governments, requiring participation from two-thirds of the homeowners and approval from over half. Community management regulations shall apply to these requirements (if any).

Residents' committees temporarily performing the duties of homeowners' committees shall follow the established practices of the homeowners' committees. This temporary period shall not exceed one year, during which the sub-district office and township government will work to quickly form or re-elect a new homeowners' association board.

Section 10 The Pudong New Area shall implement a response system to address residents' concerns and needs efficiently. Residents' committees shall assess and respond to community needs under the guidance of appropriate district government departments, sub-district offices, and township governments.

Sub-district offices and township governments shall guide residents' committees in identifying and assisting vulnerable populations, including the elderly, children in difficulty, pregnant women, seriously ill patients, disabled individuals, and others requiring support, and compile lists of these individuals and their needs, ensuring targeted interventions and assistance.

When resident issues require coordination with district government departments to address residents' needs, sub-district and township governments shall promptly engage the appropriate departments, which are to assign dedicated staff to manage and resolve the issues. For issues involving multiple departments, the Pudong New Area People's Government shall create and enhance a coordinated service system to effectively address and resolve problems.

Section 11 Sub-district offices and township governments in the Pudong New Area shall develop and implement plans to establish integrated operations and response hubs (or sites) in residential communities, enhance the integrated operations and response processes, continually refine procedures for detecting, responding to, managing, and providing feedback on emergencies and illegal activities, and ensure efficient and comprehensive incident management.

Together with appropriate district government departments and their regional areas responsible for community management matters, sub-district offices and township governments in the Pudong New Area shall utilize these hubs (or sites) to promote collaborative and co-governed community management.

第十二条 浦东新区应急管理、房屋管理、卫生健康等部门应当指导街道办事处、镇人民政府建立住宅小区应急管理制度，完善平急转换机制，储备应急救援队伍，每年定期组织开展专业培训和应急演练，合理安排应急救援场地和基本生活保障物资，提高住宅小区突发事件处置和应急动员能力。

浦东新区街道办事处、镇人民政府应当将物业服务企业纳入应急处置工作体系，提供物资、资金等保障和支持，会同房屋管理、建设交通、应急管理、消防救援、卫生健康、绿化市容等部门指导物业服务企业建立平时和应急状态下的物业服务工作职责清单，定期组织物业服务工作人员开展专业培训和应急演练。

居民委员会在突发事件应急处置中难以及时召集居民会议并形成决议的，应当以多种方式听取居民意见，共同协商并实施临时性管理措施。紧急情况消除后，应当立即召开居民会议或者停止实施临时性管理措施。

第十三条 浦东新区人民政府应当建立老旧小区更新改造投入机制，制定更新改造分步推进计划，改善老旧小区居住条件和生活环境。

浦东新区应当建立老旧小区物业服务的财政扶持机制，明确资金补助条件和标准，加强老旧小区保安、保洁等物业服务。支持有条件的街镇探索区域化、连片化的物业服务模式，推动物业服务区域合并，整体提升老旧小区物业服务水平。

第十四条 浦东新区应当结合城市更新、区域功能提升等工作，按照政府主导、规划引领、尊重民意、市场运作的原则，统筹规划指标、土地供应等，制定计划加快实施城中村改造；加大对城中村公共安全、公共卫生、人居环境、违法建筑等的规范和整治力度。支持在城中村引入专业物业服务管理。

Section 12 Pudong New Area emergency management, housing management, and health departments shall guide sub-district offices and township governments in developing community-specific emergency preparedness system. This includes improving the transition process between daily and emergency models, maintaining emergency rescue teams, organizing annual professional training and drills, arranging emergency rescue sites and essential support materials, and enhancing the overall capability of residential communities to manage and respond to emergencies.

Sub-district offices and township governments in the Pudong New Area shall integrate property management enterprises into the emergency response system by providing these enterprises with necessary materials, funding, and support. In collaboration with housing management, construction and transportation, emergency management, fire rescue, health, and landscaping and city appearance departments, they shall help property management enterprises create a detailed list of responsibilities for both normal and emergency situations, and organize regular professional training and emergency drills for property management staff.

If a residents' committee cannot promptly convene a meeting and reach a resolution during an emergency, it shall gather residents' opinions through various methods. The committee shall collaboratively develop and implement temporary management activities. Once the emergency is resolved, the committee shall either hold a meeting or discontinue the temporary management activities.

Section 13 The Pudong New Area People's Government shall establish a support process for refurbishing aging and deteriorating residential communities, outlining phased improvement plans to enhance living conditions and environments.

The Pudong New Area shall create financial support systems for maintaining property management services in these areas, specifying eligibility for subsidies and enhancing essential services like security and maintenance. Neighborhoods suitable for regional property management approaches shall explore merging management operations to improve overall service.

Section 14 The Pudong New Area shall integrate urban renewal with regional function enhancement by following principles of government leadership, planning guidance, public input, and market dynamics. This involves coordinating planning indicators, land supply, and other factors to develop and expedite urban village refurbishing plans. Efforts are to be intensified to address public safety, public health, living conditions, and illegal buildings in urban villages, and support is to be provided for the introduction of professional property management services.

浦东新区应当加强对商业办公项目、厂房擅自改变房屋结构和规划用途等违法行为的整治。对在整治期间尚有居民实际居住的商业办公用房（以下称类住宅），应当纳入社区治理和居民委员会自治。

对类住宅、城中村的相关管理及执法，适用本规定关于住宅小区的相关规定。

第十五条 浦东新区街道办事处、镇人民政府、居民委员会应当建立住宅小区安全隐患排查机制，定期排查老旧房屋、楼道堆物、高空坠物、非机动车违规充电、违规群租等安全隐患。

浦东新区街道办事处、镇人民政府应当会同区人民政府相关部门建立住宅小区安全隐患联动整治机制，发现安全隐患的，应当及时督促整改，拒不整改或者整改不符合规定的，及时启动执法程序，必要时通过联合执法等方式开展整治。

第十六条 浦东新区人民政府应当按照“一支队伍管执法”的原则，决定将与住宅小区密切相关且基层能够有效承接的行政执法事项，交由街道办事处、镇人民政府行使，并定期组织评估。决定应当向社会公布。

街道办事处、镇人民政府所属综合行政执法机构以街道办事处、镇人民政府名义，具体承担本辖区内住宅小区的综合执法工作。

第十七条 住宅小区内有关单位和个人违法搭建建筑、损坏承重结构、破坏房屋建筑立面、违法改变房屋原始设计等危害房屋安全的，物业服务企业应当予以劝阻、制止，留存相关资料；劝阻、制止无效的，应当在二十四小时内通过城市网格化管理平台报告。

The Pudong New Area shall intensify efforts to address illegal activities such as unauthorized alterations to building structures and improper use of commercial office and factory buildings. During the correction period, commercial office buildings used as residences (the "quasi-residential buildings") shall be incorporated into community governance and managed by residents' committees.

The management and law enforcement of regulations for quasi-residential buildings and urban villages shall comply with the guidelines outlined for residential communities in these Provisions.

Section 15 Pudong New Area sub-district offices, township governments, and residents' committees shall establish a safety inspection process to identify and address hazards in communities, such as aging and deteriorating buildings, blocked exits, falling debris, unsafe electric vehicle charging, and illegal over-occupancy.

In collaboration with appropriate district government departments, sub-district offices and township governments shall enforce corrective actions for detected safety risks, demanding prompt compliance. If correction is refused or does not meet the required standards, law enforcement procedures shall be promptly initiated. Joint enforcement actions may be taken as necessary to ensure compliance.

Section 16 The Pudong New Area People's Government shall adhere to the principle of "law enforcement under one team" by assigning administrative enforcement closely related to residential communities, which can be effectively managed at the local level, to sub-district offices or town governments. Regular assessments shall be organized, and the decisions shall be made public to society.

Comprehensive enforcement authorities associated with sub-district offices and township governments shall carry out enforcement duties concerning community affairs within their jurisdictions.

Section 17 If individuals or entities in residential communities illegally construct buildings, damage structural systems or facades, or make unauthorized alterations that jeopardize building safety, property management companies shall halt these violations and document the incidents. If these efforts fail, they shall report the violations through the urban management platform within twenty-four hours.

涉及违法搭建建（构）筑物或者违反房屋装饰装修相关规定行为的，物业服务企业应当按照管理规约限制相关施工人员、建筑材料进入住宅小区。

第十八条 浦东新区城管执法部门、街道办事处、镇人民政府（以下统称综合执法部门）接到物业服务企业报告或者投诉举报的，应当在二十四小时内到现场进行调查核实，法律、法规另有特定时限要求的除外。

查处住宅小区内的违法行为时，综合执法部门的执法人员可以依法进入违法现场调查取证；业主（物业使用人）、装饰装修施工人员应当配合。必要时，公安机关应当依法予以协助。

对居民委员会、物业服务企业等单位和个人提供的照片、视（音）频等相关资料，经查证属实的，可以作为行政执法案件证据材料。

第十九条 对正在实施的违法搭建建（构）筑物、损坏房屋承重结构、破坏房屋建筑立面、擅自改变房屋原始设计等侵害业主共同利益的行为，综合执法部门应当责令当事人暂停施工，并可以暂扣施工工具和材料。

当事人拒不停止施工的，综合执法部门可以书面通知市政公用服务单位在施工作业期间按照合同规定暂时停止施工现场的水电供应；暂时停止相关市政公用服务的，不得影响居民生活。违法行为得到有效制止后，应当及时书面通知市政公用服务单位恢复施工现场的水电供应。

第二十条 对不适用简易程序，但违法事实清楚，当事人自愿认错认罚、对法律适用没有异议且主动配合整改的行政执法案件，经当事人书面提出，综合执法部门可以简化流程快速办理。

Property management companies shall, according to management regulations, restrict the entry of construction workers and building materials into residential communities when there are instances of illegal construction or violations of house decoration regulations.

Section 18 Upon receiving reports of violations from property management companies or residents, the Pudong New Area urban management and law enforcement department, sub-district offices, and township governments (the "comprehensive enforcement authorities"), shall conduct on-site inspections and verifications within twenty-four hours, unless otherwise provided by the laws and regulations.

During these investigations, enforcement officers of comprehensive enforcement authorities may enter properties to collect evidence and perform inspections, which homeowners (or property users) and construction workers shall facilitate. Assistance from the public security department may be requested if necessary.

Documentary evidence like photos and videos provided by residents' committees and property management companies may be used in administrative enforcement proceedings if authenticated.

Section 19 For ongoing unauthorized construction, structural damages, unauthorized alterations, or facade modifications that impact homeowners' common interests, comprehensive enforcement authorities shall order an immediate cessation of activities and may temporarily seize construction materials and equipment.

If the party involved refuses to cease construction, comprehensive enforcement authorities may issue a written notice to the municipal public utility organizations to temporarily suspend water and electricity supplies to the construction site, as outlined in the contract. This suspension shall not impact residents' daily lives. Upon cessation of the illegal activity, comprehensive enforcement authorities shall promptly notify the municipal public utility organizations in writing to restore water and electricity services to the construction site.

Section 20 For administrative law enforcement cases that are not subject to streamlined procedures but where the facts of the violation are clear, comprehensive enforcement authorities may simplify and expedite the settlement of the case if the involved party admits their wrongdoing, accepts the punishments, raises no objections to the application of law, and actively cooperates in correction, upon written notice from the party involved.

综合执法部门应当依照法律规定采用直接送达、留置送达、邮寄送达和公告送达等方式送达法律文书。对于有关违法建（构）筑物的法律文书，采用直接送达方式无法送达的，综合执法部门可以邀请见证人到场，将相关法律文书在住宅小区公告栏和涉案建（构）筑物出入口等显著位置张贴公示，同时以电话、短信等方式将法律文书的主要内容通知当事人，张贴公示之日起十日视为送达。

第二十一条　综合执法部门依法作出要求当事人履行排除妨碍、恢复原状等义务的行政决定，当事人逾期不履行，经催告仍不履行，其后果已经或者将危害交通安全、公共安全、造成环境污染或者破坏自然资源的，综合执法部门可以代履行，或者委托没有利害关系的第三人代履行。

综合执法部门依法作出责令改正等行政决定后，符合申请强制执行条件的，可以向人民法院申请强制执行。人民法院依法裁定准予强制执行的，可以交由综合执法部门组织实施，并派员现场指导监督。

对于违法搭建建（构）筑物、损坏房屋承重结构、破坏房屋建筑立面、擅自改变房屋原始设计、违规群租等行为，综合执法部门可以持生效法律文件向不动产登记机构申请将有关事项记载于不动产登记簿。当事人完成整改的，综合执法部门应当及时向其出具证明文件；当事人申请抵押、转移登记的，应当提交证明文件。

第二十二条　浦东新区人民政府及其相关部门、街道办事处、镇人民政府应当依托城市运行“一网统管”平台，及时采集并动态更新实有人口、实有房屋等信息，并在“社区云”平台实现信息共享。

街道办事处、镇人民政府应当加快推动住宅小区数字治理应用场景建设，加强相关信息数据的分析研判和运用，提高服务水平和管理效率。

Comprehensive enforcement authorities shall serve the legal instruments through personal delivery, service at the recipient's address, mail, or announcement. For instruments on illegal buildings (or structures) where personal delivery is not feasible, they may invite witnesses to observe the posting of the instruments, post and disclose the documents at prominent locations such as the residential community bulletin board and the building's entrances and exits. The involved party shall be notified of the document's main contents via telephone or text message. The instruments are considered to have been served ten days upon posting and disclosure.

Section 21 If the party fails to complete legally mandated corrective actions within the specified deadlines, and such failure leads to potential or actual harm to transportation, public security, or the environment, comprehensive enforcement authorities may carry out the said actions directly in lieu of the party or entrust an uninterested third party to do so.

If the conditions for compulsory enforcement are met, comprehensive enforcement authorities may apply for compulsory enforcement to the people's court. The court may issue a ruling to authorize such authorities to execute the enforcement, with court personnel providing on-site oversight and guidance.

For confirmed cases of illegal construction, structural integrity breaches, unauthorized facade alterations, or illegal over-occupancy, comprehensive enforcement authorities, with proper legal instruments, may request that these violations be recorded in the real estate registry. Upon satisfactory resolution, certificates of compliance shall be issued, which are to be presented for any future property mortgage or assignment.

Section 22 The Pudong New Area People's Government and its associated departments, along with sub-district offices and township governments, shall utilize the integrated online platform to manage and update real-time population and housing information, facilitating information sharing through a community cloud platform.

Sub-district offices and township governments shall advance the implementation of digital governance within communities, enhancing the analytical and operational use of data to improve service delivery and administrative efficiency.

综合执法部门因执法活动所需，可以通过大数据平台直接共享使用其他部门已纳入共享需求清单的数据信息；未纳入共享需求清单的，可以通过大数据平台发出协助通知书，有关部门应当在收到协助通知书的五个工作日内告知。

第二十三条 浦东新区人民政府和街道办事处、镇人民政府应当加强住宅小区治理和综合执法相关工作所需人员、经费、技术、装备、场所等保障。

支持街道办事处、镇人民政府和居（村）民委员会开展无违建创建活动，并将创建结果纳入街镇年度绩效考核。

市城管执法部门应当会同浦东新区城管执法部门，加强对街道办事处、镇人民政府开展住宅小区综合执法工作的指导、监督，提升正规化、专业化、职业化水平。

第二十四条 浦东新区有住宅小区的村民委员会参照本规定关于居民委员会的要求执行。

第二十五条 本规定自 2022 年 11 月 1 日起施行。

When necessary for enforcement activities, comprehensive enforcement authorities may access shared data from other departments stored on the big data platform. For unlisted data, they may request cooperation through the platform, with responses required within five business days.

Section 23 The Pudong New Area People's Government, alongside sub-district offices and township governments, shall bolster support for staff, funding, technology, equipment, and facilities dedicated to enhancing community management and enforcement operations.

Projects aimed at removing illegal construction are to be initiated by sub-district offices and township governments and residents' (or villagers') committees, with outcomes contributing to the annual performance evaluations of these administrative regions.

The municipal urban management and law enforcement department shall work with the Pudong New Area urban management and law enforcement department to improve the guidance and oversight of sub-district offices and township governments in residential law enforcement, aiming to enhance standardization, specialization, and professionalism.

Section 24 Villagers' committees within the Pudong New Area that manage residential communities shall be subject to these Provisions on resident's committees *mutatis mutandis*.

Section 25 These Provisions shall take effect from November 1, 2022.

上海市浦东新区优化揭榜挂帅机制促进新型研发机构发展若干规定

Several Provisions for the Pudong New Area of Shanghai Municipality on Enhancing Open Competition and Advancing New Research and Development Institutions

上海市浦东新区优化揭榜挂帅机制促进新型研发机构发展若干规定

（2022 年 10 月 28 日上海市第十五届人民代表大会常务委员会第四十五次会议通过）

第一条 为了深入实施创新驱动发展战略，优化揭榜挂帅机制，营造新型研发机构良好的发展环境，推动浦东新区建设国际科技创新中心核心区，根据有关法律、行政法规的基本原则，结合浦东新区实际，制定本规定。

第二条 在浦东新区通过优化揭榜挂帅机制吸引科技领军人才承接创新项目，培育发展新型研发机构以及相关的促进、管理和保障等活动，适用本规定。

本规定所称创新项目，包括科学研究、技术开发、技术攻关、成果转化、示范应用、产业化等项目。

第三条 市人民政府应当支持浦东新区率先推进科技体制机制创新，建立促进新型研发机构发展的统筹协调机制，支持浦东新区持续优化创新创业环境、提升科技创新公共服务水平。

市科技、经济信息化、发展改革、财政、国有资产监管、审计等部门根据自身职责和本规定，支持浦东新区开展创新项目揭榜挂帅和新型研发机构发展等工作。

Several Provisions for the Pudong New Area of Shanghai Municipality on Enhancing Open Competition and Advancing New Research and Development Institutions

(Adopted at the 45th Session of the 15th Shanghai Municipal People's Congress Standing Committee on October 28, 2022)

Section 1 The Several Provisions for the Pudong New Area of Shanghai Municipality on Enhancing Open Competition and Advancing New Research and Development Institutions (these "Provisions") are formulated to advance the innovation-driven development strategy, improve the open competition system, create an optimal environment for new research and development institutions, and position the Pudong New Area as a leading international science and technology innovation hub, pursuant to the basic principles of applicable laws and administrative regulations, and in light of the actual circumstances in the Pudong New Area.

Section 2 These Provisions shall apply to activities aimed at attracting top science and technology talent and establishing new R&D institutions, which include facilitating, managing, and supporting such activities through the enhanced open competition system in the Pudong New Area.

"Innovation projects" in these Provisions include, but are not limited to, scientific research, technical development, technological breakthroughs, results transformation, pilot projects, and industrialization projects.

Section 3 The Municipal People's Government shall support the Pudong New Area in leading technological innovation, establishing a coordination framework to promote new R&D institutions, and enhancing the environment for innovation and entrepreneurship to elevate public services in scientific and technological innovation.

The municipal departments, including but not limited to, science and technology, economy and information technology, development and reform, finance, state-owned asset regulation, and auditing take charge of supporting the open competition system for innovation projects and the development of new R&D institutions in the Pudong New Area pursuant to these Provisions.

市规划资源、人力资源社会保障、公安、民政、地方金融监管、税务等部门以及海关等单位按照各自职责和本规定，支持新型研发机构在浦东新区发展。

第四条 浦东新区人民政府应当统筹协调本行政区域创新项目揭榜挂帅和促进新型研发机构发展的重大事项，增强自主创新能力，搭建为揭榜挂帅活动提供服务的公共平台，吸引社会力量参与和科技人才集聚，营造有利于创新的生态环境。

浦东新区科技经济部门负责创新项目揭榜挂帅的具体推进工作和新型研发机构的促进发展工作，完善项目、基地、人才、资金一体化调度和配置机制，提高承担国家和本市重大战略任务的能力。

浦东新区其他相关部门应当按照各自职责和本规定，共同做好创新项目揭榜挂帅的推进和新型研发机构的促进发展工作。

第五条 在浦东新区设立非营利性、公益性的创新项目揭榜挂帅公共服务平台（以下简称服务平台），承担汇集发布创新项目信息、组织实施创新项目揭榜挂帅等事项，并提供相关的公共服务。

服务平台应当按照专业化、社会化的运作要求委托专门机构运营，与有关企业、机构、产业基金和创投基金等开展合作，接受区科技经济部门监督管理。

通过服务平台开展创新项目揭榜挂帅活动的规则由浦东新区人民政府制定。服务平台应当建立信息公开制度，明确服务内容和监督办法，并向社会公布。

The municipal departments, including but not limited to, planning and resources, human resources and social security, public security, civil affairs, local financial regulation, taxation, and customs support the development of new R&D institutions in the Pudong New Area to the extent of their designated responsibilities and these Provisions.

Section 4 The Pudong New Area People's Government shall coordinate significant activities on the open competition system and the development of new R&D institutions, develop independent innovation capabilities, establish public platforms to support open competition, engage societal participation, and attract technological professionals, thereby creating a favorable environment for innovation.

The Pudong New Area science and economic development department takes charge of specifically advancing the open competition system and facilitating new R&D institutions, refining the integration and coordination of projects, bases, professionals, and enhancing the capacity to manage major national and municipal strategic tasks.

Other appropriate Pudong New Area departments shall collaborate to advance the open competition system and the development of new R&D institutions based on their roles and these Provisions.

Section 5 A non-profit, public interest service platform (the "Service Platform") for the open competition system is to be created in the Pudong New Area to handle tasks such as compiling and disseminating information on innovation projects, implementing the open competition system, and delivering associated public services.

Service Platform shall be operated by specialized organizations in compliance with professional and community standards and in collaboration with interested entities, institutions, industrial funds, and venture capitals, overseen by the Pudong New Area science and economic development department.

The Pudong New Area People's Government shall develop rules for conducting innovation projects through the Service Platform, which features a transparent information disclosure system, clearly defined service provisions and oversight procedures, all made publicly accessible.

第六条 服务平台应当选聘科技创新领域知名专家组成专家委员会，建立专家库。专家委员会负责对服务平台组织开展创新项目揭榜挂帅等活动提供决策咨询。专家库中的专家根据相关参与方的需求对创新项目的发布、申报、评鉴、揭榜等活动提供专业支持。专家委员会和专家库的名单向社会公布。

第七条 在服务平台上发布的创新项目应当面向全社会征集，聚焦重点领域突破、关键核心技术攻关和重大成果转化，具备策源性强、影响力大和带动面广等特点。

本市政府部门、国有企业、事业单位的创新项目可以在服务平台上公开发布，但依法需要保密的除外。支持其他企业和社会组织的创新项目在服务平台上公开发布。

在服务平台上发布创新项目的，应当列明完成项目需要的科研能力要求、项目考核和评审验收标准、经费拨付和管理等事项。

第八条 创新项目申报主体应当按照项目需求提交方案，说明项目组织形式、首席科学家或其他重要科技领衔人、团队组成等，证明科研能力等情况。

不得以国籍、年龄、资历、学历和工作经历、单位属性等作为国内外人才和团队在浦东新区参与创新项目揭榜挂帅的资格条件。

第九条 创新项目发布方应当对申报主体提交的方案和有关情况开展尽职调查和评鉴，确定一个申报主体作为揭榜方承接创新项目。

无法确定唯一主体的，可以采用赛马制方式择优选择多个申报主体承接创新项目、各自独立揭榜攻关，并按合同约定开展科研活动。

Section 6 The Service Platform shall form an expert committee by recruiting acclaimed innovation experts and create an expert directory, both of which is to be disclosed to the public. The expert committee advises on the platform's operations on open competition, and the experts in the directory provide professional assistance for activities such as project disclosure, application, evaluation, and management, tailored to participant needs.

Section 7 Innovation projects listed on the Service Platform shall be open for submissions from the broader community, targeting breakthroughs in critical technological areas, tackling key technological challenges, and converting significant research findings into practical applications, marked by distinct originality and extensive impact.

Innovation projects by municipal government agencies, state-owned enterprises, and public institutions may be listed unless required by law to be kept confidential. Submissions from private businesses and social organizations are encouraged.

Each innovation project listed on the Service Platform shall detail essential scientific capabilities, standards for project evaluation and completion, funding allocation, and management procedures.

Section 8 Applicants for innovation projects shall submit a detailed proposal outlining the project's organizational methods, chief scientists and other key leading research expert, team members, and their capability to conduct scientific research.

The open competition in the Pudong New Area is open to both domestic and international professionals unrestricted by such conditions as nationality, age, tenure, educational background, work experience, or type of employer.

Section 9 The project publisher shall be responsible for strictly evaluating proposals and submissions from applicants and selecting suitable contractor(s) for the innovation project.

If no single contractor stands out, multiple candidates may be engaged following the horse racing system, where each one independently strives to achieve scientific breakthroughs based on the terms of the contract.

第十条 鼓励参与创新项目揭榜挂帅活动的企业、单位在浦东新区开展有关科技成果转化和应用，实现集聚发展。

浦东新区应当采取措施，引进和培育符合创新规律、提升创新效能、满足创新需求的新型研发机构，并实施依章程管理的组织体系和治理结构。支持新型研发机构在浦东新区参与创新项目揭榜挂帅活动。

第十一条 创新项目发布方和揭榜方可以依法约定科技成果的知识产权归属。创新项目科技成果转化和应用符合本市和浦东新区发展战略定位的，市、区相关科技创新基金等应当提供支持，并按程序纳入用地保障范围。浦东新区应当给予融资担保、财政补助等政策支持。

鼓励社会资本与浦东新区政府投资基金合作，对在浦东新区实施的科技成果转化、示范应用、产业化项目等进行投资。浦东新区政府投资基金的投资收益，可以用于激励奖补。

支持社会力量通过设立基金、捐赠、股权投资等方式，重点支持新型研发机构开展科学研究、技术开发和技术攻关等活动。

第十二条 支持揭榜挂帅的创新项目建立以结果为导向的经费拨付机制，项目完成并通过验收的，按照合同约定拨付剩余资金。

支持新型研发机构对使用财政科研经费的创新项目实行包干制和负面清单管理。负面清单由财政部门会同有关部门根据财政资金来源予以编制。在承诺遵守科研伦理道德和作风学风诚信要求、经费除负面清单列明的禁止支出项目外全部用于本项目研究工作相关支出的基础上，有权自主管理和使用项目经费。

使用社会资金的创新项目，由发布方和揭榜方在相关合同中约定经费使用方式。

Section 10 Enterprises and other entities participating in the open competition are encouraged to transform and apply scientific and technological advancements within the Pudong New Area to facilitate clustered development.

The Pudong New Area shall adopt certain strategies to establish new R&D institutions that embody the principles of innovation, enhance innovation efficiency, meet innovation demands, and comply with organizational norms and governance as outlined in their charters. New R&D institutions are encouraged to participate in the open competitions in the Pudong New Area.

Section 11 Publishers and contractors of innovation projects may agree on the ownership of intellectual property works derived from technological advancements lawfully. When such innovations align with the strategic goals of municipal and Pudong New Area development, appropriate science and technology innovation funds shall provide support and integrate them into land use protection systems per rules and procedures. The Pudong New Area shall offer support such as financial guarantees or subsidies.

Social investments in partnership with the Pudong New Area People's Government's investment funds to support the conversion, pilot projects, and industrial application of scientific and technological achievements are encouraged. Financial incentives and subsidies from the earnings of these funds may be used.

Social support for new R&D institutions such as funding, donations, and equity investments aimed at facilitating scientific research, technical development, and innovation is encouraged.

Section 12 Innovation projects under the open competition system are encouraged to adopt a result-oriented funding allocation process. Remaining funds after project completion and approval are to be distributed as outlined in the contract.

New R&D institutions are encouraged to implement a lump-sum funding scheme and a negative list system for government-funded innovation projects. The negative list shall be prepared by the finance department in collaboration with pertinent departments according to financial sources. New R&D institutions have the autonomy to manage and use project funds provided that they adhere to the ethics of scientific research as well as the honesty of work and study styles, and ensure that funds are used solely for project-related expenses aside from those on the negative list.

Contracts between publishers and contractors are to outline the specific uses of funds for innovation projects financed by social capital.

第十三条 浦东新区对新型研发机构培养、引进的相关人才，提供居留和出入境、落户、安居、医疗保险、子女教育等服务保障。在浦东新区新型研发机构工作的紧缺急需人才，按照规定享受浦东新区提供的财政补贴。支持浦东新区的新型研发机构按规定与高等学校联合培养研究生。

符合条件的境外人员可以担任浦东新区新型研发机构法定代表人。

第十四条 使用财政资金出资购置、建设大型科学仪器设施的管理单位，应当按照规定为浦东新区新型研发机构提供共享服务。

鼓励浦东新区新型研发机构与境外研究开发机构合作开展技术研究，通过举办国际性学术会议、科技创新展会、科技创新大赛等方式进行国际科技合作交流。

浦东新区新型研发机构进口设备、材料的，按照规定享受关税和进口环节增值税减免政策。

第十五条 支持浦东新区新型研发机构实行任务为导向的绩效评价管理模式。对运用财政性资金设立的新型研发机构，可以实行综合预算管理；对其他新型研发机构，可以以研发和服务活动的公共性、稀缺性和引领性等评价结果，择优给予财政补助。

支持对浦东新区承担战略性任务的新型研发机构，建立以创新绩效为核心的中长期综合评价机制。

第十六条 浦东新区应当按照支持创新、权责一致、尽职免责、失职追责的原则，探索建立符合创新项目特点的容错机制，按照相关合同的约定开展监督。

Section 13 The Pudong New Area provides comprehensive services such as residency, entry and exit, settlement, housing, medical insurance, and children's education support for professionals recruited or nurtured by new R&D institutions. Essential professionals in urgent need may receive financial subsidies as authorized by the Pudong New Area. Collaborative graduate education programs between the new R&D institutions and higher education institutes are to receive support.

Eligible foreign nationals may act as representatives by operation of law for new R&D institutions in the Pudong New Area.

Section 14 Managers who use government funds to acquire and develop major scientific devices shall ensure these resources accessible to new R&D institutions in the Pudong New Area.

New R&D institutions are encouraged to collaborate with international counterparts in conducting scientific research and technological development through activities such as hosting global academic conferences, innovation exhibitions, and technology competitions.

New R&D institutions importing essential materials and devices into the Pudong New Area are entitled to lawful exemptions and reductions on tariffs and import value-added tax.

Section 15 The Pudong New Area is to implement performance evaluation systems tailored to achieving specific goals for new R&D institutions, employing a comprehensive budget approach for those established with government funding; other institutions may receive financial subsidies based on assessments of public benefits, innovation scarcity, and leadership in research and development.

A long-standing, comprehensive evaluation system focusing on innovation outcomes is to be developed for new R&D institutions undertaking strategic projects in the Pudong New Area.

Section 16 The Pudong New Area shall explore creating a fault-tolerance system tailored to the unique needs of innovation projects, based on principles of supporting innovation, aligning authority with responsibility, protecting those who have performed their duties from liability, and holding accountable those guilty of negligence. Oversight is conducted pursuant to the contractual terms.

第十七条 本规定有关用语的含义：

（一）揭榜挂帅，是指创新项目向社会公开发布，由科技领军人才作为项目负责人挂帅并组织团队提供解决方案，并以科研技术成果产出来兑现的非周期性科研资助机制。

（二）经费包干，是指由项目负责人按照规定或者约定，对项目资金自主管理使用的模式。

（三）赛马制，是指对创新项目在开展揭榜挂帅过程中实行择优选择、并行攻关、合同约定的组织管理方式。

第十八条 本规定自 2022 年 12 月 1 日起施行。

Section 17 The definitions for the terms in these Provisions:

(1) Open Competition System: A dynamic research funding process that publicly solicits innovation projects, spearheaded by leading scientists and technologists who assemble teams to develop solutions, dependent on producing tangible scientific and technological outputs.

(2) A Lump-sum Funding Scheme: A funding arrangement that permits project leaders to independently manage and utilize grants as outlined by laws or contractual terms.

(3) Horse Racing System: A competitive, organizational strategy for the open competition system that selects top candidates through a contest, facilitates simultaneous research efforts, and establishes binding agreements.

Section 18 These Provisions shall take effect from December 1, 2022.

上海市浦东新区促进无驾驶人智能网联汽车创新应用规定

Provisions for the Pudong New Area of Shanghai Municipality on Facilitating the Innovation and Application of Connected and Autonomous Vehicles

上海市浦东新区促进无驾驶人智能网联汽车创新应用规定

（2022年11月23日上海市第十五届人民代表大会常务委员会第四十六次会议通过）

第一条　为了进一步规范和促进浦东新区无驾驶人智能网联汽车创新应用，推动产业高质量发展，保障道路交通安全，根据有关法律、行政法规的基本原则，结合浦东新区实际，制定本规定。

第二条　本规定适用于在浦东新区行政区域内划定的路段、区域开展无驾驶人智能网联汽车道路测试、示范应用、示范运营、商业化运营等创新应用活动以及相关监督管理工作。

本规定所称的无驾驶人智能网联汽车，是指车内不配备驾驶人和测试安全员的智能网联汽车。

第三条　浦东新区无驾驶人智能网联汽车创新应用活动应当坚持鼓励创新、包容审慎、循序渐进的原则，实行分级分类管理，按照从低风险场景到高风险场景、从简单类型到复杂类型的要求，确保安全有序、风险可控。

第四条　市人民政府应当建立完善促进智能网联汽车产业发展的工作协调机制和政策措施，优化创新应用环境。

市经济信息化、交通、公安等部门建立智能网联汽车测试与应用工作推进机制，协调推进全市智能网联汽车测试与应用工作，指导浦东新区智能网联汽车创新应用工作，并按照各自职责做好相关管理工作。

Provisions for the Pudong New Area of Shanghai Municipality on Facilitating the Innovation and Application of Connected and Autonomous Vehicles

(Adopted at the 46th Session of the 15th Shanghai Municipal People's Congress Standing Committee on November 23, 2022)

Section 1 The Provisions for the Pudong New Area of Shanghai Municipality on Facilitating the Innovation and Application of Connected and Autonomous Vehicles (these "Provisions") are formulated to regulate and enhance the development and application of connected and autonomous vehicles (CAVs), boost the sector's high-quality growth, and ensure traffic safety within the Pudong New Area, pursuant to the basic principles of applicable laws and administrative regulations, and in light of the actual circumstances in the Pudong New Area.

Section 2 These Provisions shall apply to innovation and application involving CAVs, including road tests, pilot projects, pilot operations, commercial operations, and administrative oversight within designated roads and zones in the Pudong New Area.

"CAVs" in these Provisions refer to intelligent connected vehicles that operate autonomously without a driver or a safety inspector.

Section 3 The CAVs innovation and application activities in the Pudong New Area shall comply with principles of fostering innovation, inclusivity, prudent management, and systematic progression to maintain safety, orderliness, and manage risks effectively, scaling from low-risk to high-risk contexts and from simple to complex systems.

Section 4 The Municipal People's Government shall develop and refine work processes and policies to bolster the CAVs sector, fostering an environment conducive to innovation and application.

Municipal departments responsible for economy and information technology, transportation, and public security, among others, shall develop a work process to facilitate the testing and application of CAVs throughout this Municipality, directing and overseeing their application in the Pudong New Area to the extent of their duties.

市发展改革部门负责协调智能网联汽车创新应用相关新型基础设施建设等工作。

浦东新区人民政府、中国（上海）自由贸易试验区临港新片区管理委员会（以下简称临港新片区管委会）应当建立促进智能网联汽车创新应用的工作机制，制定配套政策，落实支持措施，并按照各自职责具体负责辖区内的智能网联汽车创新应用管理工作。

市规划资源、市场监管、网信、通信管理等部门以及浦东新区科技经济、建设交通、公安、规划资源、大数据管理等部门按照各自职责，做好浦东新区智能网联汽车创新应用相关管理工作。

第五条 开展无驾驶人智能网联汽车道路测试、示范应用、示范运营的企业应当申请安全性自我声明的确认。无驾驶人智能网联汽车经安全性自我声明确认的，可以向公安机关交通管理部门申领车辆号牌；取得车辆号牌的，可以上道路行驶；经交通部门审核同意的，方可从事道路运输示范运营活动。

第六条 申请安全性自我声明确认的企业应当符合以下要求：

（一）具有独立法人资格；

（二）具备相关技术能力；

（三）具备符合道路测试、示范应用、示范运营等相应条件的车辆；

（四）配备远程监控系统和紧急接管人员，紧急接管人员应当具备无驾驶人智能网联汽车的操控能力和相应准驾车型的机动车驾驶证，经过专业知识、现场操作和应急处置培训；

（五）按照有关规定已经投保或者承诺投保机动车交通事故责任强制保险和一定金额的商业保险。

The municipal development and reform department oversees the coordination of building essential infrastructure for CAVs innovation and application.

The Pudong New Area People's Government and the Lin-gang Special Area Administration Committee of the China (Shanghai) Pilot Free Trade Zone shall develop systems to facilitate the innovation and application of CAVs, create and implement supportive policies, and manage CAVs innovation and application activities within their jurisdictions.

Departments responsible for planning and resources, market regulation, cybersecurity, and communication management, alongside those managing technology and economy, construction, construction and transportation, public security, planning and resources, and big data, among others, in the Pudong New Area shall enhance the governance of CAVs innovation and application to the extent of their authorization.

Section 5 Enterprises shall acquire the safety commitment endorsement before initiating CAVs road tests, pilot projects, or pilot operations. Upon obtaining this endorsement, the enterprises may request vehicle plates from the public security department's traffic division; vehicles may operate on public roads after acquiring such plates, and with transportation agency's approval, begin pilot transport operations.

Section 6 To receive a safety commitment endorsement, enterprises shall:

(1) be an independent juristic person;

(2) possess the necessary technical capabilities;

(3) own vehicles fit for road tests, pilot projects, and pilot operations;

(4) equip vehicles with a remote monitoring system and emergency specialists trained and licensed to operate CAVs, skilled in professional knowledge, onsite operations, and emergency responses; and

(5) obtain required automobile liability insurance and adequate commercial insurance as required.

第七条 开展道路测试活动，申请安全性自我声明确认的车辆应当符合以下要求：

（一）具备最小风险运行模式，满足功能安全、信息安全等技术标准和要求，设计运行范围覆盖道路测试场景；

（二）配备处于无驾驶人状态的显示装置以及发生故障或者事故后的警示装置，设置符合标准的夜间反光装置；

（三）按照有关规定经过有驾驶人智能网联汽车道路测试并达到规定里程或者时间，且未发生交通违法行为以及因车辆原因造成的安全事故，人工接管率符合规定值。

开展高风险道路测试的，应当经过规定里程或者时间的低风险道路测试，且未发生严重交通违法行为以及因车辆原因造成的安全事故，人工接管率符合规定值。

第八条 开展具有试点、试行效果的载人、载货示范应用活动，申请安全性自我声明确认的车辆应当经过规定里程或者时间的道路测试，且未发生交通违法行为以及因车辆原因造成的安全事故，人工接管率符合规定值。

第九条 开展载人、载货或者特定场景作业的示范运营活动，申请安全性自我声明确认的车辆应当符合以下要求：

（一）符合开展示范运营所需的技术性能、外廓尺寸、轴荷、质量、安全性能等标准或者规范；

（二）经过规定里程或者时间的示范应用，且未发生交通违法行为以及因车辆原因造成的安全事故，人工接管率符合规定值。

Section 7 Before road tests commence, vehicles shall meet the following requirements to be eligible to apply for a safety commitment endorsement:

(1) operate in a minimal-risk mode, comply with safety and data security standards, and address the designated road test contexts;

(2) be equipped with autonomous mode indicators and systems for warning of malfunctions or accidents and meet standards for night visibility; and

(3) have undergone the road test for the CAV with a driver present and have met the designated mileage or time requirements, with no traffic violations or accidents caused by the vehicle, and with the manual takeover rate meeting the prescribed value.

Before conducting high-risk road tests, vehicles shall first pass low-risk tests within designated mileage or time without serious violations or accidents, achieving the required manual takeover rate.

Section 8 Before beginning pilot projects that involve transporting people or goods, vehicles applying for the safety commitment endorsement shall pass road tests within predefined mileage or time without traffic violations or accidents, achieving the specified manual takeover rate.

Section 9 Before starting pilot operations involving passenger or freight transport, or context-specific activities, vehicles shall:

(1) comply with the necessary standards for technical performance, dimensions, axle load, quality, and safety for pilot operations; and

(2) complete pilot projects within the set mileage or time without traffic violations or accidents, achieving the required manual takeover rate.

第十条　申请开展无驾驶人智能网联汽车道路测试、示范应用、示范运营安全性自我声明确认的，由市经济信息化、交通、公安等部门和浦东新区科技经济部门、临港新片区管委会按照各自职责，组织有关部门、第三方机构和专家，对相应阶段的安全性自我声明进行确认。

浦东新区科技经济部门、临港新片区管委会负责收取企业提交的安全性自我声明和相关证明材料，并将是否确认的决定书面告知企业。

涉及跨区域事项的，市经济信息化、交通、公安等部门应当加强对浦东新区科技经济、建设交通、公安等部门以及临港新片区管委会的业务指导和沟通协调。

第十一条　有关主管部门对安全性自我声明进行确认时，可以将企业在浦东新区以外地区的测试结果作为参考依据，简化相关测试流程和测试项目。

开展无驾驶人智能网联汽车道路测试、示范应用、示范运营达到规定里程或者时间，且未发生交通违法行为以及因车辆原因造成的安全事故，人工接管率符合规定值的，企业可以向浦东新区科技经济部门或者临港新片区管委会提出同一阶段同一型号车辆批量申请确认，并提交一致性技术参数、性能和安全检测报告。有关主管部门应当组织第三方机构进行一致性抽查，并根据抽查结果做出决定。

第十二条　企业取得安全性自我声明确认的，可以向市公安机关交通管理部门提交申领车辆号牌需要的有关材料，申领临时行驶车号牌和车辆识别标牌。

临时行驶车号牌有效期届满的，可以凭有效的安全性自我声明和其他相关材料，申领新的临时行驶车号牌。在临时行驶车号牌有效期内取得下一阶段安全性自我声明确认的，无需申领新的临时行驶车号牌。

Section 10 When an application is submitted for endorsing the safety commitment of CAVs road tests, pilot projects, or pilot operations, the municipal economy and information technology, transportation, and public security departments, along with the Pudong New Area technology and economy department and the Lin-gang Special Area Administration Committee, coordinate with appropriate departments, third-party agencies and experts to review and endorse the specific safety commitment to the extent of their duties.

The Pudong New Area technology and economy department or the Lin-gang Special Area Administration Committee takes charge of processing the submissions for safety commitments and the associated evidence from enterprises, providing written notification of the results.

Cross-regional issues shall be managed through improved guidance, communications, and coordination between municipal and Pudong New Area departments of technology and economy, construction and transportation, public safety, as well as the Lin-gang Special Area Administration Committee, among others.

Section 11 Competent authorities may approve the safety commitment based on test results obtained outside the Pudong New Area to streamline testing processes and methods.

Enterprises may request batch endorsement for vehicles undergoing similar stages of testing or pilot projects from the Pudong New Area technology and economy department or the Lin-gang Special Area Administration Committee. Submissions shall include technical specifications, performance, and safety evaluation reports, confirming that the vehicles have met the required mileage or time without traffic violations and accidents, and maintained the required manual takeover rate. Competent authorities shall coordinate with third-party agencies to perform consistency evaluations and make decisions based on the results of the evaluations.

Section 12 Enterprises that have acquired the safety commitment endorsement may request a temporary vehicle license plate and a vehicle identification plate from the municipal public security department's traffic division after submitting the necessary documents following the receipt of a safety commitment endorsement.

Enterprises may request to renew a temporary vehicle license plate with a valid safety commitment and associated documents if the existing one is going to expire; no new request is necessary if the safety commitment endorsement for the subsequent stage is acquired during the validity of the current plate.

第十三条 无驾驶人智能网联汽车经道路测试安全性自我声明确认并且取得临时行驶车号牌、车辆识别标牌的，可以上道路行驶从事测试活动，但不得搭载与测试活动无关的人员和用于配重以外的货物。

第十四条 无驾驶人智能网联汽车经示范应用安全性自我声明确认并且临时行驶车号牌在有效期内的，按照规定搭载相关人员或者货物，但不得超出车辆的额定乘员和核定载质量，不得搭载危险货物。搭载相关人员或者货物的，应当向服务对象明示可能存在的风险，采取必要的安全措施。

第十五条 开展无驾驶人智能网联汽车示范运营活动的企业，应当符合以下要求：

（一）具备相应的道路运输经营资质或者条件，或者与具备相应道路运输经营资质的企业合作；

（二）具备与经营业务相适应并经检测合格的车辆；

（三）提出相对固定的运营区域和运营时段；

（四）具有健全的安全管理制度。

企业凭经确认的示范运营安全性自我声明、有效期内的临时行驶车号牌、运营方案以及其他相关材料，向浦东新区建设交通部门或者临港新片区管委会申请办理相关车辆营运证件。

取得前款规定的车辆营运证件的，可以利用无驾驶人智能网联汽车从事示范运营活动，并可以收费。依法纳入政府定价范围的收费实行政府定价或者政府指导价，其他收费实行市场调节价。收费标准应当在运营方案中载明，面向不特定对象收费的，收费标准应当向社会公示。

Section 13 CAVs with a safety commitment endorsement for road tests, a temporary license plate, and a vehicle identification plate are permitted to conduct testing on public roads but are prohibited from transporting passengers or goods unrelated to the test, except for counterweights.

Section 14 CAVs with an endorsed pilot project safety commitment and a valid temporary license plate may transport passengers or goods per regulations, ensuring they do not exceed designated capacities and weight limits, or transport hazardous materials, with a requirement to inform all passengers about potential risks and necessary safety precautions.

Section 15 Enterprises shall meet the following requirements before commencing pilot operations of CAVs:

(1) hold or collaborate with entities possessing the necessary road transport operation credentials;

(2) own vehicles that meet operational standards and have passed required inspections;

(3) clearly define operational areas and schedules; and

(4) implement a comprehensive safety management system.

Enterprises shall apply to the Pudong New Area's transportation department or the Lin-gang New Area Administration Committee for vehicle operation permits with an endorsed safety commitment, a temporary license plate, an operation plan, and other necessary documents.

Enterprises that have obtained vehicle operation permits may use CAVs for pilot operations and charge for these services. Charges set or guided by the government shall be within the ranges set by the government, while other charges are based on market dynamics. Pricing details shall be included in the operation plan or publicly disclosed if the services are available to the public.

第十六条　获得产品准入或者具备同等条件的产品认定的无驾驶人智能网联汽车，经公安机关交通管理部门登记，可以取得车辆号牌、行驶证等登记凭证。

利用符合前款要求的无驾驶人智能网联汽车从事商业化运营的企业，应当取得道路运输经营资质。车辆应当与经营业务相适应，并经检测合格，依法取得车辆营运证件。

商业化运营的收费管理，按照有关法律、法规的规定执行。

第十七条　浦东新区科技经济部门和临港新片区管委会应当加强对无驾驶人智能网联汽车运行的日常监督管理，并采取措施强化后台监管。

开展无驾驶人智能网联汽车道路测试、示范应用、示范运营的企业应当按照规定安装监控装置，将相关数据接入指定的数据平台，实时上传到市级数据平台，并定期向浦东新区科技经济部门或者临港新片区管委会提交创新应用情况报告。

第十八条　开展智能网联汽车创新应用的路段、区域，由市交通部门会同市公安、经济信息化、通信管理等部门根据道路基础条件和实际需要划定并组织开展验收。验收通过后，应当向社会公布，并在该路段、区域及周边设置相应标识和安全提示。

前款所称的路段、区域，是指用于社会机动车辆通行的路段、区域。

支持在浦东新区逐步扩大智能网联汽车创新应用的路段、区域范围，支持特定区域全域开放，丰富测试与应用场景。

第十九条　浦东新区科技经济、建设交通部门和临港新片区管委会应当统筹规划、协调推动建设车路协同基础设施和车路协同云控平台，支持车路协同基础设施在安全可控的条件下与云控平台、路侧信号控制设施、智能网联汽车实现信息共享。

Section 16 CAVs authorized for access or under equivalent conditions may obtain vehicle registration, including a license plate and driving license, from the public security department's traffic division.

Enterprises deploying CAVs for commercial use shall meet defined operational prerequisites, ensure vehicles are suitable for commercial use, pass required inspections, and legally acquire vehicle operation permits.

Fees for commercial operations are subject to applicable laws and regulations.

Section 17 The Pudong New Area technology and economy department and the Lin-gang Special Area Administration Committee shall intensify ongoing oversight and management of CAVs operations, implementing effective background monitoring approaches.

Enterprises engaging in road tests, pilot projects, or pilot operations of CAVs shall install and use prescribed monitoring devices, connect to the designated platform and share data with municipal platforms in real time, and regularly report on innovation application activities to the Pudong New Area technology and economy department or the Lin-gang Special Area Administration Committee.

Section 18 The municipal transportation department shall cooperate with municipal public security, economy and information technology, and communication management departments to plan and manage approved roads and areas for CAV innovation, taking into account road conditions and practical requirements. These areas shall be publicly disclosed following approval, with appropriate signage and safety notifications installed.

The said roads and areas are designated for use by civilian vehicles.

The progressive expansion of road sections and regional coverage for CAV innovation applications in the Pudong New Area, including the full opening of specific areas to improve testing and use case contexts, are to be encouraged.

Section 19 The technology and economy and construction and transportation departments in the Pudong New Area shall cooperate with the Lin-gang Special Area Administration Committee to plan and support the development of Vehicle-to-Everything (V2X) infrastructure alongside a cloud-based control platform. Such cooperation shall include facilitating safe and controllable data sharing between V2X infrastructure and its cloud-based platform, alongside managing control facilities for roadside signals and CAVs.

车路协同基础设施和车路协同云控平台应当实现数据交互加密、通信网络防护、实时安全监测，有效防范数据篡改、数据泄露和网络攻击等风险。

第二十条 本市根据国家有关主管部门的授权，支持开展智能网联汽车创新应用的企业在浦东新区特定区域开展高精度地图应用试点。市和浦东新区规划资源部门应当加强对高精度地图应用试点工作的指导和监督管理。

开展智能网联汽车创新应用的企业应当按照有关规定，严格保护高精度地图数据安全。

第二十一条 开展无驾驶人智能网联汽车道路测试、示范应用、示范运营的企业对智能网联汽车进行可能影响车辆功能、性能的软件升级（包括远程升级）或者硬件变更的，应当向浦东新区科技经济部门或者临港新片区管委会报告。

发生影响车辆安全性能的重大升级或者变更的，企业应当提交新的安全性自我声明进行再次确认。

第二十二条 无驾驶人智能网联汽车上道路行驶的，应当具有显著标识，按照要求放置、粘贴临时行驶车号牌和车辆识别标牌，遵守道路交通安全法律、法规的有关通行规定。

开展无驾驶人智能网联汽车载人示范应用、示范运营，应当在有关主管部门的指导下有序推进。

第二十三条 开展无驾驶人智能网联汽车创新应用的企业应当加强车辆远程动态监管。

V2X infrastructure and the cloud-based control platform shall facilitate interactive data encryption, network communication protection, and real-time security monitoring, and prevent risks such as data tampering, disclosure, and cyberattacks.

Section 20 This Municipality encourages enterprises focused on CAV innovation in designated areas of the Pudong New Area to undertake pilot projects using high-definition maps, subject to approval by national competent authorities. The municipal and the Pudong New Area planning and resources departments shall oversee and manage these pilot projects.

Enterprises involved in CAV innovation shall strictly comply with applicable regulations to ensure the security of high-definition map data.

Section 21 Enterprises engaged in CAV road tests, pilot projects, or pilot operations shall report any software upgrades (including remote upgrades) or hardware changes that may affect vehicle performance to the Pudong New Area technology and economy department or the Lin-gang Special Area Administration Committee.

Should these changes impact vehicle safety performance significantly, the enterprise shall secure a new safety commitment endorsement.

Section 22 CAVs shall display clear signage, mount temporary license and vehicle identification plates as required, and comply with traffic safety laws and regulations during operation.

Competent authorities shall manage the structured rollout of CAV pilot projects and operations.

Section 23 Enterprises developing CAV innovations shall enhance their remote vehicle monitoring capabilities.

在恶劣天气、道路施工、大型活动等情形下，企业应当根据相关管理部门要求及时调整运行计划。公安机关依法实施现场临时管制时，企业应当按照公安机关的指令，立即采取避让、暂停运行、终止运行等处置措施。

第二十四条　开展无驾驶人智能网联汽车创新应用的企业应当按照网络安全相关法律、法规和信息安全标准的强制性要求，建立网络安全管理制度，落实网络安全等级保护制度，采取技术措施和其他必要措施，提高网络安全保护水平，保障网络安全稳定运行。

第二十五条　开展无驾驶人智能网联汽车创新应用的企业应当按照数据安全相关法律、法规要求，建立健全全流程数据安全和个人信息保护管理制度，落实数据安全和个人信息保护责任。发生或者可能发生涉及国家安全、个人信息等数据泄露、损毁、丢失等情况的，有关企业应当立即采取补救措施，按照规定及时告知用户并向有关主管部门报告。

开展创新应用过程中收集和产生的重要数据，应当依法在境内存储；因业务需要，确需向境外提供的，应当按照国家有关规定进行安全评估。个人信息数据的出境安全管理，按照有关法律、行政法规的规定执行。

第二十六条　开展创新应用期间，无驾驶人智能网联汽车发生故障的，企业应当按照有关技术要求作出判断，采取相应措施确保车辆处于安全状态。

创新应用企业应当将相关故障信息传输至指定的监管平台，并保存至少一年。

Enterprises shall adjust operation plans swiftly in response to adverse weather, road construction, major events, or similar circumstances as directed by appropriate departments. If the public security department imposes temporary controls, the enterprise shall take immediate actions such as rerouting, pausing, or ceasing operations as directed.

Section 24 Enterprises shall develop a cybersecurity management system, comply with cybersecurity classifications, and enact technical and other necessary actions to boost security, ensuring the safe and stable functioning of their networks by complying with cybersecurity laws and mandatory information security standards.

Section 25 Enterprises shall create and maintain robust data security and personal information protection systems, ensuring their effective implementation pursuant to data security laws and regulations. In the event of a data breach, damage, or loss affecting national security or personal information, enterprises shall take prompt corrective action, inform affected individuals, and report to competent authorities.

Critical data gathered through innovation applications shall be stored domestically as required by law. International data transfers for business purposes shall pass a safety assessment in line with national guidelines, and personal data transfers abroad shall comply with applicable laws and administrative regulations.

Section 26 In case of a CAV malfunction during application trials, enterprises shall evaluate the issue based on technical standards and take appropriate safety actions.

These enterprises shall deliver the fault data to the designated regulatory platform and maintain it for at least one year.

第二十七条 开展创新应用期间，无驾驶人智能网联汽车发生交通事故的，企业应当立即暂停车辆运行、开启危险警示装置，报警并视情派员现场处置；事故发生后两小时内，应当将事故发生前至少九十秒的视频信息上传至指定的数据平台。

开展无驾驶人智能网联汽车创新应用的企业应当在有关主管部门全程参与下对事故过程进行技术分析并形成事故分析报告。相关事故过程信息和事故分析报告应当及时报送浦东新区公安机关交通管理部门，并保存至少一年。

第二十八条 无驾驶人智能网联汽车在开展创新应用期间发生交通违法行为的，由公安机关按照道路交通安全法律、法规对车辆所有人或者管理人进行处理。

第二十九条 无驾驶人智能网联汽车在开展创新应用期间发生交通事故的，由公安机关交通管理部门按照道路交通安全法律、法规进行交通事故责任认定。

无驾驶人智能网联汽车发生交通事故并造成损害，依法应由智能网联汽车一方承担责任的，由该无驾驶人智能网联汽车所属的企业先行赔偿，并可以依法向负有责任的自动驾驶系统开发者、汽车制造者、设备提供者等进行追偿。已经投保机动车交通事故责任强制保险、商业保险的，按照相关规定执行。

无驾驶人智能网联汽车以及车路协同云控平台采集的数据，经公安机关交通管理部门调查核实无误后，可以作为认定交通违法行为和认定交通事故责任的依据。

Section 27 Should a CAV be involved in a traffic accident during an application trial, the enterprise shall immediately halt operations, activate warning systems, and secure the accident scene. Within two hours, they shall upload video footage spanning at least 90 seconds before the accident to an assigned data platform.

The enterprises shall conduct a technical review of the accident under the full participation of competent authorities and produce an accident analysis report. This report and details of the accident shall be submitted expediently to the Pudong New Area public security department's traffic division and retained for no less than one year.

Section 28 If a CAV violates traffic regulations during trials, the public security department shall take action against the vehicle owners or the manager pursuant to road safety laws.

Section 29 In cases of traffic accidents involving CAVs during trials, the public security department's traffic division shall assess liability pursuant to road safety laws and regulations.

If such accidents result in damages attributed to CAVs, the vehicle owner is required to offer initial recompense, with the option to seek further compensation from developers, manufacturers, and device providers of the autonomous driving system pursuant to law. Applicable regulations shall apply to vehicles covered by compulsory liability or commercial insurance.

CAV and V2X cloud-based control platform-collected data may be utilized in determining liability for traffic violations and accidents post-verification by the public security department's traffic division.

第三十条 利用无驾驶人智能网联汽车开展道路货物运输经营的，企业应当投保承运人责任保险；开展旅客运输服务的，应当投保车上人员责任保险。

鼓励相关行业组织、企业等联合设立风险基金。鼓励保险公司开发适应无驾驶人智能网联汽车特点的保险产品。

第三十一条 无驾驶人智能网联汽车道路测试、示范应用、示范运营期间有下列情形之一的，由浦东新区科技经济部门或者临港新片区管委会暂停有关企业的相关创新应用活动，责令其限期整改；完成整改后，方可恢复相关创新应用活动：

（一）无驾驶人智能网联汽车经过测试不符合要求的；

（二）开展创新应用的企业、车辆或者紧急接管人员等发生变化，不再符合规定要求的；

（三）未按照安全性自我声明载明的阶段、时段、路段等开展相关创新应用活动的；

（四）违反载人、载货有关规定的；

（五）未按照规定将相关数据上传至指定的数据平台的；

（六）发生软件升级、硬件变更，未按照规定报告的；

（七）车辆发生故障或者交通事故，未按照规定采取相应措施的；

（八）未按照规定传输和保存车辆故障、事故信息，或者未提交事故分析报告的；

（九）存在重大软件、硬件系统性缺陷的；

（十）发生网络安全或者数据安全事故的。

Section 30 Before engaging CAVs in road freight or passenger services, enterprises shall secure carrier or passenger liability insurance, respectively.

Industry groups and enterprises are encouraged to form risk pools, and insurers are encouraged to develop CAV coverage options.

Section 31 If enterprises fail to comply during CAV road tests, pilot projects, or pilot operations due to any listed circumstances, the Pudong New Area technology and economy department or the Lin-gang Special Area Administration Committee shall mandate a correction period before applications can resume.

(1) CAVs that fall short during testing;

(2) changes in enterprises, vehicles, or emergency response staff that violate established criteria;

(3) discrepancies in following allocated stages, schedules, or designated areas noted in the safety commitment;

(4) breach of passenger or freight transport regulations;

(5) failure to upload crucial data to designated platforms;

(6) non-disclosure of essential software or hardware upgrades;

(7) inadequate actions taken following vehicle malfunctions or traffic accidents;

(8) insufficient transmission or archiving of malfunction or accident data, or non-submission of the accident analysis reports;

(9) significant systemic defects in software or hardware; or

(10) cybersecurity or data breach incidents.

开展无驾驶人智能网联汽车道路测试、示范应用、示范运营的车辆有下列情形之一的，由浦东新区科技经济部门或者临港新片区管委会暂停该车辆或者同型号车辆的相关创新应用活动，责令其限期整改；完成整改后，方可恢复相关创新应用活动：

（一）未按照要求放置车辆识别标牌的；

（二）发生三次以上一般道路交通违法行为，或者发生不按照交通信号指示通行、违反标志标线指示、逆向行驶等严重道路交通违法行为的；

（三）发生道路交通事故并承担同等及以上责任的。

第三十二条 无驾驶人智能网联汽车道路测试、示范应用、示范运营期间有下列情形之一的，由浦东新区科技经济部门或者临港新片区管委会终止有关企业的相关创新应用活动，相关号牌、标牌和营运证件失效：

（一）暂停创新应用活动后，拒不整改或者经整改仍不符合要求的；

（二）提供虚假的安全性自我声明或者数据、信息、报告等材料的；

（三）对国家安全、公共安全造成危害，或者程序设计违反伦理要求、存在重大安全风险的。

开展无驾驶人智能网联汽车道路测试、示范应用、示范运营的车辆有下列情形之一的，由浦东新区科技经济部门或者临港新片区管委会终止该车辆或者同型号车辆的相关创新应用活动；情节严重的，终止有关企业的相关创新应用活动：

（一）发生三次以上不按照交通信号指示通行、违反标志标线指示、逆向行驶等严重道路交通违法行为的；

（二）发生造成人员伤亡的道路交通事故，并承担主要或者全部责任的。

The Pudong New Area technology and economy department or the Lin-gang Special Area Administration Committee shall suspend the innovation application of the vehicle or its type and mandate correction within a specified timeframe if the road test, pilot projects, or operation of CAVs involves any of the following:

(1) improperly displayed vehicle identification plate;

(2) three or more general traffic violations, or serious offenses such as running traffic signals, ignoring signs or markings, or driving in the wrong direction; or

(3) involvement in traffic accidents with equivalent or greater liability.

Section 32 The Pudong New Area technology and economy department or the Lin-gang Special Area Administration Committee shall terminate the innovation application, voiding vehicle license and identification plates, and the autonomous vehicle permit if any of the following occur during the road test, pilot projects, or operation of CAVs:

(1) non-compliance with correction requirements post-suspension;

(2) submission of falsified commitments, data, or reports; or

(3) compromising national security or public safety, or the program design breaching ethical standards, or posing significant security risks.

The Pudong New Area technology and economy department or the Lin-gang Special Area Administration Committee shall terminate the innovation application for the vehicle or its type under any of the following circumstances during CAV road tests, pilot projects, or operations. If the violations are serious, the enterprise's innovation application shall be terminated:

(1) having committed three or more general traffic violations, or serious offenses such as running traffic signals, ignoring signs or markings, or driving in the wrong direction; or

(2) involvement in road traffic accidents with primary or full liability.

安全性自我声明未经确认或者未取得临时行驶车号牌、相关车辆营运证件擅自开展相关活动的，由浦东新区科技经济部门或者临港新片区管委会责令立即终止相关活动，并由有关主管部门依法进行处理。

第三十三条 无人配送、无人清扫等无人驾驶装备上道路行驶，参照适用道路交通安全法律、法规有关非机动车的通行规定。无人驾驶装备道路测试、示范运营等具体管理规定，由浦东新区、临港新片区管委会在市有关主管部门的指导下制定。

第三十四条 本规定自2023年2月1日起施行。

If the safety commitment is not endorsed or the temporary vehicle license plate or autonomous vehicle permit is not obtained, the Pudong New Area technology and economy department or the Lin-gang Special Area Administration Committee shall order an immediate halt to the activities, with competent authorities addressing the matter lawfully.

Section 33 Road safety laws on non-motor vehicles similarly apply to the operation of autonomous devices used for deliveries or cleaning on public roads. The Pudong New Area and the Lin-gang Special Area Administration Committee, under the guidance of municipal competent authorities, shall develop detailed rules governing the testing and application of these devices.

Section 34 These Provisions shall take effect from February 1, 2023.

上海市浦东新区固体废物资源化再利用若干规定

Several Provisions for the Pudong New Area of Shanghai Municipality on the Recycling of Solid Wastes

上海市浦东新区固体废物资源化再利用若干规定

（2022年12月21日上海市第十五届人民代表大会常务委员会第四十七次会议通过）

第一条 为了推动浦东新区“无废城市”建设，加快形成与城市绿色发展相适应的固体废物处理模式，率先实现固体废物从源头分类到资源化再利用的全过程治理，全面提升资源化再利用的效率和水平，根据有关法律、行政法规的基本原则，结合浦东新区实际，制定本规定。

第二条 本规定适用于浦东新区行政区域内固体废物资源化再利用的相关活动。

第三条 浦东新区应当按照统筹规划、合理布局、政府引导、多元共治的原则，打造循环畅通、高效利用、生态友好、智慧创新的固体废物资源化再利用样板，在实现原生生活垃圾零填埋的基础上，率先实现固体废物近零填埋。

第四条 市人民政府应当加强固体废物资源化再利用工作的领导，深化与国家有关部门的协作，统筹协调浦东新区固体废物资源化再利用工作中的重大事项。

浦东新区人民政府应当加强本行政区域固体废物资源化再利用工作的领导，建立分工明确、权责明晰、协同增效的综合管理体制机制，推进落实相关工作。

Several Provisions for the Pudong New Area of Shanghai Municipality on the Recycling of Solid Wastes

(Adopted at the 47th Session for the 15th Shanghai Municipal People's Congress Standing Committee on December 21, 2022)

Section 1 The Several Provisions for the Pudong New Area of Shanghai Municipality on the Recycling of Solid Wastes (these "Provisions") are formulated to develop a zero-waste city, develop an effective solid waste management model, ensure comprehensive management from source separation to recycling, and increase the efficiency and effectiveness of recycling operations, pursuant to the basic principles of applicable laws and administrative regulations, and in light of the actual circumstances in the Pudong New Area.

Section 2 These Provisions shall apply to all solid waste recycling activities within the administrative boundaries of the Pudong New Area.

Section 3 The Pudong New Area shall develop an effective, eco-friendly solid waste recycling program based on systematic planning, efficient organization, governmental guidance, and multi-stakeholder governance to achieve near-zero landfill use, starting with the elimination of landfilling unprocessed household waste.

Section 4 The Municipal People's Government shall enhance its leadership in solid waste recycling, coordinate with appropriate national departments, and manage critical issues of solid waste recycling in the Pudong New Area.

The Pudong New Area People's Government shall bolster solid waste recycling efforts within its jurisdiction, develop a comprehensive enforcement system with defined roles and responsibilities, and help implement the initiatives.

第五条 市发展改革、绿化市容、规划资源、生态环境、住房城乡建设管理、经济信息化、商务、农业农村、交通、财政等部门应当按照规定履行各自职责，完善政策措施，深化制度创新，支持和保障浦东新区固体废物资源化再利用工作。

浦东新区发展改革、绿化市容、规划资源、生态环境、建设交通、科技经济、商务、农业农村、财政等部门按照各自职责，做好相关工作。

第六条 浦东新区应当构建固体废物资源化再利用体系，建立健全固体废物资源化再利用制度，明确政府、企业、个人等各类主体的责任，推动实现生产、流通、消费、处理各环节的绿色低碳循环发展。

第七条 浦东新区人民政府应当组织开展固体废物资源化再利用处置能力调查评估，按照应用尽用、能用尽用的要求，编制固体废物资源化再利用专项规划，明确发展目标、指标体系、主要任务、重点领域、项目布局、保障措施等内容。

第八条 浦东新区人民政府应当建立健全以资源产出率、资源化再利用率为核心指标的固体废物资源化再利用指标体系，并与绿色发展指标体系、“无废城市”建设指标体系相衔接。

第九条 浦东新区应当采取措施，支持企业采用先进的生产工艺和设备，减少工业固体废物的产生量；提高工业固体废物综合利用效率，推行绿色设计，提高产品可拆解性、可回收性；结合产业实际情况，确定重点行业和重点领域，落实生产者责任延伸制度，建成废弃产品逆向回收体系。

浦东新区支持高端再制造、智能再制造产业发展。

Section 5 Municipal departments including but not limited to development and reform, landscaping and city appearance, planning and resources, ecology and environment, housing and urban-rural development, economy and information technology, commerce, agriculture and rural development, transportation, and finance, shall perform their specific duties, refine policies, foster innovation, and support recycling efforts in the Pudong New Area.

Departments in the Pudong New Area, such as the development and reform, landscaping and city appearance, planning and resources, ecology and environment, construction and transportation, science and economy, commerce, agriculture and rural development, and finance, shall diligently perform their respective duties.

Section 6 The Pudong New Area shall enhance and expand the recycling system for solid waste, assigning clear responsibilities to government entities, businesses, and individuals, and facilitating sustainable and low-carbon practices throughout production, distribution, consumption, and disposal processes.

Section 7 The Pudong New Area People's Government shall manage the evaluation of recycling and disposal capacities for solid waste and develop a specific plan that outlines objectives, performance metrics, primary tasks, key areas, project designs, and supporting activities to maximize the use of the available resources.

Section 8 The Pudong New Area People's Government shall develop and enhance key performance indicators for solid waste recycling, focusing on resource efficiency and recycling rates. These indicators shall align with the goals of sustainable development and the zero-waste city initiative.

Section 9 The Pudong New Area shall support businesses in adopting advanced production technologies and processes to reduce industrial solid waste significantly, facilitate eco-design and improve product disassembly and recyclability, enforce comprehensive producer responsibility, and establish industry-specific reverse logistics systems for recycling products in key sectors and fields.

The Pudong New Area encourages the development of advanced and smart remanufacturing industries.

第十条 浦东新区应当促进主要农业固体废物全量利用，推动农作物秸秆、蔬菜废弃物、绿林废弃物多元化利用，加强废弃农膜和农药包装废弃物回收利用，推进畜禽粪污资源化利用。

第十一条 浦东新区应当逐步实现建筑垃圾全面资源化再利用，装修垃圾、拆房垃圾、建筑废弃混凝土应当全量收集，进入资源化再利用设施进行处置；制成的资源化再利用产品按照有关规定实施强制使用制度。

浦东新区可以在本市建筑垃圾资源化再利用产品强制使用要求的基础上，进一步拓展使用范围，提高使用比例。

浦东新区应当在市政建设项目中推广使用符合要求的建筑垃圾资源化再利用产品。

第十二条 浦东新区人民政府以及有关部门应当采取措施，畅通生活垃圾可回收物回收利用渠道，建立规范有序的回收利用链条，培育和支持主体企业集约化发展，鼓励标准化、规范化、连锁化经营。

浦东新区推广回收新技术、新模式，支持再生资源回收企业建立在线交易平台，实现线上交废与线下回收有机结合。

浦东新区应当探索湿垃圾资源化新工艺，拓展资源化利用方向，打通产品出路，提升利用价值。

第十三条 浦东新区应当加快固体废物资源化再利用体系建设，遵循环境友好的原则，按照规划和标准，设置可回收物交投服务点、中转站、集散场，建设生活垃圾、建筑垃圾、工业固体废物等资源化再利用设施，并将生活垃圾、建筑垃圾等固体废物分类收集设施纳入城市基础设施和公共设施范围。

Section 10 The Pudong New Area shall support the use of major agricultural solid wastes such as crop straws, vegetable waste, and garden waste, improve the recycling of agricultural plastic films and pesticide containers, and advocate for livestock and poultry manure recycling.

Section 11 The Pudong New Area shall aim to gradually achieve the comprehensive recycling of construction and demolition waste, and ensure complete collection and recycling of renovation waste, demolition debris, and concrete. Recycled products shall comply with a mandatory usage policy.

The Pudong New Area may increase the scope and utilization rates of these products under the mandatory usage policy.

The Pudong New Area shall promote the application of suitable recycled construction waste products in municipal projects.

Section 12 The Pudong New Area People's Government and appropriate departments shall develop an organized and efficient recycling network for residential recyclables, facilitate the expansion of specialized businesses, and encourage standardized, regulated, and franchised operations across the industry.

The Pudong New Area is to introduce innovative recycling technologies and models, support businesses in creating online platforms for recyclable resources, and integrate digital waste management strategies with traditional recycling activities.

The Pudong New Area shall explore new recycling methods for household food waste, expand the recycling initiatives, develop markets for recycled materials, and increase the value obtained from recycling.

Section 13 Following eco-friendly principles and standards, the Pudong New Area shall expedite the advancement of solid waste recycling infrastructure, including setting up collection services, transfer stations, and distribution hubs and incorporating facilities for residential and construction waste and industrial solid waste recycling into urban and public infrastructures.

第十四条 浦东新区应当鼓励和支持固体废物资源化再利用项目建设和企业稳定发展，在土地全生命周期管理中，更加注重环境效益和社会效益。

第十五条 按照本市和浦东新区固体废物资源化再利用发展需求，在浦东新区建设老港、黎明等固体废物资源化再利用园区。

老港园区应当建设成为固体废物综合处置战略保障基地、资源循环利用示范基地、环保科创科普先导基地、智慧绿色生态基地。

市和浦东新区人民政府可以指定特定主体负责固体废物资源化再利用园区的统一规划、统一开发建设、统一运营调度、统一管理服务。

浦东新区应当充分考虑固体废物资源化再利用园区的地理位置、目标定位及发展需求，规划配套园区周边的公共设施和道路交通设施。

第十六条 固体废物资源化再利用园区应当建立健全生态环保指标体系，运用先进的工艺设计、污染防治和低碳技术，减少污染物排放总量和碳排放总量。

鼓励固体废物资源化再利用园区通过整合、升级园区内的各类设施、资源、能源，逐步建立覆盖物质、能源、水等循环系统，实现资源能源利用效率的最大化。

探索老港、黎明等园区资源化再利用企业开展电力市场化交易模式创新。

第十七条 本市应当建立健全固体废物资源化再利用标准体系。市绿化市容、住房城乡建设管理、经济信息化、农业农村、交通等部门负责组织编制各自职责范围内固体废物资源化再利用相关标准和规范。

Section 14 The Pudong New Area shall support and encourage the development and consistent growth of solid waste recycling projects and businesses, emphasizing ecological and social benefits throughout the land lifecycle management.

Section 15 Solid waste recycling parks, including Laogang Park and Liming Park, are to be developed to meet the strategic needs of this Municipality and the Pudong New Area.

Laogang Park shall be built into a strategic hub for comprehensive solid waste disposal, a model for resource recycling, a pioneering site for environmental protection and technological innovation, and an example of smart, sustainable, eco-friendly operations.

The Municipal and the Pudong New Area People's Governments may appoint specific entities to take charge of coordinated planning, development, management, and operations of these solid waste recycling parks.

The Pudong New Area shall fully consider the geographic location, strategic significance, and development needs of the recycling parks, ensuring they are supported by surrounding public facilities and transportation infrastructure.

Section 16 Solid waste recycling parks shall develop and refine ecological and environmental protection metrics, adopting advanced processing designs, pollution control, and low-carbon technologies to minimize pollutant and greenhouse gas emissions.

These parks are encouraged to consolidate and enhance their facilities, resources, and energy systems, progressively creating a comprehensive recycling network for materials, energy, and water to maximize resource use and energy efficiency.

Research is carried out on a market-based electricity transaction system for recycling companies in parks such as Laogang Park and Liming Park.

Section 17 This Municipality shall refine and develop recycling standards. Municipal departments including but not limited to landscaping and city appearance, housing and urban-rural development, economy and information technology, agriculture and rural development, and transportation departments shall coordinate to establish pertinent standards and guidelines for solid waste recycling to the extent of their duties.

浦东新区应当建立固体废物资源化再利用产品使用制度。党政机关、事业单位应当优先使用资源化再利用产品。鼓励和引导单位和个人使用各类资源化再利用产品。

第十八条 浦东新区应当在规划产业用地中划出一定比例用地，专门用于发展固体废物资源化再利用产业。

资源化再利用园区新增的资源化再利用项目，其建设用地指标和耕地占补平衡指标由市级统筹安排。

对固体废物资源化再利用项目，可以采用“带方案”出让方式或者“带方案”租赁方式供地。工业用地出让起始价可以按照工业用地出让最低价标准执行。

第十九条 确需整体实施、整体建设的固体废物资源化再利用项目，在不突破国家出让规模底线要求和明确项目开竣工要求的前提下，鼓励创新优化土地供应方式。

第二十条 市规划资源部门应当加强老港园区国土资源利用计划统筹，在符合国土空间规划、落实国土空间用途管制总体要求的前提下，优先分配老港园区规划产业用地指标，保障固体废物资源化再利用项目实施。

老港园区内的储备土地由土地储备机构委托市人民政府指定的特定主体进行前期开发。前期开发的费用，应当列入土地收储成本。

第二十一条 浦东新区固体废物资源化再利用建设项目的环境影响评价，按照分类管理的规定，报浦东新区生态环境部门审批或者备案。

浦东新区生态环境部门可以对相同类型的固体废物资源化再利用建设项目环境影响评价，实施一次性受理和集中审批。

The Pudong New Area shall set guidelines for using products made from recycled solid waste, with government agencies, public institutions, and business entities and individuals encouraged to prioritize these products in support of sustainable practices.

Section 18 The Pudong New Area shall designate specific industrial zones for solid waste recycling operations.

Land allocation for construction and cultivated land credits for new recycling projects shall be managed by this Municipality, focusing on the needs of recycling parks.

Land arrangements for recycling projects may involve conditional transfers or leases, with pricing set at the minimum rates established for industrial land transfers.

Section 19 This Municipality shall consider advanced or optimized land supply models for solid waste recycling projects requiring comprehensive implementation, ensuring compliance with national standards for project scopes and timelines.

Section 20 The municipal planning and resources department shall improve the coordinated utilization of national land resources in Laogang Park, ensuring that land allocations are focused on solid waste recycling projects in line with national spatial planning and regulatory guidelines.

Reserved land in Laogang Park shall be allocated for initial development by designated entities, managed by the land reserve department, and the costs will be covered by the budget for land banking.

Section 21 The environmental impact assessment for solid waste recycling projects in the Pudong New Area is to be submitted to the Pudong New Area ecology and environment department for review or filing, as required by classified management guidelines.

The Pudong New Area ecology and environment department may facilitate expedited reviews for similar recycling projects by implementing batch processing and streamlined submission procedures.

浦东新区固体废物资源化再利用园区已完成规划环境影响评价且有效落实规划环境影响评价有关措施的，建设项目环境影响评价手续可以按照规定予以简化。

第二十二条 浦东新区推进固体废物资源化再利用建设项目环境影响评价和排污许可“两证合一”办理，实现两项行政许可一套材料、一口受理、同步审批、一次办结。

市生态环境部门可以根据国家固定污染源排污许可分类管理名录，结合区域污染物减排和固体废物资源化再利用等实际情况，制定浦东新区排污许可管理细化名录，在浦东新区先行先试。

第二十三条 鼓励固体废物资源化再利用园区按照集约建设、共享治污的原则，探索由政府投资或者政府组织、多元投资，配套建设可供多个市场主体共享的污染治理设施或者集中工艺设施，实现污染物统一收集、集中治理、稳定达标排放。

第二十四条 浦东新区应当通过碳普惠、碳认证等制度，鼓励和支持固体废物资源化再利用企业充分发挥碳减排效益，推动企业实现减污降碳协同增效。

第二十五条 市和浦东新区人民政府应当加大固体废物资源化再利用的财政扶持力度，安排相关资金支持资源化再利用项目、园区基础设施及公共配套项目建设。

鼓励社会资本参与资源化再利用项目建设，积极引导金融机构通过绿色金融工具、不动产投资信托基金等，为符合条件的固体废物资源化再利用项目提供融资服务。

固体废物资源化再利用企业依法享受税收优惠政策。

If an effective environmental assessment has already been performed during the planning stage, simplified procedures may apply to projects in the recycling parks.

Section 22 The Pudong New Area shall implement a consolidated permit system for environmental impact assessments and pollutant discharge permits in solid waste recycling projects, streamlining the process with a single submission, unified acceptance, joint review, and simultaneous completion.

The municipal ecology and environment department may compile a specific pollutant discharge permit list for the Pudong New Area as a pilot scheme, tailored to local needs for pollution control and solid waste recycling.

Section 23 Solid waste recycling parks are encouraged to explore the establishment of shared pollution control facilities or integrated processing systems, financed either through government funding or diverse investment models, to support intensive development and collective pollution management, ensuring consistent, centralized, and compliant pollutant management.

Section 24 The Pudong New Area shall motivate solid waste recycling enterprises to maximize carbon reduction benefits through inclusive carbon projects and a carbon certification program, aligning pollution reduction with carbon offset initiatives

Section 25 The Municipal and the Pudong New Area People's Governments shall increase financial support for solid waste recycling by allocating funds for recycling projects, park infrastructure, and supportive public infrastructure development.

Non-government investment in these recycling initiatives are to be encouraged, and financial institutions are to be prompted to offer financial support services for eligible projects using sustainable finance tools and real estate investment trusts.

Solid waste recycling enterprises are to enjoy preferential tax treatment under the law.

第二十六条　浦东新区应当加大科技投入，加快固体废物资源化再利用新技术、新材料、新工艺、新设备的研发和推广。

老港园区应当推进固体废物环保科创中心建设，实现科技研发、中试验证、研制试制、展示交流等功能，形成自主的核心技术和能力体系。

第二十七条　浦东新区应当推进智慧化建设，拓展智慧化应用场景，运用大数据分析模型，通过数据采集、储存、应用、查询，实现固体废物资源化再利用全方位、全过程、全覆盖的智慧化管理。

浦东新区应当支持固体废物资源化再利用园区结合产业功能布局建设完善智慧化设施和系统，推进园区数字化转型，提升园区生产和运营管理效能。

第二十八条　浦东新区应当建立固体废物资源化再利用领域的信用管理机制，形成信用评价标准，依法对相关企业予以信用激励或惩戒。

第二十九条　本规定自 2023 年 2 月 1 日起施行。

Section 26 The Pudong New Area shall enhance investment in science and technology to accelerate the development of innovative technologies, materials, processes, and devices for solid waste recycling.

Laogang Park shall prioritize developing a hub for environmental protection and innovation in solid waste management, supporting R&D, pilot testing, scale-up trials, exhibitions and exchanges, and fostering the development of independent core technologies and capabilities.

Section 27 The Pudong New Area shall advance intelligent operations by expanding the application of intelligent systems and employing comprehensive data analysis to create an integrated, intelligent management system for solid waste recycling to realize complete data collection, storage, processing, and access throughout all phases of recycling.

The Pudong New Area shall support solid waste recycling parks in upgrading intelligent systems, integrating industrial functions, facilitating digital transformation, and improving production and operation efficiency.

Section 28 The Pudong New Area shall introduce a credit management system for solid waste recycling, create evaluation standards, and apply legal incentives for or impose penalties on companies pursuant to law.

Section 29 These Provisions shall take effect from February 1, 2023.

上海市健全浦东新区生态环境保护制度若干规定

Several Provisions of Shanghai Municipality on Improving the Ecological and Environmental Protection System in the Pudong New Area

上海市健全浦东新区生态环境保护制度若干规定

（2023年6月20日上海市第十六届人民代表大会常务委员会第三次会议通过）

第一条 为了打造人与自然和谐共生的美丽浦东，进一步健全源头预防、过程控制、损害赔偿、责任追究的生态环境保护制度，根据有关法律、行政法规的基本原则，结合浦东新区实际，制定本规定。

第二条 浦东新区建立健全生态文明建设领导机制，实行生态环境保护党政同责、一岗双责。

浦东新区人民政府应当构建以绿色发展为导向的生态文明建设目标考核体系，建立区级生态环境保护工作监督和责任追究机制，对本级人民政府有关行政管理部门和街道办事处、镇人民政府的环境保护职责履行和目标完成情况进行监督，并依法追究相关单位和责任人的责任。

浦东新区生态环境、发展改革、科技经济、建设交通、规划资源、农业农村、城管执法、财政等部门以及管理局（管理委员会）、街道办事处、镇人民政府应当按照规定履行各自职责，完善政策措施，深化制度创新，做好生态环境保护相关工作。

Several Provisions of Shanghai Municipality on Improving the Ecological and Environmental Protection System in the Pudong New Area

(Adopted at the 3rd Session of the 15th Shanghai Municipal People's Congress Standing Committee on June 20, 2023)

Section 1 The Several Provisions of Shanghai Municipality on Improving the Ecological and Environmental Protection System in the Pudong New Area (these "Provisions") are formulated to enhance source prevention, process control, compensation, and accountability within the ecological and environmental protection framework and build a harmoniously coexisting human and natural environment in Pudong, pursuant to the basic principles of applicable laws and administrative regulations, and in light of the actual circumstances in the Pudong New Area.

Section 2 The Pudong New Area shall develop a robust ecological civilization system, assigning environmental protection responsibilities equally among Party committees and governments and carry specific environmental duties alongside their regular responsibilities.

The Pudong New Area People's Government shall implement a performance assessment system focused on sustainable development, establish a district-level oversight and accountability structure for ecological and environmental protection, oversee the fulfillment of environmental duties and achievement of goals by the competent departments under the Pudong New Area People's Government, sub-district offices, and township governments, and hold the pertinent entities and responsible persons liable pursuant to law.

Pudong New Area departments, including ecology and environment, development and reform, science and economy, construction and transportation, planning and resources, agriculture and rural development, urban management and law enforcement, and finance departments, along with the administrative bureau (or administration committee), sub-district offices, and township governments, shall perform their duties to refine policies and deepen institutional innovation to ensure effective ecological and environmental protection.

第三条 浦东新区将碳达峰、碳中和纳入经济社会发展全局，建立健全减少污染排放、降低温室气体排放等的激励约束机制，推动经济社会发展全面绿色转型。

浦东新区生态环境部门应当推动大气污染物源排放清单与温室气体排放清单协同编制，推进温室气体和污染物排放协同控制。编制建设项目环境影响报告书（表）和产业园区规划环境影响报告书时，应当按照国家和本市有关规定将碳排放纳入环境影响评价范围。

第四条 浦东新区已完成相关区域规划环境影响评价、有效落实规划环境影响评价结论与审查意见的区域，可以实施规划环境影响评价与建设项目环境影响评价联动。区域内符合条件的建设项目可以实行简化办理环境影响评价手续等措施。

浦东新区生态环境部门可以依行政相对人的申请同步办理本行政区域内环境影响评价审批与排污许可审批。

第五条 浦东新区应当统筹农村生态环境治理、农村基础设施建设与农业绿色发展。

浦东新区探索推行农田退水规范化管理，防治农业面源污染。浦东新区农业农村部门应当优化畜禽、水产养殖空间布局，加强畜禽、水产养殖污染防治以及对使用化肥、农药的监督管理和指导。

第六条 浦东新区生态环境部门应当会同相关部门建立持久性有机污染物、内分泌干扰物、抗生素等新污染物管控机制，按照国家和本市规定采取禁止、限制、限排、强制清洁生产审核等环境风险管控措施，加强对新污染物在生产、加工、使用、处置等环节的管控和治理。

Section 3 The Pudong New Area shall incorporate peak carbon dioxide emissions and carbon neutrality goals into its broader economic and social development strategies, enhance systems to incentivize reductions in both pollution and greenhouse gas emissions, and facilitate a comprehensive sustainable transformation across economic and social sectors.

The Pudong New Area ecology and environment department shall lead in integrating and managing the emission inventories for greenhouse gases and air pollutants, reinforcing the coordinated reduction of both pollutant types. Carbon emissions shall be included in the environmental impact assessment reports (or forms) required by both national and municipal regulations for all construction projects and industrial park developments.

Section 4 In regions of the Pudong New Area where environmental impact assessments of planning have been completed and enforced, the environmental impact assessment for construction projects may be coordinated with the planning assessment. The environmental impact assessment may be simplified for eligible construction projects in the regions

Upon request, the Pudong New Area ecology and environment department may process applications for environmental impact assessments and pollutant discharge permits within its jurisdiction concurrently.

Section 5 The Pudong New Area shall streamline ecological and environmental governance in rural areas, focusing on infrastructure development and sustainable agricultural practices.

The Pudong New Area shall implement standardized management of agricultural runoff to curb non-point source agricultural pollution. The Pudong New Area agriculture and rural development department shall adjust land zoning for livestock, poultry, and aquaculture to minimize environmental impact, and oversee and guide the application of chemical fertilizers and pesticides.

Section 6 In cooperation with the appropriate departments, the Pudong New Area ecology and environment department shall implement robust controls over emerging pollutants like persistent organic pollutants, endocrine disruptors, and antibiotics, enforce environmental risk regulations through prohibition, restriction, discharge limitation, and mandatory cleaner production certifications, and manage pollutants across their production, processing, use, and disposal as mandated by national and municipal regulations.

第七条　浦东新区生态环境部门应当加强企业环境信息披露的监督管理。除国家规定应当进行环境信息披露的企业以外，浦东新区环境风险重点管控单位、属于全国碳排放权交易市场覆盖行业的温室气体重点排放单位也应当披露相关环境信息。

浦东新区环境风险重点管控单位、属于全国碳排放权交易市场覆盖行业的温室气体重点排放单位的名单由浦东新区生态环境部门按照规定确定并公布，其监管要求和法律责任按照企业环境信息依法披露管理的规定执行。

第八条　违反国家规定造成生态环境损害的单位或者个人，应当依法承担生态环境损害修复和赔偿责任。

浦东新区人民政府是本行政区域内生态环境损害赔偿权利人。街道办事处、镇人民政府负责所辖区域生态环境损害赔偿具体工作；浦东新区有关行业主管部门负责跨区域、重大的生态环境损害赔偿具体工作。浦东新区相关行业主管部门应当加强对街道办事处、镇人民政府的业务指导。

依法登记的环保公益性组织可以应邀以磋商第三人、修复监督人等身份参与生态环境损害赔偿工作。

第九条　对于生态环境损害事实简单、责任认定无争议、损害较小的案件，在浦东新区探索生态环境损害鉴定电子化评估工作。

在生态环境损害赔偿磋商阶段可以组织开展听证。经磋商达成生态环境损害赔偿协议的，可以依法向有管辖权的人民法院申请司法确认。赔偿协议的履行情况作为生态环境行政处罚的裁量因素。

第十条　责任人应当依法赔偿相关损失并承担生态环境损害赔偿范围内的相关费用。

Section 7 The Pudong New Area ecology and environment department shall oversee and regulate the disclosure of environmental data by organizations. Beyond nationally mandated disclosures, key organizations involved in environmental risk management and major greenhouse gas emitters under the national carbon credits trading scheme shall report pertinent environmental information.

The Pudong New Area ecology and environment department shall identify and disclose lists of key organizations subject to environmental risk management and those in sectors under the national carbon credits trading scheme. Their regulatory requirements and legal liabilities shall be enforced based on the regulations governing the disclosure of organizations' environmental information.

Section 8 Entities or individuals responsible for unauthorized ecological or environmental damage shall restore affected areas or provide appropriate compensation pursuant to law.

The Pudong New Area People's Government is entitled to ecological and environmental damage compensation within its jurisdiction. Sub-district offices and township governments manage the localized environmental damage compensations, and the appropriate Pudong New Area departments shall handle significant and cross-regional cases, offering guidance to sub-district offices and township governments.

Legally registered non-profit environmental organizations may be included as third-party consultants or supervisory entities in the compensation process for ecological damages.

Section 9 The Pudong New Area is to pilot electronic assessments for straightforward, undisputed ecological and environmental damage cases with minor impact.

During compensation negotiation for ecological and environmental damages, hearings may be organized. If parties reach a settlement through the negotiation, they can seek legal endorsement from the people's court. Compensation agreement performance may influence the discretion applied in the administrative penalties.

Section 10 Responsible persons shall cover all losses and expenses associated with ecological damage as required by law.

生态环境损害可以修复的，责任人应当修复至生态环境受损前的基线水平或者生态环境风险可接受水平。生态环境损害无法修复的，在符合有关生态环境修复法规政策和规划的前提下，可以开展替代修复或者通过认购碳汇等提高生态效益的方式履行义务，实现生态环境及其服务功能等量恢复。

浦东新区探索建立生态环境公益基金制度，保障生态环境修复等公益事项的开展。

第十一条 违反国家规定故意污染环境、破坏生态造成严重后果的，依法承担惩罚性赔偿责任。惩罚性赔偿数额一般不超过生态环境受到损害至修复完成期间服务功能丧失导致的损失、生态环境功能永久性损害造成的损失的三倍。

第十二条 浦东新区人民政府和相关检察机关应当建立健全生态环境损害赔偿与公益诉讼衔接协调机制。浦东新区生态环境、城管执法、规划资源、建设交通、农业农村等部门与相关检察机关应当加强沟通协调，开展生态环境信息共享、线索移送、专业咨询、支持起诉等工作协作。

第十三条 浦东新区城管执法部门开展生态环境事项现场检查时，可以按照相关技术规范要求现场采样，监测数据可以作为行政执法的证据。浦东新区生态环境部门可以委托具有相应资质的环境监测机构按照国家和本市规定开展监测，出具监测数据。监测数据经审核的，方可作为生态环境监督管理和执法的证据使用。

浦东新区生态环境、农业农村、城管执法等部门可以采用自动监测监控、遥感监测、能耗监控、雷达监控、视频监控等技术手段进行生态环境监督检查。

If ecological and environmental damage can be restored, the responsible persons shall restore it to the baseline condition or an acceptable level of ecological and environmental risk. If restoration is not possible, alternative methods, such as subscribing to carbon credits or other practices, may be used to enhance ecological benefits pursuant to applicable laws, policies, and restoration plans to ensure equivalent recovery of the ecosystem and its functions.

The Pudong New Area is to explore the creation of a non-profit funding system dedicated to ecological and environmental restoration, aimed at supporting public interest projects.

Section 11 Parties who unlawfully and intentionally pollute the environment or destroy the ecology, causing material adverse effects, shall be liable for punitive damages pursuant to law. The amount of punitive damages shall not exceed three times the loss caused by service failure or the permanent damage to ecological and environmental functions from the time of the incident to the completion of restoration.

Section 12 The Pudong New Area People's Government and the procuratorate shall enhance coordination systems that connect ecological and environmental damage compensation with public interest litigation. Cooperation shall be enhanced among the procuratorates and the departments responsible for ecology and environment, urban management and law enforcement, planning and resources, construction and transportation, and agriculture and rural development, among others, including but not limited to sharing environmental data, exchanging investigative leads, expert consultation, and providing litigation support.

Section 13 The Pudong New Area urban management and law enforcement department may conduct on-site sampling during ecological and environmental inspections as per technical specifications. The resulting monitoring data may be used as evidence for administrative law enforcement. The Pudong New Area ecology and environment department may entrust certified environmental monitoring organizations to carry out monitoring pursuant to national and municipal regulations. Monitoring data may only be used as evidence for ecological regulation and enforcement after verification.

Pudong New Area departments including but not limited to ecology and environment, agriculture and rural development, urban management law enforcement, may utilize advanced monitoring technologies such as automated, remote sensing, energy consumption, radar, and video surveillance to oversee and inspect the ecological environment.

第十四条 环境影响评价机构、环境监测机构以及从事环境监测设备和防治污染设施维护、运营等第三方机构，未按照法律、法规和相关技术规范的要求提供有关环境服务活动，或者在有关环境服务活动中弄虚作假的，除法律、行政法规另有规定的，由浦东新区城管执法部门责令停业整顿，处十万元以上一百万元以下的罚款，并对其主要负责人处二万元以上二十万元以下的罚款。对造成的环境污染和生态破坏负有责任的，除依法予以处罚外，还应当与造成环境污染和生态破坏的其他责任者承担连带责任。

建设单位、施工单位未按照规定取得证明，在噪声敏感建筑物集中区域夜间进行产生噪声的建筑施工作业，受到罚款处罚，被责令改正，拒不改正的，浦东新区城管执法部门可以自责令改正之日的次日起，按照原处罚数额实施按日连续处罚。

第十五条 本规定自 2023 年 8 月 15 日起施行。

Section 14 If environmental assessment organizations, monitoring organizations, or third-party operators responsible for managing environmental monitoring devices or pollution prevention facilities fail to meet legal, regulatory, or technical standards, or engage in fraudulent activities, the Pudong New Area urban management and law enforcement department shall order suspension of all activity and corrections. Fines of RMB 100,000 to RMB 1,000,000 shall be imposed on organizations, and RMB 20,000 to RMB 200,000 on responsible individuals. In addition to being subject to legal penalties, those causing environmental pollution and ecological damage shall be held jointly and severally liable, along with other accountable parties.

If an employer or contractor fails to obtain the required permits and carries out nighttime construction in noise-sensitive areas, resulting in fines and orders for correction, and refuses to comply, the Pudong New Area urban management and law enforcement department may impose consecutive daily fines equal to the original amount, starting from the second day since the correction order.

Section 15 These Provisions shall take effect from August 15, 2023.

上海市促进浦东新区标准化创新发展若干规定

Several Provisions of Shanghai Municipality on Promoting the Development of Standardization Innovation in the Pudong New Area

上海市促进浦东新区标准化创新发展若干规定

（2023 年 7 月 25 日上海市第十六届人民代表大会常务委员会第四次会议通过）

第一条 为了促进浦东新区标准化创新发展，提升标准国际化水平，推动标准制度型开放，引领高质量发展，根据有关法律、行政法规的基本原则，结合浦东新区实际，制定本规定。

第二条 浦东新区标准化创新发展应当对标国际最高水平，结合经济社会发展的实际情况和未来趋势，依托科创策源、产业集聚优势，率先在人工智能、集成电路、生物医药、民用航空和现代服务业等领域制定具有国际先进水平的标准，构建结构合理、重点突出、符合高质量发展要求的标准体系。

第三条 市人民政府应当加强对标准化创新发展工作的领导，健全标准化工作协调机制，深化与国家有关部门的协作，统筹协调浦东新区标准化创新发展工作中的重大事项。

浦东新区人民政府应当建立健全标准化创新发展促进工作机制，推动标准化创新发展。

第四条 市标准化行政主管部门负责统筹本市标准化创新发展促进工作，依托标准化部市合作及议事协调机制，协调推进浦东新区标准化创新发展。

Several Provisions of Shanghai Municipality on Promoting the Development of Standardization Innovation in the Pudong New Area

(Adopted at the 4th Session of the 16th Shanghai Municipal People's Congress Standing Committee on July 25, 2023)

Section 1 The Several Provisions of Shanghai Municipality on Promoting the Development of Standardization Innovation in the Pudong New Area (these "Provisions") are formulated to improve standardization innovation, enhance international recognition of the standards, promote open standards systems, and drive high-quality development, pursuant to the basic principles of applicable laws and administrative regulations, and in light of the actual circumstances in the Pudong New Area.

Section 2 The standardization innovation in the Pudong New Area shall align with leading international standards, integrate current and future socioeconomic trends, capitalize on strengths in scientific and technological innovation and industrial clusters, initiate international-level standards in sectors such as artificial intelligence, integrated circuits, biopharmaceutical medicines, civilian aviation, and modern services, and create a coherent, targeted standards system to support high-quality development.

Section 3 The Municipal People's Government shall intensify its leadership role in standardization innovation development by creating effective coordination processes, enhancing collaboration with national agencies, and coordinating significant standardization innovation initiatives in the Pudong New Area.

The Pudong New Area People's Government shall develop and refine a comprehensive system to facilitate standardization innovation development and improve the development of new standards.

Section 4 The municipal standardization administration coordinates support for standardization innovation and development across this Municipality, leveraging the municipal cooperation process to advance the standardization innovation in the Pudong New Area.

浦东新区标准化行政主管部门具体负责推进、实施本行政区域内标准化创新发展工作。

市和浦东新区发展改革、经济信息化、商务、教育、科技、农业农村、人力资源社会保障、地方金融监管、国有资产管理、知识产权等部门在各自职责范围内，共同促进浦东新区标准化创新发展。

第五条 浦东新区标准化行政主管部门和科技经济、商务、农业农村等行业主管部门应当引导社会团体、企业、科研机构参与国家标准、行业标准、地方标准以及国际标准的研究和制定，采用境内外先进标准，推进本市相关标准在境外实施应用；鼓励推出团体标准、企业标准的外文版文本。

浦东新区人民政府应当为外商投资企业依法平等参与标准制定工作提供服务和保障。

第六条 浦东新区人民政府应当建立标准化行政主管部门与科技经济部门、相关产业主管部门的联动机制，推进产业链、创新链、供应链与标准链融通，引导科研机构、高等院校、企业等在科技创新和实施产业项目时，推进标准同步布局、同步研制、同步应用，将标准作为科技计划重要产出，实现科技、标准与产业的有效衔接和互动。

第七条 浦东新区企业、科研机构、高等院校、金融基础设施运营机构或者标准化技术组织等，可以相互联合或者与境内外其他企业或者组织联合，形成标准创新联合体，共同制定企业联合标准。企业联合标准属于企业标准。

鼓励制定高于推荐性标准相关技术要求、体现引领性的企业联合标准，鼓励制定具有国际先进水平的企业联合标准。

The Pudong New Area standardization administration shall actively support and implement standardization innovation initiatives within its jurisdiction.

Municipal departments including but not limited to development and reform, economy and information technology, commerce, education, science and technology, agriculture and rural development, human resources and social security, local financial regulation, state-owned assets management, and intellectual property, shall cooperate to advance the standardization innovation in the Pudong New Area.

Section 5 The Pudong New Area standardization administration shall cooperate with industry regulatory agencies, including technology and economy, commerce, and agriculture and rural development departments, to lead social groups, enterprises, and research institutions in developing and adopting national, industry, local, and international standards to support the international application of municipal standards and encourage the publication of group and enterprise standards in multiple languages.

The Pudong New Area People's Government shall ensure that foreign-invested businesses have equitable and lawful opportunities to contribute to the standards development process.

Section 6 The Pudong New Area People's Government shall create a coordinated process among its standardization administration, technology and economy, and industry regulatory departments to integrate industrial, innovation, supply, and standards chains, to guide research institutions, universities, and businesses to align the development and application of standards with scientific and technological plans and emphasize that standards are key outputs in scientific innovation and industrial projects, ensuring effective integration and interaction between science, standards, and industry.

Section 7 Enterprises, research institutions, higher education institutions, financial infrastructure operators, and standardization organizations in the Pudong New Area may form partnerships among themselves or with domestic or international organizations to become standards consortiums and develop consensus standards, classified as enterprise standards.

Developing consensus standards that surpass existing technical standards and meet international benchmarks is encouraged, particularly those showcasing advanced technical capabilities.

形成标准创新联合体的各方可以协商确定企业联合标准的制定、权属和执行等事项。

第八条 企业联合标准应当在编号后发布。

企业联合标准的编号由企业标准代号（Q）/ 联合标准代号（LH）、标准创新联合体代号、顺序号和年代号组成，其中标准创新联合体代号可以用汉语拼音字母、阿拉伯数字或者两者兼用组成。

企业联合标准可以以标准创新联合体的名义发布。

第九条 企业联合标准由形成标准创新联合体的各方自愿执行或者按照约定供境内外其他企业或者组织自愿采用。

鼓励形成标准创新联合体的各方执行企业联合标准。执行企业联合标准的企业或者组织应当进行自我声明公开，公开其执行的标准编号和名称，以及产品、服务的功能指标和产品的性能指标。鼓励相关企业或者组织通过企业标准信息公共服务平台，进行自我声明公开。

执行企业联合标准的企业或者组织生产的产品、提供的服务不符合其自我声明公开标准的技术要求的，依法承担民事责任。

第十条 根据"上海标准"评价的技术规范，企业联合标准经自愿申请，并经具备法定条件的第三方机构评价，符合国内领先、国际先进要求的，可以在标准文本上使用"上海标准"标识。

禁止利用企业联合标准设置不合理技术贸易壁垒，禁止利用企业联合标准实施妨碍商品、服务自由流通等排除、限制市场竞争的行为。

第十一条 市和区标准化行政主管部门应当对企业联合标准的制定进行指导和监督，对标准实施进行监督检查。

Partners in these consortiums may negotiate the development, ownership, and application processes for these standards.

Section 8 Consensus standards shall be disclosed after receiving a distinct identifier.

The identifier shall include the enterprise standard code (Q), consensus standard code (LH), standards consortium identifier, sequence number, and year code. The standards consortium's identifier may consist of Chinese Pinyin, Arabic numerals, or both.

Consensus standards may be disclosed under the standards consortium's name.

Section 9 Adoption of consensus standards by consortium members or by other domestic and international businesses or organizations is voluntary or based on mutual agreements.

Standards consortium members are encouraged to implement consensus standards. Enterprises or organizations that adopt these standards shall disclose the standards' identifiers, names, functional indicators of products or services, and performance metrics. They are encouraged to submit self-declarations through the enterprise standards information public service platform.

Enterprises or organizations that implement consensus standards shall assume civil liability if their products or services do not meet the technical requirements of their self-declared standards.

Section 10 Consensus standards documents may use the "Shanghai Standards" logo after applying and meeting both international and domestic advanced criteria, as assessed by eligible third-party agencies.

Consensus standards shall not establish unfair technical trade barriers or practices that restrict the free movement of goods and services or diminish market competition.

Section 11 The municipal and district standardization administrations shall guide and oversee the development of consensus standards and inspect their implementation.

企业联合标准的技术要求低于强制性国家标准的相关技术要求的，由市或者区标准化行政主管部门责令限期改正；逾期不改正的，由市标准化行政主管部门废止相关标准，并在标准信息公共服务平台上公示。

企业联合标准未按照本规定进行编号的，由市或者区标准化行政主管部门责令限期改正；逾期不改正的，由市标准化行政主管部门撤销相关标准编号，并在标准信息公共服务平台上公示。

执行企业联合标准的企业或者组织未依法公开其执行的标准的，由市或者区标准化行政主管部门责令限期改正；逾期不改正的，在标准信息公共服务平台上公示。

利用企业联合标准实施妨碍商品、服务自由流通等排除、限制市场竞争的行为的，依照《中华人民共和国反垄断法》等法律、行政法规的规定处理。

第十二条　浦东新区人民政府可以围绕城市数字化转型、基本公共服务、社会治理等方面，将具有区域特点的管理模式形成标准化指导性技术文件。

市标准化行政主管部门会同市级相关部门对浦东新区人民政府制定标准化指导性技术文件工作进行指导，成效显著且条件成熟的可以予以推广。

第十三条　浦东新区人民政府应当支持浦东新区社会团体、企业、科研机构打造标准数字化平台或者通过市级标准化服务平台，将相关标准转化为机器可读取、可解析的数据，提升标准实施与产品质量管理的协同性、便捷度。

If consensus standards do not meet mandatory national standards, the municipal or district standardization administrations shall mandate their correction within a set timeframe. Failure to comply may lead to the revocation of these standards by the municipal standardization administration and the revocation will be disclosed to the public via the enterprise standards information public service platform.

If consensus standards are not assigned an identifier as required, the municipal or district standardization administrations shall mandate corrections within a specified period. If corrections are not made, the municipal standardization administration shall revoke the identifier and publicly disclose the revocation on the enterprise standards information public service platform.

If enterprises or organizations that implement consensus standards fail to publicly disclose these standards as required, the municipal or district standardization administrations shall order corrections within a specified period. If the corrections are not made, a record of non-compliance will be published on the enterprise standards information public service platform.

Using consensus standards to exclude or restrict market competition, including but not limited to impeding the free circulation of goods and services, shall be subject to the applicable laws and administrative regulations such as the Anti-Monopoly Law of the People's Republic of China.

Section 12 The Pudong New Area People's Government may develop technical guidelines on standardization for subjects like urban digital transformation, fundamental public services, and social governance to create regional management models.

The municipal standardization administration shall provide guidance to the Pudong New Area People's Government's technical guidelines on standardization in collaboration with appropriate municipal departments and facilitate their wider adoption if they prove effective and conditions are favorable.

Section 13 The Pudong New Area People's Government shall encourage the creation of a digital standards platform by social groups, enterprises, and research institutions, or the use of an existing city-wide service platform to make standards machine-readable, thereby improving the implementation synergy and regulation of standards implementation and product quality.

第十四条 浦东新区人民政府鼓励技术、知识产权等交易机构为与标准相关的交易提供登记、评估、撮合、结算等服务。交易机构应当制定交易规则和其他有关业务规则，并向社会公开。

第十五条 鼓励金融机构在浦东新区探索开展标准融资增信业务，将标准制定、执行情况纳入企业融资信用评估，提升企业融资额度及便利度。

第十六条 市标准化行政主管部门应当按照国家部署，鼓励和支持社会团体、企业、科研机构等加强与相关国际标准组织对接交流，深度参与标准化国际交流与合作。支持集成电路、生物医药、人工智能等重点领域标准化机构在浦东新区落户。

浦东新区人民政府应当鼓励国际标准组织技术委员会、分技术委员会、工作组以及国际性专业标准组织分支机构、办事机构等在浦东新区落户，并提供相应支持。

在浦东新区举办标准领域国际性会议等活动的，市和浦东新区相关部门应当提供信息沟通、人员来往便利等支持。

第十七条 市标准化行政主管部门和经济信息化、商务、科技、农业农村等行业主管部门应当支持浦东新区聚焦区域重点产业、行业，培育相关标准化技术组织，发挥其在国际、国内标准研究、制定和推广等方面的组织和管理作用。

第十八条 构建浦东新区多层次标准化人才体系。市和浦东新区人民政府及相关部门支持浦东新区通过多种形式培养国际标准化人才，开展国际标准化教育培训实训活动；鼓励科研人员提高标准化技能和专业知识；鼓励教育、科研机构等设置标准化学科专业，或者在相关学科专业方向领域开设标准化相关课程，在职业能力评价、职称评定中优化完善标准化人才的激励机制。

Section 14 The Pudong New Area People's Government encourages technology, intellectual property, and other agencies to offer registration, evaluation, matchmaking, and settlement services for standard-specific transactions. These agencies should develop and publicly disclose the transaction rules and other business guidelines.

Section 15 Financial institutions are encouraged to develop financing and credit enhancement services related to standardization in the Pudong New Area, incorporating standards development and compliance as part of the evaluation process to facilitate and enhance access to business financing.

Section 16 The municipal standardization administration shall encourage and support social groups, enterprises, and research institutions to enhance their engagement with international standards organizations and to play a larger role in international standards exchanges and collaboration. Standardization organizations in key sectors such as integrated circuits, biopharmaceutical medicines, and artificial intelligence are also encouraged to establish a presence in the Pudong New Area.

The Pudong New Area People's Government shall facilitate support for international standards organization technical committees, technical committee branches, and working groups, as well as the branches and agencies of international standards organizations, to establish a presence and provide support in the Pudong New Area.

Assistance shall be provided to host international standards forums in the Pudong New Area, facilitating the exchange of information and participant mobility.

Section 17 The municipal standardization administration and appropriate industry regulatory departments, including economy and information technology, commerce, agriculture, and rural development will support the Pudong New Area's focus on critical sectors by aiding the development of standardization organizations dedicated to preparing and promoting both domestic and international standards.

Section 18 The Pudong New Area is to establish a multi-tiered system for standards professionals. The Municipal and the Pudong New Area People's Governments, along with appropriate departments, will support the Pudong New Area in training international standards professionals through international education, training, and practices. Higher education institutions and research institutions are encouraged to create standards majors, develop standards courses, and enhance incentive systems for standards professionals in vocational assessments and title evaluations.

浦东新区人民政府应当将国际标准化专家纳入区级人才政策的支持范围。对符合要求的国际标准化专家及其团队提供居留和出入境、来华工作、落户、安居等服务便利，对其相关创新、创业项目等提供支持；依托标准化专家资源开展标准化工作培训和指导服务，搭建标准化工作交流平台。

第十九条 浦东新区标准化专项资金按照规定对参与浦东新区标准化创新发展相关工作的单位给予资助或者奖励。

鼓励社会力量通过设立基金、捐赠、股权投资等方式，支持标准化创新发展工作。

第二十条 本规定自 2023 年 10 月 14 日起施行。

The Pudong New Area People's Government shall include international standards experts in its talent policy, provide services to facilitate their residency, entry and exit, work permits, settlement, and housing, support their innovation and entrepreneurial projects, utilize their expertise for training and guidance in standards work, and set up a platform for exchanging ideas and experiences in the field.

Section 19 The Pudong New Area ad hoc standardization fund is to provide necessary subsidies or rewards to organizations engaged in the standardization innovation in the Pudong New Area.

Social contributions to standardization efforts by investments such as fund creation, donations, or equity investments are encouraged.

Section 20 These Provisions shall take effect from October 14, 2023.

上海市促进浦东新区融资租赁发展若干规定

Several Provisions of Shanghai Municipality on Promoting Financial Leasing in the Pudong New Area

上海市促进浦东新区融资租赁发展若干规定

（2023 年 7 月 25 日上海市第十六届人民代表大会常务委员会第四次会议通过）

第一条 为了促进浦东新区融资租赁高质量发展，发挥金融服务实体经济功能，推动国际金融中心核心区建设，根据有关法律、行政法规的基本原则，结合浦东新区实际，制定本规定。

第二条 本规定适用于住所地在浦东新区的融资租赁公司（以下统称“融资租赁公司”）的促进发展、管理服务等活动。

第三条 浦东新区人民政府应当建立融资租赁行业促进发展和监督管理相协调的工作机制，研究制定推动行业发展的政策措施。

市和浦东新区金融、发展改革、财政、市场监管、生态环境、公安、知识产权等部门和中国（上海）自由贸易试验区临港新片区（以下简称“临港新片区”）管理委员会应当按照工作职责，完善配套政策，支持和促进融资租赁行业发展。

浦东新区融资租赁行业的监督管理按照国家和本市相关规定执行。

第四条 支持浦东新区银行业金融机构按照国家金融管理部门在沪机构要求，对在先进制造业、战略性新兴产业、绿色产业等重点领域开展业务的融资租赁公司加大授信规模。

融资租赁公司在符合国家和本市政策导向的领域开展业务的，市地方金融监管部门可以结合监管评级情况，按照有关规定对其业务集中度和关联度的监管限制进行适当放宽。

Several Provisions of Shanghai Municipality on Promoting Financial Leasing in the Pudong New Area

(Adopted at the 4th Session of the 16th Shanghai Municipal People's Congress Standing Committee on July 25, 2023)

Section 1 The Several Provisions of Shanghai Municipality on Promoting Financial Leasing in the Pudong New Area (these "Provisions") are formulated to promote the quality development of financial leasing, ensure the finance serves the real economy, and advance the development of the central area of Shanghai as an international financial hub, pursuant to the basic principles of applicable laws and administrative regulations and in the light of the actual circumstances in the Pudong New Area.

Section 2 These Provisions shall apply to such activities as promoting, administering and serving the financial leasing companies ("Companies") domiciled in the Pudong New Area.

Section 3 The Pudong New Area People's Government shall establish a working process to promote the development, supervision and administration of financial leasing industry and enact policies and measures to advance the industry.

The municipal and the Pudong New Area departments including but not limited to financial regulation, development and reform, finance, market regulation, ecology and environment, public security, intellectual property, along with Lin-gang Special Area Administration Committee of the China (Shanghai) Pilot Free Trade Zone ("Lin-gang Special Area Administration") shall refine the policies to support and advance the financial leasing industry to the extent of their own responsibilities.

The supervision and administration of the financial leasing industry in the Pudong New Area shall be subject to the relevant provisions of the state and this Municipality.

Section 4 The banking institutions in the Pudong New Area are to be encouraged to expand credit supply for the Companies engaging in services of key sectors including but not limited to advanced manufacturing, strategic and emerging industries, and green industry in line with the requirements of the Shanghai branch of the national financial regulatory authority

Where the Companies operate in areas that are in line with national and local policy guidelines, the municipal local financial regulation authorities may properly relax the regulatory restrictions on its business focus and relevance based on their regulatory ratings and relevant provisions.

第五条 支持融资租赁公司将环境、社会和治理因素纳入内部治理和业务决策，完善管理流程，提升自身的环境、社会和治理表现，推动融资租赁业务服务绿色低碳转型发展。

支持本市融资租赁行业协会制定绿色融资租赁业务指引。融资租赁公司遵循绿色融资租赁业务指引开展业务的，浦东新区发展改革、金融、生态环境、财政等部门和临港新片区管理委员会给予相应的激励和支持。

第六条 国家金融管理部门在沪机构优化离岸融资租赁对外债权登记制度，支持融资租赁公司发展离岸融资租赁业务，鼓励融资租赁公司在涉外经营活动中优先使用人民币结算。

国家金融管理部门在沪机构支持融资租赁公司在境内以外币形式收取租金，鼓励浦东新区银行业金融机构优化业务审核方式，支持融资租赁公司探索外币租金收入的流转使用。

综合保税区内的融资租赁公司进出口飞机、船舶和海洋工程结构物等大型设备涉及跨关区的，在确保有效监管和执行现行相关税收政策的前提下，可以实行海关异地委托监管。

第七条 融资租赁公司按照规定开展专利权等无形资产融资租赁业务的，应当取得租赁标的相关权利，建立健全适应无形资产特点的价值评估和定价体系，合理确定租金水平。

融资租赁公司应当密切监测无形资产价值对融资租赁债权的风险覆盖水平，科学确定无形资产价值，制定有效的风险应对措施。

第八条 融资租赁公司开展飞机、船舶等航运融资租赁业务的，银行业金融机构可以采取货物贸易超期限特殊退汇业务免于事前登记等经常项目便利化措施。

Section 5 The Companies are supported to incorporate environmental, social and governance (ESG) factors into internal governance and business decision-making, improve the management process, boost ESG performance, and advance green development of financial leasing services.

The financial leasing industry association is supported to formulate guidelines on green financial leasing business. If the Companies follow the guidelines, the Pudong New Area departments including but not limited to reform and development, financial regulation, ecology and environment, and finance, and the Lin-gang Special Area Administration will give incentives and support.

Section 6 The Shanghai branch of the national financial regulatory authority is to optimize the foreign debt registration system for offshore financial leasing, support the Companies to develop offshore financial leasing services, and encourage the Companies to prioritize RMB settlements in overseas businesses.

The Shanghai branch of the national financial regulatory authority is to support the Companies to collect rents in foreign currencies, encourage the financial institutions in the Pudong New Area to improve the review process, and support the Companies to explore the methods of using the collected rents in foreign currencies.

Where the Companies in the comprehensive bonded area import and export large equipment including but not limited to aircraft, vessel and marine engineering structures across customs areas, such import and export may be subject to remote customs control if effective supervision and implementation of current taxation policies are ensured.

Section 7 The Companies engaging in financial leasing of intangible assets including patents according to relevant provisions shall possess the rights over the leased assets, establish a sound value assessment and pricing system suitable for intangible assets, and reasonably determine the rents.

The Companies shall closely monitor the coverage of intangible assets' risk on the lease, determine the value of intangible assets and take effective measures against the risk.

Section 8 Where the Companies engaging in aviation and shipping financial leasing of aircraft, vessels, and the like, the banking institutions may adopt facilitation measures, including but not limited to, the pre-registration exemption for foreign exchange refund for overdue goods.

融资租赁公司将从境外购买的飞机、船舶或者设备等租赁给境外承租人的，国家金融管理部门在沪机构在确保业务真实性审查的基础上，简化审批内容，优化管理措施。

第九条 融资租赁公司开展机动车融资租赁业务的，可以就其享有所有权的本市号牌机动车向浦东新区公安机关交通管理部门申请抵押登记。首次办理机动车抵押登记的，应当提交公司营业执照原件和公章样章申请备案；之后办理机动车抵押登记或者解除抵押登记时，提交的主体资格证明可以是加盖公章的营业执照复印件。

第十条 市和浦东新区药品监管部门应当健全与融资租赁相适应的医疗器械经营许可和备案制度，支持融资租赁公司将业务范围拓展至按照固定资产管理的各类医疗器械。

融资租赁公司办理医疗器械经营许可证时，可以同时合并办理第二类医疗器械经营备案，无需另行提交备案申请表和纸质材料。

融资租赁公司从事医疗器械融资租赁活动的，应当建立覆盖医疗器械融资租赁全过程的质量管理体系，加强医疗器械融资租赁产品信息追溯管理。

第十一条 支持融资租赁公司依法设立项目子公司，市场监管部门应当提供便利。

支持融资租赁公司按照规定发行各类债券，通过银行间和交易所等市场发行债务融资工具。

支持融资租赁公司开展资产证券化业务，依法通过境内外多层次资本市场上市、挂牌，开展并购重组，增强资金实力。

Where the Companies lease the aircraft, vessels, or equipment purchased from overseas to overseas lessees, the Shanghai branch of the national financial regulatory authority shall simplify the approval procedures and optimize the administration measures if the authenticity of such lease is verified.

Section 9 The Companies engaging in the financial leasing of vehicles may apply for mortgage registration of their owned license plates issued in this Municipality with the Pudong New Area public security department's traffic division. When applying for such registration for the first time, the company shall submit the original business license and the sample business seal; a business license copy with the business seal may be allowed in any subsequent mortgage registration or deregistration.

Section 10 The municipal and the Pudong New Area medical products administrations shall improve the medical devices licensing and record-filing mechanisms compatible with financial leasing development, and support the Companies to extend financial leasing services to all kinds of medical devices that are usually under fixed assets administration.

The Companies may file for Class Ⅱ medical device services at the time when a medical device business license is applied, and no further application form and paper materials are needed.

The Companies engaging in the financial leasing of medical devices shall establish a full-cycle quality management system and improve information tracking of the leased medical devices.

Section 11 The Companies are supported to set up subsidiaries lawfully, and the market regulation authority shall provide convenience.

The Companies are supported to issue bonds according to relevant provisions and issue debt instruments on the inter-bank market and exchanges.

The Companies are supported to engage in asset securitization business, to list and trade on multi-level capital markets both domestically and internationally lawfully, and to carry out mergers, acquisitions, and restructuring to enhance their financial strength.

第十二条　国家金融管理部门在沪机构支持具备条件的融资租赁公司申请接入金融信用信息基础数据库。

融资租赁公司接入金融信用信息基础数据库的，应当按照规定做好征信合规和数据安全等工作。

第十三条　融资租赁公司应当按照诚信原则开展融资租赁业务活动。承租人逾期支付租金的，融资租赁公司可以按照法律规定或者合同约定解除融资租赁合同。

融资租赁合同解除后，融资租赁公司可以采取合法方式收回租赁物，并及时采取委托评估或者通过公开市场拍卖等方式确定租赁物价值。

第十四条　融资租赁公司应当规范服务收费。融资租赁公司与承租人就收取服务费用作出约定的，应当按照约定提供质价相符的服务，不得违反约定将应当由出租人承担的义务转化为有偿服务。

融资租赁公司应当依法向承租人明示服务费、手续费、咨询费等各类费用收费情况。

第十五条　本市充分发挥人民法院与金融监管部门、金融基础设施运营机构等的协同治理作用，加强金融治理协同，深化金融治理合作，防范化解金融风险，支持融资租赁行业监管规则发挥效用，保障融资租赁行业规范健康发展。

第十六条　支持建立健全融资租赁行业纠纷解决机制，加强人民法院、司法行政机关、仲裁机构、专业调解组织、行业协会、公证机构的沟通与对接，完善诉讼与非诉讼相衔接的“一站式”融资租赁纠纷解决机制。

Section 12 The Shanghai branch of the national financial regulatory authority is to support eligible Companies in applying for access to the key financial credit information database.

The Companies that have access to the key financial credit information database shall comply with the regulations and ensure compliance with credit reporting and data security requirements.

Section 13 The Companies shall conduct financial leasing business in good faith. If the lessee fails to make timely rental payments, the Companies may terminate the financing leasing contract pursuant to law or contractual terms.

After the termination of the financial leasing contract, the Companies may legally repossess the leased assets and promptly assess the value of such assets through third-party evaluation or other methods such as public market auctions.

Section 14 The Companies shall regulate their service charges. The Companies shall provide services commensurate with the agreed-upon quality and price when charging service fees to lessees, and shall not, in violation of the agreement, convert obligations that shall be borne by the lessor into paid services.

The Companies shall lawfully inform lessees of the charging details such as service fees, handling fees, and consultation fees.

Section 15 This Municipality fully leverages the role of the people's courts, financial regulatory authorities, financial infrastructure operators, and other relevant entities for collaborative governance, strengthen coordinated financial governance, deepen financial governance cooperation, prevent and resolve financial risks, support the effective implementation of regulatory rules in the financial leasing industry, and ensure the healthy and regulated development of the financial leasing industry.

Section 16 The financial leasing industry is supported to establish and improve the dispute resolution mechanism, to strengthen communication and coordination among the people's courts, judicial administration, arbitration institutions, professional mediation organizations, industry associations, and notary public offices, and to enhance the "one-stop" financial leasing dispute resolution mechanism that integrates litigation and non-litigation approaches.

支持本市融资租赁行业协会在行业规范、自律管理、诉源治理和纠纷调解等方面发挥作用。

第十七条 本市有关人民法院、仲裁机构在审判、仲裁活动中应当尊重融资租赁行业交易习惯，发布融资租赁典型案例，为融资租赁行业发展营造良好法治环境。

支持浦东新区人民法院在融资租赁案件审判中深化示范判决机制，推动审判与执行的有效衔接，维护融资租赁各方当事人合法权益。

第十八条 住所地在临港新片区（浦东新区范围以外）的融资租赁公司，参照适用本规定。

第十九条 本规定自2023年10月1日起施行。

The financial leasing industry association of this Municipality is supported to engage in such works as industry regulation, self-discipline, dispute source management, and dispute mediation.

Section 17 People's courts and arbitration institutions in this Municipality shall follow the established practices of the financial leasing industry and publish typical cases to create a predictable law-based environment for the financial leasing industry development.

The Pudong New Area People's Court is supported to deepen the model judgment mechanism in financial leasing litigation, promote effective coordination between the trial and enforcement, and safeguard lawful rights and interests of all parties to financial leasing cases.

Section 18 These Provisions shall apply *mutatis mutandis* to the Companies domiciled in the Lin-gang Special Area (outside the administrative area of the Pudong New Area).

Section 19 These Provisions shall take effect from October 1, 2023.

第二编　管理措施

Part Ⅱ　Management Measures

浦东新区人民代表大会常务委员会关于率先构建经济治理、社会治理、城市治理统筹推进和有机衔接的治理体系的决定

Decision of the Pudong New Area People's Congress Standing Committee on Leading the Development of a Coordinated and Integrated Economic, Social, and Urban Governance System

浦东新区人民代表大会常务委员会关于率先构建经济治理、社会治理、城市治理统筹推进和有机衔接的治理体系的决定

（2021 年 10 月 29 日浦东新区第六届人民代表大会常务委员会第四十五次会议通过）

为贯彻落实《中共中央　国务院关于支持浦东新区高水平改革开放打造社会主义现代化建设引领区的意见》，在浦东新区率先构建经济治理、社会治理、城市治理统筹推进和有机衔接的治理体系（以下简称“治理体系”），加快提升社会主义现代化建设引领区善治效能，依据《上海市人民代表大会常务委员会关于加强浦东新区高水平改革开放法治保障制定浦东新区法规的决定》，结合本区改革创新实践需要，特作如下决定：

一、本区率先构建“治理体系”，是指在充分发挥市场在资源配置中的决定性作用和激发社会发展活力的前提下，通过政府积极引导市场主体和社会主体多元参与经济治理、社会治理、城市治理各方面全过程，进一步统筹治理需求和治理资源，充分运用现代科技，强化治理供需衔接、治理职责衔接、治理流程衔接，全面推动治理手段、治理模式、治理理念创新。

二、本区在率先构建“治理体系”过程中应当坚持党的全面领导，深入践行以新发展理念为导向的系统治理；坚持以人民为中心，强化以协同高效为路径的综合治理；坚持以法治为引领，强化以制度创新为基础的依法治理；坚持严守风险底线，强化以事前防范为重点的源头治理。

Decision of the Pudong New Area People's Congress Standing Committee on Leading the Development of a Coordinated and Integrated Economic, Social, and Urban Governance System

(Adopted at the 45th Session of the 6th Pudong New Area People's Congress Standing Committee on October 29, 2021)

The Decision of the Pudong New Area People's Congress Standing Committee on Leading the Development of a Coordinated and Integrated Economic, Social, and Urban Governance System (this "Decision") is formulated to effectively implement the Opinions of the Communist Party of China Central Committee and the State Council on Supporting the High-level Reform and Opening-up to Establish a Pilot Area for Modern Socialism in the Pudong New Area and to spearhead the development of an integrated and coordinated economic, social, and urban governance system (the "governance system") in the Pudong New Area. This development is aimed at improving governance and operational efficiency within the modern socialism pilot area, pursuant to the Decision of the Shanghai Municipal People's Congress Standing Committee on Formulating Regulations to Improve Law-based Safeguards for High-level Reform and Opening-up in the Pudong New Area, and grounded in the transformative reforms and innovative practices utilized in the Pudong New Area:

Ⅰ. Leading the development of a "governance system" using market forces for decisive resource allocation and stimulating social development, the Pudong New Area will proactively guide market participants and other entities to carry out economic, social, and urban governance at all stages and in all aspects. This initiative will further align governance demands with resources, use modern technology, and improve connections between governance supply, demand, responsibilities, and processes, comprehensively promoting innovation in governance methods, models, and philosophies.

Ⅱ. Throughout the process of pioneering the "governance system," the Pudong New Area will act under the guidance of the Party to promote systematic governance under new developmental ideologies; be based on people-oriented principles and improve integrated governance emphasizing synergy and efficiency; follow the rule of law as its guiding principles and strengthen law-based governance based on institutional innovation; proactively address risks and highlight precautions for foundational governance.

三、区人民政府应当按照“谁主管谁牵头”原则，在各行业或者领域内明确由一个政府部门履行综合治理牵头部门职责，并将相关市场主体、社会主体纳入职责体系。

综合治理牵头部门应当及时收集各类市场主体和社会主体治理需求，统筹政府、市场、社会各类治理资源；构建分级联动响应机制；组织开展跨部门、跨层级、跨主体综合治理以及治理效能考核等工作，建立健全职责明确、协同高效的行业或者领域综合治理制度。

由区审批制度改革部门、地区工作部门、发展改革部门、大数据管理部门、城市运行管理部门组成牵头工作小组，协调构建“治理体系”。

四、区人民政府应当优化企业专属网页和个人专属网页建设，提升惠企惠民政策及服务信息精准推送能力，健全受理、处理和反馈机制。各部门各单位应当持续畅通人民建议征集点、人大代表联系人民群众平台、政协委员协商活动站、大调研走访、联勤联动站、来信来访、家门口服务站、专属网页等问题反映渠道，搭建完善“线上＋线下”“网上＋掌上”的立体化需求收集渠道。

五、各部门各单位应当围绕群众和市场主体需求，全面梳理各行业、领域、区域涉及经济、社会、城市治理的各类治理要素，把治理要素作为基本单元，加快形成标准化、规范化、数字化的问题发现和派单机制、处置流程和处置标准，以服务对象为中心推动业务流程跨部门、跨层级协同联动，引导政府、市场、社会同向发力，加快形成共建、共治、共享的治理格局。

Ⅲ. The Pudong New Area People's Government shall follow the principle of designated leadership when assigning specific government agencies to lead the comprehensive management of each sector or field and integrate market participants and other entities into the responsibility system.

The designated comprehensive management agencies shall promptly gather the governance requirements of market participants and other entities, and coordinate the diverse governance resources from government, market, and public sources; develop processes for integrated command over resource allocation; organize comprehensive management across departments, levels of government, and entities; conduct effectiveness assessments; and establish and refine efficient governance systems with specific sector or field responsibilities.

A multi-department coordination group is to be created, consisting of the district examination and approval system reform agencies, regional coordination agencies, development and reform agencies, big data management departments, and urban operations management agencies to coordinate and develop the governance system.

Ⅳ. The Pudong New Area People's Government shall advance the development of specialized websites for both businesses and residents, improve capacities for personalized information services and targeted policy benefits for businesses and individuals, and refine request acceptance, processing, and feedback processes. All departments and organizations shall expand their public complaint and report channels, incorporating platforms for public feedback, platforms facilitating communications between NPC deputies and local residents, CPPCC public participation meetings, extensive research and site visits, public safety community forums, petition systems, comprehensive services, and exclusive webpages, in addition to building and refining a comprehensive, multichannel system for collecting demands that integrates online and offline, as well as web and mobile methods.

Ⅴ. All departments and organizations shall prioritize the needs of the public and market participants, systematically organize all governance elements involved in economic, social, and urban governance across sectors, fields, and areas, and accelerate the development of standardized, normalized, and digitized processes for identifying issues, task delegation, management procedures, and management standards. These processes are to be centered around governance elements and promote interdepartmental and cross-level collaboration focused on service recipients, guiding the government, market, and the public to align efforts and develop a governance model characterized by collaboration, joint participation, and shared benefits.

综合治理牵头部门应当围绕“高效处置一件事”，梳理涉及的治理要素与治理职责，健全涵盖信息传递、事件处置、结果反馈的闭环管理流程。

六、区人民政府应当建立健全治理场景标准化开发机制，归集各治理场景使用的算法技术与分析模型，结合现代管理理念和有效措施，进行规范管理与统一调度，推动部门间数据共享和集约利用。

七、综合治理牵头部门应当加强城市感知体系建设规划，加快推动政府、市场、社会共同参与高风险行业、领域或者区域物联感知设施建设，引导高风险行业市场主体提供必要的生产经营数据，共同防范和化解行业风险。

八、牵头工作小组应当科学设置效能评价指标，将效能评价指标嵌入业务流程各个环节，生成评价报告。综合治理牵头部门应当建立健全评价结果应用机制，探索依据效能评价结果科学配置人力、财力、土地、环境、能耗等要素资源的路径。

九、支持中国（上海）自由贸易试验区临港新片区基于一体化信息管理服务平台建立健全两网融合、风险防范场景联合共建、数据共享公用机制，促进浦东新区和临港新片区治理场景的互通互用和数据的开放共享。

十、区人民政府应当依据本决定制定相应的实施细则，并按照有关规定备案。

十一、区人大常委会通过听取和审议专项工作报告、开展专项监督检查等方式，加强对本决定实施情况的监督。

十二、本决定自 2021 年 11 月 1 日起施行。

The designated comprehensive management agency shall prioritize efficient and thorough resolution of all issues, organize governance elements and responsibilities, and improve the closed-loop management process covering information disclosure, incident management, and reporting results.

Ⅵ. The Pudong New Area People's Government shall institute and refine a standardized development framework for management use cases, incorporate algorithmic technologies and analytical models across different use cases, and implement standardized management and coordinated schedules through modern management principles and effective strategies to promote data-sharing and comprehensive inter-agency use.

Ⅶ. The designated comprehensive management agency shall advance the planning and development of the urban perception system, encourage joint efforts from the government, market, and public sectors to construct IoT-based perception infrastructure in high-risk industries and regions, and guide market participants in these sectors to supply the production and operational data necessary to collaboratively prevent and mitigate industry risks.

Ⅷ. The multi-department coordination group shall define evidence-based performance assessment metrics for each part of the business process, and publish assessment reports. Additionally, the group is to develop and refine processing methods for assessment results, and research strategies for the effective allocation of human, financial, land, environmental, and energy resources based on such assessment results.

Ⅸ. The Lin-gang Special Area of the China (Shanghai) Pilot Free Trade Zone is to receive support to establish and improve public processes to facilitate multi-network integration, collaborative risk prevention processes, and data sharing via the central information management service platform, thus promoting network interoperability and management data sharing between the Pudong New Area and the Lin-gang Special Area.

X. The Pudong New Area People's Government shall make supplementary rules pursuant to this Decision and file for record as required.

Ⅺ. The Pudong New Area People's Congress Standing Committee strengthens oversight of this Decision's enforcement through methods such as listening to and reviewing ad hoc work reports and ad hoc oversight reviews.

Ⅻ. This Decision shall take effect from November 1, 2021.

浦东新区促进商事调解若干规定

Several Provisions of the Pudong New Area on the Promotion of Commercial Mediation

浦东新区促进商事调解若干规定

（2022 年 6 月 30 日上海市浦东新区第七届人民代表大会常务委员会第三次会议通过）

第一条 为了进一步优化营商环境，促进市场化法治化商事调解，建设具有国际影响力和吸引力的国际商事纠纷解决中心，根据中共中央、国务院《关于支持浦东新区高水平改革开放打造社会主义现代化建设引领区的意见》和全国人大常委会、上海市人大常委会的有关决定，结合浦东新区实际，制定本规定。

第二条 本规定适用于纳入浦东新区调解组织和调解员名册的调解主体所开展的商事调解活动及其监督管理。

第三条 本规定所称的商事调解，是指由调解组织、调解员协助平等主体的自然人、法人和非法人组织友好解决商事领域合同纠纷和其他财产权益纠纷的调解活动。

第四条 设立为公司、个人独资企业、合伙企业的调解组织，应当依法向市场监管部门申请登记。

设立为社会服务机构的调解组织，应当依法向民政部门申请登记。

设立为其他不具备法人资格的调解组织，法律、法规规定可以向司法行政部门申请登记或者备案的，依照其规定。

第五条 浦东新区支持境外知名调解机构在符合境内监管要求条件下，提供国际商事调解服务，并在本区依法设立业务机构。

Several Provisions of the Pudong New Area on the Promotion of Commercial Mediation

(Adopted at the 3rd Session of the 7th Pudong New Area People's Congress Standing Committee of Shanghai Municipality on June 30, 2022)

Section 1 The Several Provisions of the Pudong New Area on the Promotion of Commercial Mediation (these "Provisions") are formulated to further improve the business environment, promote a market-oriented and law-based commercial mediation process, and establish a globally influential and appealing commercial dispute resolution center, pursuant to the Opinions of the Communist Party of China Central Committee and State Council on Supporting the High-level Reform and Opening-up to Establish a Pilot Area for Modern Socialism in the Pudong New Area, along with decisions of the National People's Congress Standing Committee and the Shanghai Municipal People's Congress Standing Committee, and in light of the actual circumstances in the Pudong New Area.

Section 2 These Provisions shall apply to commercial mediation activities carried out by entities enrolled in the Pudong New Area mediation organization and mediator registry and their regulation.

Section 3 "Commercial mediation" in these Provisions refers to activities in which mediation organizations and mediators assist individuals, juristic persons, and unincorporated organizations in amicably resolving contractual disputes and other property disputes within the commercial sector.

Section 4 Mediation organizations organized as corporations, sole proprietorships, or partnerships shall lawfully register with the appropriate market regulation authority.

Mediation organizations organized as social organizations shall lawfully register with the appropriate civil affairs department.

Formation of mediation organizations without juristic personality may register with or file with the judicial administration if the laws or regulations permit.

Section 5 The Pudong New Area is to facilitate well-known foreign mediation agencies to provide international commercial mediation services and establish operations within the area, subject to the regulatory requirements in the Chinese Mainland.

第六条 浦东新区探索与国际通行规则接轨，支持调解员个人在符合境内监管要求条件下，采用线上或者线下方式参与国际商事调解活动。鼓励律师、仲裁员等专业人士在国际商事调解活动中充分发挥个人作用，提升服务能力和国际竞争力。

第七条 浦东新区成立相关调解行业协会，发挥行业指导作用，吸纳各类调解组织、调解员参与行业治理，培育扶持调解组织发展，加强调解组织建设，提升调解工作水平。

第八条 区司法行政部门建立调解组织和调解员名册，应当制定相应的名册管理办法。在浦东新区开展商事调解活动的调解组织、调解员，可以向区司法行政部门申请加入名册。

区司法行政部门应当对调解行业协会和纳入名册的调解组织、调解员加强指导和管理。纳入名册的调解组织、调解员开展或者参与商事调解活动的管理办法，由区司法行政部门根据实际情况另行制定或者提请相关部门制定。

第九条 调解组织应当建立健全执业管理、利益冲突审查、收费与财务管理、投诉查处、年度考核、档案管理等制度，对其聘任的调解员在执业活动中遵守职业道德、执业纪律的情况进行监督。

调解组织应当制定调解规则，并向社会公开。

第十条 调解员应当品行端正、公道正派、勤勉尽责，熟悉商事法律法规、商事交易规则、商事交易习惯。

调解组织聘任调解员，应当及时报送区司法行政部门备案。

第十一条 调解组织、调解员开展商事调解活动，不得违反法律、法规的强制性规定，不得违背公序良俗。

Section 6 In line with international best practices, the Pudong New Area supports mediators in participating in international commercial mediation both online and offline, subject to domestic regulatory requirements, and encourages professionals such as attorneys and arbitrators to utilize their expertise to improve the quality of their services and global competitiveness in international commercial mediation.

Section 7 The Pudong New Area is to form a mediation industry association to guide the mediation sector, encouraging involvement from various mediation organizations and mediators to promote industry governance, support the development of mediation organizations, facilitate the development of mediation organizations, and improve the overall quality of mediation services.

Section 8 The judicial administration of the Pudong New Area is to maintain a mediation organization and mediator registry and develop appropriate management procedures for such. Mediation organizations and mediators engaged in commercial mediation within the Pudong New Area may file a request to enroll into this registry with the judicial administration of the Pudong New Area.

The judicial administration of the Pudong New Area is to improve management practices and guidance for mediation associations and enrolled mediation organizations and mediators; the judicial administration of the Pudong New Area, or other appropriate departments, shall develop specific management procedures for these mediation activities based on local conditions.

Section 9 Mediation organizations shall develop and maintain policies covering practice management, conflict of interest assessments, financial management, complaint resolution, annual performance reviews, and record management. They shall ensure mediators to adhere to professional ethics and discipline during their practice activities.

Mediation organizations shall create publicly accessible mediation rules.

Section 10 Mediators shall demonstrate good character, impartiality, diligence, and a thorough understanding of commercial law, transaction regulations, and business practices.

Mediation organizations shall promptly report the hiring of any new mediators to the judicial administration of the Pudong New Area.

Section 11 Mediation organizations and mediators shall comply with all applicable legal and regulatory requirements, and uphold public order and morality in their commercial mediation activities.

第十二条 调解组织、调解员和相关工作人员，对调解过程、调解协议和在调解过程中知悉的商业秘密以及当事人个人信息等事项负有保密义务。法律、法规另有规定的，依照其规定。

第十三条 浦东新区支持各类调解组织在区司法行政部门指导下建立健全预授权调解、单边承诺调解等小额商事纠纷快速调处机制，更好实现纠纷的高效率、低成本、便利化解决。

浦东新区鼓励各类商事行业协会引导成员单位基于自愿原则事先授权调解组织适用小额商事纠纷快速调处机制。

第十四条 经调解，当事人就纠纷解决达成全部或者部分和解的，调解组织、调解员应当制作调解协议。调解协议具有民事合同性质。

调解协议应当载明下列事项：

（一）当事人的基本信息；

（二）商事纠纷的主要事实、争议事项；

（三）当事人达成和解的内容、履行方式、期限等。

第十五条 当事人同意进行无争议事实记载的，调解员应当如实记录，并经当事人确认。

第十六条 以给付为内容的调解协议，当事人可以申请公证机构依法赋予强制执行效力。

第十七条 当事人可以在调解协议中约定仲裁条款，并选定仲裁机构裁决确认调解协议的效力。

第十八条 当事人达成调解协议的，可以依法共同向有管辖权的人民法院申请司法确认。

调解协议中具有金钱或者有价证券给付内容的，债权人可以依法向有管辖权的人民法院申请支付令。

Section 12 Unless otherwise provided by laws and regulations, mediation organizations, mediators, and any of their employees involved shall keep the mediation process, agreements, other party's trade secrets, or other party's personal information obtained during the mediation process confidential.

Section 13 The Pudong New Area supports the development of streamlined mediation processes for small commercial disputes guided by the judicial administration of the Pudong New Area, such as pre-approved or unilateral mediation, to ensure efficient, cost-effective, and easy resolution.

The Pudong New Area is to encourage industry associations to guide their members to voluntarily adopt new streamlined mediation processes when resolving small commercial disputes.

Section 14 Upon achieving a full or partial settlement via mediation, the mediator or mediation organization shall create a mediation agreement, which is to be recognized as a civil contract.

The mediation agreement shall outline the:

(1) description of the parties involved;

(2) main facts of the dispute and disputed matters; and

(3) settlement terms, performance methods, and time limits.

Section 15 If the parties agree to have the agreed facts recorded, mediators shall be required to accurately record such facts and obtain confirmation from all parties involved.

Section 16 Parties may request notarization to ensure that mediation agreements involving financial obligations are legally enforceable.

Section 17 Parties may insert arbitration clauses in their mediation agreements and select an arbitration institution to verify the agreement's validity.

Section 18 Parties that reach a mediation agreement may jointly request judicial confirmation from the competent people's court.

Creditors in mediation agreements involving monetary or securities transactions may petition the competent people's court to enforce payment.

第十九条 从事商事调解业务，可以向当事人收取合理费用，收费标准应当符合价格管理的有关规定，并向社会公开。

第二十条 区人民政府及其相关部门可以根据实际需要，在法律、法规规定的范围内，出台便利、促进、保障商事调解开展的鼓励措施。

纳入名册的调解组织、调解员，可以依照相关规定享受扶持政策。

第二十一条 区人民政府及其相关部门应当建立商事调解信息系统，运用网络化、信息化等方式促进商事调解发展，搭建多元化纠纷化解平台，并向社会公开商事调解组织、调解员的相关信息。

第二十二条 本规定自 2022 年 7 月 15 日起施行。

Section 19 Participants in mediation may incur reasonable fees for commercial mediation services, which should comply with established pricing regulations and be publicly disclosed.

Section 20 The Pudong New Area People's Government and appropriate departments may issue preferential policies to support and ensure the development of commercial mediation, in compliance with legal and regulatory systems.

Enrolled mediation organizations and mediators may lawfully benefit from such preferential policies.

Section 21 The Pudong New Area People's Government and its departments shall set up a commercial mediation information system using information technologies to facilitate mediation progress, create a multi-channel dispute resolution platform, and publicly disclose information on mediators and mediation organizations involved.

Section 22 These Provisions shall take effect from July 15, 2022.

浦东新区生态环境信用评价办法

Procedures of the Pudong New Area on the Administration of Ecology and Environment Credit Assessment

浦东新区生态环境信用评价办法

（2022 年 7 月 29 日浦府管规〔2022〕1 号印发）

第一条 目的与依据

为规范企事业单位生态环境信用评价管理工作，强化生态环境保护主体责任，加快构建生态环境信用体系，持续优化营商环境，根据《中华人民共和国环境保护法》《上海市环境保护条例》等法律法规规定，结合浦东新区实际，制定本办法。

第二条 定义

本办法所称生态环境信用评价，是指浦东新区生态环境局（以下简称“区生态环境局”）根据企事业单位生态环境行为信息，按照规定的指标、方法和程序，对其进行生态环境综合信用评价，确定其信用等级并向社会公布，供社会监督和应用的活动。

本办法所称生态环境行为信息，是指企事业单位在生产经营活动中遵守环境法律、法规、规章、规范性文件、环境标准以及履行环保社会责任的情况，并通过法律文书、行政公文等予以记录的行为信息。

第三条 总体要求

生态环境信用评价应当遵循依法依规、审慎适度、客观公正、公开透明的原则，体现政社共治、分类监管的改革理念。

Procedures of the Pudong New Area on the Administration of Ecology and Environment Credit Assessment

(PGMM [2022] No.1, July 29, 2022)

Section 1 Purpose and Basis

The Procedures of the Pudong New Area on the Administration of Ecology and Environment Credit Assessment (these "Procedures") are formulated to regulate the administration of ecology and environment credit assessments for enterprises and public institutions, specify responsibilities for ecological and environmental protection, accelerate the development of an ecology and environment credit system, and continuously improve the business environment, pursuant to the Environmental Protection Law of the People's Republic of China, Regulations of Shanghai Municipality on Environmental Protection, and in light of the actual circumstances in the Pudong New Area.

Section 2 Definitions

"Environmental credit assessment" in these Procedures refers to the comprehensive environmental assessments carried out by the Pudong New Area Ecology and Environment Bureau (the "Pudong Ecology and Environment Bureau") on enterprises' and public institutions' environmental conduct records using specific metrics, methods, and procedures to determine their credit rating. These ratings are subsequently made public to facilitate public oversight and large-scale use.

"Environmental conduct records" in these Procedures refer to documented legal or official records of an enterprises's or public institution's compliance with environmental laws, regulations, practices, and standards, as their fulfillment of environmental protection responsibilities during routine operations.

Section 3 General Requirements

Ecology and environment credit assessments shall be carried out in a legal, prudent, and objective manner, and shall be impartial and transparent, following principles of collaborative governance between government and society, as well as tiered regulation.

第四条 职责分工

区生态环境局负责制定管理制度和评价指标，组织开展本行政区域内企事业单位生态环境信用评价工作。

中国（上海）自由贸易试验区管理委员会保税区管理局（以下简称“保税区管理局”）负责对辖区内企事业单位开展生态环境信用评价，将评价结果定期抄送区生态环境局。

第五条 评价对象

浦东新区行政区域内的下列企事业单位应当纳入生态环境信用评价范围：

（一）应当取得排污许可证的；

（二）其他纳入评价年度上海市重点排污单位管理名录的。

鼓励未纳入上述范围的企事业单位自愿申请参加生态环境信用评价。

第六条 评价指标

企事业单位生态环境信用评价指标包括生态环境执法信息、生态环境司法信息、环境管理信息和社会责任信息等四类。

生态环境执法信息、生态环境司法信息和环境管理信息用于信用减分。社会责任信息用于信用加分。

第七条 信息获取

企事业单位生态环境行为信息按照“谁产生、谁归集、谁负责”的原则进行归集，由区生态环境局及保税区管理局通过相关业务系统、数据库等渠道获取。

Section 4 Division of Responsibilities

The Pudong Ecology and Environment Bureau is responsible for developing management systems and assessment metrics, as well as coordinating ecology and environment credit assessments for enterprises and public institutions within its jurisdiction.

The Bonded Areas Office of the China (Shanghai) Pilot Free Trade Zone Administration (the "Bonded Areas Office") is responsible for carrying out ecology and environment credit assessments on enterprises and public institutions under its jurisdiction, and regularly report assessment results to the Pudong Ecology and Environment Bureau.

Section 5 Assessment Subjects

Enterprises and public institutions within the Pudong New Area jurisdiction that are subject to ecology and environment credit assessment include:

(1) those required to obtain a pollutant discharge permit; and

(2) those listed in the Shanghai key pollutant discharge management list during the assessment year.

Enterprises and public institutions not included in annual assessments are encouraged to voluntarily participate in ecology and environment credit assessments.

Section 6 Assessment Metrics

Ecology and environment credit assessment metrics for enterprises and public institutions cover ecological and environmental law enforcement records, judicial records, environmental administration records, and social responsibility records.

Ecological and environmental law enforcement records, judicial records, and environmental administration records may result in deductions from the credit score, while social responsibility records may be credited positively.

Section 7 Access to Information

Ecological and environmental activity records for enterprises and public institutions shall be collected following the principle of those who produce and collect them being accountable for the records or obtained by the Pudong Ecology and Environment Bureau and the Bonded Areas Office through the specific business systems or databases.

第八条 评价方式

区生态环境局、保税区管理局每年至少开展1次生态环境信用评价，探索建立实时评价、动态更新机制。

企事业单位生态环境信用评价实行计分制，生态环境信用评价的初始分值为70分。企事业单位在评价周期内，存在单个生态环境违法违规行为涉及多个指标的，按照分值最高指标予以计分；存在多个生态环境违法违规行为的，按照相应指标分别计分，累计计算。

评价指标、分值计算、信用评定等具体规定由区生态环境局另行制定，并动态调整。

第九条 信用等级

企事业单位的生态环境信用等级依据实际计分情况，分为四个等级：

（一）A级：生态环境信用分值90分及以上。

（二）B级：生态环境信用分值60—89分。

（三）C级：生态环境信用分值40—59分。

（四）D级：生态环境信用分值39分及以下。

第十条 评价公示

区生态环境局、保税区管理局应当通过浦东新区人民政府网站、信用中国（上海浦东）等渠道，公示拟作出的生态环境信用评价结果，并告知复核申请途径，公示期不少于10个工作日。企事业单位生态环境信用评价结果为C级、D级的，区生态环境局、保税区管理局应当书面告知其评价结果。

Section 8 Assessment Methods

The Pudong Ecology and Environment Bureau and the Bonded Areas Office shall carry out at least one ecology and environment credit assessment annually and consider the development of real-time evaluation and dynamic updating processes.

Ecology and environment credit assessments for enterprises and public institutions shall follow a scoring system, starting with a base score of 70. If an ecological and environmental violation takes place during the assessment period involving multiple metrics, the highest score metric is to be used; scores for enterprises and public institutions committing multiple violations is to accumulate based on the metrics.

The Pudong Ecology and Environment Bureau shall formulate and adjust rules for specific assessment metrics, score calculations, and credit assessments as needed.

Section 9 Credit Rating

Ecology and environment credit ratings for enterprises and public institutions are categorized into four grades based on their actual scores:

(1) Grade A: Ecology and environment credit score of 90 or above;

(2) Grade B: Ecology and environment credit score of 60 to 89;

(3) Grade C: Ecology and environment credit score of 40 to 59; and

(4) Grade D: Ecology and environment credit score of 39 or below.

Section 10 Assessment Disclosure

The Pudong Ecology and Environment Bureau and the Bonded Areas Office shall publish ecology and environment credit assessment results via channels, such as on the websites of the Pudong New Area People's Government and Credit China (Shanghai Pudong). The disclosure period shall be no less than ten business days and include information on how to request a review. Enterprises and public institutions who receive a Grade C or Grade D score shall be notified of the assessment results in writing by the Pudong Ecology and Environment Bureau or the Bonded Areas Office.

第十一条　复核申请

企事业单位对评价结果有异议的，自评价结果公示期满之日起10个工作日内书面向区生态环境局或者保税区管理局提出复核申请，并提交相关证据材料。

区生态环境局或者保税区管理局应当自收到复核申请之日起3个工作日内完成复核，并将结果告知企事业单位。

企事业单位生态环境信用评价过程中需要现场核查、监测或者鉴定的，前述时间不计入复核期限。

第十二条　技术支持

区生态环境局、保税区管理局可以委托第三方生态环境信用评价服务机构开展资料收集、信息核实等生态环境信用评价辅助工作。

第十三条　信用修复

失信企事业单位纠正其生态环境失信行为后，可以申请生态环境信用修复，生态环境信用修复具体规定由区生态环境局会同相关部门另行制定。失信企事业单位完成信用修复后，失信信息不再用于信用减分。

第十四条　结果公布

区生态环境局通过浦东新区人民政府网站、信用中国（上海浦东）等渠道，向社会公布企事业单位生态环境信用评价结果。

第十五条　结果共享

公众可以通过信用中国（上海浦东）查询企事业单位生态环境信用评价结果。区生态环境局应当将企事业单位生态环境信用评价结果共享给开展联合奖惩的相关职能部门，并纳入区公共信用信息服务平台、城管执法信息平台等相关信息平台。

Section 11 Requests for Review

Enterprises and public institutions that disagree with their assessment results may submit a written request for review to the Pudong Ecology and Environment Bureau or the Bonded Areas Office within ten business days following the expiration of the disclosure period, along with the necessary supporting documentation.

The Pudong Ecology and Environment Bureau or the Bonded Areas Office shall complete the review within three business days of receiving the request and notify the requesting enterprises or public institution of their decision.

The time taken to complete any on-site verification, monitoring, or assessments necessary during the ecology and environment credit assessment shall not be counted toward the review period.

Section 12 Technical Support

The Pudong Ecology and Environment Bureau and the Bonded Areas Office may commission third-party service providers to assist with tasks supporting the ecology and environment credit assessment, such as data collection and information verification.

Section 13 Credit Repair

Enterprises and public institutions that remedy their ecological and environmental violations may request credit repair. The specific procedures for ecological and environmental credit repair shall be developed separately by the Pudong Ecology and Environment Bureau, in cooperation with the appropriate departments. Following remediation, records of the violations shall no longer result in credit deductions.

Section 14 Disclosure of Results

The Pudong Ecology and Environment Bureau shall publish the enterprise and public institution ecology and environment credit assessment results via channels such as the Pudong New Area People's Government and Credit China (Shanghai Pudong) websites.

Section 15 Sharing of Results

The general public may access the ecology and environment credit assessment results for enterprises and public institutions through Credit China (Shanghai Pudong). The Pudong Ecology and Environment Bureau shall share these results with the appropriate departments for joint incentives and penalties, and upload them to information platforms, including the district public credit information service platform and the urban management and law enforcement information platform.

第十六条　分类监管

区生态环境局、区城管执法局、保税区管理局等部门和单位对不同生态环境信用等级的企事业单位，实施以下分类监管措施：

（一）被评定为A级的，固定污染源监管等级不变，“双随机、一公开”的抽查频次适当减少；连续3年均评定为A级的，申请纳入上海市生态环境监督执法正面清单。

（二）被评定为B级的，固定污染源监管等级不变，“双随机、一公开”的抽查频次不变。

（三）被评定为C级的，固定污染源监管等级提高一个级别，“双随机、一公开”的抽查频次适当增加。

（四）被评定为D级的，固定污染源监管等级提高两个级别，“双随机、一公开”的抽查频次增加，并启动提示约谈或者警示约谈程序，督促失信企事业单位履行相关义务、消除不良影响。

第十七条　联合奖惩

区相关部门和单位在实施行政许可、行政处罚、行政检查、监督抽验、政府采购、财政投资公共工程建设项目招标、基础设施和公共事业特许经营活动、财政性资金项目安排、国有土地使用权出让、执行投资税收和价格等优惠政策、科研管理、表彰奖励等过程中，依法运用企事业单位生态环境信用评价等级信息。

支持行业协会和金融机构参考企事业单位生态环境信用评价结果，采取适当的守信激励和失信惩戒措施。

Section 16 Tiered Regulation

The Pudong Ecology and Environment Bureau, the Pudong Urban Management and Law Enforcement Bureau, and the Bonded Areas Office and others shall implement tiered regulation of enterprises and public institutions based on their ecology and environment credit ratings:

(1) Organizations rated Grade A are to be subject to the same degree of regulation for fixed pollution sources, with appropriately reduced sampling and disclosures; those rated Grade A for three consecutive years may be enrolled into the Shanghai Ecological and Environmental Regulation and Law Enforcement Positive List.

(2) Organizations rated Grade B are to be subject to the same degree of regulation for fixed pollution sources, with the same sampling and disclosure frequency.

(3) Organizations rated Grade C are to have their regulation level for fixed pollution sources increased by one level, with an appropriate increase in sampling and disclosure frequency.

(4) Organizations rated Grade D are to have their regulation level for fixed pollution sources increased by two levels, with increased sampling and disclosure frequency; prompt interviews or warning interviews are to be initiated to encourage these organizations to fulfill their obligations and mitigate any negative impacts.

Section 17 Joint Incentives and Penalties

The appropriate district departments shall lawfully use enterprise and public institution ecology and environment credit assessment results when administering permissions, penalties, inspections, sampling, government procurement, tenders for public construction projects, infrastructure, and public utility franchises funded by the government, as well as the organization of government projects, assignment of leasehold estates for state-owned land, investment incentives, preferential pricing, scientific research, and recognition, among others.

Industry associations and financial organizations are encouraged to refer to the ecology and environment credit assessment results to implement appropriate incentives and penalties for compliant and non-compliant behaviors.

第十八条 信息安全管理

区生态环境局以及相关部门应当加强生态环境信用信息安全管理，依法依规认定、记录、归集、共享、披露和使用相关信息，建立完善生态环境信用信息查询、使用登记和审查制度，依法依规保护企事业单位及其工作人员的商业秘密和个人隐私。

第十九条 行政责任

行政机关工作人员未履行本办法规定职责和相关要求，造成严重后果的，由其所在单位或者上级主管部门依法给予政务处分。

第二十条 施行时间

本办法自 2022 年 9 月 1 日起施行，有效期至 2027 年 8 月 31 日。

Section 18 Information Security Management

The Pudong Ecology and Environment Bureau and other appropriate departments shall lawfully improve ecological and environmental credit information security management practices, identify, record, collect, share, disclose, and use any necessary information, and create and improve systems for ecology and environment credit information inquiries, registrations, and reviews, while lawfully protecting the trade secrets and personal privacy of such enterprises or public institutions and their employees.

Section 19 Administrative Responsibility

Any administrative department employee who fails to fulfill the duties and requirements specified in these Procedures, resulting in material adverse effects, shall be subject to disciplinary action by the department that employs them or the superior department lawfully.

Section 20 Validity Period

These Procedures shall take effect from September 1, 2022, and remain valid until August 31, 2027.

浦东新区加强滴水湖水域保护和滨水公共空间建设管理若干规定

Several Provisions of the Pudong New Area on Improving the Protection and Management of Water Areas and Waterfront Public Spaces Development in Dishui Lake

浦东新区加强滴水湖水域保护和滨水公共空间建设管理若干规定

（2022 年 7 月 29 日上海市浦东新区第七届人民代表大会常务委员会第四次会议通过）

第一条 为进一步保护和提升滴水湖水域水环境品质，促进和保障滴水湖滨水公共空间高水平建设和智慧化管理，打造流域清洁、亲水宜人、智慧生态、韧性低碳的一流滨水区和旅游度假区，根据《上海市人民代表大会常务委员会关于加强浦东新区高水平改革开放法治保障制定浦东新区法规的决定》，结合改革创新实际，制定本规定。

第二条 本规定适用于滴水湖水域保护和滴水湖滨水公共空间规划、建设、开放以及相关的管理工作。

滴水湖水域是指位于浦东新区范围内的滴水湖主湖区及春涟河、夏涟河、秋涟河、冬涟河、赤风港、橙和港、黄日港、绿丽港、青祥港、蓝云港和紫飞港河道水域。

滴水湖滨水公共空间（以下简称滨水公共空间），是指滴水湖水域周围对社会公众开放，具有观光休憩、科教文创、运动健身、商贸服务等公共活动功能的空间。具体范围由中国（上海）自由贸易试验区临港新片区管理委员会（以下简称临港新片区管委会）根据相关规划确定，并向社会公布。

Several Provisions of the Pudong New Area on Improving the Protection and Management of Water Areas and Waterfront Public Spaces Development in Dishui Lake

(Adopted at the 4th Session of the 7th Pudong New Area People's Congress Standing Committee of Shanghai Municipality on July 29, 2022)

Section 1 The Several Provisions of the Pudong New Area on Improving the Protection and Management of Water Areas and Waterfront Public Spaces Development in Dishui Lake (these "Provisions") are formulated to better protect and improve water quality at Dishui Lake, ensure advanced construction and intelligent management of its waterfront public spaces, and create a premier lakeside and resort destination characterized by pristine waters, eco-friendly practices, resilience, and low-carbon emissions, pursuant to the Decision of the Shanghai Municipal People's Congress Standing Committee on Formulating Regulations to Improve Law-based Safeguards for High-level Reform and Opening-up in the Pudong New Area, and in light of contemporary reform and innovation initiatives.

Section 2 These Provisions shall apply to the protection of Dishui Lake waters and the planning, development, accessibility, and management of its public waterfront spaces.

The Dishui Lake water area includes the lake itself and the adjacent Chunlian River, Xialian River, Qiulian River, Donglian River, Chifeng Port, Chenghe Port, Huangri Port, Luli Port, Qingxiang Port, Lanyun Port, and Zifei Port within the Pudong New Area.

The Dishui Lake Waterfront Public Spaces ("Waterfront Public Spaces") encompasses the areas surrounding the lake designated for public activities including sightseeing, recreation, education, cultural activities, sports, and commercial purposes. The exact boundaries are as determined and disclosed by the Lin-gang Special Area Administration Committee of the China (Shanghai) Pilot Free Trade Zone (the "Lin-gang Special Area Administration Committee").

第三条 滴水湖水域保护和滨水公共空间建设管理，应当遵循水陆统筹、规划引领、绿色发展、智慧管理、共享共治的原则。

第四条 浦东新区人民政府应当与临港新片区管委会加强协作，并按照职责承担滴水湖水域保护相关行政事务。

浦东新区人民政府加强与临港新片区管委会河（湖）长制工作协同联动，按照各自职责共同推进滴水湖水域保护。

浦东新区生态环境、建设交通、公安、应急管理等有关部门在各自职责范围内依法支持临港新片区管委会开展滴水湖水域水上交通、岸线利用管理、公共安全和应急管理等工作。

浦东新区人民政府及其有关部门应当支持临港新片区管委会承担以下主要职责：

（一）组织编制滨水公共空间专项规划以及滴水湖水域和滨水公共空间文体商旅、智慧城市、慢行交通等专项规划；

（二）组织制定滨水公共空间利用设计导则等专项导则以及滨水公共空间设施建设导则、滴水湖和滨水公共空间风貌管控标准；

（三）组织制定滨水公共空间管理规范和政策；

（四）统筹清水廊道基础设施建设和监管，持续提升滴水湖水环境质量；

（五）加强滴水湖水域生态系统的整体保护和污染防治，增强水域水源涵养能力；

（六）统筹建设滨水公共空间，提升科教文创、商业、旅游、体育、休闲娱乐等功能；

Section 3 Protection of the Dishui Lake water area and the development and management of Waterfront Public Spaces shall comply with the principles of comprehensive land and water management, planned initiatives, green development, intelligent management, and comprehensive governance.

Section 4 The Pudong New Area People's Government shall improve cooperation with the Lin-gang New Area Administration Committee, and administer matters pertinent to the protection of Dishui Lake.

The Pudong New Area People's Government shall strengthen its collaboration with the river (lake) protection program administered by the Lin-gang Special Area Administration Committee, with each working together to protect the waters of Dishui Lake to the extent of their duties.

Appropriate departments in the Pudong New Area, such as the ecology and environment, construction, transportation, public safety, and emergency management departments, shall lawfully support the Lin-gang Special Area Administration Committee in administering water transportation, shoreline utilization, public safety, and emergency responses within Dishui Lake.

The Pudong New Area People's Government and its appropriate departments shall cooperate with the Lin-gang Special Area Administration Committee to take charge of:

(1) development of specialized plans for both the Waterfront Public Spaces and broader water areas, focusing on culture, sports, commerce, resorts, smart city initiatives, and pedestrian traffic;

(2) creation of design guidelines for Waterfront Public Spaces and construction diagrams for facilities in such areas, along with aesthetic standards for both Dishui Lake and its waterfront spaces;

(3) development of management standards and policies for Waterfront Public Spaces;

(4) coordination of infrastructure projects, such as the Clear Water Corridor, to continually improve Dishui Lake water quality;

(5) enhancement of ecosystem conservation and pollution prevention in Dishui Lake, and improving its water retention capabilities;

(6) comprehensive planning for the development of Waterfront Public Spaces, improving offerings related to education, culture, commerce, tourism, sports, and entertainment;

（七）推动绿色低碳发展，建设绿色低碳示范区；

（八）提升智能化数字化治理水平，建设数字化应用场景体系和智能化应用支撑体系；

（九）其他综合管理职责。

南汇新城镇人民政府依法负责滨水公共空间区域内的秩序管理、辖区内的雨污混接行为监督管理等工作。

第五条　根据滴水湖水域水体净化和生态景观需要，加强生物多样性研究，种植和投放适宜的水生动植物，防治有害外来物种，预防蓝藻等有害藻类，保护滴水湖水域水生态环境。在不影响防洪安全和景观游览的前提下，可以在滴水湖水域设置外来污染物的阻拦设施。

第六条　遵循节水优先、保护生态、智慧调度、定向补水的原则，加强清水廊道口门管理，制定并逐步完善水资源调度方案，建立滴水湖水系调度模型，建设水资源智慧调度系统，改善水资源调蓄和水动力条件，确保滴水湖水域生态用水。

第七条　探索实行岸线分区分类管控，科学合理划分岸线区域，严格管控岸线开发利用强度和方式，依法整治破坏水域岸线的违法违规行为，实现水域、岸线、码头等资源的优化配置、集约开发和可持续利用。

第八条　根据滨水公共空间的特点和需求，统筹规划建设高品质的基础设施、公共服务设施、商业配套设施、应急保障设施，营造布局合理、功能匹配、风貌协调、安全舒适的魅力水岸空间。

鼓励社会公众依托相关设施开展水上旅游、水上体育、文艺演出、文化展示等活动，促进科教文创、商业、旅游、体育、休闲娱乐等功能融合发展。

(7) advancement of green and low-carbon development initiatives, including the creation of demonstration zones;

(8) improvement of smart and digital management capabilities, and creation of digital use cases and smart application support systems; and

(9) other comprehensive management tasks.

The Nanhui New Town People's Government shall lawfully ensure public order in the Waterfront Public Spaces and oversee combined sewer overflow management within its jurisdiction.

Section 5 Biodiversity research shall be increased to support water purification and ecological landscaping in Dishui Lake. Appropriate aquatic plants and animals are to be introduced, invasive species controlled, efforts made to prevent harmful algae blooms like cyanobacteria, and the aquatic ecology is to be protected. Pollution control devices are to be installed as necessary, without compromising flood controls or aesthetic appeal.

Section 6 The administration of Clear Water Corridor access points shall be improved following the principles of water conservation, ecological protection, intelligent operation, and targeted supplementation. Additionally, a water resource scheduling plan is to be developed and progressively refined, a water system management model for Dishui Lake be created, a smart scheduling system for water resources be implemented, and conditions for water management, storage, and hydrodynamics be optimized to ensure ecological use of water resources.

Section 7 Research shall be conducted on the viability of zoned and categorized shoreline management, ensuring shorelines are sufficiently demarcated based on reasonable criteria. Shoreline construction intensity and methods are to be strictly controlled to prevent activities that damage these resources, aiming for optimal allocation, intensive development, and sustainable utilization of resources such as water, shorelines, and docks.

Section 8 All strategic planning and construction of high-quality infrastructure, public service, business amenities, and emergency facilities shall be based on the characteristics and needs of Waterfront Public Spaces, allowing for functional, well-organized, appealing, coordinated, and safe waterfront spaces.

Designated facilities shall be used to encourage participation in water tourism, sports, artistic performances, and cultural exhibitions, thereby promoting an integrated approach to science, education, culture, creativity, commerce, tourism, sports, and entertainment.

鼓励和支持在滨水公共空间区域内及相邻的交通枢纽，合理布局集商业、休闲、旅游等购物和体验功能的大型商业综合体。

第九条 建设绿色低碳示范区，探索水陆统筹，规划空间紧凑、功能复合、景观融合的城市布局形态，全面推进海绵公园等碳汇系统建设，全面推行建设项目绿色建筑要求，全面应用新能源交通，全面提高可再生能源规模化利用，降低环境负荷，打造低能耗低排放的城市公共空间。

第十条 依托城市运行“一网统管”平台，采集生态环境、安全运行、公共秩序、市容环境、防洪防涝等数据信息，建立文体商旅资源管理、景观设施管理、用地资源管理、船舶动态管理、人流分布管理等多个场景应用单元，实现资源调度、实时监控、动态跟踪、趋势预测等智慧管理；加强气象、水务、海洋等信息共享，建立防汛灾情预报预警和实时报送信息系统。

第十一条 加强滴水湖水域和滨水公共空间区域内的水上交通安全等公共安全统筹保障工作。

建立生态环境类、自然灾害类和公共安全类等突发事件的应急联动工作机制，并与国家突发事件应急体系全面对接。

第十二条 在滴水湖水域和滨水公共空间区域内进行游泳、垂钓、烧烤、燃放烟花爆竹等活动的，应当在规定的特定区域、特定时间段内进行，并符合活动秩序要求。

不得实施影响公共秩序、公共安全、生态环境等行为。未经相关管理部门同意不得实施养殖、捕捞、投放外来物种等行为。

滨水公共空间区域内应当按照规定设置警示、禁止等安全标识。安全标识应当明显、统一和易辨识。

The strategic placement of large commercial complexes that integrate shopping and experiential offerings, such as commerce, recreation, and tourism, near Waterfront Public Spaces and adjacent transport hubs are encouraged and facilitated.

Section 9 Efforts shall be made to create a green and low-carbon demonstration area; research urban layouts that integrate land and water management, efficient space planning, and functional landscaping; promote carbon sink projects like sponge parks; enforce green building standards; adopt new energy transport solutions; and expand the use of renewable energy to reduce environmental impact and create a low-energy, low-emission urban space.

Section 10 Administration shall be based on the integrated online platform to collect data on ecology and environment, safety operations, public order, urban aesthetics, and flood prevention, among other areas; multifunctional use scenario modules for cultural, sporting, commercial, and tourist resources, landscape amenities, land use, vessel movements, and crowd management are to be created; smart management is to be achieved through resource scheduling, real-time monitoring, dynamic tracking, and trend prediction; meteorology, water, and oceanography information sharing is to be improved; and an information system for flood disaster forecasting, warnings, and real-time reporting is to be developed.

Section 11 Policies shall be refined to ensure the safety of water traffic in Dishui Lake and its Waterfront Public Spaces.

An integrated process for emergency response shall be developed for ecological disturbances, natural disasters, and public safety incidents, ensuring alignment with the national emergency response system.

Section 12 Activities including swimming, fishing, barbecuing, and fireworks in Dishui Lake and its Waterfront Public Spaces shall be restricted to specific areas and times, and shall follow the guidelines for orderly conduct.

Activities that disrupt public order, safety, or the ecology, and environment are prohibited, as well as the introduction of any non-native species, fish farming, and fishing without proper authorization from the competent department.

Conspicuous, standardized, and easily recognizable safety signs shall be installed in Waterfront Public Spaces to indicate the different warnings and prohibited activities as required.

第十三条 鼓励企事业单位、社会团体和社会公众参与滴水湖水域保护和滨水公共空间规划、建设、开放等活动。

对涉及滴水湖水域保护和滨水公共空间规划、建设、开放和管理的重大事项，有关部门应当采取向社会公示等多种方式，广泛听取公众意见。

建立滨水公共空间志愿服务工作长效机制，依托区域内的志愿服务站点，组织志愿者队伍开展宣传、引导、咨询以及秩序维护等活动。

在滨水公共空间区域内组织开展各类活动的，应当自觉维护公共秩序和公共安全。

第十四条 支持设立专家咨询委员会，组织专业机构和人员为滴水湖水域和滨水公共空间重大发展战略、公共决策、统筹规划、建设开发、智慧治理、文化建设等工作提供专业咨询意见。

第十五条 本规定自2022年8月15日起施行。

Section 13 Enterprises, public institutions, social organizations, and the general public are encouraged to participate in the protection of Dishui Lake and the planning, development, and opening of its Waterfront Public Spaces.

The appropriate departments shall extensively solicit public opinions on significant issues concerning the protection of Dishui Lake or the planning, development, opening, and management of its Waterfront Public Spaces through methods including public disclosure.

A sustainable local volunteer service system is to be created for Waterfront Public Spaces, relying on volunteers from local volunteer service sites for outreach, guidance, consultations, maintenance, and other appropriate activities.

Organizers of activities in Waterfront Public Spaces shall actively ensure public order and safety.

Section 14 The creation of an expert advisory panel to organize professional agencies and individuals to provide expert opinions on major developmental strategies, public policy decisions, comprehensive planning, construction, smart governance, and cultural initiatives for Dishui Lake and its Waterfront Public Spaces are to receive support.

Section 15 These Provisions shall take effect from August 15, 2022.

浦东新区推进特色产业园区高质量发展若干规定

Several Provisions of the Pudong New Area on Promoting High-quality Development of Specialized Industrial Parks

浦东新区推进特色产业园区高质量发展若干规定

（2022年9月23日上海市浦东新区第七届人民代表大会常务委员会第七次会议通过）

第一条 为建设优势更优、特色更特、强项更强的特色产业园区，集聚产业创新要素资源，优化全产业链生态环境，打造世界级产业集群，促进浦东新区产业高质量发展，根据中共中央、国务院《关于支持浦东新区高水平改革开放打造社会主义现代化建设引领区的意见》、上海市人大常委会《关于加强浦东新区高水平改革开放法治保障制定浦东新区法规的决定》以及相关规定，结合浦东新区实际，制定本规定。

第二条 本规定适用于浦东新区经市或者区产业部门认定的特色产业园区的各项支持保障及监督管理活动。

第三条 推进特色产业园区高质量发展，应当紧扣浦东新区产业发展战略，坚持规划引领、聚焦特优、头部带动、全链协同、可持续发展的原则。

第四条 区人民政府应当加强对特色产业园区高质量发展工作的领导，建立协调推进机制，统筹、协调、决定相关重大事项。

Several Provisions of the Pudong New Area on Promoting High-quality Development of Specialized Industrial Parks

(Adopted at the 7th Session of the 7th Pudong New Area People's Congress Standing Committee of Shanghai Municipality on September 23, 2022)

Section 1 The Several Provisions of the Pudong New Area on Promoting High-quality Development of Specialized Industrial Parks (these "Provisions") are formulated to facilitate the construction of specialized industrial parks with greater competitiveness, distinctive features, and strategic advantages, consolidate innovative industry elements, optimize the entire industrial chain ecosystem, create world-class industrial clusters, and promote the high-quality development of industries in the Pudong New Area, pursuant to the Opinions of the Communist Party of China Central Committee and State Council on Supporting the High-level Reform and Opening-up to Establish a Pilot Area for Modern Socialism in the Pudong New Area, the Decision of the Shanghai Municipal People's Congress Standing Committee on Formulating Regulations to Improve Law-based Safeguards for High-level Reform and Opening-up in the Pudong New Area and other applicable provisions, and in light of actual circumstances in the Pudong New Area.

Section 2 These Provisions shall apply to the support, warranty, and regulatory activities for specialized industrial parks in the Pudong New Area as recognized by the municipal or district industrial departments.

Section 3 The Pudong New Area industrial development strategy shall be followed, and the principles of planning as guidance, specializations and advantages, executive leadership, whole-chain coordination, and sustainable development shall be prioritized to promote the high-quality development of the specialized industrial parks.

Section 4 The Pudong New Area People's Government shall be responsible for the high-quality development of specialized industrial parks, creating a coordination and promotion system, and the overall planning, coordination, and decision-making on pertinent major issues.

区产业部门负责特色产业园区发展规划编制、考核评价等相关工作。区发展改革部门负责产业布局研究、改革事项统筹协调等相关工作。区规划资源部门负责空间规划编制、土地收储出让、建设项目土地指标统筹协调等相关工作。区生态环境部门负责产业园区规划环评编制和建设项目水系、绿地、林地指标统筹协调等相关工作。区建设交通部门负责房屋征收、建设项目征收安置房源指标统筹协调等相关工作。

区财政、人力资源社会保障、应急管理、金融、国有资产监督管理等其他有关部门在各自职责范围内，协同开展相关工作。

各相关管理局（管委会）、镇人民政府负责协调推进本辖区特色产业园区发展相关工作。特色产业园区开发运营主体在各相关管理局（管委会）、镇人民政府指导下做好具体实施工作。

第五条　区产业部门应当会同发展改革等有关部门，聚焦集成电路、生物医药、人工智能等领域世界级产业集群以及重点优势产业建设，编制浦东新区特色产业园区发展规划，明确指导思想、总体目标、重点工作、实施步骤、保障措施等内容。

特色产业园区开发运营主体应当根据浦东新区特色产业园区发展规划，编制本园区产业发展规划以及阶段性推进计划，明确园区亩产、效益、能耗、环境等方面的目标任务。

第六条　区产业部门制定区级特色产业园区创建标准，评定区级特色产业园区，并指导、推荐其申报创建市级特色产业园区。

The district industrial department is responsible for the work including but not limited to specialized industrial park development planning, preparation, assessment, and evaluation. District development and reform department's responsibilities include, but are not limited to, researching industry layouts, overall planning, and coordination of reform initiatives. The district planning and resources department shall administer the preparation of spatial planning, land acquisition, reserves, and assignment, and coordinate land quotas for construction projects, among others. The district ecology and environment department shall carry out environmental impact assessments on industrial park planning, and coordinate water systems, green space, and forestland quotas for construction projects, among others. The district construction and transportation department shall take charge of housing eminent domain and coordinate housing exchange credits for construction projects, among others.

Other district departments, including fiscal, human resources and social security, emergency management, financial regulation, and state-owned assets regulation departments, shall cooperate with the work while carrying out their routine duties.

All appropriate administrative bureaus (or administration committees) and township people's governments shall be responsible for coordinating and promoting the development of specialized industrial parks in their jurisdictions. Specialized industrial park development and operation entities shall be responsible for specific implementations under the guidance of appropriate administrative bureaus (or administration committees) and township people's governments.

Section 5 The district industrial department shall cooperate with the development and reform department and other departments to prioritize the construction of world-class industrial clusters and competitive industries such as integrated circuits, biopharmaceuticals, and artificial intelligence. It shall prepare a development plan for specialized industrial parks in the Pudong New Area, outlining guiding principles, overall objectives, critical tasks, implementation steps, and supporting policies.

Specialized industrial park development and operation entities shall prepare an industrial development plan and a phased advancement plan based on the Pudong New Area specialized industrial park development plan, defining targets and tasks related to aspects including but not limited to yield per acre, economic efficiency, energy consumption, and environmental impact.

Section 6 The district industrial department shall develop standards for the construction of district-level specialized industrial parks, evaluate them, and provide guidance and recommendations for their use in municipal-level specialized industrial parks.

各相关管理局（管委会）、镇人民政府应当建立特色产业园区储备库，对具有一定发展潜力但尚未达到创建标准的产业园区进行服务指导，加快培育为区级特色产业园区。

第七条 创新特色产业园区运营方式，支持品牌化、专业化、国际化的各类园区开发运营主体或者行业领先的社会资本，以服务输出、搭建平台、合作运营等方式，参与特色产业园区高质量发展工作。

第八条 支持特色产业园区建设创新创业服务平台，构建小试中试平台、孵化器、加速器全链条产业服务体系，为入驻项目提供创业孵化、技术评估、产权交易、成果转化和投融资等服务。

推动大企业开放创新中心、企业技术中心等创新平台向行业开放资源，强化共性技术的研发和供给。

第九条 支持各相关管理局（管委会）、镇人民政府对辖区内特色产业园区实施与贡献联动的扶持政策。按照综合贡献度，对引进的功能性平台给予相应扶持。

支持专业化招商、产业链招商、产业基金招商等多途径招商模式，鼓励和吸引各类社会主体参与投资促进和企业服务，推进特色产业园区投资促进服务工作。

引导特色产业园区内的中小企业向专业化、精细化、特色化、新颖化发展，支持其开展关键核心技术、共性基础技术和新产品的产业技术攻关，补齐核心领域、关键环节短板。

第十条 浦东新区对特色产业园区内产业项目建设提供土地空间、资源性指标等方面优先保障支持。

All appropriate administrative bureaus (or administration committees) and township people's governments shall create development reserves for specialized industrial parks, provide guidance for industrial parks that have development potential but do not currently meet construction standards, and facilitate the recognition of district-level specialized industrial parks.

Section 7 Efforts shall be made to innovate the specialized industrial park operation model, and support branded, specialized, and international park development and management entities or industry-leading social investors to participate in high-quality development through service delivery, platform development, and collaborative operations.

Section 8 Creation of innovation and entrepreneurship service platforms for specialized industrial parks shall be faciliated. An integrated industrial service system, including small and medium-sized testing platforms, incubators, and accelerators is to be created. These platforms and service systems provide services such as entrepreneurship support, business incubation, technology assessment, property transactions, commercialization of deliverables, investment, and financing for new projects.

Large organizations are encouraged to share their innovation centers, technology centers, and other innovation platforms with the industry to enhance research and development and the availability of generic technologies.

Section 9 The administrative bureaus (or administration committees) and township people's governments involved shall enforce integrated support policies for contributions to specialized industrial parks within their jurisdiction. New functional platforms are to receive support based on their overall contribution.

A range of investment attraction models are to be encouraged, covering professional, industrial chain, and industrial fund investment attraction. Public organizations are to be encouraged and invited to participate in investment attraction and business services, thereby enhancing investment attraction services for specialized industrial parks.

Small and medium-sized enterprises in specialized industrial parks are to receive guidance to progress toward specialization, refinement, uniqueness, and innovation, and receive support to carry out industrial technology research on core technologies, basic generic technologies, and new products, thereby addressing gaps in core areas and key processes.

Section 10 The Pudong New Area shall prioritize support for industrial construction projects in specialized industrial parks such as land and resource quotas.

支持特色产业园区采用新型混合用地方式出让土地，明确混合用地主导用途、兼容用途类型及比例。

特色产业园区内产业用地地价按照底线原则管理，综合产业政策和项目绩效情况，经集体决策确定产业用地出让起始价。

符合产业规划的优质项目，可以在战略预留区落地，无需补划预留区面积。建立成片预留区启动打开会商机制，完善全过程管理体系。

特色产业园区内经区人民政府认定的重大产业项目建设涉及的新增建设用地、征收安置房源、水系占补平衡、林地占补平衡、绿地占补平衡等资源性指标，由区级层面统筹配置。

第十一条 特色产业园区的市政道路、河道、绿化和社会事业项目等基础设施建设，根据重点产业项目推进的时序安排，所在镇人民政府财力承担确有困难的，经区人民政府同意后，可以由区级财力统筹支持。

支持特色产业园区建设高品质公共服务配套设施，依托高品质社区和高水平文化设施，营造宜业、宜居、宜学的生活环境，打造产业与城市融合发展的示范区。

第十二条 支持特色产业园区纳入上海张江国家自主创新示范区范围，享受相关扶持政策。

支持将特色产业园区的重点产业企业纳入市相关部门的重点企业目录，享受相关扶持政策。

第十三条 对首次被认定为市级或区级特色产业园区的所在镇人民政府，可以给予一定奖励。

对年度综合评价优秀的市级或区级特色产业园区开发运营主体，可以给予一定奖励。

Specialized industrial parks are to receive land assignment support using new mixed-use land management methods, specifying primary and secondary use types and their proportions.

Industrial land pricing in specialized industrial parks follows the bottom-line principle, with starting prices for industrial land assignments determined collectively based on industrial policies and project effectiveness.

High-quality projects aligned with industrial planning may use the strategic reserved area without the need for additional reserved space. An integral reserved area is to be created to initiate a consultation process and enhance the overall management system.

Resource quotas, such as those for new construction land, housing for permanent taking and resettlement, and the balanced allocation and replenishment of water, forestland, and green space involved in the construction of major industrial projects in specialized industrial parks recognized by the Pudong New Area People's Government, are to be allocated at the district level.

Section 11 Infrastructure construction, including for municipal roads, waterways, greening, and social projects in specialized industrial parks shall proceed based on the schedule of key industrial projects and may receive financial support from district sources with the approval of the Pudong New Area People's Government if the township people's government where the park is located faces financial pressure.

The development of high-quality public service facilities within specialized industrial parks is to receive support to create a living, working, and learning environment suitable for high-quality communities and cultural facilities, building a demonstration zone for integrated industrial and urban development.

Section 12 Specialized industrial parks are encouraged to participate in the Shanghai Zhangjiang National Independent Innovation Demonstration Zone and may benefit from the pertinent support policies.

Key industry organizations within specialized industrial parks may be added to the competent municipal department's list of key enterprises and may benefit from pertinent support policies.

Section 13 Township people's governments where parks are first recognized as municipal or district-level specialized industrial parks may be eligible for specific incentives.

The development and operation entities of municipal or district-level specialized industrial parks may be eligible for incentives following an excellent annual evaluation.

第十四条 支持引领区产业母基金等政府引导基金、浦东科创母基金等私募股权基金以及其他基金为特色产业园区内符合产业导向的企业提供资本支持。

鼓励金融机构为园区内符合产业导向的企业提供金融创新产品服务，对符合产业导向的企业提供政策性融资担保支持。

第十五条 浦东新区为特色产业园区内符合条件的人才提供居留和出入境、落户、安居、医疗保险等服务保障。

在浦东新区特色产业园区工作的紧缺急需人才，按照规定享受相应支持。

第十六条 本规定相应支持保障措施的专项管理办法由区人民政府或其相关工作部门另行制定。

本规定自 2022 年 10 月 15 日起施行。

Section 14 Support is provided to develop government-backed funds, such as industrial master funds in the pilot zones, private equity funds such as the Pudong Science and Innovation Master Fund, and other funds, to provide financial support to those organizations in specialized industrial parks that comply with industry guidelines.

Financial institutions are encouraged to offer innovative financial products and services to enterprises based in specialized industrial parks that comply with industry guidelines, and provide policy-backed financing guarantees to enterprises that comply with industry guidelines.

Section 15 The Pudong New Area shall offer residency, entry and exit, settlement, housing, and health insurance support services for eligible professionals working in specialized industrial parks.

Essential individuals working in specialized industrial parks of the Pudong New Area may be eligible for support pursuant to applicable provisions.

Section 16 The Pudong New Area People's Government or its pertinent departments shall make specific administrative procedures to support and enforce these Provisions.

These Provisions shall take effect from October 15, 2022.

浦东新区住宅小区建筑物外墙墙面以及建筑附属构件脱落隐患治理办法

Procedures of the Pudong New Area on Addressing Potential Hazards of Falling Facades and Other Architectural Features of Residential Compound Buildings

浦东新区住宅小区建筑物外墙墙面以及建筑附属构件脱落隐患治理办法

（2022年10月28日浦府管规〔2022〕2号印发）

第一条　目的与依据

为进一步规范浦东新区行政区域内住宅小区建筑物外墙墙面以及建筑附属构件脱落隐患（以下简称“脱落隐患”）治理工作，切实保障人民群众人身、财产安全，根据《物业管理条例》《上海市住宅物业管理规定》《上海市房屋使用安全管理办法》等法律、法规、规章规定，结合浦东新区实际，制定本办法。

第二条　治理原则

脱落隐患治理应当遵循预防为主、防治结合、确保安全、责任明晰、属地监管的原则。

第三条　部门职责

浦东新区建设和交通委员会（以下简称“区建交委”）负责统筹协调住宅小区脱落隐患治理工作，承担业主大会成立前脱落隐患治理活动中专项维修资金的归集和日常使用管理，建立健全全区脱落隐患抽查检测机制，并落实区级安全抽查检测资金。

浦东新区物业管理事务中心负责指导脱落隐患治理相关专项维修资金使用，编制年度安全抽查检测资金预算，开展住宅小区安全抽查检测工作。

Procedures of the Pudong New Area on Addressing Potential Hazards of Falling Facades and Other Architectural Features of Residential Compound Buildings

(PGMM [2022] No.2, October 28, 2022)

Section 1 Purpose and Basis

The Procedures of the Pudong New Area on Addressing Potential Hazards of Falling Facades and Other Architectural Features of Residential Compound Buildings (these "Procedures") are formulated to standardize the management of potential hazards of falling facades and architectural features of residential compound buildings ("fall hazards"), and to effectively safeguard the personal and property safety of residents, pursuant to the Property Management Regulations, Regulations of Shanghai Municipality on Residential Property Management, and Procedures of Shanghai Municipality on the Administration of Residential Safety, and in light of the actual circumstances in the Pudong New Area.

Section 2 Management Principles

Fall hazards management shall follow the principles of prioritizing prevention, integrating prevention and resolution, ensuring safety, specific responsibilities, and local regulation.

Section 3 Department Responsibilities

The Construction and Transportation Committee of Pudong New Area (the "District Construction and Transportation Committee") takes charge of the coordination of fall hazards management in a residential area, manage the collection and daily allocation of ad hoc maintenance funds for fall hazards prior to the creation of a homeowners' meeting, develop and improve the district fall hazards inspection and testing processes, and manage district-level funds allocated for safety inspection sampling.

The Pudong New Area Property Management Center is responsible for guiding the use of ad hoc maintenance funds for managing fall hazards, preparing the annual budget for safety inspection sampling, and carrying out sampling in residential areas.

第四条 街镇与居委会职责

街道办事处、镇人民政府负责综合协调、处理本辖区住宅小区脱落隐患治理工作，履行下列职责：

（一）建立应急处置工作机制，处理跟踪脱落隐患紧急维修相关事务；

（二）开展脱落隐患抽查检测，编制脱落隐患治理年度工作计划，落实相关资金费用；

（三）加强对业主大会、业主委员会履行房屋使用安全责任的指导和监督，督促其依法开展脱落隐患治理工作，协调其在脱落隐患治理中依法使用维修资金；

（四）加强相关法律法规宣传，增强全社会防范脱落隐患的安全意识。

居民委员会依法协助街道办事处、镇人民政府开展脱落隐患治理工作，加强对业主大会、业主委员会的指导和监督，引导其以自治方式规范运作。

第五条 脱落隐患治理责任主体

房屋所有权人为脱落隐患治理责任人。房屋所有权人下落不明或者房屋权属不清的，房屋使用人为脱落隐患治理责任人。

物业服务企业应当按照规定开展脱落隐患治理工作。

鼓励脱落隐患治理责任人通过购买公众责任险等相关责任保险，增强抵御风险、保障安全的能力。

第六条 房屋质量保修责任主体

房屋建设单位应当依法全面承担房屋质量保修责任。鼓励房屋建设单位投保房屋质量相关责任险、财产险，增强抵御风险的能力。

Section 4 Sub-district Offices, Township Governments, and Residents' Committee Responsibilities

Sub-district offices and township governments are responsible for the comprehensive coordination and management of the fall hazards within their jurisdictions, and will perform the following duties:

(1) create an emergency response system for urgent repairs of fall hazards and monitor ongoing issues;

(2) conduct inspection sampling of fall hazards, prepare an annual management plan for addressing such hazards, and ensure proper allocation of the necessary funds;

(3) improve guidance and oversight of homeowners' meetings and homeowners' committees in performing their safety duties when using the property, ensuring lawful management of potential hazards and the legal use of maintenance funds; and

(4) promote awareness of pertinent laws and regulations to increase public safety awareness against fall hazards.

Residents' committees cooperate with sub-district offices and township governments to resolve fall hazards, and improve guidance and oversight of homeowners' meetings and committees, helping them self-regulate.

Section 5 Entities Responsible for Addressing Fall Hazards

The property owner is responsible for addressing fall hazards. If the property owner cannot be located or property rights are undetermined, the user of the property is responsible for addressing fall hazards.

Property management companies are responsible for resolving fall hazards as required.

All responsible entities are encouraged to improve their risk management and safety by acquiring liability insurance such as public liability insurance.

Section 6 Parties Responsible for Housing Quality Warranties

Property developers shall be fully responsible for housing quality warranties as required by law. They are also encouraged to obtain insurance that covers housing quality and property risks to further improve their risk management capabilities.

第七条 日常巡查

物业服务企业应当结合住宅小区实际情况，定期对建筑物外墙墙面以及建筑附属构件进行日常巡查；汛期前以及遇台风、暴雨等极端天气时应当加大巡查频次。

物业服务企业在日常巡查中发现脱落隐患的，应当如实记录脱落隐患发生部位、隐患状态等信息，并在24小时内向业主委员会、居民委员会报告。

业主大会决定实施自行管理的，自行管理执行机构应当按照本条规定开展日常巡查。

第八条 常规检查

业主大会、业主委员会应当定期对建筑物外墙墙面以及建筑附属构件进行常规安全检查，频次不得少于每年一次。

存在下列情形之一的，可以每半年检查一次，或者汛期前完成一次全覆盖检查：

（一）建筑物外墙墙面以及建筑附属构件使用年限20年（含）以上的；

（二）建筑物使用马赛克等外墙瓷质贴面材料或者外墙使用水泥基无机保温砂浆系统的；

（三）建筑附属构件采用易脱落装饰构件的；

（四）区人民政府确定的其他情形。

业主大会、业主委员会可以委托专业检测单位对建筑物外墙墙面以及建筑附属构件进行安全检测，检测报告应当如实记录、留存备查并在出具后24小时内向居民委员会报告。

Section 7 Routine Inspections

Property management companies shall carry out regular inspections of facades and architectural features as needed by residential areas. Inspection frequencies shall be increased prior to flood seasons or severe weather such as typhoons or heavy rainstorms.

The location and condition of any fall hazards identified by property management companies during inspections shall be accurately documented and reported to the homeowners' committees and residents' committees within twenty-four hours.

If the homeowners' meeting decides to self-regulate, the managing organization is responsible for carrying out routine inspections pursuant to these Procedures.

Section 8 Regular Safety Checks

Homeowners' meetings and committees shall perform regular safety reviews of building facades and architectural features, at least once annually.

More frequent inspections, such as bi-annual inspections or comprehensive inspections, may be required to be completed prior to flood seasons for any of the following:

(1) building facade and architectural features over twenty years old;

(2) facades constructed out of mosaic or other porcelain tile materials, or contain synthetic thermal mortar;

(3) architectural features comprising items prone to falling; or

(4) other circumstances determined by the Pudong New Area People's Government.

Homeowners' meetings and committees may entrust professional testing agencies for building facade and architectural feature safety inspections, and such organizations are required to accurately record their findings for reference and submit their report to the residents' committee within twenty-four hours of completion.

第九条 抽查检测

街道办事处、镇人民政府应当加强脱落隐患抽查检测工作，可以通过购买服务等方式，委托专业检测单位进行安全检测，每年安全抽查检测比例不低于5%。抽查检测结果应当以书面形式告知业主委员会、居民委员会。

区建交委可以通过购买服务等方式，委托专业检测单位对住宅小区进行安全抽查检测，每年安全抽查检测比例不高于5%，抽查检测结果应以书面形式告知各相关街道办事处、镇人民政府。

第十条 脱落隐患风险等级

脱落隐患风险分为以下三个等级：

（一）低风险：建筑物外墙墙面未见明显空鼓、起壳、脱落等损伤，建筑附属构件设施完好，建筑物外墙墙面以及建筑附属构件无变形、腐蚀、老化和脱落风险的；

（二）中风险：建筑物外墙墙面有明显的空鼓、起壳或者渗漏，建筑附属构件存在变形、腐蚀或者老化情况的；

（三）高风险：建筑物外墙墙面有明显的开裂、脱落，建筑附属构件变形、腐蚀、松动、老化严重且有脱落风险，已发生建筑物外墙墙面以及建筑附属构件脱落，以及其他严重危及人身财产安全的。

第十一条 防范与治理措施

存在中风险等级脱落隐患的，物业服务企业或者自行管理执行机构应当采取相应防范措施，向所在地业主委员会、居民委员会报告，并启动脱落隐患治理工作。

存在高风险等级脱落隐患的，物业服务企业或者自行管理执行机构应当立即采取以下应急防范措施：

Section 9 Sampling Inspection

Sub-district offices and township governments shall improve the sampling test methods for fall hazards. They may outsource to professional agencies for annual sampling inspections, with sampling being carried out on at least 5% of buildings annually. Inspection results shall be promptly reported to homeowners' committees and residents' committees in writing.

The District Construction and Transportation Committee may outsource to professional agencies to conduct annual sampling safety inspections of residential areas, ensuring that at least 5% of buildings are inspected. Inspection results are to be submitted in writing to the appropriate sub-district offices and township governments.

Section 10 Risk Classification of Fall Hazards

Fall hazard risks are classified into three categories:

(1) Low risk: no significant damage such as bulging, peeling, or falling observed on exterior walls, with intact building features and no deformation, corrosion, aging, or fall risks on the façade or architectural features;

(2) Medium risk: clear bulging, peeling, or leakage observed on the building facade or architectural features, showing deformation, corrosion, aging, or loosening; and

(3) High risk: significant cracking, and falling observed on building facades and severe deformation, corrosion, loosening, and aging of architectural features with fall hazards; buildings facades or architectural features have previously fallen, or other serious personal and property safety risks.

Section 11 Prevention and Addressment Methods

Property management companies or self-managing organizations shall take appropriate precautions for medium risk fall hazards, report to local homeowners' committees and residents' committees, and begin risk addressment of fall hazards.

Immediate emergency action shall be taken for high risks fall hazards:

（一）设置警戒线、警示牌等安全防范警戒标识，调整通行路线；

（二）通过在住宅小区主要出入口张贴公告、线上媒介发布等方式提示风险；

（三）其他应急防范措施。

第十二条　保修期内的检测鉴定与维修

建筑物保修期内发生不明原因外墙墙面开裂、脱落且影响公共安全等情形的，房屋建设单位应当委托符合条件的房屋检测鉴定单位进行检测鉴定。

建筑物保修期内发生外墙墙面空鼓、开裂、脱落或者建筑附属构件脱落等情形的，房屋建设单位应当进行排查、制定维修方案，并按照规定将排查结果和维修方案在物业管理区域内公示。

建筑物保修期内发生外墙墙面以及建筑附属构件质量问题的，房屋建设单位应当及时维修，并向物业服务企业或者自行管理执行机构提供相关维修资料。维修后的保修期限，按照国家和本市的相关规定执行。

物业服务企业、自行管理执行机构或者业主大会在日常巡查、常规检查中发现存在本条第二款情形的，应当以书面形式告知房屋建设单位。

第十三条　一般维修流程

出现中风险等级脱落隐患的，物业服务企业或者自行管理执行机构应当在 20 日内制定脱落隐患治理方案，并经业主大会表决通过后，开展脱落隐患治理工作。

第十四条　紧急维修程序的启动

出现高风险等级脱落隐患的，物业服务企业或者自行管理执行机构应当立即向业主委员会、居民委员会、街镇房屋管理机构报告，并申请启动紧急维修流程。

(1) add safety barricades, warning signs, and other precautionary markers, and adjust traffic routes;

(2) issue risk warnings via announcements posted at main entrances and exits of residential areas or online media; and

(3) other emergency precautions

Section 12 Warranty Period Inspections, Risk Identification, and Maintenance

Property developers shall be required to entrust certified inspection agencies to inspect and assess any cracks or crumbling of building facades that endanger public safety that occur during the warranty period and whose causes are unknown.

If there are signs of hollowing, cracking, or falling off, or if architectural features fall off during the warranty period, the property developers shall carry out an inspection, prepare repair plans, and disclose their findings and plans within the managed property.

Property developers shall be required to promptly resolve any facade or architectural feature quality issues arising during the warranty period. Repairs carried out shall be documented, and such documentation shall be submitted to the appropriate property management companies or self-managing organizations. Warranty terms shall follow applicable national and municipal provisions following the completion of all repairs.

Property management companies, self-managing organizations or homeowners' meetings shall be required to notify the property developers in writing upon discovering any of the issues outlined in Paragraph 2 of this Section during routine inspections

Section 13 General Maintenance Process

Property management companies or self-managing organizations shall prepare fall hazards addressment plans within twenty days since identifying any medium risk fall hazards, which shall be implemented upon approval by the homeowners' meeting.

Section 14 Initiating Emergency Repairs

High risk fall hazards shall be immediately reported to the appropriate homeowners' committees, residents' committees, and property management organizations under the jurisdiction of sub-district offices or township governments by property management companies or self-managing organizations, as well as a request to initiate emergency repairs.

第十五条　紧急维修方案编制与实施

开展高风险等级脱落隐患紧急维修的，业主委员会应当按照本市规定，委托符合条件的房屋检测鉴定单位对脱落隐患进行检测和维修方案编制。

房屋检测鉴定单位应当在20日内完成检测和维修方案编制。对隐患问题突出、处置难度较大的项目，区建交委可以根据需要组织专家对维修方案进行技术评审。

业主委员会应当在7日内对维修方案进行审核，并按照相关流程选择有资质的施工单位开展维修。业主委员会未在7日内审核同意的，且已出现影响房屋正常使用或者居民人身财产安全情形的，街道办事处、镇人民政府可以组织代为维修。

第十六条　紧急维修项目监管

物业服务企业或者自行管理执行机构应当配合施工单位做好施工现场管理，并配合业主委员会、居民委员会做好居民解释、告知工作。

第十七条　紧急维修审价验收与费用列支

业主委员会应当委托符合条件的第三方专业机构开展紧急维修项目工程造价审价、组织验收，并按照规定从专项维修资金中列支维修费用。

尚未成立业主委员会的，物业服务企业或者自行管理执行机构经工程造价审价、街镇房屋管理机构审核同意，凭审价报告和区建交委出具的支取通知，从专项维修资金中列支维修费用。

街道办事处、镇人民政府组织代为维修的，凭审价报告和区建交委出具的支取通知，从专项维修资金中列支维修费用。

Section 15 Emergency Repair Plan Creation and Implementation

Homeowners' committees shall contract certified property inspection organizations to inspect the fall hazards and prepare repair plans for high risk fall hazards pursuant to municipal regulations.

The property inspection organization shall complete the inspection and repair plan within twenty days. Repair plans for complex issues with significant hazards may be reviewed by experts organized by the District Construction and Transportation Committee.

Homeowners' committees shall review the repair plan within seven days and select a certified contractor to complete the repairs. If the plan is rejected and safety is compromised, sub-district offices and township governments may organize repairs on behalf of the homeowners' committees.

Section 16 Emergency Repair Project Regulation

Property management companies or self-managing organizations shall assist the contractors with construction site management and collaborate with homeowners' committees and residents' committees to inform the residents of the details.

Section 17 Emergency Repair Costs Reviewing and Expenditure

Homeowners' committees are required to hire certified third-party agencies to assess emergency repair project costs, organize approval, and allocate funds from ad hoc maintenance accounts as required.

Without homeowners' committees, property management companies or self-managing organizations may fund the repairs using ad hoc maintenance funds following the completion of the repair project cost assessment and approval from the sub-district or township government property management departments based on the cost assessment report and the funding approval notice issued by the District Construction and Transportation Committee.

Repair costs for repairs organized by sub-district offices or township governments independently may be funded using ad hoc maintenance funds based on the cost assessment report and the withdrawal approval issued by the District Construction and Transportation Committee.

第十八条　缺位补足机制

业主委员会无法正常运作且业主大会无法召开的，在街道办事处、镇人民政府的指导和监督下，居民委员会可以代为组织实施相关工作。

在业主大会、业主委员会设立或者恢复正常运作前，由物业服务企业或者自行管理执行机构实施常规检查等脱落隐患治理工作。

第十九条　监督管理

区建交委应当强化对脱落隐患治理工作的监督管理，定期组织对脱落隐患防范和治理情况开展专项监督检查，优化脱落隐患治理工作诉求响应、数据共享、监测预警、应急处置等流程。

对于已发生过建筑物外墙墙面以及建筑附属构件脱落的房屋以及前期排查发现存在中、高等级脱落隐患的房屋，区建交委应当建立“一楼一档”，并实行挂牌督办、限期维修、销项管理。

第二十条　社会参与

鼓励市民主动报告脱落隐患情况，对于经审核确实存在高风险等级脱落隐患，且未在前期巡查、检查、抽查中发现的，可以对报告人给予精神奖励或者物质奖励，具体实施办法由各街道办事处、镇人民政府另行制定。

支持物业管理行业协会开展脱落隐患治理问题调研，指导区内物业服务企业提高脱落隐患治理水平。

对未按照法定职责进行脱落隐患治理，致使社会公共利益受到重大损害的相关责任主体，鼓励相关行业协会等社会组织依法提起公益诉讼。

Section 18 Alternative Processes

Where homeowners' committees are unable to operate normally and the meetings of homeowners' associations cannot be convened, residents' committees may organize and carry out the work on behalf of the homeowners' committees under the guidance and oversight of sub-district offices and township governments.

Property management companies or self-managing organizations may carry out routine inspections and address all fall hazards until a homeowners' meeting or homeowners' committee can be convened or resume regular operations.

Section 19 Oversight and Management

The District Construction and Transportation Committee shall improve oversight and management of fall hazards and their resolution, organize regular, ad hoc oversight and reviews of fall hazards prevention controls, and improve procedures such as those for responding to fall hazards addressment requests, data sharing, monitoring and warning, and emergency responses.

The District Construction and Transportation Committee shall create a record for each property with a history of facade or architectural feature damage or with confirmed medium or high fall hazards identified during past inspections, and implement signboard oversight, ensure all repairs are completed within the required deadline, and enforce output management.

Section 20 Public Participation

Residents are encouraged to actively report fall hazards, and may be eligible for recognition or rewards for reporting previously unnoticed verified high-risk fall hazards, pursuant to the specific rules issued by the sub-district offices or township governments.

Property management associations are encouraged to carry out research on solutions to fall hazards and guide local property management companies to improve their fall hazards management capabilities.

Associations are encouraged to file public interest litigation against fall hazards due to the neglect of the responsible parties, with the lack of lawful fall hazards addressment posing a material damage to the public interest.

第二十一条　信用管理

有关部门应当按照国家、本市和本区信用管理等规定，将房屋建设单位、物业服务企业等主体在脱落隐患排查、检测、维修等治理过程中未尽到相关责任而被行政处罚的信息，归集到公共信用信息服务平台，并依法对失信主体采取联合惩戒措施。

第二十二条　指引条款

违反本办法规定的行为，法律、法规、规章有相应行政处罚规定的，依照有关法律、法规、规章处理。

第二十三条　施行日期

本办法自 2022 年 12 月 1 日起施行，有效期至 2027 年 11 月 30 日。

Section 21 Credit Management

The appropriate agencies shall disclose any administrative penalties incurred by property developers or management companies for neglecting their duties in identifying, assessing, repairing, or otherwise addressing fall hazards on the social credit lookup platform, and take joint disciplinary actions against violators pursuant to national, municipal, and Pudong New Area credit regulations.

Section 22 Governing Law

Where applicable laws, regulations, or rules prescribe administrative penalties for violations of these Procedures, such violations shall be addressed in accordance with the relevant legal provisions.

Section 23 Validity Period

These Procedures shall take effect from December 1, 2022, and remain valid until November 30, 2027.

浦东新区国有建设用地垂直空间分层设立使用权若干规定

Several Provisions of the Pudong New Area on the Creation of Air Space Use Right for Leasehold Estates to State-owned Construction Land

浦东新区国有建设用地垂直空间分层设立使用权若干规定

（2022 年 11 月 7 日 浦府管规〔2022〕3 号印发）

第一条 目的依据

为规范本区国有建设用地垂直空间使用权分层设立，保障地表、地上、地下空间的国有建设用地使用权人合法权益，提升国有建设用地综合利用效率，促进城市空间结构优化、功能完善和品质提升，根据《中华人民共和国民法典》《中华人民共和国城乡规划法》《中华人民共和国土地管理法》《上海市城乡规划条例》《上海市地下空间规划建设条例》《上海市城市更新条例》等法律、法规，制定本规定。

第二条 适用范围

本规定适用于本行政区域内国有建设用地垂直空间分层设立使用权，以及相关规划、利用、建设、登记等活动。

第三条 基本原则

根据规划利用空间界限，国有建设用地使用权可以在国有建设用地垂直空间的地表、地上、地下分层设立。

国有建设用地垂直空间分层设立使用权，应当坚持科学统筹规划、集约节约利用、层次空间协调、公共利益优先的原则。

Several Provisions of the Pudong New Area on the Creation of Air Space Use Right for Leasehold Estates to State-owned Construction Land

(PGMM [2022] No.3, November 7, 2022)

Section 1 Purpose and Basis

The Several Provisions of the Pudong New Area on the Creation of Air Space Use Right for Leasehold Estates to State-owned Construction Land (these "Provisions") are formulated to regulate the creation of air space use right for leasehold estates to state-owned construction land in this district in order to protect the legal rights of leaseholders holding title to the surface, above-ground, and underground state-owned construction land leasehold estates, improve the overall utilization efficiency of state-owned construction land, and facilitate urban spatial structure, functionality, and quality improvements, pursuant to the Civil Code of the People's Republic of China, Urban and Rural Planning Law of the People's Republic of China, Regulations of Shanghai Municipality on Urban and Rural Planning, Regulations of Shanghai Municipality on Underground Space Planning and Construction, Shanghai Regulations on Urban Redevelopment, and other applicable laws and regulations.

Section 2 Applicable Scope

These Provisions shall apply to the creation of air space use right for leasehold estates to state-owned construction land and the related planning, utilization, construction, and registration activities within this administrative area.

Section 3 Basic Principles

The state-owned construction land use right may be granted divisibly in leasehold estates to surface, aboveground, and underground spaces on state-owned construction based on the boundaries defined in spatial plans.

The creation of air space use right for leasehold estates to state-owned construction land shall follow the principles of strategic and comprehensive planning, efficient and economical utilization, spatial coordination, and prioritizing the public interest.

第四条 政府职责

区人民政府加强本区国有建设用地垂直空间分层设立使用权工作的领导，建立健全统筹协调机制，研究、协调、决策国有建设用地垂直空间分层设立使用权以及相关规划、利用、建设、登记等活动中的重大事项。

第五条 部门职责

区规划资源部门负责本区国有建设用地垂直空间分层设立使用权相关工作。

区人民政府其他有关职能部门以及各镇人民政府、街道办事处和相关管理局（管委会）按照各自职责，协同做好国有建设用地垂直空间分层设立使用权相关工作。

第六条 规划编制要求

区人民政府组织编制有关控制性详细规划时，应当按照规定和需要明确国有建设用地垂直空间层次、性质、功能、高度、深度、规模、互联互通以及基础设施、公共服务设施配套等要求。

第七条 设立要求

国有建设用地垂直空间分层利用的，应当依法取得相应的国有建设用地使用权。

国有建设用地垂直空间分层设立使用权，应当符合相应的国土空间规划以及节约资源、保护生态环境的要求，遵守法律、法规、规章关于土地用途的规定，充分考虑相邻空间的发展需要和相互衔接，不得损害已经设立的用益物权。

Section 4 Government Duties

The Pudong New Area People's Government is to improve the regulation over the creation of air space use right for leasehold estates to state-owned construction land, create and refine a comprehensive coordination process to research, coordinate, and issue decisions on major matters related to the creation of air space use right for leasehold estates to state-owned construction land and other major matters such as planning, utilization, construction, and registration.

Section 5 Department Duties

The district planning and resources department is responsible for all work related to the creation of air space use right for leasehold estates to state-owned construction land within its jurisdiction.

Other appropriate departments of the Pudong New Area People's Government, along with township governments and sub-district offices, and pertinent administrative bureaus (or administration committees) coordinate while carrying out work related to the creation of air space use right for leasehold estates to state-owned construction land to the extent of their responsibilities.

Section 6 Requirements for Preparing Plans

The Pudong New Area People's Government shall specify requirements for air space such as characteristics, function, height, depth, scale, connectivity, as well as infrastructure and public facilities on state-owned construction land based on applicable regulations and actual needs when preparing the necessary detailed management plans.

Section 7 Leasehold Creation Requirements

The use of air space on state-owned construction land shall require lawfully obtaining a leasehold estate to state-owned construction land.

The creation of air space use right for leasehold estates to state-owned construction land shall conform to the applicable territorial spatial plans, resource preservation and environmental protection requirements, comply with land use laws, fully consider developmental needs and interconnectivity of adjacent spaces, and not infringe upon existing usufruct.

第八条 分层供地

国有建设用地垂直空间分层设立使用权的，应当分别对照相应空间的规划批准用途，实行分层供地，依法确定出让、划拨等不同的供地方式。国有建设用地使用权出让，按照国家有关规定采用招标、拍卖、挂牌或者协议等方式进行。

第九条 储备地块地下空间统一建设后供地

政府储备土地属于集中开发区域的，可以按照控制性详细规划的要求，对该地块地下空间进行整区域统一建设，经竣工验收合格，形成土建预留工程后，采取“带地下工程”方式将该地下空间与地表、地上空间的国有建设用地使用权统一供应，或者分别设立地表、地上、地下国有建设用地使用权，予以单独供应。

第十条 供地后委托实施地下空间统一建设

鼓励实行地下空间区域性整体开发建设。

国有建设用地分宗出让给不同主体的，国有建设用地使用权人可以通过协议方式，委托一个主体对一定区域地下空间实行整区域统一建设，并符合以下要求：

（一）地下建设工程设计方案和工程规划许可充分考虑各宗地地下空间的分割条件，合理确定地下工程布局；

（二）各宗地地下空间分割界线与地上权属界线相协调；

（三）其他统一建设要求。

第十一条 连通便利及协议

国有建设用地垂直空间开发利用中，因出入口、地上连廊、地下通道等建设，需要利用其他既有国有建设用地的，相关国有建设用地使用权人应当进行协商，达成协议，并按照有关规定办理国有建设用地审批手续。

Section 8 Granting Air Space Use Right

Air space use right for leasehold estates to state-owned construction land shall be granted in compliance with the approved use purposes for the space. Methods for such grant, such as assignment or allocation, shall be determined by law. Leasehold estates for state-owned construction land are to be assigned through methods such as bidding, auction, direct sale, or by agreement pursuant to applicable national regulations.

Section 9 Supply of Developed Integrated Underground Spaces on Reserved Land

Integrated construction of underground spaces on land reserved by the government within designated development zones may take place based on the detailed planning requirements. Following approval and completion of preliminary works, leasehold estates for underground spaces on state-owned construction land may be assigned together with those for surface and aboveground spaces on the same on state-owned construction land. Alternatively, leasehold estates for surface, aboveground, or underground spaces on state-owned construction land may be created and assigned separately.

Section 10 Post-supply Integrated Construction Entrusting for Underground Spaces

The development of partially complete underground spaces is encouraged.

If leasehold estates to state-owned construction land are assigned to multiple entities, the holder of the leasehold estate to the state-owned construction land may contract a single entity to generally develop the underground spaces in a designated area, subject to specific requirements:

(1) design plans and planning permits for underground construction projects must fully consider subdivision conditions for each estate and properly layout underground structures;

(2) underground space boundaries for each estate must align with those of the aboveground spaces; and

(3) other comprehensive construction requirements.

Section 11 Streamlined Access and Agreements

State-owned construction land leaseholders shall negotiate and enter into agreements with the appropriate leaseholders when the development and use of air space for leasehold estates to state-owned construction land requires access to other leaseholder estates for entrances, exits, skywalks, and tunnels, among others, and shall submit the necessary state-owned construction land review documents pursuant to applicable provisions.

协议中应当具体约定地上或者地下空间的地面出入口、工程连通设施以及地下桩基等配套设施和构筑物的权属、使用方式、维修养护等内容。

区规划资源部门以及其他有关单位应当做好相关指导、协调工作。

第十二条 结合地面建筑开发地下空间

国有建设用地使用权已经出让或者划拨，并由地表、地上空间的国有建设用地使用权人结合地面建筑一并开发建设地下空间的，该国有建设用地使用权人按照国家和本市有关规定，通过出让或者划拨等方式取得上述范围内地下空间的国有建设用地使用权，土地用途按照规划审批方案确定。

第十三条 出让年限

国有建设用地垂直空间使用权出让年限，应当按照法律、法规规定的不同用途确定。

地表、地上空间的国有建设用地使用权人结合地面建筑一并开发建设地下空间的，其地下空间的国有建设用地使用权出让终止日期应当与地表、地上空间的国有建设用地使用权出让终止日期相一致。地表、地上空间的国有建设用地使用权按照用途有不同最高年限的，地下空间的国有建设用地使用权不得超过地表、地上空间的国有建设用地使用权最高年限对应的终止日期。

第十四条 出让价格确定

国有建设用地垂直空间使用权出让价格，应当遵循分层利用、区别用途、层次空间协调的原则，按照土地价格评估技术规范，经市场评估、出让人集体决策后确定。

The agreements shall specify ownership, usage, and maintenance, among others, for necessary facilities and features, including but not limited to entrances, exits, engineering connection facilities, and underground pile foundations, in both aboveground and underground spaces.

The district planning and resources department and other appropriate departments shall provide the necessary guidance and coordination.

Section 12 Integrated Construction of Surface and Underground Spaces

Lessees who have previously acquired leasehold estates for state-owned construction land via lease or allocation and have developed surface or aboveground spaces are permitted to extend their leasehold interests to include underground spaces connected to ground-level buildings on state-owned construction land through leasing or allocation pursuant to national and municipal regulations, with the land usage as determined by the review plans.

Section 13 Lease Term

Lease terms for air space use right on state-owned construction land shall be determined based on the different use purposes as defined by law.

Expiration dates for underground spaces in leasehold estates for surface and aboveground spaces on state-owned construction land held by leaseholders who develop underground spaces together with surface-level buildings shall be the same as those for the surface and aboveground leasehold estates. If surface and aboveground spaces have different lease terms based on their use purposes, leasehold estates for underground spaces on state-owned construction land shall not exceed the expiration date for the corresponding surface and aboveground space leasehold estates to state-owned construction land.

Section 14 Determination of Leasehold Price

Leasehold prices for air space use right on state-owned construction land shall be determined according to the principles of stratified usage, differentiated purposes, and spatial coordination. Prices are to be calculated based on technical land valuation standards, market assessments, and collective determinations by lessors.

第十五条　出让合同的补充完善

区规划资源部门可以根据国有建设用地垂直空间开发利用需求和管理需要，经与受让人协商，对国有建设用地使用权出让合同中的特别约定条款内容予以补充、完善。

第十六条　审批要求

国有建设用地垂直空间使用权审批应当符合国家和本市有关规定。

本区有关单位应当按照“放管服”改革以及优化营商环境的要求，进一步简化相关审批材料、缩减审批时限、优化审批环节，提高审批效能。

第十七条　登记

国有建设用地垂直空间使用权按照不动产登记有关规定进行登记。

本区探索完善垂直空间地表、地上、地下国有建设用地使用权范围不完全对应情形下的登记规则。

第十八条　施行日期

本规定自2022年12月15日起施行，有效期至2027年12月14日。

Section 15 Amendments to Leasehold Agreements

The district planning and resources department may amend and revise lease agreements for state-owned construction land leaseholds following negotiations with the applicable lessees pursuant to air space utilization and management requirements for state-owned construction land.

Section 16 Review Requirements

Reviews of leasehold estates for air space use right on state-owned construction land shall comply with applicable national and municipal provisions.

The competent departments in the Pudong New Area shall be responsible for streamlining the review documents, shorten review deadlines, optimize review procedures, and enhance review efficiency in compliance with requirements for streamlining government services and business environment optimization.

Section 17 Registration

Leasehold estates for air space use right on state-owned construction land shall be registered pursuant to applicable real estate registration regulations.

The Pudong New Area advances the development of registration guidelines for circumstances where the permitted activities for air spaces in surface, aboveground, and underground leasehold estates to state-owned construction land do not fully align.

Section 18 Validity Period

These Provisions shall take effect from December 15, 2022, and remain valid until December 14, 2027.

浦东新区户外招牌管理若干规定

Several Provisions of the Pudong New Area on the Administration of Outdoor Signage

浦东新区户外招牌管理若干规定

（2022年12月14日浦府管规〔2022〕6号印发）

第一条　目的和依据

为了加强浦东新区户外招牌全过程管理，维护市容环境整洁有序，保障城市公共安全，根据上海市人民代表大会常务委员会《关于促进和保障浦东新区综合配套改革试点工作的决定》《关于促进和保障浦东新区改革开放再出发实现新时代高质量发展的决定》《关于加强浦东新区高水平改革开放法治保障制定浦东新区法规的决定》《上海市市容环境卫生管理条例》和其他有关法律、法规和规章的规定，结合浦东新区实际，制定本规定。

第二条　适用范围

本规定适用于浦东新区行政区域内户外招牌的设置及其监督管理活动。

设置国家机关、人民团体标识标牌的，按照国家和本市有关规定执行。利用户外招牌发布广告的，按照户外广告相关规定执行。

第三条　定义

本规定所称户外招牌，是指在自有或者租赁的办公、生产经营场所建（构）筑物外立面及用地范围内设置，用于表明其名称、字号、标识等内容或者建筑物名称的户外设施。

第四条　管理职责

区绿化市容局是本行政区域内户外招牌行业主管部门，负责本辖区内户外招牌设置的协调、指导和监督管理工作。

Several Provisions of the Pudong New Area on the Administration of Outdoor Signage

(PGMM [2022] No.6, December 14, 2022)

Section 1 Purpose and Basis

The Several Provisions of the Pudong New Area on the Administration of Outdoor Signage (these "Provisions") are formulated to improve the comprehensive management of outdoor signage in Pudong New Area, maintain a tidy and orderly urban appearance and ensure public safety in Shanghai Municipality, pursuant to the Standing Committee of Shanghai Municipal People's Congress Decision on Supporting Comprehensive Management Reforms in the Pudong New Area Pilot Zone, Decision on Supporting and Safeguarding Reform and Opening-up in the Pudong New Area for High-quality Development in the New Era, Decision on Drafting Regulations to Improve Rule-based Safeguards for High-level Reform and Opening-up in the Pudong New Area, Regulations of Shanghai Municipality on Urban Appearance and Environmental Sanitation Management, and other applicable laws, regulations and rules, and in light of the actual circumstances in the Pudong New Area.

Section 2 Applicable Scope

These Provisions shall apply to the installation and regulation of outdoor signage within the administrative area of the Pudong New Area.

Signage for government departments and social organizations shall comply with applicable national and municipal provisions. The use of outdoor signage for advertising shall be governed by specific outdoor advertising provisions.

Section 3 Definitions

"Outdoor signage" in these Provisions refers to outdoor equipment installed on the exterior surfaces or within the property boundaries of privately owned or leased spaces used for office, manufacturing, or business purposes to display elements such as the business name, trade name, logo, or name of the building.

Section 4 Management Responsibilities

As the competent department for outdoor signage in this administrative area, the district landscaping and city appearance administration shall be responsible for coordinating, guiding, overseeing, and managing the outdoor signage installations within the administrative area.

各镇政府、街道办事处、自贸区保税区管理局、度假区管委会（以下简称“区域管理责任单位”）在区绿化市容局的指导下，负责本辖区户外招牌相关具体管理工作。

区规划资源局、区建交委、区文体旅游局、区市场监管局、区应急管理局、区城管执法局等部门按照各自职责，协同实施本规定。

第五条 设置导则

区绿化市容局应当组织编制本辖区主要道路沿线和景观区域、历史风貌区等重点区域内以及文物保护单位、优秀历史建筑等重要建（构）筑物上的户外招牌设置导则。

鼓励区域管理责任单位在区绿化市容局的指导下，根据实际情况，编制前款规定范围以外的户外招牌设置导则。

户外招牌设置导则应当根据技术规范进行编制，体现区域环境、建筑风格以及业态特点，为设置者展现个性和创意提供空间，避免样式、色彩、字体等同质化。

第六条 设置要求

户外招牌设置应当符合户外招牌技术规范和设置导则的要求。

户外招牌设置不得有下列情形：

（一）损害城市容貌或者建（构）筑物形象；

（二）妨碍他人生产经营或者居民正常生活，影响他人对建（构）筑物合法使用；

（三）利用违法建筑、危险房屋，以及危及建（构）筑物或者其他设施安全；

（四）利用树木或者损毁绿地；

（五）妨碍无障碍设施使用；

Each township government, sub-district office, free trade zone bonded area office, and resort management committee ("regional management responsible parties") take charge of outdoor signage management in their jurisdiction under the guidance of the district landscaping and city appearance administration.

The district planning and resources, transportation and construction, culture, sports, and tourism, market regulation, emergency management, and urban governance and enforcement departments are to jointly implement these Provisions to the extent of their duties.

Section 5 Installation Guidelines

The district landscaping and city appearance administration shall create guidelines for installing outdoor signage along primary roads and key areas such as those for sightseeing, historical sites, and significant buildings (or structures) such as historical and cultural landmarks.

Regional management responsible parties are encouraged to create additional guidelines for outdoor signage in other locations based on local conditions, under the guidance of the district landscaping and city appearance administration.

The installation guidelines for outdoor signage shall be developed based on technical standards, reflecting the local environment, architectural styles, and business traits, and allow for creativity and personalization to avoid uniformity in style, color, or font, among others.

Section 6 Installation Requirements

The installation of outdoor signage shall conform to the technical standards and guidelines provided.

The following are prohibited in the installation of outdoor signage:

(1) compromising the city appearance or the exterior of buildings (or structures);

(2) interfering with third-party business operations or daily life of residents, or infringing upon the lawful use of the buildings (or structures) by others;

(3) using illegally built or hazardous equipment, posing a risk to the safety of the buildings (or structures) or other equipment;

(4) using trees or damaging green spaces;

(5) blocking accessibility facilities;

（六）垂直设置于建（构）筑物外立面，且招牌面积大于0.5平方米；

（七）设置于建（构）筑物屋顶、围墙顶部，或者超出建筑物女儿墙部位；

（八）法律、法规、规章、标准以及技术规范规定的其他情形。

第七条 分类信息登记

在本行政区域内设置户外招牌，应当办理户外招牌设置信息登记。

符合以下四类情形的户外招牌，设置人应当在设置前办理信息登记：

（一）在历史文化风貌区或者风貌保护街坊内、风貌保护道路或者风貌保护河道沿线、文物保护单位或者优秀历史建筑上设置；

（二）设置箱体式整体结构户外招牌、高度大于2.5米的独立式户外招牌；

（三）超过建（构）筑物3层或者在建（构）筑物10米以上部位设置；

（四）市政府确定的可能影响公共安全的其他情形。

除前款规定的四类情形外，设置人应当在户外招牌设置后10个工作日内办理信息登记。鼓励设置人在户外招牌设置前办理信息登记。

第八条 事前信息告知与服务指导

区绿化市容局和区域管理责任单位应当通过业主自治、商户自治、物业管理、网格化管理等多种途径，告知户外招牌设置信息登记要求。

区建交委核发建筑外立面装修施工许可、街道办事处或者镇政府对限额以下小型建设项目实施安全监管、企业服务窗口提供市场主体登记服务时应当告知户外招牌设置信息登记要求。

(6) involving installing signage vertically on building (or structure) exteriors, with the signage area exceeding 0.5 square meters;

(7) involving installing signage atop building (or structure) roofs, walls, or extending beyond parapet walls; and

(8) other circumstances provided by laws, regulations, rules, norms, and technical standards.

Section 7 Categorized Information Registration

Installations of outdoor signage within this administrative area shall be registered.

The signage installation under the following circumstances requires registration before installation:

(1) located in historical, cultural, or scenic zones, along scenic routes or waterways, or on significant historical or cultural landmarks;

(2) standalone outdoor signage with a self-contained box taller than 2.5 meters;

(3) installation higher than the third floor, or over 10 meters high on buildings (or structures); or

(4) other circumstances designated by the Municipal People's Government as impacting public safety.

Registrations shall be completed within ten business days following the signage installation, except under the four circumstances described above. Registration before the installation of outdoor signage is favored.

Section 8 Pre-installation Information Disclosure and Service Guidance

The district landscaping and city appearance administration and the regional management responsible parties shall disclose registration requirements for outdoor signage installation through approaches such as property owner and vendor self-management, property management, and comprehensive management systems.

When the transportation and construction committee issues permits for facade renovation, sub-district offices or governments oversee the safety of smaller construction projects below specified limits, or the commercial service center provides registration services for market entities, they shall inform the registration requirements for outdoor signage.

区绿化市容局和区域管理责任单位应当采用多种方式，为设置人知悉户外招牌设置基本要求、技术规范、设置导则以及相应法律责任等内容提供便利，并根据设置人需求提供针对性服务指导。

第九条 设置人责任

设置人对户外招牌设施的质量和安全负有主体责任。

设置人应当加强对户外招牌设施的日常管理，对户外招牌设施进行维护保养，保持户外招牌设施整洁、完好、美观。图案、文字、灯光等显示不全或者破损、缺失、污浊、腐蚀、陈旧的，应当及时修复或者更换。

对于存在安全隐患或者失去使用价值的户外招牌设施，设置人应当及时整修或者拆除。在台风、暴雨、暴雪、雷电等灾害性天气警报和气象灾害预警信号发布后，设置人应当加强对户外招牌设施的安全检查，采取相应的安全防范措施，消除安全隐患。

第十条 设施载体所有权人责任

户外招牌设施所在建（构）筑物等载体的所有权人（以下简称“所有权人”）与设置人不一致的，所有权人应当督促设置人依法设置、维护管理户外招牌设施。设置人违法设置或者未履行维护管理责任的，所有权人应当及时报告区域管理责任单位。

第十一条 安全检测

属于本规定第七条第二款第一项至第四项规定情形的，设置人应当按照规定委托专业检测单位，对设置满两年的户外招牌设施每年进行安全检测，并向所在地的区域管理责任单位提交安全检测报告。

第十二条 设施拆除

因搬迁、退租等原因不再需要户外招牌的，设置人应当自行拆除户外招牌设施。

The district landscaping and city appearance administration and regional management responsible parties shall disclose and specify fundamental requirements, technical standards, installation guidance, and associated legal obligations for outdoor signage installations through various means, providing targeted guidance based on the installer's needs.

Section 9 Installer Responsibility

Installers are the principal parties responsible for the quality and safety of outdoor signage.

Installers are required to strengthen routine management and maintenance of outdoor signage, maintaining them in a clean, intact, and visually appealing condition, and must promptly repair or replace any parts of the signage, such as patterns, characters, or lights, that are incomplete, damaged, corroded, or outdated.

Installers shall carry out comprehensive safety inspections of their outdoor signage for safety hazards or remove outdoor signage that no longer serves a purpose in response to weather alerts or metrological early warnings, such as for typhoons, heavy rains, blizzards, or lightning storms, and take the appropriate safety precautions to mitigate potential risks.

Section 10 Property Owner Responsibilities

If the owner of a building (structures) with outdoor signage (the "property owner") is not the installer, they are required to ensure that the installer complies with all legal standards for installation, maintenance, and management. The property owner shall promptly report any non-compliant installation or lack of maintenance or management conducted by the installer to the regional management responsible parties.

Section 11 Safety Check

Installers are required to contract a professional inspection service provider to conduct safety checks on outdoor signage that has been installed for more than two years, particularly under circumstances outlined in Paragraphs 1 through 4 of Section 7 of these Provisions. A comprehensive safety check report shall be submitted to the regional management responsible party of the installation location.

Section 12 Signage Removal

Installers are required to remove any outdoor signage that is no longer needed due to relocation or termination of tenancy.

所有权人与设置人不一致，且设置人未自行拆除户外招牌设施的，所有权人应当予以拆除。所有权人可以委托物业服务企业组织拆除。

第十三条 安全保障

区绿化市容局、区域管理责任单位应当加强户外招牌设施安全检查，可以通过购买服务等方式，委托专业检测单位对户外招牌设施进行安全抽检。区绿化市容局负责全区户外招牌设施的抽检，每年安全抽检比例不低于2%；区域管理责任单位负责本辖区内户外招牌设施的抽检，每年安全抽检比例不低于20%。必要时，可以组织实施户外招牌设施的集中安全检查和整治。

台风、暴雨、暴雪、雷电等灾害性天气警报和气象灾害预警信号发布后，区域管理责任单位应当启动相关应急预案，及时督促设置人采取相应的安全防范措施，消除安全隐患。

鼓励设置人运用新技术、新工艺、新材料，提高户外招牌安全管理水平，保障户外招牌设施安全。

第十四条 协调机制

区绿化市容局与区域管理责任单位在日常管理工作中，不断完善事前、事中、事后协同管理工作机制：

（一）区绿化市容局应当与区城管执法局、区建交委、区规划资源局、区市场监管局、区文体旅游局、区应急管理局、区域管理责任单位等单位建立信息共享机制，动态掌握街面业态布局、商户开办、建设项目施工、建筑外立面装修等信息，及时开展户外招牌设置指导、监督工作。

If the property owner is not the installer and the installer does not remove the signage, the property owner shall take charge of the removal and may entrust a property management company to remove outdoor signage.

Section 13 Safety Assurance

The district landscaping and city appearance administration and regional management responsible parties shall conduct frequent safety checks of outdoor signage, such as outsourcing sampling safety checks to professional inspection agencies. The district landscaping and city appearance administration takes charge of conducting sampling safety checks across the entire district, with an annual sampling ratio of no less than 2%, while regional management responsible parties take charge of sampling checks of outdoor signage in this jurisdiction, maintaining an annual sampling ratio of no less than 20%. Comprehensive safety assessments and corrections of outdoor signage may be carried out as necessary.

Following the issuance of severe weather alerts and meteorological early warnings, such as for typhoons, rainstorms, blizzards, or lightning storms, regional management responsible parties shall initiate the emergency response procedures and promptly require installers to take appropriate safety precautions to prevent safety risks.

Installers are encouraged to adopt new technologies, processes, and materials to improve the management of outdoor signage safety and ensure their structural integrity.

Section 14 Coordinating Process

The district landscaping and city appearance administration and regional management responsible parties shall continually enhance the pre-installation, installation, and post-installation coordination process during daily management:

(1) The district landscaping and city appearance administration shall create an information-sharing process with other departments, including the district urban management and enforcement, transportation and construction committee, planning and resources, market regulation, culture, sports and tourism, emergency management, and regional management responsible parties to guide and oversee the commercial layout, business setups, construction projects, and facade renovation, providing prompt guidance and oversight for outdoor signage installations.

（二）区绿化市容局应当协同区域管理责任单位加强对商业密集、人流量大、设施安全风险高等重要路段的监督抽查。发现问题设施的，督促设置人及时整改。

（三）区域管理责任单位应当及时维护和更新户外招牌智能化综合管理平台数据信息，并依托数据库进行协同管理。

第十五条　信用监管

设置人和相关单位违反本规定的，有关部门应当按照国家和本市规定，将相关失信信息归集到公共信用信息服务平台，并依法采取惩戒措施。

第十六条　行政处罚

违反本规定的，按照《上海市市容环境卫生管理条例》等法规、规章有关规定进行处罚。

第十七条　行政责任

区绿化市容局、区域管理责任单位以及其他有关部门及其工作人员有下列行为之一的，依法对直接负责的主管人员和其他直接责任人员给予处分：

（一）未按照本规定履行安全抽检等职责的；

（二）对发现、投诉或者举报的违法行为不依法查处的；

（三）违法实施行政处罚的；

（四）其他滥用职权、玩忽职守、徇私舞弊的行为。

第十八条　施行日期

本规定自 2023 年 2 月 1 日起施行，有效期至 2028 年 1 月 31 日。

(2) In collaboration with the regional management responsible parties, the district landscaping and city appearance administration shall increase oversight and the frequency of sampling checks in areas with high business density, pedestrian traffic, and equipment safety risks, and require installers to promptly correct any identified issues.

(3) Regional management responsible parties shall maintain and update outdoor signage data on the smart integrated management platform to facilitate database collaborative management.

Section 15 Credit Regulation

If installers or organizations violate these Provisions, appropriate departments shall collect details of the violation and upload such to the public credit information service platform pursuant to national and municipal law, and lawfully enforce any necessary disciplinary actions against violators.

Section 16 Administrative Penalties

Violations of these Provisions shall be subject to penalties as provided in the Regulations of Shanghai Municipality on Urban Appearance and Environmental Sanitation Management.

Section 17 Administrative Liability

If the district landscaping and city appearance administration, regional management responsible parties, or any other appropriate departments or their employees engage in any of the following conduct, individuals directly responsible and others with direct responsibilities shall face disciplinary actions:

(1) failing to perform required safety checks as specified by these Provisions;

(2) failing to investigate and address violations observed, complained about, or reported pursuant to law;

(3) illegally imposing administrative penalties; or

(4) engaging in abuse of power, dereliction of duty, playing favoritism and committing irregularities.

Section 18 Validity Period

These Provisions shall take effect from February 1, 2023, and remain valid until January 31, 2028.

浦东新区建设项目资源性指标统筹配置实施办法

Procedures of the Pudong New Area on Implementing the General Allocation of Resource Credits for Construction Projects

浦东新区建设项目资源性指标统筹配置实施办法

（2022 年 11 月 15 日浦府管规〔2022〕4 号发布，根据 2024 年 2 月 8 日印发的《浦东新区人民政府关于修改〈浦东新区建设项目资源性指标统筹配置实施办法〉的通知》修改后重新发布）

第一条　（目的和依据）

为了提高建设项目资源利用效率，统筹协调推进浦东新区经济发展和生态文明建设，根据《中共中央　国务院关于支持浦东新区高水平改革开放打造社会主义现代化建设引领区的意见》《上海市人民代表大会常务委员会关于加强浦东新区高水平改革开放法治保障制定浦东新区法规的决定》以及相关规定，结合浦东新区实际，制定本办法。

第二条　（适用范围）

本办法适用于浦东新区范围内建设项目资源性指标（以下简称“资源性指标”）的统筹配置以及相关监督保障活动。

前款所称的资源性指标，是指土地指标（含新增建设用地指标和耕地占补平衡指标）、征收安置房源指标、水系占补平衡指标、绿地占补平衡指标、林地占补平衡指标。

Procedures of the Pudong New Area on Implementing the General Allocation of Resource Credits for Construction Projects

(PGMM [2022] No.4, November 15, 2022, and revised on February 8, 2024)

Section 1 [Purpose and Basis]

The Procedures of the Pudong New Area on Implementing the General Allocation of Resource Credits for Construction Projects (these "Procedures") are formulated to enhance resource utilization efficiency in construction projects, promote economic development, and advance ecological civilization in the Pudong New Area, pursuant to the Opinions of the Communist Party of China Central Committee and State Council on Supporting the High-level Reform and Opening-up to Establish a Pilot Area for Modern Socialism in the Pudong New Area and the Decision of the Shanghai Municipal People's Congress Standing Committee on Formulating Regulations to Improve Law-based Safeguards for High-level Reform and Opening-up in the Pudong New Area, and other applicable provisions, and in light of the actual circumstances in the Pudong New Area.

Section 2 [Applicable Scope]

These Procedures shall apply to the general allocation of resource credits for construction projects in the Pudong New Area, including activities related to regulation and support.

"Resource credits" in these Procedures include land credits (including land credits for new construction and mitigation credits for the use and restoration of arable land), housing credits for expropriation and resettlement, water system mitigation credits, green area mitigation credits, and forest land mitigation credits.

第三条 （总体要求）

资源性指标统筹配置应当坚持“整体政府”理念，遵循“总量管控、占补分离、动态平衡”的原则，严守生态环境保护底线，深化制度创新，加快流程再造，通过资源性指标计划管理和适度超前储备，推动资源性指标由建设主体自行筹措向行业主管部门统一供给的转变，形成生态环境、自然资源和建设项目全面统筹、协调推进的工作格局。

资源性指标统筹周期由区人民政府与市相关主管部门协商确定。

第四条 （适用统筹配置的项目）

下列建设项目适用资源性指标的统筹配置：

（一）能源、交通、水利等重大基础设施项目；

（二）科技、文化、教育、卫生、体育、生态环境等重大公共事业项目；

（三）保障性安居工程建设项目；

（四）区人民政府组织实施的土地储备项目；

（五）区人民政府认定的其他建设项目。

第五条 （职责分工）

区人民政府受市人民政府委托负责填堵河道的审批工作。

区规划资源部门负责建设项目土地指标的全区统筹、储备、配置、审核报批等管理工作。

区生态环境部门负责全区水系、绿地、林地占补平衡指标的统筹、储备、配置以及建设项目填堵河道的审核报批等工作；接受市绿化市容部门委托，承担绿地、林地占补平衡方案的审批工作。

区住房保障部门负责全区征收安置房源的统筹、储备、配置等工作。

Section 3 [General Requirements]

Resource credit allocation shall be managed through an integrated government approach following the principles of capacity control, differentiation of use and restoration, and dynamic equilibrium. This approach shall firmly uphold ecological and environmental thresholds, facilitate systemic innovations, streamline process redesign, and the transition from internal procurement by construction companies to centralized management by the appropriate department through credit administration policies and the creation of appropriate active reserves to form a cohesive operational environment blending ecology, environment, natural resources, and construction projects.

Strategic cycles for allocating resource credits shall be determined through discussions with competent municipal authorities led by the Pudong New Area People's Government.

Section 4 [Projects Subject to General Allocation]

Construction projects subject to general resource credit allocation include:

(1) major infrastructure projects such as those for energy, transportation, and water conservation;

(2) major public service initiatives in fields such as science and technology, culture, education, health, sports, environmental, and ecological protection;

(3) affordable housing developments;

(4) land reserve projects carried out by the Pudong New Area People's Government; and

(5) other construction projects designated by the Pudong New Area People's Government.

Section 5 [Assignment of Responsibilities]

The Municipal People's Government shall commission the Pudong New Area People's Government to take charge of reviewing the filling and blocking of any watercourses.

The district planning and resources department shall administer land credits for construction projects, including but not limited to planning, reserves, allocation, and review requests within the district.

The district ecology and environment department shall administer the planning, reserves, and allocation of mitigation credits for water systems, green areas, and forest land within the district, and review watercourse filling and blocking requests in construction projects, as well as review green area and forest land mitigation credit requests with the authorization of the municipal landscaping and city appearance administration.

The district housing department shall take charge of general housing planning, reserves, and allocation within the district, among others.

区发展改革、财政部门根据区国民经济和社会发展规划，负责将新增资源性指标统筹项目纳入区政府年度投资计划和年度重大建设项目投资计划。

镇人民政府应当配合区资源性指标统筹配置部门推进本辖区内资源性指标项目建设。

第六条 （联席会议机制）

区人民政府建立资源性指标统筹配置工作联席会议机制，研究并协调解决资源性指标统筹配置工作重大问题。联席会议办公室设在区重大工程建设指挥部办公室，具体负责联席会议日常工作。

第七条 （需求计划编制）

建设主体应当根据区国民经济和社会发展规划，编制资源性指标统筹配置五年规划、三年滚动计划和年度需求计划，配合做好资源性指标配置与落实工作。

第八条 （指标统筹联动）

浦东新区设立建设项目全过程管理平台（以下简称“联动平台”），开展资源性指标的征询、受理、反馈、监测评估、统筹配置等工作，实现规划联动、计划联动、项目联动。

区资源性指标统筹配置部门应当根据联动平台反馈和建设项目实际需求，配置相关资源性指标。

第九条 （土地指标统筹）

区规划资源部门应当根据国土空间总体规划，采用统筹周期内总量管控的模式对建设项目土地指标进行统筹，确保统筹周期内永久基本农田数量不减少、质量有提升、布局更优化。

The district development and reform department and the finance department shall integrate comprehensive planning projects for new resource credits into the Pudong New Area People's Government's annual and primary construction project investments pursuant to national socioeconomic development planning.

Township governments shall cooperate with the district resource credit planning and allocation department to facilitate the organization and allocation of resource credits for projects within their jurisdictions.

Section 6 [Multi-department Coordination Group]

The Pudong New Area People's Government is to establish a multi-department coordination group for the comprehensive management of resource credits to analyze and address major issues in the allocation of resource credits. A coordination group office is to be set up within the district's major project management headquarters, which takes charge of the routine work carried out by the multi-department coordination group.

Section 7 [Preparing Demand Plans]

Developers shall prepare five-year, three-year update, and annual resource credit demand plans pursuant to district economic and social development planning, to support the effective allocation and realization of credits.

Section 8 [Integrated Planning of Credits]

A full process management platform (the "integrated platform") for construction projects in the Pudong New Area is to be created to facilitate consultation, request, report, oversight, and assessment processes, as well as the comprehensive planning of resource credits, among others, ensuring dynamic integration of planning, projects, and schemes.

The district resource credit planning and allocation department shall allocate the necessary credits based on reports received through the integrated platform as needed by actual projects.

Section 9 [Comprehensive Planning of Land Credits]

The district planning and resources department shall create a comprehensive plan for land credits based on the overall territorial space management plan, implementing aggregate control over the comprehensive planning period and ensuring that the amount of permanent basic farmland remains unchanged, its quality improves, and its layout is optimized.

区规划资源部门应当结合全域土地综合整治、高标准农田建设、建设用地减量化和一般整理复垦等工作，持续开展永久基本农田整备区建设。建设项目选址确实无法避让耕地保护空间的，应当按照量质并重原则，编制整理方案调整布局，调整成果纳入市城市空间基础信息平台。

区规划资源部门应当在统筹周期的最后一个年度明确下一个统筹周期内土地指标的总量需求，并报送市规划资源部门。

第十条 （征收安置房源指标统筹）

区住房保障部门应当建立区征收安置房源资源库，根据建设主体实际房源需求，配置征收安置房源。

第十一条 （填堵河道水系平衡指标统筹）

区生态环境部门会同区发展改革部门拟定、落实新开区级和镇级河道储备和建设计划，建立区河湖面积资源库；指导镇人民政府开展镇级河道建设，形成的河湖面积在用于镇级项目后富余部分纳入区河湖面积资源库。

建设项目水系占补平衡应当保障区域防汛排涝安全和水环境质量，确保统筹周期内全区河湖面积只增不减。建设项目在填堵具有防汛功能的非规划河道时，应当确保现状水系沟通，防汛功能不降低。

填堵河道原则上在项目内实现平衡。新建、改建、扩建的桥梁工程，建设主体在建设项目立项时应当将其垂直投影面内及上下游各三十米河道纳入项目建设内容，按河道规划同步选址、同步建设；上下游各三十米河道选址时可因地制宜，并与周边水系成网成体系；产生的河湖面积用于本项目填堵河道水系平衡。房屋建设项目应当尽量结合景观规划优先在项目红线内布置河湖等水体，并在规划阶段落实相关水体指标。

In support of comprehensive land consolidation efforts, development of high-quality farmland, reduction of construction land, and general consolidation and reclamation, the district planning and resources department shall continue to create designated zones for permanent basic farmland. If the location of a construction project overlaps with arable land protection areas, a land consolidation plan shall be prepared to maintain a balance between quantity and quality, with adjustments documented on the municipal urban spatial information platform.

During the final year of the planning cycle, the district planning and resources department shall assess the total demand for land credits for the forthcoming period and submit this department to the municipal planning and resources department.

Section 10 [Comprehensive Planning for Expropriation and Resettlement Credits]

The district housing department shall set up housing reserves for expropriation and resettlement, allocating credits based on the actual needs of developers.

Section 11 [Comprehensive Planning of Filled and Blocked Watercourse System Mitigation Credits]

The district ecology and environment department and the district development and reform department shall formulate and implement district and township-level plans for watercourse reserves and construction to establish river and lake area resource reserves within the district, and guide township governments in watercourse development, which uses river and lake areas in town-level projects and incorporates any surplus space into the district reserves for river and lake resources.

Mitigation and compensation for the water systems used by construction projects shall conform to district flood control safety and water quality standards, ensuring only increases, not decreases, in river and lake areas within the district throughout the planning period. When filling or blocking non-planned watercourses with flood control features, construction projects shall preserve the integrity of the existing water network and not affect its flood control capabilities.

All watercourses filled or blocked during a project shall generally be compensated. Developers shall be required to incorporate space within the air space and thirty meters both upstream and downstream into construction plans for newly constructed, modified, or expanded bridge projects upon approval. They shall select sites and begin construction at the same time based on the watercourse plans. Adjustments may need to be made every thirty meters upstream and downstream to align with conditions in the surrounding water network; river and lake areas affected by filled or blocked watercourses shall also be compensated. Housing projects shall, where feasible, include landscape plans that prioritize the inclusion of rivers and lakes within project boundaries, using the necessary water credits during the planning phase.

第十二条 （绿地占补平衡指标统筹）

区生态环境部门会同区发展改革部门拟定、落实用于占绿补偿项目的储备和建设计划，建立区绿地资源库。

区生态环境部门应当按照计划安排区级和镇级绿地补建项目，确保统筹周期内补建面积不少于因占用绿地而减少的绿化面积。

建设项目原则上在项目内实现占补平衡，确实无法达到法定绿地率或者无法实现占补平衡的，应当缴纳绿地易地补偿费或者绿化补建费。各类新建、改建建设项目超出法定绿地率部分，应当纳入区绿地资源库。纳入区绿地资源库用于绿化补偿的项目进库后绿地率不得减少。

鼓励学校、医院、产业园等房屋建设项目在满足配套技术要求外，通过建设立体绿化、屋顶绿化等方式增加绿化面积。

第十三条 （林地占补平衡指标统筹）

区生态环境部门根据各建设主体占林需求计划，会同区相关部门拟定、落实补林项目储备计划和建设计划，建立区林地资源库。

区生态环境部门应当按照造林规划和计划，负责指导和安排项目建设主体开展林地补建，确保统筹周期内补建面积不少于因占用林地而减少的森林植被面积。

新建道路红线范围内超出法定绿地率且满足林地标准的可以用于林地平衡；河道两侧陆域控制线内满足林地标准的可以用于林地平衡。

城镇开发边界外已落实土地储备的和其他未利用的土地，经区规划资源部门确认可以作为补建林用地。由区土地储备机构、镇人民政府提供且经区生态环境部门会同相关部门确认可以用于补建林的土地，其土地权属不变。

Section 12 [Comprehensive Planning of Green Area Mitigation Credits]

The district ecology and environment department and the district development and reform department shall plan and implement compensation projects for green areas to establish green area reserves within the district.

The district ecology and environment department shall take charge of organizing district and town-level green area compensation projects based on the plan, ensuring that newly compensated areas match or exceed the areas impacted by green area mitigation within the allocation period.

Construction projects shall, in principle, balance the use of green areas with their restoration. Projects that fail to achieve the required green area ratio or equivalent compensated green area shall be subject to fees for green space relocation or supplement. Any portions of new or reconstructed projects exceeding the legally required green space ratios are to be added to the district green area reserve and shall not result in a reduction of green areas following their addition.

Housing development projects, including but not limited to those for school, hospital, and industrial park developments, are encouraged to increase green space through methods such as vertical and rooftop gardening, provided these approaches meet applicable technical standards.

Section 13 [Comprehensive Planning of Forest Land Mitigation Credits]

The district ecology and environment department shall, together with other appropriate departments, draft and implement reserve and construction plans for forest compensation projects based on developer forestry needs, and establish a district forest land reserve.

Following afforestation guidelines, the district ecology and environment department shall guide and arrange developers in supplementing forest land, ensuring that the compensated area matches or exceeds the area of forest cover impacted within the planning period.

New roads within project boundaries that surpass the legally required green space ratio and meet forest standards may contribute to forest land compensation; areas within watercourse control zones that meet forest land criteria may contribute to forest land compensation.

Land outside urban development boundaries designated for land reserves or other unused land may be used for forest compensation once approved by the district planning and resources department. Land designated by the district land reserve department or township governments for forest compensation, and verified by the district ecology and environment department and the appropriate agencies, shall retain its original ownership status.

镇域内补建林面积可以认定为镇人民政府年度林地建设面积考核指标。

第十四条 （土地指标配置）

建设主体取得房屋土地权属调查报告后可以提出土地指标需求申请，区规划资源部门应当在收到申请后十个工作日内反馈统筹配置初步意见，并在收到农转用组卷材料后三十日内完成审核、报批。

第十五条 （征收安置房源指标配置）

项目储备库阶段，建设主体取得土地权属调查边界确认后可以向区房屋征收部门提出启动房屋征收前期调查摸底申请，区房屋征收部门应当在收到申请后三十日内完成前期调查摸底。建设主体可以根据前期摸底情况向区住房保障部门提出征收安置房源需求申请，区住房保障部门应当在十个工作日内反馈统筹配置初步意见。

项目实施库阶段，区房屋征收部门应当在建设项目征收土地预公告发布后规定时间内完成房屋调查确认工作。建设主体应当根据房屋调查结果、房型配比合理要求和房源配置方案，向区住房保障部门提出征收安置房源调拨申请。区住房保障部门应当根据申请，按照就地、就近原则，在十个工作日内完成征收安置房源配置工作。

第十六条 （填堵河道水系平衡指标配置）

项目储备库阶段，建设主体在初步排摸填堵河道情况后向区生态环境部门征询水系平衡意见，区生态环境部门应当在二十日内反馈统筹配置初步意见。

Compensated forest land within a township may be taken into account in the annual evaluation of the township government's forest land development performance.

Section 14 [Allocation of Land Credits]

After acquiring property rights assessment reports, developers may request land credits. The district planning and resources department shall provide preliminary opinions on planning credits within ten business days of receiving a request and complete the review and approval process for converting agricultural land within thirty days of receiving the necessary documentation.

Section 15 [Allocation of Expropriation and Resettlement Housing Credits]

During the project reserve phase, developers may verify land ownership boundaries and initiate preliminary reviews on expropriation with the district housing expropriation department, which shall complete these preliminary investigations within thirty days of receiving the request. Based on the results of the review, developers may submit a request to the district housing department, which manages resources for expropriation and resettlement, and the district housing department shall issue its initial opinions on the comprehensive planning within ten business days.

During project implementation, the district housing expropriation department shall finalize housing reviews and confirmations within the designated period following the public notice of expropriation for construction projects. Developers shall then apply to the district housing department for distribution of housing in exchange for taken properties based on survey results, appropriate housing type matching, and allocation plan. The district housing department shall then be responsible for allocating the final expropriation and resettlement credits within ten business days.

Section 16 [Allocation of Mitigation Credits for Watercourse System Filling and Blocking]

During the project reserve phase, developers shall negotiate water system compensation with the district ecology and environment department following initial watercourse filling and blocking reviews, with the district ecology and environment department providing preliminary allocation opinions within twenty days.

项目实施库阶段，建设主体应当根据统筹配置初步意见，委托专业机构编制项目填堵河道论证方案，并征询区生态环境部门意见。区生态环境部门应当在十个工作日内反馈配置意见，意见应当包括统筹配置的河道名称、平衡数量和项目实施计划等内容。配置意见可以作为编制前期概算的依据。

建设项目取得工程可行性研究报告批复后，建设主体可以通过“一网通办”向区生态环境部门提出填堵河道申请，区生态环境部门应当在十个工作日内完成填堵河道的审核、报批。

第十七条 （绿地、林地占补平衡指标配置）

项目储备库阶段，建设主体在初步排摸项目占用绿地、林地情况后向区生态环境部门征询占补平衡意见，区生态环境部门应当在二十日内核准占绿占林性质，反馈统筹配置初步意见。占用规划绿地、规划林地的建设项目应当在规划绿地和规划林地外进行平衡。

项目实施库阶段，建设主体应当根据统筹配置初步意见向区生态环境部门申报绿地、林地占补平衡指标。区生态环境部门应当在十个工作日内反馈配置意见。

建设项目按照规定取得相关批复后，建设主体可以通过“一网通办”向区生态环境部门提出占用绿地、林地申请，区生态环境部门应当在收到申请后七个工作日内作出决定。

第十八条 （事中事后监管）

区资源性指标统筹配置部门应当加强农用地转建设用地、填堵河道、占用绿地和林地、征收安置房源等事项的事中、事后监管。

During project implementation, developers shall entrust professional organizations to prepare demonstration plans for watercourse filling and blocking based on initial allocation opinions, and consult the district ecology and environment department for further guidance. The district ecology and environment department shall provide allocation opinions within ten business days, which shall include details such as the watercourse name, areas to be compensated, and project implementation plan. These allocation opinions may serve as the basis for preparing preliminary budget estimates.

Upon approval of construction project feasibility studies, developers may submit a request for watercourse filling and blocking to the district ecology and environment department via the integrated online government service platform, with the district ecology and environment department completing the review within ten business days.

Section 17 [Allocation of Mitigation Credits for Green and Forested Areas]

During the project reserve phase, developers shall negotiate the mitigation and compensation of green and forested areas with the district ecology and environment department following initial site reviews, with the department assessing the nature of the impacted green areas and forest lands and providing preliminary allocation opinions within twenty days. Compensation for construction projects impacting designated green or forested areas must occur outside of these designated areas.

During project implementation, developers may submit a request for green and forest area mitigation and compensation credits based on initial allocation opinions to the district ecology and environment department, which shall issue its allocation opinions within ten business days.

Upon approval of a construction project, developers may submit a request for the use of green and forested areas to the district ecology and environment department via the integrated online government service platform, and the district ecology and environment department shall issue their decision within seven business days.

Section 18 [Regulation During and After Project Development]

The district resource credit planning and allocation department shall improve regulation both during and after project development such as converting agricultural land to construction land, filling and blocking watercourses, and using green and forest lands, as well as expropriation and resettlement housing.

区城市管理行政执法部门、街道办事处、镇人民政府按照本办法加强日常执法巡查，开展建设项目违法用地、填堵河道、占用绿地和林地等执法工作。

第十九条 （建设主体责任）

建设主体应当加强项目储备库、实施库阶段的研究，通过优化方案推动资源性指标在项目内实现平衡，减少资源性指标占用，并按照区资源性指标统筹配置部门的要求，上报资源性指标的需求数量和需求计划。

第二十条 （风险防控机制）

区资源性指标统筹配置部门应当严守生态保护红线，规范实施资源性指标统筹配置工作。资源性指标的统筹配置情况，纳入领导干部自然资源资产离任审计。

区资源性指标统筹配置部门应当对资源性指标占补情况开展年度监测评估和统筹周期内中期监测评估，并将评估结果报送区联席会议。区联席会议根据评估结果和实际需求调整区资源性指标储备计划、建设计划和永久基本农田整备区建设实施计划。

区资源性指标统筹配置部门发现指标资源库出现严重隐患的，应当及时提请区联席会议决策，并调整项目建设计划或者终止项目建设。

第二十一条 （纳入绩效考核）

区人民政府对区资源性指标统筹配置部门指标统筹、配置效率以及镇人民政府执行情况进行跟踪督查，并将督查结果纳入该单位的年度绩效考核。

District urban management and law enforcement departments, sub-district offices, and township governments shall increase regular enforcement inspections and enforce regulations against the unauthorized use of land for construction projects, watercourse dredge and fill, and the use of green and forested areas.

Section 19 [Developer Responsibilities]

Developers shall increase research and reviews during project planning and implementation phases, encourage the rational use of resource credits within projects through optimized plans, minimize the unauthorized use of the resource credits, and report resource credit needs and planning details pursuant to the district resource credit planning and allocation department's requirements.

Section 20 [Risk Prevention and Control Process]

The district resource credit planning and allocation department shall enforce strict compliance with ecological protection redlines and regulate resource credit planning and allocation, among others. Resource credit planning and allocation are to be included in audits of natural resource asset administration in connection with leadership transitions.

The district resource credit planning and allocation department shall carry out annual and ongoing monitoring and evaluation of resource mitigation credits during the planning period, reporting the results of such evaluations to the district multi-department coordination group. The district multi-department coordination group shall adjust reserve and development plans for district resource credits and permanent basic farmland based on evaluation results and actual needs.

If the district resource credit planning and allocation department identifies significant risks within the resource reserves, it shall promptly report to the district multi-department coordination group for a decision and adjust or terminate the project development plan or construction as necessary.

Section 21 [Incorporating Performance Evaluations]

The Pudong New Area People's Government shall conduct follow-up oversight and assessments on the district resource credit planning and allocation department's resource credit planning administration and allocation efficiency, as well as the township government's enforcement, incorporating the assessment results into their annual performance evaluation.

第二十二条 （财政保障）

区发展改革、财政部门应当统筹做好建设项目资源性指标资源库资金保障工作。

统筹用于区财力建设项目水系平衡的镇级河道建设成本计入区财力建设项目的前期概算。用于其他投资主体项目水系平衡的区级、镇级河道建设前期费用和工程费用按照投资机制由相关主体分别承担。

统筹用于建设项目补建绿地所发生的前期费用和工程费用计入建设项目前期概算。

因补建林地产生的前期费用和工程费用纳入建设项目前期概算。补建公益林地的后续养护管理和土地流转等费用由区生态环境部门按照区林地管理相关规定执行。

第二十三条 （施行日期）

本办法自 2024 年 3 月 1 日起施行，有效期至 2027 年 12 月 14 日。

Section 22 [Financial Provisions]

The district development and reform department and the finance department shall cooperate to secure financial support for the construction project resource credit reserve.

Watercourse compensation costs for financial development projects within the region are included in the district's preliminary financial development project budgets. Preliminary expenses and construction costs for district and town-level watercourse developments to facilitate investment in other water system compensation projects shall be borne by the appropriate entities based on the investment process.

Preliminary expenses and construction costs for green area compensation related to construction projects are included in the construction projects' preliminary budget estimates.

Similar preliminary expenses and construction costs for forest land compensation shall be included in the preliminary construction project budget estimates, with ongoing management and land transition costs for forest land relocation subject to the applicable forestry management regulations issued by the district ecology and environment department.

Section 23 [Validity Period]

These Procedures shall take effect from March 1, 2024, and remain valid until December 14, 2027.

浦东新区促进存量产业用地提质增效若干规定

Several Provisions of the Pudong New Area on Improving the Quality and Efficiency of Underutilized Industrial Land

浦东新区促进存量产业用地提质增效若干规定

（2022年12月12日浦府管规〔2022〕5号印发）

第一条 目的和依据

为引导产业用地资源高效配置，加快存量产业用地盘活，促进产业高质量发展，根据《中共中央 国务院关于支持浦东新区高水平改革开放打造社会主义现代化建设引领区的意见》《上海市人民代表大会常务委员会关于加强浦东新区高水平改革开放法治保障制定浦东新区法规的决定》以及相关规定，结合浦东新区实际，制定本规定。

第二条 适用范围

本规定适用于促进浦东新区存量产业用地提质增效的各项支持保障及监督管理活动。

本规定所称的存量产业用地，是指通过划拨、出让、租赁、二级市场转让等方式取得的工业、研发及仓储用地。

第三条 基本原则

促进存量产业用地提质增效，应当坚持产业用途、绩效优先、多元参与、市场主导、协同监管的原则。

第四条 推进机制

区政府加强对促进存量产业用地提质增效工作的领导，建立协调推进机制，统筹、协调、决定相关重大事项。

Several Provisions of the Pudong New Area on Improving the Quality and Efficiency of Underutilized Industrial Land

(PGMM [2022] No.5, December 12, 2022)

Section 1 Purpose and Basis

The Several Provisions of the Pudong New Area on Improving the Quality and Efficiency of Underutilized Industrial Land (these "Provisions") are formulated to guide the efficient allocation of industrial land resources, accelerate the revitalization of underutilized industrial land, and advance the high-quality development of industries, pursuant to applicable laws and regulations, including the Opinions of the Communist Party of China Central Committee and State Council on Supporting the High-level Reform and Opening-up to Establish a Pilot Area for Modern Socialism in the Pudong New Area, the Decision of the Shanghai Municipal People's Congress Standing Committee on Formulating Regulations to Improve Law-based Safeguards for High-level Reform and Opening-up in the Pudong New Area, and in light of the actual circumstances in the Pudong New Area.

Section 2 Applicable Scope

These Provisions shall apply to all supportive and regulatory activities aimed at improving the quality and efficiency of underutilized industrial land in the Pudong New Area.

"Underutilized industrial land" in these Provisions refers to industrial or R&D and land designated for warehouses that has been acquired through methods such as allocation, assignment, lease, or secondary market transactions.

Section 3 Basic Principles

Improvements in the quality and efficiency of underutilized industrial land shall follow the principles of industrial usage, prioritizing performance, diverse participation, market orientation, and coordinated regulation.

Section 4 Support Process

The Pudong New Area People's Government shall enhance its leadership role, establish a coordination process, plan, coordinate and make decisions on major issues related to improving the quality and efficiency of underutilized industrial land.

区产业部门负责资源利用效率评价、产业准入标准及监管协议制定、产业项目统筹推进等相关工作。区规划资源部门负责空间规划引导、土地管理、项目落地保障等相关工作。区发展改革部门负责产业发展总体战略制定、综合政策研究等相关工作。区生态环境部门负责推进产业园区规划环评编制、重大产业项目的水系、绿地和林地的资源性指标统筹等相关工作。区国有资产监督管理部门负责协调国有企业参与存量产业用地提质增效等相关工作。

区建设交通、财政、市场监管、应急管理等其他有关部门在各自职责范围内，协同开展相关工作。

管理局（管委会）、镇政府作为辖区内统筹协调的责任主体，负责具体项目的推进实施及监督管理。

第五条 资源利用效率评价及应用

区产业部门会同发展改革、规划资源、生态环境等有关部门，定期组织开展资源利用效率调查，形成优先支持类、鼓励提升类、调整转型类、整治淘汰类的评价结果，为全区促进存量产业用地提质增效工作提供基础支撑。

本区发挥政府配置资源的引导作用，根据资源利用效率评价结果，在产业准入、用地保障、技术改造、能源价格、财税政策、信贷政策等方面，支持优质项目创新发展和提升能级，促进低效项目调整改造和转移腾退。

管理局（管委会）、镇政府结合资源利用效率评价结果，建立本辖区促进存量产业用地提质增效的重点项目库，制定推进计划并加快实施。

The district industrial department takes charge of evaluating resource efficiency, setting industry access standards, providing regulatory guidance, and supporting industrial projects. The district planning and resource department provides guidance on spatial planning, land management, and project support. The district development and reform department is responsible for preparing the overall industry development strategy and carrying out the necessary research on integrated policies. The ecology and environment department takes charge of preparing environmental impact assessments for industrial park planning and planning resource credits for water systems, green space, and forest land in major industrial projects. The district state-owned assets regulatory administration takes charge of coordinating state-owned enterprises to improve the quality and efficiency of underutilized industrial land.

Other competent departments, including but not limited to those for district transportation, finance, market regulation, and emergency management, shall collaborate to carry out the work to the extent of their duties.

Administrative bureaus (or administration committees) and township governments take charge of the overall coordination, implementation, and management of projects within their duties.

Section 5 Assessment of Resource Uses and Utilization Efficiency

The district industrial department shall collaborate with the development and reform, resource planning, and ecology and environment departments to carry out regular assessments of resource utilization efficiency. This involves classifying projects for priority support, recommending improvements, adjustments for transition, or termination, providing fundamental support in support of underutilized industrial land quality and efficiency improvements within the district.

The Pudong New Area shall guide resource allocation, recommend the adjustment, conversion, assignment, or termination of inefficient projects, while supporting innovative development and capacity improvements for high-quality projects in terms of industry access, land use support, technological innovations, energy pricing, fiscal and taxation policies, and credit policies.

Administrative bureaus (or administration committees) and township governments use the resource utilization assessments to create a key project database to enhance and expedite the implementation of initiatives aimed at improving the quality and efficiency of underutilized industrial land in their jurisdictions.

第六条 严格准入管理

区产业部门会同发展改革、规划资源、生态环境等有关部门，落实坚持产业用途要求，按照产业导向和区域规划定位，定期完善促进存量产业用地提质增效的准入标准，坚持以科技论英雄、以亩产论英雄、以效益论英雄、以能耗论英雄、以环境论英雄的绩效导向，强化项目准入审核，将准入条件纳入土地出让合同。

第七条 支持工业上楼新模式

在产业主管部门组织论证可行的前提下，支持未纳入全生命周期管理的存量工业用地项目在签订产业监管协议后，建设功能复合楼宇，形成集生产、研发、中试、展示、销售、配套为一体的综合高效利用的产业空间，可以出租给符合产业导向和区域规划定位的项目。促进存量产业用地提质增效，工业用地容积率不低于 2.0，通用类研发用地容积率不低于 3.0。工业企业工业用地经批准提升容积率不再补缴土地款。

对已纳入全生命周期管理的产业项目类存量工业用地，在开展产业用地绩效评估的基础上，经区政府审核同意后，可以调整为标准厂房类工业用地。

第八条 支持优质低价的标准厂房和通用研发类物业供给

支持国有企业发挥主导带动作用，可以通过收购存量产业项目等方式参与促进存量产业用地提质增效工作。

鼓励国有企业利用自有存量产业用地建设优质低价的标准厂房和通用研发类物业。经批准实施容积率提升而增加使用面积的标准厂房、通用研发类物业，在满足企业自用以外，可以用于支持科技型初创企业入驻，并落实租赁管理要求。

Section 6 Strict Access Management

In collaboration with appropriate departments like the development and reform, planning and resources, and ecology and environment departments, the district industrial department shall strictly implement industrial use requirements and regularly revise access standards to improve the quality and efficiency of underutilized industrial land in accordance with industrial and regional planning directives, prioritizing performance-based criteria, including scientific and technological innovation, yield per acre, economic benefits, energy use, and environmental impact. This department shall improve project access review processes and integrate these standards into land leasehold agreements.

Section 7 Supporting New Urban Manufacturing Models

Projects for underutilized industrial land not covered by complete lifecycle management are encouraged to develop multi-functional buildings that effectively integrate production, R&D, prototype testing, exhibition, sales, and support services into a cohesive industrial space after entering into an industrial regulatory agreement, based on feasibility studies carried out by the jurisdictional industry agencies. This space may be leased to projects that align with industrial and regional planning directives. Industrial land plot ratios for underutilized industrial land quality and efficiency improvement projects must be at least 2.0, and no less than 3.0 for land designated for general R&D. Industrial corporations granted industrial land after being approved for an increased plot ratio shall not be charged additional land fees.

Underutilized industrial land under complete lifecycle management may be reclassified as standard industrial land with the approval of the Pudong New Area People's Government following an industrial land use performance assessment.

Section 8 Support for High-quality, Low-cost Standard Factory Building and General R&D Property Development

State-owned enterprises are encouraged to play a leading role and participate in efforts to improve the quality and efficiency of underutilized industrial land through measures such as acquiring existing industrial projects.

State-owned enterprises are encouraged to develop high-quality, low-cost standard factory buildings and general R&D properties on their own underutilized industrial land. In addition to the organization's own use, these buildings and properties may be designated to technology start-ups subject to administrative regulations after an increase in plot ratio is approved.

第九条 支持节余空间租赁

支持已纳入全生命周期管理的存量产业用地项目的厂房、研发类物业，在满足企业自用以外，经批准后可以出租给科技型初创企业或者孵化器、加速器运营机构，并限定租赁价格。

第十条 支持多元主体参与

支持具有招商资源和运营经验的园区开发运营企业、社会资本等各类市场主体，通过收购、与土地原权利人合作等方式，参与存量产业用地的开发建设、园区的运营管理等活动。

第十一条 支持收储重新出让

区政府可以根据产业发展需要，依法对存量产业用地进行收储，重新进行产业用地出让。

产业用地重新出让价格实行底线管理原则，综合产业政策和项目绩效情况，经集体决策确定产业用地出让起始价，起始价可以低于成本价。

第十二条 支持零星工业用地转型

根据浦东新区产业发展需要，工业用地可以通过补缴土地出让金，经依法批准调整为研发用地。

产业用地土地出让金，经区政府集体决策，可以按照分期方式补缴，最长时间不超过两年，且须在不动产登记前缴清。补缴金额综合考虑土地取得成本、公共要素贡献等因素确定。

第十三条 支持集中成片区域高质量转型

支持管理局（管委会）、镇政府选取成片、相对完整区域的存量产业用地，划定集中成片转型区域，制定实施方案，通过集中收储等方式推进产业高质量发展。

Section 9 Support for the Leasing of Surplus Spaces

Factory buildings and R&D properties on projects under underutilized industrial land complete lifecycle management may lease surplus spaces to technology start-ups or incubator or accelerator operators based on the enterprise's own needs for such spaces and upon approval. Lease prices shall be capped.

Section 10 Encouraging Diverse Participation

Market entities, including but not limited to park development and management companies with investment attraction resources and operation experience, as well as market investors, are encouraged to participate in the development and management of underutilized industrial land and park operations through acquisitions or collaborations with the original leasehold estate holders.

Section 11 Support for Reclaim and Re-leasing

The Pudong New Area People's Government may reclaim underutilized industrial land and re-lease it based on industrial development requirements lawfully.

The new lease price for the industrial land shall follow the principle of threshold management, with the starting price collectively determined based on industrial and project performance, which may be less than the initial cost price.

Section 12 Support for Small-scale Industrial Land Conversions

Industrial land in the Pudong New Area may be converted to R&D land upon approval, subject to industrial development needs and the payment of an additional conversion fee.

Following a collective decision by the Pudong New Area People's Government, the conversion fee for industrial land may be paid in installments, not exceeding two years in duration, and shall be fully settled before the registration of such land. The additional land conversion fee is based on factors like land acquisition cost and elements contributed to the public.

Section 13 Support for the High-quality Conversion of Large Land Areas

Administrative bureaus (or administration committees) and township governments shall receive support in selecting underutilized industrial land in large, generally open spaces, clearly demarcating these areas for conversion, developing an implementation plan, and encouraging high-quality industrial development through centralized land reclaiming, among others.

第十四条　发挥产业监管协议效能

存量产业用地提质增效项目的实施，应当签订产业监管协议并纳入土地出让合同，明确项目的准入类别、投资强度、产出效率、节能环保、履约承诺、投产时间、违约责任等约定事项。

管理局（管委会）、镇政府负责落实项目推进的日常监管，定期对监管协议的履约情况进行核查，并将核查情况报送区产业、规划资源等部门。

第十五条　全生命周期监管

区政府统筹组织各相关部门、管理局（管委会）、镇政府落实全生命周期监管，实行产业用地系统化、精细化和动态化利用管理，对项目在用地期限内的利用状况开展全过程动态评估和监管。

第十六条　部门协同监管

本区建立统一的存量产业用地监管信息系统，将产业用地的指标要求、利用绩效等信息纳入系统，健全信息共享、部门协同的动态监管机制。

加强对涉地股权转让等行为的联合监管，推行企业诚信体系建设。对违反法定义务的失信主体，在项目审批、核准、备案以及融资抵押等方面进行监管。

加强对违规违约用地行为的联动监管，多部门提前介入，从源头上遏制产业用地“用非所用”等情况发生，保障产业用地的产业属性。

第十七条　实施细则

本规定相应支持保障措施的专项实施细则由区政府或者区产业、规划资源等相关工作部门另行制定。

第十八条　施行日期

本规定自 2023 年 1 月 15 日起施行，有效期至 2028 年 1 月 14 日。

Section 14 Effective Use of Industrial Regulatory Agreements

Projects aimed at enhancing the quality and efficiency of underutilized industrial land shall begin with an industrial regulatory agreement, which shall be integrated into the leasehold estate contracts. These agreements shall specify agreed-upon matters such as access categories, investment intensity, output efficiency, energy conservation, environmental protection, performance obligations, production timelines, and liability for non-compliance.

Administrative bureaus (or administration committees) and township governments are responsible for the routine regulation of these projects, regularly reviewing the performance of regulatory agreements, and reporting review findings to the appropriate agencies, including the district industry and planning and resources departments.

Section 15 Whole-life Cycle Regulation

The Pudong New Area People's Government shall coordinate and organize the appropriate departments, administrative bureaus (or administration committees), and township governments to implement systematic, intensive, and dynamic land use management across the entire lifecycle, carry out land use assessments, and regulate land use throughout the term of the project lease.

Section 16 Coordinated Regulation Between Agencies

A general regulatory information system for underutilized industrial land is to be created within the district, incorporating data such as land use metrics and utilization performance. The dynamic regulation process for information sharing and coordination between agencies is to be refined.

Joint regulation of activities such as land equity assignments is to be intensified, and a business credit lookup system be developed. Entities that fail to fulfill their legal project review, approval, filing, and mortgage financing obligations, among others, shall be subject to regulatory action.

Joint regulation of non-compliant land use in violation of land use agreements is to be increased, with multiple departments intervening early to prevent misuse of industrial land from the outset and ensure its industrial features are maintained.

Section 17 Implementation Guidelines

The implementation guidelines detailing the supportive actions outlined in these Provisions shall be developed separately by the Pudong New Area People's Government or other appropriate departments, such as the district industry or planning and resources departments.

Section 18 Validity Period

These Provisions shall take effect from January 15, 2023, and remain valid until January 14, 2028.

浦东新区大宗商品仓单登记中心管理办法
（试行）

Procedures of the Pudong New Area on Bulk Commodities Warehouse Receipts Registration Center (Trial)

浦东新区大宗商品仓单登记中心管理办法（试行）

（2022 年 12 月 26 日浦府管规〔2022〕7 号印发）

第一条　目的与依据

为了建设全国性大宗商品仓单登记中心，提升大宗商品价格影响力，加快推进现代流通方式，增强全球资源配置能力，更好地服务和引领实体经济发展，根据中共中央、国务院《关于支持浦东新区高水平改革开放打造社会主义现代化建设引领区的意见》《关于加快建设全国统一大市场的意见》以及上海市人大常委会《关于加强浦东新区高水平改革开放法治保障制定浦东新区法规的决定》等规定，结合浦东新区实际，制定本办法。

第二条　适用范围

本办法适用于设立于浦东新区的上海大宗商品仓单登记有限责任公司的机构运营以及相关监督管理活动。

第三条　机构定位

浦东新区支持上海大宗商品仓单登记有限责任公司建设大宗商品仓单登记中心（以下简称“仓单登记中心”），发挥全国性大宗商品流通领域基础性平台作用，为大宗商品仓单提供集中登记、查询等相关服务。

第四条　基本原则

仓单登记中心的相关活动，遵循公平自愿、诚实守信、便捷高效、安全可控、风险自担的原则。

Procedures of the Pudong New Area on Bulk Commodities Warehouse Receipts Registration Center (Trial)

(PGMM [2022] No.7, December 26, 2022)

Section 1 Purpose and Basis

The Procedures of the Pudong New Area on Bulk Commodities Warehouse Receipts Registration Center (Trial) (these "Procedures") are formulated to create a national warehouse receipt registration center for bulk commodities to enhance the influence of bulk commodity prices, accelerate the modernization of circulation methods, enhance global resource allocation capabilities, and better serve and advance the development of the real economy, pursuant to the Opinions of the Communist Party of China Central Committee and State Council on Supporting the High-level Reform and Opening-up to Establish a Pilot Area for Modern Socialism in the Pudong New Area, Opinions on Expediting the Development of a National Integrated Market, and Decision of the Shanghai Municipal People's Congress Standing Committee on Drafting Regulations to Improve Rule-based Safeguards for High-level Reform and Opening-up in the Pudong New Area and other applicable provisions, and in light of the actual circumstances in the Pudong New Area.

Section 2 Applicable Scope

These Procedures shall apply to the operation, regulation, and management of Shanghai Bulk Commodity Warehouse Receipt Registration LLC formed in the Pudong New Area.

Section 3 Center Positioning

The Pudong New Area supports the development of Shanghai Bulk Commodity Warehouse Receipt Registration Center LLC's bulk commodity warehouse receipt registration center (the "warehouse receipt registration center") as a foundational platform for national commodity circulation, providing commodity warehouse receipt services, including integrated registration and inquiry.

Section 4 Basic Principles

The warehouse receipt registration center's activities shall follow the principles of fairness, voluntariness, integrity, efficiency, safety, and assumption of risks by participants.

第五条 部门职责

区商务委、区金融局、区市场监管局等相关部门按照各自职责做好仓单登记中心运营活动的相关指导、服务和监督管理工作。

第六条 机构运营条件

仓单登记中心应当具备下列条件：

（一）开展业务活动所必需的营业场所、业务设施、营运资金、专业人员；

（二）健全的法人治理结构；

（三）辐射全国的数字化信息系统平台；

（四）完善的风险管理与内部控制制度；

（五）机构运营所需的其他条件。

第七条 机构运营规则

仓单登记中心应当制定本中心仓单登记、查询等活动运营规则，明确仓单登记流程、业务规则、信誉评价、风险管理、内部控制、商业秘密保护、股东利益回避等内容。

仓单登记中心应当在运营规则制定或者修改完成后 7 个工作日内报送区商务委、区金融局。

第八条 仓单登记信息系统建设

仓单登记中心应当基于区块链等技术建设大宗商品仓单登记信息系统，汇集全国大宗商品仓单登记信息，推进区域间信息互联、互通、互认、共享。

第九条 机构服务内容

仓单登记中心提供下列服务：

（一）仓单注册、流转、更正、注销等登记服务；

Section 5 Department Responsibilities

The district commerce committee, finance department, market regulation administration, and other appropriate departments shall provide guidance, service, and oversight of the operations of the warehouse receipt registration center to the extent of their duties.

Section 6 Operating Conditions of the Center

The warehouse receipt registration center shall maintain:

(1) adequate business premises, equipment, operation capital, and professional employees for business operation;

(2) a robust corporate governance structure;

(3) a comprehensive national digital information system;

(4) an extensive risk management and internal control system; and

(5) all necessary operational requisites for conducting business.

Section 7 Operating Rules of the Center

The warehouse receipt registration center shall develop operational rules governing activities such as warehouse receipt registration and inquiry. These rules shall define the processes for warehouse receipt registration, business protocols, credit evaluation, risk management, internal controls, protection of trade secrets, and procedures for recusal of shareholders in cases of conflicts of interest.

These rules shall be submitted by the warehouse receipt registration center to the district commerce committee and the finance department within seven business days following their creation or any amendments.

Section 8 Development of a Warehouse Receipt Registration Information System

The warehouse receipt registration center shall develop a warehouse receipt registration information system using technologies such as blockchain to compile national bulk commodity warehouse receipt registration data to facilitate data integration, access, recognition, and sharing across different areas.

Section 9 Center Services

The warehouse receipt registration center shall provide the following services:

(1) registration services, such as the registration, assignment, correction, and termination of warehouse receipts;

（二）仓单登记信息的查询服务；

（三）与仓单登记相关的其他服务。

第十条 业务参与主体

下列单位为仓单登记中心的业务参与主体：

（一）存货人、仓单持有人等权利人；

（二）提供仓储服务并签发仓单的仓储企业或者机构；

（三）以仓单为标的进行现货交易的合规交易场所；

（四）提供融资服务的金融机构；

（五）提供商品质量检测的质检机构；

（六）与仓单登记业务相关的其他主体。

第十一条 业务参与主体注册

仓单登记中心应当建立仓单业务参与主体注册目录制度。

业务参与主体应当在仓单登记中心注册，并遵守仓单登记中心相关运营规则。

第十二条 风险管控

仓单登记中心应当采取下列措施，加强仓单登记业务的风险防范和控制：

（一）制定风险防范制度和内部控制制度；

（二）建立技术系统，制定由业务参与主体等各方共同遵守的技术标准和规范；

（三）建立业务参与主体等各方准入标准和风险评估体系；

（四）制定业务应急预案和信息安全应急预案。

第十三条 重要信息报送

仓单登记中心应当向区商务委、区金融局报送以下信息：

(2) inquiry services for warehouse receipt registration information; and

(3) other warehouse receipt services.

Section 10 Business Participants

Business participants in the warehouse receipt registration center include:

(1) right holders such as custodians and warehouse receipt holders;

(2) warehousing entities or organizations that provide storage services and issue warehouse receipts;

(3) legal transaction platforms where spot transactions are based on warehouse receipts;

(4) financial institutions that offer financing;

(5) quality assurance agencies that conduct commodity quality checks; and

(6) other parties involved in warehouse receipt registration.

Section 11 Business Participant Registration

The warehouse receipt registration center shall establish a directory registration system for warehouse receipt business participants.

Participants shall register with the warehouse receipt registration center and comply with its operation rules.

Section 12 Risk Control

To prevent and control risks associated with warehouse receipt registration, the warehouse receipt registration center shall:

(1) develop risk management and internal control systems;

(2) establish technical systems, and technical standards and norms for all parties, including business participants;

(3) create access and risk assessment systems for various parties, including business participants; and

(4) develop emergency response strategies for operation and information security.

Section 13 Reporting Important Information

The warehouse receipt registration center shall report the following to the district commerce committee and the finance department:

（一）年度财务报告、审计报告、市场运行情况分析报告；

（二）年度工作报告、工作计划；

（三）其他需要报送的重要事项。

第一项信息应当于年度结束后 4 个月内报送，第二项信息应当于年度结束后 1 个月内报送，第三项信息应当在合理时间内报送。

第十四条　重大事件报告

遇到下列重大事件或者重大隐患的，仓单登记中心应当在 24 小时内向区商务委、区金融局等部门报告，同时做好后续情况跟踪报告：

（一）仓单登记中心运行过程中发生的重大生产安全事故、网络与信息安全事件；

（二）仓储企业或者机构出现重大经营风险，面临潜在破产清算、重组等风险；

（三）存货人、仓单持有人等权利人的货物被侵占或者挪用；

（四）仓单流转中出现的重大异常事件；

（五）重大的负面舆情、群体性事件、诉讼事项；

（六）其他可能影响市场安全稳定运行、损害相关主体合法权益的重大事件。

第十五条　诚信管理

仓单登记中心应当建立业务参与主体诚信档案，按照规定提供诚信信息查询服务，并依法将相关信息归集至公共信用信息服务平台。

第十六条　相关主体责任

仓单登记中心应当加强自我管理、完善服务机制，引导业务参与主体进行自律管理。

(1) annual financial and audit reports, and market analysis reports;

(2) annual work progress reports and plans; and

(3) other significant matters requiring submission.

The above information (1) shall be reported within four months of year-end, information (2) within one month, and information (3) within a time deemed reasonable.

Section 14 Reporting Critical Incidents

Upon the occurrence of the following critical incidents, the warehouse receipt registration center shall promptly report to the district commerce committee, finance department, and other competent departments within twenty-four hours, and make follow-up reports:

(1) incidents involving critical operational safety, network, or information security risks during the operation of the warehouse receipt registration center;

(2) material operational risks such as bankruptcy, wind-up, or restructuring of warehousing entities or the organizations involved;

(3) encroachment or misappropriation of assets owned by rights holders such as custodians and warehouse receipt holders

(4) material anomalies during warehouse receipt transfer;

(5) material public relations problems, mass incidences, or legal actions; and

(6) other significant events affecting market safety, stability, or the legal rights and interests of the parties involved.

Section 15 Credit Management

The warehouse receipt registration center shall maintain credit records for business participants, provide credit inquiry services as required, and lawfully compile the data into the public credit information service platform.

Section 16 Participant Liability

The warehouse receipt registration center shall manage itself, enhance the service system, and encourage self-regulation among business participants.

仓储企业或者机构应当保证其签发仓单的合法、真实、准确、完整。因仓储企业或者机构原因导致仓单权利人名下仓单相关信息有误或者因保管不善造成仓单对应的仓储物毁损、灭失而产生的损失和法律后果，依法由仓储企业或者机构承担。

第十七条 监督管理

区商务委、区金融局、区市场监管局应当按照各自职责，对仓单登记中心和在仓单登记中心开展业务的单位以及个人进行监督管理。被监管的单位以及个人应当予以配合，如实提供有关文件和资料，不得拒绝、阻碍和隐瞒。

第十八条 施行日期

本办法自2023年2月1日起施行，有效期至2025年1月31日。

Warehousing entities or organizations shall ensure the legality, authenticity, accuracy, and integrity of all warehouse receipts issued, and shall be held liable for any damages or losses incurred to rights holders arising from incorrect information or poor custody of the stored commodities listed in the warehouse receipts if such consequences result from the actions of the warehousing entities or organizations.

Section 17 Supervision

The district commerce committee, finance department, and market regulation administration shall supervise the warehouse receipt registration center and all business entities and individuals conducting business at the warehouse receipt registration center. The entities and individuals under supervision shall cooperate, provide accurate documentation, and not refuse, obstruct, or withhold information.

Section 18 Validity Period

These Procedures shall take effect from February 1, 2023, and remain valid until January 31, 2025.

浦东新区生态空间保护利用若干规定

Several Provisions of the Pudong New Area on the Protection and Utilization of Ecological Spaces

浦东新区生态空间保护利用若干规定

（2022 年 12 月 28 日浦府管规〔2022〕8 号印发）

第一条 目的和依据

为规范土地节约集约利用，进一步加强生态空间要素保护，优化城市生态环境，推动超大城市高质量发展，满足人民高品质生活需求，根据有关法律法规以及《上海市人民代表大会常务委员会关于加强浦东新区高水平改革开放法治保障制定浦东新区法规的决定》等规定，结合浦东新区实际，制定本规定。

第二条 适用范围

本规定适用于浦东新区生态空间保护利用活动及其相关节约集约用地管理工作。

本规定所称生态空间，是指市和区国土空间规划、生态空间专项规划确定的农田、林地、湿地、湖泊河道水系、近郊绿环、生态间隔带、生态走廊、外环绿带、公园绿地、楔形绿地等功能空间。

第三条 总体要求

浦东新区生态空间保护利用应当坚持人与自然和谐共生，坚持生态惠民，以保护生态功能为主，合理开发、科学利用生态空间的各种资源，确保生态空间不减少、生态功能不降低、生态保障不打折。

第四条 管理职责

区政府统筹协调有关部门推进本行政区范围内的生态空间保护利用工作。

Several Provisions of the Pudong New Area on the Protection and Utilization of Ecological Spaces

(PGMM [2022] No.8, December 28, 2022)

Section 1 Purpose and Basis

The Several Provisions of the Pudong New Area on the Protection and Utilization of Ecological Spaces (these "Provisions") are formulated to regulate the efficient and sustainable use of land, enhance ecological space protection, optimize the urban ecology and environment, support high-quality metropolitan development, and fulfill citizen demands for a high-quality life, pursuant to the Decision of the Shanghai Municipal People's Congress Standing Committee on Formulating Regulations to Improve Law-based Safeguards for High-level Reform and Opening-up in the Pudong New Area and other applicable provisions, and in light of the actual circumstances in the Pudong New Area.

Section 2 Applicable Scope

These Provisions shall apply to the protection, utilization, and integrated land use management of ecological spaces in the Pudong New Area.

"Ecological space" in these Provisions refers to functional areas such as farmland, forest land, wetlands, lakes and river systems, suburban green belts, ecological buffer zones, ecological corridors, Outer Ring green belts, park green spaces, and green wedges as determined by municipal and district spatial and ecological space plans and other ad hoc plans.

Section 3 General Requirements

The protection and utilization of ecological space in the Pudong New Area shall pursue harmony between human and nature and ecological benefits, prioritize ecological protection, rationally develop and utilize various ecological space resources to ensure no reduction in ecological space, no diminishment of ecological functions, and no compromise in ecological safeguards.

Section 4 Administrative Responsibilities

The Pudong New Area People's Government coordinates appropriate departments to enhance the protection and utilization of ecological spaces within the administrative areas.

区生态环境部门负责生态空间保护利用项目组织推进、指导和监督工作。

区规划资源部门负责生态空间保护利用的规划和土地管理工作。

区人力资源社会保障部门负责生态空间保护利用项目涉及被征地人员就业和社会保障等工作。

区发展改革、农业农村、建设交通、财政、城市管理综合执法等部门以及区域管理局（管委会）、街道办事处、镇政府应当在各自职责范围内履行相关职能，协同推进生态空间保护利用工作。

第五条　公众参与

浦东新区建立健全生态空间规划、保护、利用、开放和管理的公众参与机制，依法保障公众的知情权、参与权、表达权和监督权。

对涉及生态空间规划、保护、利用、开放和管理的重大事项，区生态环境、规划资源等部门应当采取多种方式，广泛听取公众意见。

第六条　规划引领

生态空间保护利用项目选址应当坚持规划引领，以市和区国土空间规划、生态空间专项规划为依据。

区、镇政府应当根据相关规划，结合生态空间保护利用需求，推动土地资源合理布局、高效利用。

第七条　项目管理

区生态环境部门应当会同区发展改革、规划资源、农业农村等部门，根据市和区国土空间规划、生态空间专项规划等，结合生态宜居、提升重要河湖生态功能等实际，提出生态空间保护利用项目实施清单和年度生态空间保护利用项目实施计划（以下简称“实施计划”），报区政府批准后组织实施。

The district ecology and environment department is responsible for the organization, support, guidance, and regulation of protection and utilization projects in ecological spaces.

The district resource planning department is responsible for planning and land management for the protection and utilization of ecological space.

The district human resources and social security department takes charge of safeguarding the employment and welfare of individuals affected by land expropriation for ecological space protection and utilization projects.

District development and reform, agriculture and rural affairs, construction and transportation, finance, and urban management and enforcement departments, along with zone administrative bureaus (or administrative committees), sub-district offices, and township governments, shall fulfill their obligations to the extent of their duties and collaborate on matters related to ecological space protection and utilization.

Section 5 Public Participation

The Pudong New Area is to enhance processes for public involvement in ecological space planning, protection, utilization, opening, and management to lawfully safeguard citizens' rights to information, participation, expression, and oversight.

The district ecology and environment department and planning and resources department, among others, shall use different methods to actively solicit public opinions on significant matters related to ecological space planning, protection, utilization, opening, and management.

Section 6 Planning Guidance

Site selection for ecological space protection and utilization projects shall comply with existing planning guidance and municipal and district spatial planning and plans for ecological spaces.

District and township governments shall manage and allocate land resources efficiently and rationally based on appropriate planning and ecological space protection and utilization needs.

Section 7 Project Management

The district ecology and environment department shall collaborate with the development and reform, planning and resources, and agriculture and rural affairs departments to develop and annually update a list and plan for the implementation of ecological space protection and utilization projects (the "implementation plan") focused on ecological sustainability and river and lake ecological functionality improvements for approval by the Pudong New Area People's Government, in line with municipal and district space planning and ecological space planning.

第八条 项目实施主体

区政府应当按照公开、公平、公正的原则组织遴选，确定与区域范围内生态空间保护利用要求相适应的单位作为生态空间保护利用项目实施主体（以下简称“项目实施主体”）。

第九条 保护利用方案

项目实施主体应当根据控制性详细规划、专项规划或者郊野单元村庄规划，编制生态空间保护利用方案，并按规定报市、区政府或者相关部门批准后实施。

保护利用方案应当包括以下内容：

（一）保护利用范围及功能定位；

（二）土地现状调查和生态要素现状调查；

（三）土地使用性质的规划控制和调整、自然资源空间优化方案；

（四）生态环境、景观保护与山水林田湖草综合整治要求；

（五）配建公共服务设施有关情况；

（六）集体经济组织及其成员权益保障方案；

（七）其他保护利用内容。

城市更新涉及生态空间保护利用项目的，可以不专门编制保护利用方案，但应当在更新方案中编制生态空间保护利用专章，明确前款规定的相关内容。

第十条 方案编制基本要求

项目实施主体编制生态空间保护利用方案或者生态空间保护利用专章（以下统称“保护利用方案”），应当充分考虑河、湖、林、草、田、湿等生态要素现状，有序引导生态空间内土地用途向有利于生态功能提升的方向转变，提高生态空间的完整性和连通性。

Section 8 Project Implementing Parties

The Pudong New Area People's Government shall conduct an open, fair, and impartial selection process to appoint eligible parties that meet ecological space protection and utilization requirements for managing ecological space protection and utilization projects ("project implementing parties") within the zone.

Section 9 Protection and Utilization Plan

Project implementing parties are required to develop an ecological space protection and utilization plan based on regulatory, detailed, specialized, or rural zoning and village plans, which are subject to the approval of municipal and district governments, or other competent departments prior to implementation.

The protection and utilization plan shall cover:

(1) scope and functions of the protection and utilization;

(2) analysis of the current state of land and ecological elements;

(3) strategies to control and adjust the nature of land use and optimize the spatial allocation of natural resources;

(4) requirements for ecology and environment and landscape protection, and integrated management of mountains, waters, forests, and grasslands;

(5) information on the allocation and construction of public amenities;

(6) compensation plans for collective economic organizations and their members; and

(7) other information related to protection and utilization.

Urban development projects involving ecological spaces shall include a specific chapter addressing the above aspects in their overall development plan rather than creating a separate protection and utilization plan.

Section 10 Basic Requirements for Plan Preparation

Project implementing parties shall comprehensively consider the conditions of existing ecological elements, such as rivers, lakes, forests, grasslands, fields, and wetlands, when preparing ecological space protection and utilization plans or specific chapters to manage the orderly use of land within ecological spaces toward enhancing ecological functions and ensure integrity and connectivity in ecological places.

生态空间内规划设置公共服务设施的，应当与生态环境相协调。

第十一条 保护利用效益

生态空间保护利用应当强化生态敏感区和生态景观等保护，根据生态空间的特点，结合乡村振兴、文化遗产保护、生态清洁小流域治理等工作，满足生态保护、功能匹配、布局合理、风貌协调和安全舒适等要求，提升生态空间保护利用的综合效益。

第十二条 耕地保护

生态空间保护利用应当严格落实永久基本农田保护制度，严格遵守耕地保护规定，严格管控一般耕地转为其他农用地。确实无法避让、需将永久基本农田以外的耕地转为其他农用地的，应当选择质量较低、零星分散、难以长期稳定利用的耕地，并按规定报批。

浦东新区通过持续推进建设用地减量化和一般整理复垦等方式，统筹补充优质耕地资源，确保国土空间规划确定的本行政区域内的耕地数量不减少、质量不降低。

第十三条 差别化土地政策

为进一步优化生态空间布局，改善生态环境，区规划资源部门实行生态空间差别化土地政策时，应当强化用途管制，确保土地性质长期不变。

纳入实施计划的生态空间保护利用项目，确需征收农民集体土地，且实施后用地性质不属于国家规定的建设用地范围的，按照现行法律和政策，落实被征地农民权益保障工作，不办理农用地和未利用地转为建设用地审批手续，由区规划资源部门报区政府办理生态空间保护利用项目边界确认以及用地手续。

Any plans for installing public amenities within ecological spaces shall be designed to complement the surrounding ecological environment.

Section 11 Protection and Utilization Benefits

Ecological space protection and utilization efforts shall prioritize safeguarding ecologically sensitive areas and landscapes by fulfilling ecological protection, functionality matching, aesthetic appeal, and safety and comfort requirements, and supporting rural revitalization and cultural heritage protection and small watershed management initiatives based on the characteristics of the ecological space, thereby maximizing the overall benefits of ecological space protection and utilization.

Section 12 Farmland Protection

Permanent basic farmland protection policies and farmland protection regulations shall be strictly followed, alongside stringent controls over the conversion of general farmland into other types of agricultural land, prioritizing low-quality, fragmented, and unsustainable land if the conversion of permanent basic farmland into other agricultural land is unavoidable, which shall be reported for review as required.

The Pudong New Area focuses on strategically enhancing high-quality farmland by continually reducing construction and general land reclamation activities, ensuring no reduction in both the quantity and quality of farmlands in the administrative area designated by national spatial planning.

Section 13 Differentiated Land Policy

The district resource planning department shall enforce differentiated land use policies for ecological spaces to further improve and optimize the layout of ecological spaces while increasing land use controls to ensure the long-term sustainability of the land.

If the expropriation of collective farmland is necessary to fulfill any ecological space protection and utilization projects outlined in the implementation plan, and the land is not to be converted to nationally designated construction land, the rights of affected farmers are to be protected under applicable laws and policies. Conversion of agricultural and unused land into construction land shall not proceed, and the district planning and resources department shall report to the Pudong New Area People's Government for boundary confirmation and land use procedures for ecological space projects.

为有效保护和科学利用生态空间，确需配建公共服务设施的，应当科学合理确定生态空间内建设活动的规模、强度和布局等，其所占用的农用地、未利用地，应当依法办理农用地和未利用地转为建设用地审批手续。

第十四条 集体经济组织及其成员的权益保障

区政府根据规定对生态空间保护利用项目的征收补偿方案进行论证，并征求被征收人的意见，充分保障被征地集体经济组织及其成员的合法权益。

区政府承担土地补偿费、青苗补偿费、地上地下建筑物及其附着物补偿费、安置补助费以及国家、本市规定的其他费用。

区政府及其相关部门落实被征地集体经济组织成员的房屋征收补偿和社会保障。对有就业需求的，提供有关就业援助政策和服务。鼓励被征地集体经济组织成员参加职业技能培训，按照规定给予培训补贴。

第十五条 开放共享

生态空间应当对社会公众开放，但因重大活动、防汛防台和其他突发事件应急处置等需要临时封闭的除外。临时封闭或者特定时间段封闭生态空间的，应当向社会公布。

项目实施主体可以在生态空间内合理设置漫步道、跑步道等慢行设施以及文化宣传、体育运动等公益性服务设施，营造可漫步、可阅读、有温度的城市生态空间。

第十六条 禁止性行为

项目实施主体应当严格按照保护利用方案开展生态空间保护利用活动，禁止在生态空间内实施下列行为：

（一）改变生态空间用途、功能或者用地性质的；

To effectively protect and reasonably manage ecological spaces, the scale, intensity, and layout of any public amenities built in ecological spaces shall be correctly and appropriately organized. Agricultural and unused lands occupied are subject to review procedures for conversion into construction land lawfully.

Section 14 Protection of Collective Economic Organizations and Members' Rights

The Pudong New Area People's Government shall justify the eminent domain and compensation plans for ecological space protection and utilization projects, seeking feedback from those affected to fully protect the legal rights and interests of the affected collective economic organizations and their members.

The Pudong New Area People's Government shall cover the costs of land compensation, crop compensation, compensation for existing buildings above and below ground and their outbuildings, resettlement subsidies, and other costs designated by national or municipal governments.

The Pudong New Area People's Government and competent departments shall provide compensation for house expropriation and social security for affected collective organization members, as well as offer targeted employment support policies and services as necessary and encourage the affected collective economic organization members to participate in vocational training using training grants provided as required.

Section 15 Openness and Sharing

Ecological spaces shall remain open to the public except during major events, flood control efforts, typhoon prevention efforts, or other emergencies that require temporary closures. Any temporary or specific period closure of ecological spaces shall be announced.

Project implementing parties may install amenities such as promenades and running tracks, as well as public welfare equipment for cultural activities and sports to foster a walkable, educational, and culturally rich urban ecological space.

Section 16 Prohibited Activities

Project implementing parties shall strictly comply with the protection and utilization plan for ecological spaces. The following activities are prohibited:

(1) changes to use, function, or land type of ecological spaces;

（二）擅自改变生态空间主导功能定位的；

（三）实施与生态系统质量提升、生态保护以及修复无关的各类开发活动；

（四）其他擅自改变保护利用方案的行为。

第十七条　智慧管理

浦东新区推动生态空间智慧建设，依托城市运行“一网统管”平台，利用视频监控、物联网监测等技术和网格化管理等方式，综合采集生态环境、安全运行、公共秩序、市容环境、防洪防涝等数据信息，实现集感知、分析、服务、指挥为一体的智慧管理。

第十八条　事中事后监管

区政府建立协同监管机制，相关部门应当加强生态空间保护利用项目的监督管理。

区生态环境部门应当就生态空间保护利用情况定期开展监督检查。

区规划资源部门应当根据土地全域管理、全要素管理和全生命周期管理要求，定期更新生态空间用地信息清单，并就土地利用状况定期开展监督检查。

区城市管理综合执法部门以及街道办事处、镇政府应当按照各自职责加强生态空间用地的日常监管，对土地违法行为责令限期改正，并依法给予行政处罚。

第十九条　行政处分

有关行政管理部门及其工作人员有滥用职权、玩忽职守、徇私舞弊行为的，对直接负责的主管人员和其他直接责任人员依法给予处分。

第二十条　施行日期

本规定自 2023 年 2 月 1 日起施行，有效期至 2028 年 1 月 31 日。

(2) unauthorized modifications to the primary functions of ecological spaces;

(3) development activities that do not enhance ecosystem quality or are not related to ecological protection and restoration; and

(4) other unauthorized actions that conflict with the protection and utilization plan.

Section 17 Smart Management

The Pudong New Area supports the intelligent development of ecological spaces through the integrated online platform for urban operations, using technologies, such as video surveillance, Internet of Things monitoring, and grid management for comprehensive ecological and environmental data collection, operation safety, public security, urban aesthetics, and flood and waterlogging prevention, to achieve smart management integrating perception, analysis, services, and command.

Section 18 Supervision During and After the Process

The Pudong New Area People's Government shall establish a coordinated process for regulation, and competent departments shall improve the oversight and administration of ecological space protection and utilization projects.

The ecology and environment department shall conduct regular monitoring and inspections to ensure the ongoing protection and utilization of ecological spaces.

The district planning and resources department shall regularly update the ecological space land use information list and conduct land use inspections pursuant to district-wide land, comprehensive, and lifecycle management requirements.

The district urban management and enforcement department, sub-district offices, and township governments shall refine processes for the daily regulation of ecological space land use to the extent of their mandate, require violators to correct their actions within a set timeframe, and enforce administrative penalties lawfully.

Section 19 Disciplinary Actions

Any abuse of power, dereliction of duty, or playing favoritism and committing irregularities by administrative departments or their employees shall be subject to disciplinary action taken against individuals directly responsible and others with direct responsibilities.

Section 20 Validity Period

These Provisions shall take effect from February 1, 2023, and remain valid until January 31, 2028.

浦东新区促进劳动人事争议一站式多元解决机制建设若干规定

Several Provisions of the Pudong New Area on Supporting the Development of a Unified Alternative Resolution System for Employment Disputes

浦东新区促进劳动人事争议一站式多元解决机制建设若干规定

（2023年4月26日上海市浦东新区第七届人民代表大会常务委员会第十三次会议通过）

第一条 为了防范化解劳动关系风险、维护劳动者合法权益、构建和谐劳动关系、助力优化营商环境、完善社会治理体系，根据《上海市人民代表大会常务委员会关于加强浦东新区高水平改革开放法治保障制定浦东新区法规的决定》以及相关规定，结合浦东新区实际，制定本规定。

第二条 浦东新区劳动人事争议一站式多元解决机制（以下简称一站式多元解决机制）建设，应当遵循法治引领、源头预防、多元共治、创新发展的原则。

第三条 本规定所称的一站式多元解决机制，是指在张江地区探索形成的“三庭五位”模式基础上建立和完善的基层调解、劳动仲裁、起诉立案、诉讼裁判、强制执行一站式全流程闭环的劳动人事争议解决机制。

第四条 区人力资源社会保障部门、人民法院负责协调推进一站式多元解决机制建设工作，制定相关建设推进计划和工作管理办法。

区司法行政部门、工会等单位应当根据各自职责，共同推进一站式多元解决机制建设工作。

各相关街道办事处、镇人民政府负责推进本辖区一站式多元解决机制建设工作，做好相关的保障工作。

Several Provisions of the Pudong New Area on Supporting the Development of a Unified Alternative Resolution System for Employment Disputes

(Adopted at the 13th Session of the 7th Pudong New Area People's Congress Standing Committee of Shanghai Municipality on April 26, 2023)

Section 1 The Several Provisions of the Pudong New Area on Supporting the Development of a Unified Alternative Resolution System for Employment Disputes (these "Provisions") are formulated to prevent and resolve employment disputes, protect lawful rights and interests of employees, facilitate streamlined employment relationships, support business environment optimization initiatives, and improve the social governance system, pursuant to the Decision of the Shanghai Municipal People's Congress Standing Committee on Formulating Regulations to Improve Law-based Safeguards for High-level Reform and Opening-up in the Pudong New Area and other applicable provisions, and in light of the actual circumstances in the Pudong New Area.

Section 2 The unified alternative dispute resolution system for employment disputes (the "unified alternative dispute resolution system") in the Pudong New Area shall emphasize law-based procedures, focus on prevention, adopt collaborative governance, and encourage innovation.

Section 3 The "unified alternative dispute resolution system" in these Provisions refers to a single comprehensive employment dispute resolution system developed based on the "three channels, five methods" model piloted in the Zhangjiang area, which covers community mediation, employment arbitration, litigation, adjudication, and enforcement.

Section 4 The district human resources and social security department and the people's court take charge of coordinating and advancing the development of a unified alternative dispute resolution system and creating appropriate development plans and management guidelines

The judicial administration and labor unions of the Pudong New Area, and other applicable organizations shall collaborate to advance the development of the unified alternative dispute resolution system to the extent of their duties.

Sub-district offices and township people's governments take charge of developing the unified alternative dispute resolution system in their jurisdictions and facilitating its operation.

各相关管理局（管委会）协同做好所在地区一站式多元解决机制建设的推进和保障工作。

第五条 区人力资源社会保障部门、人民法院应当联合司法行政部门、工会以及相关街道办事处、镇人民政府、管理局（管委会）等单位建立联席会议制度，负责研究完善工作机制、总结推广工作经验、推动统一法律适用等工作，研究并指导解决重大、疑难和群体性矛盾纠纷。

联席会议应当定期召开，由区人力资源社会保障部门、人民法院轮流召集和主持。发生特殊情况或者情况紧急的，经联席会议成员单位提议，应当及时召开临时会议，临时会议可以由提议单位召集和主持。

第六条 浦东新区支持有条件的地区建立劳动人事争议解决工作站（以下简称工作站），推动一站式多元解决机制建设。

街道办事处、镇人民政府可以单独或者联合建立工作站。鼓励地理位置相邻或者处于同一片区的街道办事处、镇人民政府联合建立工作站。

各相关单位可以采取集中进站定点办公或者巡回办公等方式开展工作。

各相关街道办事处、镇人民政府负责建设、提供、维护工作站日常办公、庭审等所需的工作场所和设施设备，并合理配置专业工作人员和志愿服务人员。

第七条 工作站应当按照调解优先、多元解纷、高效便民、案结事了的要求，完善工作流程、提升服务能级。

工作站内的巡回法庭、仲裁庭应当通过组织庭审观摩、公众开放日等形式，推进案件信息和庭审流程公开。

The appropriate administrative bureaus (or administration committees) shall collaborate to support and safeguard the development of the unified alternative dispute resolution system within their jurisdictions.

Section 5 The district human resources and social security department and the people's court shall create a multi-department coordination meeting system between judicial administration, labor unions, sub-district offices, township people's governments, bureaus (or administration committees), and other competent departments to research and refine system operations, summarize and share the best practices, ensure the standardized application of law, and analyze and guide the resolution of significant, complex, and collective disputes.

Multi-department coordination meetings shall be convened regularly with meetings held in a rotation, and chaired by the district human resources and social security department and the people's court. Temporary meeting may be convened by any multi-department coordination meeting member and chaired by the proposing department in exceptional circumstances or emergencies.

Section 6 The Pudong New Area shall support the establishment of dispute resolution centers ("Centers") in eligible areas to advance the development of the unified alternative dispute resolution system.

Sub-district offices and township people's governments may set up such Centers independently or cooperatively, and those located close to each other or in the same area are encouraged to form the Centers cooperatively.

The appropriate departments may operate using joint or circuit offices in Centers.

The responsible sub-district offices and township people's governments support the construction, facilitation, and maintenance of the location, facilities, and equipment necessary for daily operations and trials in the Centers, and for organizing any necessary professionals or volunteers.

Section 7 Centers shall refine their procedures and service capabilities to prioritize mediation, alternative resolution methods, efficient and easy processing, and conclusive dispute resolutions.

The circuit tribunals and arbitration tribunals operating within the Centers shall disclose case details and proceedings by organizing trial observations or open days for the public.

第八条 工作站应当实行全流程一窗受理、首问负责、限期答复等便利化制度。

支持并推动工作站依托信息化建设，开展全流程在线委派委托调解、音视频调解、申请调解协议司法确认等工作。

鼓励有条件的工作站推行线上线下预约制度，为当事人和社区群众进站接受咨询、解决争议等提供便利。

第九条 区人力资源社会保障部门、人民法院应当联合司法行政部门共同制定基层调解工作人员培训计划，探索人才培训创新模式，并以工作站为主要载体开展相关培训工作。

基层调解工作人员经考核合格的，可以由区劳动人事争议仲裁委员会聘任为兼职仲裁员，在工作站参与争议调解仲裁活动。

第十条 工作站应当建设成为劳动人事争议源头预防工作的重要平台、实践基地和创新策源。

区人力资源社会保障部门、人民法院应当联合相关单位定期向社会发布劳动人事争议多元解决情况年度白皮书和典型案例，强化示范引导作用。

区人力资源社会保障、人民法院、司法行政、工会等单位应当加大对劳动密集型企业、初创型小微企业等用人单位的服务指导，促进用人单位增强预防能力，强化民主管理，优化管理制度，畅通申诉渠道，注重协商解决，从源头上减少矛盾纠纷。

第十一条 区人力资源社会保障执法部门应当加强与工作站的工作衔接，并与工作站之间建立群体性纠纷及时通报和违法线索及时移送等机制。

Section 8 Centers shall implement facilitation measures such as unified acceptance, initial contact responsibility, and prompt responses.

Centers shall receive IT support and development to carry out organized or authorized online, audio, and video mediation, and request judicial confirmations of settlement agreements throughout the mediation process.

Eligible Centers are encouraged to implement both online and offline appointment systems to facilitate access for parties and community residents seeking guidance and dispute resolution.

Section 9 The district human resources and social security department and the people's court shall collaborate with the judicial administration to develop a training program for community mediators, refine employee training, and conduct the appropriate training, with the Centers serving as the primary platform.

Qualified community mediators may be appointed as part-time arbitrators by the local employment dispute arbitration committee to conduct mediation and arbitration at Centers.

Section 10 Centers shall develop into pivotal platforms, practice bases, and innovation hubs for preventing employment disputes.

The district human resources and social security department and the people's court shall collaborate with the appropriate organizations to regularly publish annual reports and highlight typical cases on the diversified resolution of employment disputes to improve guidance.

The district human resources and social security department, people's court, judicial administration, labor unions, and others shall provide employers, such as those in labor-intensive businesses and small and micro start-ups, with guidance to develop their capacity to prevent disputes, improve inclusive management, optimize management systems, streamline complaint procedures, emphasize resolution through negotiation, and minimize disputes from their occurrence.

Section 11 The district human resources and social security department's enforcement office shall improve collaboration with Centers, and establish systems for the immediate notification of collective disputes and quick relaying of evidence of violations to Centers

第十二条 区总工会统筹工会劳动关系指导员、法律援助等资源力量，指导和帮助街镇、开发区总工会依法开展参与调解、代理仲裁、代理诉讼等法律服务工作，发挥工会促进和解和稳定劳动关系的作用。

各级工会组织应当积极参与工作站工作，协助开展协商调解，引导劳动者优先采用和解、调解等方式，化解矛盾纠纷。

工作站应当发挥平台作用，支持各级工会组织常态化参与调解、仲裁和诉讼。

第十三条 浦东新区鼓励各类社会力量参与工作站相关工作。

区人力资源社会保障、司法行政、工会等单位应当支持和鼓励用人单位依法设立劳动人事争议调解组织，及时有效解决内部劳动人事争议。

各相关单位应当推动各类劳动人事争议调解组织与工作站建立对接机制，形成工作合力。

第十四条 浦东新区支持市级劳动人事争议仲裁机构以派驻庭、巡回庭等形式在工作站开展相关仲裁活动。

工作站应当为市级劳动人事争议仲裁机构进站开展工作提供服务保障。

第十五条 浦东新区支持区人力资源社会保障、人民法院、司法行政等单位，根据国家和本市有关部门授权，在工作站率先开展劳动人事争议解决程序创新试点工作。

在浦东新区进一步推广和深化一站式多元解决机制建设的，可以根据本地区劳动人事争议案件具体特点和实际情况，对本规定相关机制进行完善和优化。

第十六条 本规定自 2023 年 5 月 1 日起施行。

Section 12 The district labor union federation coordinates resources such as employment relations instructors and legal aid, guide and support labor unions in sub-districts, townships, and development zones to provide legal services like mediation, arbitration, and litigation, and emphasize the role of labor unions in facilitating settlement and stabilizing employment relations.

Labor unions at all levels shall actively participate in Center activities, assist in negotiation and mediation, and encourage employers to resolve disputes through settlement or mediation.

Centers shall also serve as platforms to support labor unions at all levels to participate in routine mediation, arbitration, and litigation.

Section 13 The Pudong New Area encourages participation in Center activities from various non-governmental organizations and the public.

The district human resources and social security department, judicial administration, labor unions, and others shall support and encourage employers to set up internal employment dispute mediation committees to lawfully resolve internal disputes promptly and effectively.

All appropriate departments shall assist in creating an integrated system among the various employment dispute mediation organizations and Centers to facilitate effective collaboration.

Section 14 The Pudong New Area supports municipal-level labor arbitration institutions to arbitrate in Centers using resident or circuit tribunals.

Centers shall facilitate the operations of municipal-level labor arbitration institutions to operate within their premises.

Section 15 The Pudong New Area supports the district human resources and social security department, people's court, judicial administration, and others to innovate employment dispute resolution procedures at Centers, as authorized by the appropriate national and municipal competent authorities.

The implementation of these Provisions may be adapted and refined based on the specific conditions and circumstances of employment disputes within this district as necessary, aiming to further advance and improve the development of the unified alternative dispute resolution system.

Section 16 These Provisions shall take effect from May 1, 2023.

上海市浦东新区免予办理强制性产品认证若干规定

Several Provisions for the Pudong New Area of Shanghai Municipality on the Compulsory Product Certification Exemption Authentication

上海市浦东新区免予办理强制性产品认证若干规定

（2023 年 5 月 30 日浦府管规〔2023〕1 号印发）

第一条（目的依据）

为了推动免予办理强制性产品认证（以下称“CCC 免办”）创新，提升贸易便利化水平，加快新兴产业协同发展，优化营商环境，根据《上海市人民代表大会常务委员会关于加强浦东新区高水平改革开放法治保障制定浦东新区法规的决定》以及相关规定，结合浦东新区实际，制定本规定。

第二条（适用范围）

本规定适用于浦东新区推进 CCC 免办相关管理服务活动。

第三条（免办情形）

有下列情形之一的，产品列入国家市场监督管理总局（以下简称“市场监管总局”）发布的强制性产品认证目录的生产者、进口商、销售商或者其代理人（以下简称“申请人”）可以通过市场监管总局“CCC 免办及特殊用途进口产品检测处理管理系统”向区市场监管局提出 CCC 免办申请：

（一）为科研、测试和认证检测所需的产品和样品；

（二）直接为最终用户维修目的所需的零部件、产品；

（三）工厂生产线、成套生产线配套所需的设备、零部件（不含办公用品）；

（四）仅用于商业展示但不销售的产品；

Several Provisions for the Pudong New Area of Shanghai Municipality on the Compulsory Product Certification Exemption Authentication

(PGMM [2023] No.1, May 30, 2023)

Section 1 [Purpose and Basis]

The Several Provisions for the Pudong New Area of Shanghai Municipality on the Compulsory Product Certification Exemption Authentication (these "Provisions") are formulated to assist in the compulsory product certification exemption authentication (the "CCC Exemption"), improve trade facilitation, speed up the integrated development of emerging industries, and enhance the business environment, pursuant to the Decision of the Shanghai Municipal People's Congress Standing Committee on Formulating Regulations to Improve Law-based Safeguards for High-level Reform and Opening-up in the Pudong New Area, and other applicable provisions, and in light of the actual circumstances in the Pudong New Area.

Section 2 [Applicable Scope]

These Provisions shall apply to the CCC Exemption administration and services in the Pudong New Area.

Section 3 [Criteria for Exemption]

Manufacturers, importers, sellers, or their agents (the "Requesters") whose products are listed in the Mandatory Product Certification Catalogue issued by State Administration for Market Regulation (the "SAMR") may request the CCC Exemption through the district market regulation administration in the SAMR's management system for the CCC Exemption, inspection, and processing of specialized product imports, under any of the following circumstances:

(1) products and samples imported for research, testing, and certification inspection;

(2) products and parts needed directly for end-user maintenance purposes;

(3) necessary equipment and parts for factory operations and complete production lines (office supplies excluded);

(4) products exclusively for commercial display and not for sale;

（五）以整机全数出口为目的进口的零部件；

（六）其他因特殊用途免予办理强制性产品认证的情形。

前款规定的产品取得《免予办理强制性产品认证证明》后，方可进口，并按照申报用途使用。

第四条（情况核实）

申请CCC免办的，申请人应当对申请材料真实性负责，不得弄虚作假。

区市场监管局可以通过资料审查、现场核查等方式对申请人、产品有关情况进行核实。

区市场监管局可以委托符合条件的第三方技术机构对申报的产品是否属于CCC目录内产品进行鉴定。

第五条（便捷通道）

申请人符合信用记录良好、追溯体系完整、CCC免办业务较为频繁等条件的，经区市场监管局认定并报请市场监管总局同意后，可以使用CCC免办便捷通道，享受自愿申报、自我承诺、自助办理的便利。

第六条（重点产业支持政策）

对集成电路、人工智能、生物医药、航空航天等重点产业研发制造企业，提供CCC免办快速办理服务，支持其成为CCC免办便捷通道使用单位。

根据市场监管总局授权，注册在浦东新区，为重点产业提供通关、仓储、运输、配送等端到端服务的供应链企业，可以申请CCC免办；符合条件的，可以使用CCC免办便捷通道。

第七条（特殊用途进口产品检测试点）

根据市场监管总局授权，浦东新区试点开展CCC免办特殊用途进口产品检测工作，经检测合格的产品可以在特定区域内用于生产和使用。

(5) parts for assembling complete equipment intended for export; or

(6) other specific use cases that justify the CCC Exemption.

The above products may only be imported after obtaining a CCC Exemption certificate and shall only be used for the declared purposes.

Section 4 [Verification]

Requesters are responsible for the authenticity of their requesting documentation and shall not engage in fraudulent practices when requesting the CCC Exemption.

The district market regulation administration may verify Requesters and product details through document reviews and on-site inspections.

The district market regulation administration may hire certified third-party technical organizations to confirm whether the declared products are listed in the CCC Catalogue.

Section 5 [Expedited Access]

Requesters with good credit records, comprehensive traceability systems, and frequent participation in the CCC Exemption activities may be eligible for expedited processing. This streamlined process involves voluntary declarations, personal commitments, and independent processing, subject to confirmation by the district market regulation administration and approval by the SAMR.

Section 6 [Supporting Policies for Key Industries]

Streamlined CCC Exemption services shall be provided for manufacturing enterprises conducting research and development in critical sectors such as integrated circuits, artificial intelligence, biomedicine, and aerospace, to support their use of expedited access.

Supply chain enterprises registered in the Pudong New Area and authorized by the SAMR that offer comprehensive services such as customs clearance, warehousing, transportation, and distribution for these key industries may request the CCC Exemption and benefit from expedited access if eligible.

Section 7 [Pilot Program for Products Imported for Specialized Purpose]

The Pudong New Area may implement a pilot program for products eligible for the CCC Exemption that are imported for specialized purposes, authorized by the SAMR, and compliant products may be permitted to be manufactured and used in designated areas.

特殊用途进口产品检测工作由市场监管总局指定的强制性产品认证检测机构承担。

第八条（核销时限）

通过 CCC 免办进口的产品，申请人应当自产品进口之日起 2 年内使用并完成核销。2 年内无法完成核销，且继续使用不存在明显安全隐患的，申请人应当在期满前 1 个月内向区市场监管局提出产品延期使用申请。每批产品延期申请仅限一次。

第九条（资料留存）

申请人应当留存加盖企业印章的申请资料等各类证明性资料，留存期限为 CCC 免办产品完成核销后 2 年。

第十条（数字化服务）

在市场监管总局支持下，浦东新区探索 CCC 免办数字化监管路径，对符合条件的便捷通道企业开放系统接口，试点信息数据的对接与自动核销。

第十一条（信用监管）

区市场监管局可以根据企业信用评价、产品风险评估等情况，对申请人实施分类管理和差异化监管。

第十二条（服务监管协同）

区人民政府建立与海关的沟通协调机制，为便捷通道使用单位 CCC 免办产品进口提供便利。

浦东新区联合长三角地区有关部门开展 CCC 免办协同监管，加快长三角地区 CCC 免办监管结果互认共享。

Inspections of products imported for specialized purposes shall be carried out by mandatory product certification organizations designated by the SAMR.

Section 8 [Verification Period]

Requesters shall complete the verification process for the CCC Exemption products within two years from the date of import. Requesters shall request an extension from the district market regulation administration when verification is not completed within two years and there are no significant safety concerns. The request shall be submitted one month prior to the expiration of the initial verification period, and requests are limited to one per batch of products.

Section 9 [Documentation Retention]

Requesters shall retain all supporting documentation, including request forms stamped with their corporate seal, for two years following the successful verification of the products under the CCC Exemption.

Section 10 [Digital Services]

With the support of the SAMR, the Pudong New Area is to develop digital regulation for the CCC Exemption, which includes providing a system contact for enterprises eligible for expedited access and initiating pilot programs for integrating information and data and automatic verification.

Section 11 [Credit Regulation]

The district market regulation administration shall implement tiered management and differentiated regulation of requesters, taking into account factors such as corporate credit evaluations and product risk assessments.

Section 12 [Service and Regulation Coordination]

The Pudong New Area People's Government is to establish a coordination process with customs to facilitate expedited access for imported products eligible for the CCC Exemption.

The Pudong New Area is to cooperate with competent departments in the Yangtze River Delta region to coordinate the CCC Exemption regulation to improve mutual recognition and results sharing across the region.

第十三条（违规处理）

超过核销期限未完成核销或者经监管发现申请人不符合本规定第三条情形的，由区市场监管局通过暂停免办受理、暂停便捷通道使用等方式予以处理。

第十四条（实施时间）

本规定自 2023 年 7 月 1 日起施行，有效期至 2026 年 6 月 30 日。

Section 13 [Violation Management]

The district market regulation administration shall suspend any processing for requesters and their eligibility for expedited access, and may take other action as necessary if they fail to complete the verification within the specified period, or if they do not meet the exemption criteria provided in Section 3 of these Provisions.

Section 14 [Validity Period]

These Provisions shall take effect from July 1, 2023, and remain valid until June 30, 2026.

浦东新区促进无人驾驶装备创新应用若干规定

Several Provisions of the Pudong New Area on Advancing the Innovative Use of Unmanned Driving Equipment

浦东新区促进无人驾驶装备创新应用若干规定

（2023 年 6 月 29 日浦东新区第七届人民代表大会常务委员会第十五次会议通过）

第一条 为了进一步规范和促进浦东新区无人驾驶装备创新应用，推动智能装备产业高质量发展，保障道路交通安全，根据《上海市人民代表大会常务委员会关于加强浦东新区高水平改革开放法治保障制定浦东新区法规的决定》以及相关规定，结合浦东新区实际，制定本规定。

第二条 本规定适用于在特定道路和区域开展无人驾驶装备测试、运营等创新应用活动以及相关监督管理工作。

本规定所称的无人驾驶装备，是指符合相关技术标准或者规范，通过智能网联系统完成自动驾驶，执行预定任务的低速轮式装备。

第三条 浦东新区无人驾驶装备创新应用活动坚持鼓励创新、包容审慎、循序渐进的原则，实行总量合理控制、分级分类管理，确保安全有序、风险可控。

第四条 浦东新区人民政府应当与中国（上海）自由贸易试验区临港新片区管理委员会（以下简称临港新片区管委会）建立促进无人驾驶装备创新应用的工作机制，在市经济信息化、交通、公安等部门指导下制定配套政策，落实支持措施，并按照各自职责具体负责辖区内的无人驾驶装备创新应用管理工作。

Several Provisions of the Pudong New Area on Advancing the Innovative Use of Unmanned Driving Equipment

(Adopted at the 15th Session of the 7th Pudong New Area People's Congress Standing Committee on June 29, 2023)

Section 1 The Several Provisions of the Pudong New Area on Advancing the Innovative Use of Unmanned Driving Equipment (these "Provisions") are formulated to standardize and advance the innovative use of unmanned driving equipment ("UDE") in the Pudong New Area, support the high-quality development of the intelligent equipment industry, and ensure road safety, pursuant to the Decision of the Shanghai Municipal People's Congress Standing Committee on Formulating Regulations to Improve Law-based Safeguards for High-level Reform and Opening-up in the Pudong New Area and applicable regulations, and in light of the actual circumstances in the Pudong New Area.

Section 2 These Provisions shall apply to the testing, operation, and other innovative activities and regulatory work involving UDE on designated roads and areas in the Pudong New Area.

"Unmanned driving equipment" in these Provisions refers to low-speed wheeled equipment that meets specific technical requirements or specifications, has autonomous driving capabilities through an intelligent network system, and performs pre-configured tasks.

Section 3 The innovative use of UDE shall comply with the principles of encouraging innovation, using inclusive and prudent management, gradual progress, controlled overall volume, and classification management to ensure safety, order, and controllable risk.

Section 4 The Pudong New Area People's Government shall cooperate with the China (Shanghai) Lin-gang Special Area Pilot Free Trade Zone Administration Committee (the "Lin-gang Special Area Administration Committee") to establish a process to advance the innovative use of UDE, develop supporting policies under the guidance of municipal departments, such as economy and information technology, transportation, and public security departments, implement the supporting policies, and regulate the innovative use of UDE innovative to the extent of their duties.

浦东新区科技经济、建设交通、公安、商务、网信、邮政管理、城管执法、市场监管、规划资源、大数据管理以及街道办事处、镇人民政府等部门和单位按照各自职责，做好浦东新区无人驾驶装备创新应用相关管理工作。

第五条 开展无人驾驶装备测试、运营的企业应当申请安全性自我声明的确认。无人驾驶装备经安全性自我声明确认的，可以向公安机关交通管理部门申领识别标牌；取得识别标牌的，可以上道路行驶；经相关主管部门审核同意的，方可从事运营活动。

第六条 申请测试安全性自我声明确认的企业应当符合以下要求：

（一）具有独立法人资格；

（二）具备相关技术能力；

（三）配置符合测试相应条件的装备；

（四）配备远程监控系统和符合本规定第八条要求的紧急接管人员，并建立相应的培训机制；

（五）按照有关规定已经投保或者承诺投保一定金额的商业第三者责任险。

申请运营安全性自我声明确认的企业还应当符合以下要求：

（一）具备配送、清扫、零售等经营业务所需的条件或者能力；

（二）配置符合运营业务条件的装备；

（三）提出固定的运营区域和运营时段；

（四）具有健全的安全管理制度。

企业凭经确认的运营安全性自我声明、有效期内的识别标牌、运营方案以及其他相关材料，向相关部门备案。

The competent departments in technology and economy, construction and transportation, public security, commerce, internet information, postal services, urban management and law enforcement, market regulation, planning and resources, and big data management, as well as sub-district offices and township governments, among others, shall regulate the innovative use of UDE in the Pudong New Area to the extent of their duties.

Section 5 Organizations involved in the testing and operation of UDE shall request a safety commitment review. Upon approval, they may register with the public security department's traffic division to receive an identification badge permitting road operations Additional approvals from the appropriate departments are required for other business operations.

Section 6 Organizations requesting a review of their safety commitment shall:

(1) possess an independent juristic personality;

(2) demonstrate appropriate technical capabilities;

(3) be equipped with appropriate testing equipment;

(4) create remote monitoring systems and employ emergency takeover technicians who meet the training and qualification criteria provided in Section 8 of these Provisions; and

(5) have purchased or committed to purchasing commercial third-party liability insurance covering the amount specified in the applicable regulations.

Organizations requesting safety commitment reviews shall further:

(1) meet the necessary conditions or capabilities for business activities such as delivery, cleaning, or retail sales;

(2) have suitable operational equipment;

(3) designate operating areas and times; and

(4) create a comprehensive safety management system.

Organizations shall register their operations with approved safety commitment reviews, valid identification badges, operational plans, and other related documentation with the appropriate departments.

第七条 申请测试、运营安全性自我声明确认的装备应当符合以下要求：

（一）符合相关测试技术规范规定的一般技术要求、封闭场地测试要求，取得第三方机构出具的相应阶段技术评估报告。

（二）具备数据缓存能力，可以存储规定时长的行驶状态及视频数据。

（三）在非高峰时段上道路行驶；特殊情况应当提出申请，经管理部门同意后方可在高峰时段行驶。

（四）开展配送、清扫、零售等运营活动，申请安全性自我声明确认的装备应当经过规定里程或者时长的测试，且未发生交通违法行为以及因装备原因造成的安全事故。

第八条 创新应用活动配备的紧急接管人员应当符合以下要求：

（一）依法与申请企业或者运营方签订劳动合同或者劳务合同；

（二）熟练掌握道路交通安全法律法规等交通安全知识；

（三）无严重精神类疾病以及其他影响操控安全的疾病；

（四）经培训，熟悉测试规程，掌握无人驾驶装备操控相关知识，具有 50 小时以上无人驾驶系统操作经验，具备紧急状态下应急处置能力，并提交相关证明材料。

第九条 企业可以向浦东新区科技经济部门或者临港新片区管委会提交安全性自我声明和相关证明材料。由浦东新区科技经济部门、临港新片区管委会组织有关部门和专家，对相应阶段的安全性自我声明进行确认并将是否确认的决定书面告知企业。

有关主管部门对安全性自我声明进行确认时，可以将企业在浦东新区以外地区的测试结果作为参考依据，简化相关测试流程和测试项目。

Section 7 Equipment subject to testing and safety commitments shall:

(1) meet the general technical specifications of associated testing technology standards and closed-field testing requirements, supported by third-party technical assessment reports;

(2) have data caching capabilities suitable for storing driving state and video data for specified durations;

(3) operate during off-peak hours, unless the competent department grants approval to operate during peak hours under exceptional circumstances; and

(4) complete testing for a specified mileage or duration on any equipment subject to a safety commitment review intended for services such as delivery, cleaning, and retail sales, maintaining a record free of traffic violations or equipment safety incidents.

Section 8 Emergency takeover technicians involved in innovative use activities shall:

(1) conclude an employment or service contract with the requesting organization or operator lawfully;

(2) possess thorough knowledge of traffic safety laws and regulations;

(3) have no serious mental health conditions or other conditions that may impair safe operations; and

(4) undergo comprehensive training, possess a thorough understanding of the testing process and UDE operations, with a minimum of fifty hours of experience with UDE systems, be skilled in emergency management, and submit documentation supporting their qualifications.

Section 9 Organizations may submit a safety commitment and supporting documentation to the Pudong New Area technology and economic development department or the Lin-gang Special Area Administration Committee for organizing appropriate developments and experts to review and approve the commitment and issue written notice of their decision to the requesting organizations.

Such competent departments may reference the results of tests carried out outside the Pudong New Area to facilitate the testing processes and projects.

第十条　开展无人驾驶装备测试、运营达到规定里程或者时长，且未发生交通违法行为以及因装备原因造成的安全事故，企业可以向浦东新区科技经济部门或者临港新片区管委会提出同一阶段同一型号装备批量申请确认，并提交一致性技术参数、性能和安全检测报告。有关主管部门应当组织第三方机构进行一致性抽查，并根据抽查结果作出决定。

第十一条　企业取得安全性自我声明确认的，可以向浦东新区公安机关交通管理部门提交申领识别标牌需要的有关材料，申领识别标牌。

识别标牌有效期届满的，可以凭有效的安全性自我声明和其他相关材料，申领新的识别标牌。在识别标牌有效期内取得下一阶段安全性自我声明确认的，无需申领新的识别标牌。

第十二条　无人驾驶装备上道路行驶的，应当遵守道路交通安全法律、法规中有关非机动车的通行规定并符合以下要求：

（一）具有显著标识，按照要求悬挂识别标牌。

（二）按照指定的时段、道路和区域行驶。

（三）在专用车道或者非机动车道内行驶；没有专用车道和非机动车道的，靠车行道的右侧行驶。

（四）在专用车道内最高行驶速度不超过 25 公里 / 小时，在其他车道内最高行驶速度不超过 15 公里 / 小时。

（五）在正常情况下禁止借道超车或者临时停车。

（六）不得搭载人员，从事测试活动的不得搭载用于配重以外的货物。

开展无人驾驶装备创新应用的企业应当加强装备远程动态监管。测试阶段，企业应当在现场配备紧急接管人员。在交通高峰、恶劣天气、道路施工、大型活动等情形下，企业应当根据相关管理部门要求及时调整运行计划。公安机关依法实施现场临时管制时，企业应当按照公安机关的指令，立即采取避让、暂停运行、终止运行等处置措施。

Section 10 Upon reaching a certain mileage or duration of testing or operations of UDE with no traffic violations or safety incidents caused by the equipment, organizations may request approval for subsequent use of identical equipment from the same batch and model at the same stage. Requests shall include consistency, performance, and security testing reports, and must be submitted to the Pudong New Area technology and economic department or the Lin-gang Special Area Administration Committee. The competent departments shall carry out consistency sampling inspections in collaboration with third-party organizations and base their decisions on the sampling results.

Section 11 Following the approval of their safety commitment reviews, organizations may request identification badges from the Pudong New Area public security department's traffic division upon submission of the necessary documentation.

Expired identification badges may be renewed subject to the submission of a valid safety commitment and other necessary documents. Organizations need not request a new badge if a safety commitment for subsequent phase safety commitment is submitted and approved within the badge's validity period.

Section 12 UDE operating on roads shall comply with trafic safety laws and regulations applicable to non-motorized vehicles and the following requirements:

(1) display the prominent identification badge as required;

(2) operate only within designated times, roads, and areas;

(3) use dedicated or non-motorized lanes, or the right side of the roadway if such lanes are unavailable;

(4) not exceed 25 km/h in dedicated lanes or 15 km/h in other lanes;

(5) refrain from overtaking or temporary parking under normal circumstances; and

(6) do not carry passengers and other goods not related to load tests during UDE testing phases.

Organizations involved in the innovative use of UDE shall improve remote monitoring of the equipment. Emergency takeover technicians shall be available on-site during testing. In conditions such as traffic congestion, severe weather, road construction, or other significant events, organizations must adjust their plans as required by the appropriate agencies. Organizations are required to comply with any temporary on-site controls issued by the public security department, such as directives for rerouting, suspending, or ceasing operations.

第十三条 浦东新区科技经济部门应当与临港新片区管委会加强对无人驾驶装备运行的日常监督管理，并采取措施强化后台监管。开展无人驾驶装备测试、运营的企业应当按照规定安装监控装置，将相关数据接入指定的数据平台，并定期向浦东新区科技经济部门或者临港新片区管委会提交创新应用情况报告。

开展无人驾驶装备测试、运营的企业对无人驾驶装备进行可能影响装备功能、性能的软件升级（包括远程升级）或者硬件变更的，应当向浦东新区科技经济部门或者临港新片区管委会报告。发生影响装备安全性能的重大升级或者变更的，企业应当提交新的安全性自我声明进行再次确认。

第十四条 开展无人驾驶装备创新应用的企业应当按照网络安全相关法律、法规和信息安全标准的强制性要求，建立网络安全管理制度，落实网络安全等级保护制度，采取技术措施和其他必要措施，提高网络安全保护水平，保障网络安全稳定运行。

开展无人驾驶装备创新应用的企业应当按照数据安全相关法律、法规要求，建立健全全流程数据安全和个人信息保护管理制度，落实数据安全和个人信息保护责任。发生或者可能发生涉及国家安全、个人信息等数据泄露、损毁、丢失等情况的，有关企业应当立即采取补救措施，按照规定及时告知用户并向有关主管部门报告。

开展创新应用过程中收集和产生的重要数据，应当依法在境内存储；因业务需要，确需向境外提供的，应当按照国家和本市有关规定进行安全评估。个人信息数据的出境安全管理，按照国家和本市有关规定执行。

Section 13 The Pudong New Area technology and economic development department shall collaborate with the Lin-gang Special Area Administration Committee to enhance daily oversight of UDE and actively increase backend oversight. Organizations involved in testing and operating UDE shall install monitoring devices, synchronize data with a designated platform, and regularly submit UDE innovative use reports to either the Pudong New Area technology and economic development department or the Lin-gang Special Area Administration Committee.

Organizations shall report any software upgrades (remote upgrades included) or hardware alterations that could affect equipment functionality or performance to the Pudong New Area technology and economic development department or the Lin-gang Special Area Administration Committee. Organizations carrying out upgrades or modifications that significantly impact safety performance shall submit a new safety commitment for approval.

Section 14 Organizations participating in UDE innovative use shall create a network security management system in accordance with mandatory cyber-security laws, regulations, and standards, implement classification management for network protection, and adopt technical and other necessary precautions to improve network security and ensure stable and secure network operations.

Organizations are also required to establish a robust comprehensive data security and personal data protection management system, and comply with data security laws to fulfill their obligations to protect data security and personal information. In the event of a data breach or the damage or loss of data pertaining to national security or personal information, organizations are required to take prompt corrective action, notify affected users, and report the incident to the competent department.

Any significant amounts of data collected or generated through the innovation or use of UDE shall be stored in the Chinese Mainland. Cross-border transfers necessary for business purposes are subject to a security assessment pursuant to national and municipal provisions, and the security of any outbound personal data shall be governed by national and municipal provisions.

第十五条 开展创新应用期间，无人驾驶装备发生故障的，企业应当按照有关技术要求作出判断，及时安排紧急接管人员进行有效处置，采取相应措施降低故障装备对道路交通造成的影响。

创新应用企业应当将相关故障信息传输至指定的监管平台，并保存至少一年。

第十六条 无人驾驶装备在开展创新应用期间发生交通违法行为的，由公安机关按照道路交通安全法律、法规、规章对装备所有人或者管理人进行处理。公安机关依法对装备采取先予扣留等处置措施的，企业应当立即派员现场处置。

开展创新应用期间，无人驾驶装备发生交通事故的，企业应当立即暂停装备运行、开启危险警示装置，报警并派员现场处置；事故发生后两小时内，应当将事故发生前至少九十秒的视频信息上传至指定的数据平台；应当在有关主管部门全程参与下对事故过程进行技术分析并形成事故分析报告。相关事故过程信息和事故分析报告应当及时报送浦东新区公安机关交通管理部门，并保存至少一年。

无人驾驶装备交通事故由公安机关交通管理部门参照道路交通安全法律、法规进行交通事故责任认定。造成损害且依法应由无人驾驶装备一方承担责任的，由该无人驾驶装备所属的企业先行赔偿，并可以依法向负有责任的自动驾驶系统开发者、装备制造者、设备提供者等进行追偿。

无人驾驶装备采集的数据，经公安机关交通管理部门调查核实无误后，可以作为认定交通违法行为和认定交通事故责任的依据。

第十七条 无人驾驶装备测试、运营期间有下列情形之一的，由浦东新区科技经济部门或者临港新片区管委会暂停有关企业的相关创新应用活动，责令其限期整改；完成整改后，方可恢复相关创新应用活动：

Section 15 In the event of a malfunction during the innovative use of UDE, organizations are required to carry out a technical evaluation based on specific technical requirements, promptly direct emergency takeover staff to address the issue, and take appropriate action to minimize traffic disruptions.

Organizations shall upload malfunction data to the designated regulatory platform and store it for at least one year.

Section 16 The public security department shall respond to any traffic violations involving UDE pursuant to applicable traffic safety laws, rules, and regulations. If the public security department's actions require temporary equipment seizure, organizations shall immediately send staff to resolve the issue.

In the event of a traffic accident involving UDE, organizations shall immediately cease operations, activate risk warning devices, report the incident to the police, and send staff to resolve the issue. Organizations shall upload video from at least ninety seconds before the incident to the designated data platform within two hours of the incident, and conduct a technical analysis together with the jurisdictional agency to produce an accident analysis report. Details of the accident and the report shall be promptly submitted to the Pudong New Area public security department's traffic division and retained for at least one year.

Liability for traffic accidents involving UDE shall be determined by the Pudong New Area public security department's traffic division pursuant to applicable road safety laws and regulations. Should any damages be incurred due to unmanned driving, the organization that owns the equipment is required to provide indemnification in advance before filing a claim against any responsible parties, including the autonomous driving system developer, equipment manufacturer, and supplier.

Data collected by UDE may be admitted by the public security department's traffic division as evidence to determine liability in traffic violations and accidents following investigation and verification.

Section 17 The Pudong New Area technology and economic development department or the Lin-gang Special Area Administration Committee may temporarily suspend organization's innovative use of UDE until corrective action is taken within the designated period if:

（一）开展创新应用的企业、装备或者紧急接管人员等发生变化，不再符合规定要求的；

（二）未按照安全性自我声明载明的阶段、时段、路段等开展相关创新应用活动的；

（三）违反载货、作业有关规定的；

（四）未按照规定将相关数据上传至指定的数据平台的；

（五）发生软件升级、硬件变更，未按照规定报告的；

（六）装备发生故障或者交通事故，未按照规定采取相应措施的；

（七）未按照规定传输和保存装备故障、事故信息，或者未提交事故分析报告的；

（八）存在重大软件、硬件系统性缺陷的；

（九）未按照规定履行网络安全、数据安全和个人信息保护义务，或者违反有关法律、法规向境外提供数据的。

开展测试、运营的装备有下列情形之一的，由浦东新区科技经济部门或者临港新片区管委会暂停该装备或者同型号装备的相关创新应用活动，责令其限期整改；完成整改后，方可恢复相关创新应用活动：

（一）未按照要求放置识别标牌的；

（二）违反本规定第十二条第一款第一项、第三项、第四项、第五项规定三次以上，发生一般道路交通违法行为三次以上，或者发生不按照交通信号指示通行、违反标志标线指示、逆向行驶等严重道路交通违法行为的；

（三）发生道路交通事故并承担同等及以上责任的。

第十八条 无人驾驶装备测试、运营期间有下列情形之一的，由浦东新区科技经济部门或者临港新片区管委会终止有关企业的相关创新应用活动，识别标牌失效：

(1) changes impacting compliance with the requirements occur within the organization, equipment, emergency takeover technicians, or other parties involved;

(2) the innovation and use deviates from the phases, periods, and road sections specified in the safety commitment;

(3) regulations on freight transportation and operations are violated;

(4) data is not uploaded to the designated data platform as required;

(5) software upgrades or hardware modifications are not reported as required;

(6) the necessary actions in response to equipment malfunctions or traffic accidents are not taken;

(7) equipment failure or accident data is not transmitted or stored as required, or accident analysis reports are not submitted;

(8) persistent significant software or hardware defects; or

(9) failure to fulfill obligations to protect network security, data security, and personal data, or data is transmitted internationally in violation of applicable regulations.

The Pudong New Area technology and economic development department or the Lin-gang Special Area Administration Committee may suspend innovative use of the equipment or equipment of the same model until corrections are made within the designated period if the equipment:

(1) fails to display an identification badge as required;

(2) incurs three or more violations of Items (1), (3), (4), or (5), Paragraph 12, Section 12 of these Provisions, commits three or more general traffic violations, such as ignoring traffic signals, violating traffic signs and markings, or driving against traffic; or

(3) is involved in a traffic accident and incurs equal or greater liability as the party at fault.

Section 18 The Pudong New Area technology and economic development department or the Lin-gang Special Area Administration Committee may terminate initiatives related to the innovative use of UDE and invalidate badges in the event of any of the following during operation or testing:

（一）暂停创新应用活动后，拒不整改或者经整改仍不符合要求的；

（二）提供虚假的安全性自我声明或者数据、信息、报告等材料的；

（三）发生重大网络安全事件的；

（四）对国家安全、公共安全造成危害，或者程序设计违反伦理要求、存在重大安全风险的。

开展无人驾驶装备测试、运营的装备有下列情形之一的，由浦东新区科技经济部门或者临港新片区管委会终止该装备或者同型号装备的相关创新应用活动；情节严重的，终止有关企业的相关创新应用活动：

（一）发生三次以上不按照交通信号指示通行、违反标志标线指示、逆向行驶等严重道路交通违法行为的；

（二）发生造成人员伤亡并承担同等及以上责任的。

安全性自我声明未经确认或者未取得识别标牌擅自开展相关活动的，由浦东新区科技经济部门或者临港新片区管委会责令立即终止相关活动，并由有关主管部门依法进行处理。

第十九条 鼓励相关行业组织、企业等联合设立风险基金。

鼓励保险公司开发适应无人驾驶装备特点的保险产品。

鼓励企业在厂区、园区、港区等非道路区域开展智能运输设备创新应用。

第二十条 本规定自 2023 年 9 月 1 日起施行。

(1) repeat non-compliance or refusal of corrective actions despite corrective efforts following initial suspension of innovative use;

(2) falsified safety commitments, data, reports, or other documents are submitted;

(3) a significant cybersecurity incident occurs; or

(4) national or public security is adversely impacted, or the program design violates ethical standards or presents significant security risks.

The Pudong New Area technology and economic development department or the Lin-gang Special Area Administration Committee may terminate the innovation and use of the equipment or any equipment of the same model, as well as innovative use by the implicated organizations, under severe circumstances if the equipment involved in testing or operation:

(1) causes three or more severe road traffic violations such as ignoring traffic signals, violating traffic signs and markings, or driving the wrong way; or

(2) causes personal injury or death and incurs equal or greater liability as the party at fault.

The Pudong New Area technology and economic development department or the Lin-gang Special Area Administration Committee may order the immediate termination of unauthorized activities if the safety commitment is deemed invalid or the necessary badge is not obtained, and shall report such matters to the appropriate departments for resolution pursuant to law.

Section 19 Industry associations and enterprises are encouraged to set up joint venture capital funds.

Insurance companies are encouraged to develop products suited to the features of UDE.

Organizations are encouraged to explore innovative uses for intelligent transport systems within non-road areas, such as factories, industrial parks, and ports.

Section 20 These Provisions shall take effect from September 1, 2023.

浦东新区推动进出境生物医药特殊物品监管服务若干规定

Several Provisions of the Pudong New Area on Facilitating the Regulation and Administration of Specialized Biopharmaceutical Products Imports and Exports

浦东新区推动进出境生物医药特殊物品监管服务若干规定

（2023 年 9 月 8 日浦府管规〔2023〕2 号印发）

第一条　（目的和依据）

为了便利企业利用进出境高风险生物医药特殊物品，提升企业生物安全控制能力，促进浦东新区生物医药产业高质量发展，根据《上海市人民代表大会常务委员会关于加强浦东新区高水平改革开放法治保障制定浦东新区法规的决定》以及相关规定，结合浦东新区实际，制定本规定。

第二条　（适用范围）

本规定适用于浦东新区生物医药企业利用进出境高风险生物医药特殊物品（以下简称“特殊物品”）开展研发、生产、使用以及相关监管服务活动。

第三条　（基本原则）

对生物医药企业开展监管服务活动应当遵循企业自律、政府监管、安全可控、便捷高效的原则。

第四条　（监管服务机制及其成员单位职责）

区人民政府统筹建立监管服务机制，与海关监管形成联动。监管服务机制成员单位包括区商务委、科经委、卫生健康委、市场监管局、生态环境局、公安分局、城管执法局以及相关管理局（管委会）、街道办事处和镇人民政府等单位。

Several Provisions of the Pudong New Area on Facilitating the Regulation and Administration of Specialized Biopharmaceutical Products Imports and Exports

(PGMM [2023] No.2, September 8, 2023)

Section 1 [Purpose and Basis]

The Several Provisions of the Pudong New Area on Facilitating the Regulation and Administration of Specialized Biopharmaceutical Products Imports and Exports (these "Provisions") are formulated to support enterprises involved in the import and export of high-risk specialized biopharmaceutical products, enhance biosecurity controls, and facilitate the high-quality development of the biopharmaceutical industry in the Pudong New Area, pursuant to the Decision of the Shanghai Municipal People's Congress Standing Committee on Formulating Regulations to Improve Law-based Safeguards for High-level Reform and Opening-up in the Pudong New Area and other applicable provisions, and in light of the actual circumstances in the Pudong New Area.

Section 2 [Applicable Scope]

These Provisions shall apply to the research and development, production, and use of high-risk specialized biopharmaceutical products ("specialized products") intended for import or export by enterprises in the Pudong New Area, including related regulatory activities.

Section 3 [Basic Principles]

The regulation of biopharmaceutical enterprises shall follow the principles of corporate self-regulation, government oversight, security under controllability, ease of use, and efficiency.

Section 4 [Regulatory Process and Member Department Responsibilities]

The Pudong New Area People's Government shall coordinate the creation of a regulatory process to operate alongside customs regulation. The regulatory process shall comprise member departments such as the district commerce committee, technology and economy commission, healthcare commission, and market regulation administration, as well as the ecology and environment department, district public security branches, urban management and law enforcement departments, and other competent departments including administrative bureaus (or administration committees), sub-district offices, and township people's governments.

区商务委应当会同监管服务机制成员单位，搭建监管服务平台、设立专家库、受理企业申请、组织开展综合评估以及其他监管服务活动。

监管服务机制成员单位依据各自职责，对生物医药企业开展相关监管服务活动。

第五条 （监管服务机制专家库）

监管服务机制设立专家库，专家名单由成员单位依据各自职责推荐并定期更新。

专家库成员参与综合评估并出具专家意见。

第六条 （监管服务平台）

监管服务机制建立监管服务平台，实行信息化管理，建立健全重大事件预警和应急处置机制。监管服务平台应当采集以下信息：

（一）企业申请综合评估的相关材料；

（二）特殊物品进出境和物流运输的过程记录；

（三）特殊物品研发和生产的过程记录；

（四）监管服务机制成员单位事中事后监管的相关记录；

（五）其他应当采集的信息。

第七条 （综合评估申请条件）

企业符合下列条件的，可以通过监管服务平台提交综合评估申请：

（一）因开展生物医药研发、生产、使用活动需要在浦东新区利用特殊物品；

（二）具有良好的信用记录，近两年未受到刑事处罚和严重行政处罚，未被列入经营异常名录、严重违法失信名单和失信被执行人名单；

The district commerce committee shall, in collaboration with other regulatory process member departments, create a regulation platform, and expert registry, process enterprise requests, and organize integrated assessments and other regulatory activities.

Member departments shall be responsible for overseeing biopharmaceutical enterprises to the extent of their duties.

Section 5 [Regulatory Expert Registry]

Regulatory export registry members shall be appointed by the member departments to the extent of their mandate, and the registry shall be updated regularly.

Expert registry members shall participate in integrated assessments and provide expert opinions.

Section 6 [Regulation Platform]

The regulation platform for the regulatory process shall implement IT-based management and maintain robust processes for early warnings and emergency responses to major events. The regulation platform shall collect:

(1) documentation submitted by enterprises for integrated assessments;

(2) records of the import, export, and transport of specialized products;

(3) records of the research, development, and production of specialized products;

(4) records of regulatory activities carried out before, during, and after regulatory process member activities; and

(5) other information subject to regulation.

Section 7 [Conditions for Integrated Assessment Requests]

Enterprises may submit requests for integrated assessments through the regulation platform if they:

(1) require the use of specialized products within the Pudong New Area for biopharmaceutical research and development, production, or use;

(2) maintain good credit records without any history of criminal or serious administrative penalties, or being enrolled into its lists for unusual operations, violations, or willful defaults;

（三）在浦东新区设有二级或者二级以上病原微生物实验室，具备与申报内容相匹配的业务规模、研发技术和项目经验；

（四）具备完善的生物安全和风险管理制度以及在研发、生产、运输、贮存和处置等环节与特殊物品相适应的生物安全控制能力；

（五）建立可全流程追溯的信息管理系统，并有专人负责特殊物品管理工作；

（六）具有 1 年以上的特殊物品进出境经验。

第八条 （综合评估）

监管服务机制成员单位应当对企业是否具备申请条件提供指导和服务。

区商务委应当组织专家对符合条件的企业及进出境特殊物品开展风险评估，专家名单应当从监管服务机制专家库中随机抽取。

监管服务机制根据风险评估结果，出具相应生物安全控制能力的综合评估意见。

第九条 （通关便利）

企业通过综合评估的，可以依法享受海关通关便利。

第十条 （物流运输管理）

企业应当在特殊物品物流运输过程中采用封签方式保证全程封装完好，在运输开始和结束节点对包装完整性进行核对检查，并保存记录。

涉及高致病性或者疑似高致病性病原微生物菌（毒）种、样本的物流运输管理，应当按照国家有关规定执行。

(3) operate level two or higher pathogenic microorganism laboratories in the Pudong New Area, with suitable business scale, technology, and experience;

(4) have robust biosafety and risk management systems and biosafety control capabilities for research, development, transport, storage, and disposal;

(5) develop an information traceability management system for specialized products and designate employees; and

(6) have at least one year of experience in managing imports and exports of specialized products.

Section 8 [Integrated Assessment]

Regulatory process member departments shall guide and assist enterprises in evaluating their eligibility for the requests.

The district commerce committee shall select experts from the regulatory process expert registry without prejudice to carry out risk assessments of eligible enterprises and the specialized products to be imported or exported.

An integrated assessment opinion on biosafety control capabilities is issued by the regulatory process based on the results of these risk assessments.

Section 9 [Customs Clearance Assistance]

Enterprises that pass the integrated assessment may benefit from customs clearance assistance pursuant to law.

Section 10 [Logistics Management]

Enterprises shall use seals when transporting specialized products to ensure packaging integrity, and inspect and record packaging integrity both at the beginning and end of transportation.

The transportation of highly pathogenic or suspected highly pathogenic microbial strains (or viruses) and samples shall be subject to applicable national laws.

第十一条　（研发和生产管理）

企业应当建立特殊物品入库、存储、取样、生产制备、包装、出库、场内运输、废弃物处理等关键环节的风险控制措施，明确责任部门和责任人员，并定期进行生物安全管理培训、演练和自我评估。

第十二条　（追溯管理）

企业应当全程使用特殊物品追溯系统，在完成特殊物品进出境申请后与监管服务平台进行对接，保证特殊物品批号、批记录等信息的一致性，确保物流运输、研发、生产过程可追溯。

第十三条　（生物安全管理）

企业应当严格按照病原微生物实验室标准、环境和职业健康安全管理等规定，建立健全生物安全管理体系，规范研发和生产活动，保障生物安全。

第十四条　（其他监管措施）

监管服务机制成员单位应当及时将企业行政处罚信息上传至监管服务平台。

企业主动披露或者监管服务机制成员单位在监管过程中首次发现企业存在生物安全管理以外问题，且企业在规定期限内完成整改的，不影响该企业特殊物品利用。

企业存在下列情形之一的，监管服务机制告知企业原综合评估意见失效，并向海关通报：

（一）在规定期限内无法按照要求完成整改的；

（二）不再符合本规定第七条规定条件的；

（三）违反本规定第十条至第十三条规定的。

第十五条　（施行日期）

本规定自 2023 年 10 月 15 日起施行，有效期至 2028 年 10 月 14 日。

Section 11 [Research, Development, and Production Management]

Enterprises shall implement risk controls for key processes involving specialized products, such as inventory entry, storage, sampling, production preparation, packaging, outbound shipping, on-site transportation, and disposal, designate responsible departments and employees, and carry out regular biosafety training, drills, and internal reviews.

Section 12 [Traceability Management]

Enterprises shall utilize the specialized product tracing system throughout the entire process, which shall be integrated with the regulatory platform following the submission of a specialized item import and export request to ensure that all specialized product details, such as the batch number and record numbers, are consistent, and to ensure traceability throughout transportation, research, and production.

Section 13 [Biosafety Management]

Enterprises shall establish a robust biosafety management system in strict compliance with pathogenic microbial lab standards, environment, and occupational health and safety regulations to regulate research, development, and production activities, and to ensure biosafety.

Section 14 [Other Regulatory Activities]

Member departments shall promptly upload any administrative penalties imposed upon enterprises to the regulatory platform.

If an enterprise voluntarily discloses issues or if regulatory process member departments discover issues beyond the enterprises' biosafety management for the first time and these are corrected within the specified period, the enterprise's use of specialized products shall not be affected.

The regulatory process shall inform the enterprise of the invalidation of the original assessment opinions and report to customs if an enterprise:

(1) fails to take corrective action within the specified period;

(2) no longer meets the conditions provided in Section 7 of these Provisions; or

(3) violates Sections 10 through 13 of these Provisions.

Section 15 [Validity Period]

These Provisions shall take effect from October 15, 2023, and remain valid until October 14, 2028.

浦东新区景观照明管理若干规定

Several Provisions of the Pudong New Area on the Administration of Landscape Lighting

浦东新区景观照明管理若干规定

（2023年10月25日浦府管规〔2023〕3号印发）

第一条　（目的和依据）

为了规范浦东新区景观照明管理，展示夜间景观形象，推动绿色低碳转型和文旅经济高质量发展，根据《上海市人民代表大会常务委员会关于加强浦东新区高水平改革开放法治保障制定浦东新区法规的决定》以及相关规定，结合浦东新区实际，制定本规定。

第二条　（适用范围）

本区行政区域内景观照明的建设、运行、维护及其相关监督管理活动，适用本规定。

本规定所称景观照明是指利用建（构）筑物以及广场、公园、公共绿化等公共场所（以下简称“载体”）设置的，以装饰、造景为目的的户外人工光照。

本规定所称景观照明设施是指用于景观照明的器具以及配电、集中控制、监控、节能等系统的设备和附属设施。

本规定所称设置者是指景观照明设施的设置主体，包括建（构）筑物、公共场所的所有权人、使用权人或者经营管理单位。

第三条　（总体要求）

浦东新区景观照明管理，遵循规划先行、政府引导、社会参与、部门协同、分类管理的原则。

Several Provisions of the Pudong New Area on the Administration of Landscape Lighting

(PGMM [2023] No.3, October 25, 2023)

Section 1 [Purpose and Basis]

The Several Provisions of the Pudong New Area on the Administration of Landscape Lighting (these "Provisions") are formulated to regulate the administration of landscape lighting in the Pudong New Area, showcase the night landscape, and support the transition to a low-carbon economy and the high-quality development of the cultural and tourism economy, pursuant to the Decision of the Shanghai Municipal People's Congress Standing Committee on Formulating Regulations to Improve Law-based Safeguards for High-level Reform and Opening-up in the Pudong New Area and other applicable provisions, and in light of the actual circumstances in the Pudong New Area.

Section 2 [Applicable Scope]

These Provisions shall apply to the construction, operation, maintenance, and regulation of landscape lighting in this administrative area.

"Landscape Lighting" in these Provisions refers to outdoor artificial illumination installed on buildings (or structures), structures, squares, parks, public green spaces, and other public spaces ("Installation Locations") for decorative and urban green space purposes.

"Landscape Lighting Equipment" in these Provisions refers to the devices used for Landscape Lighting, as well as the system equipment and supporting facilities for electrical power distribution, centralized control, monitoring, and energy conservation

"Installer" in these Provisions refers to the entities responsible for installing Landscape Lighting Equipment, including the owner, user, or operator of buildings (or structures) or public places.

Section 3 [General Requirements]

The administration of Landscape Lighting in the Pudong New Area shall comply with the principles of planned development, guidance by government, public participation, collaboration among departments, and classified management.

浦东新区应当依据景观照明规划和相关规定开展绿色低碳照明工作，制定照明节能目标，严格控制景观照明的范围、亮度和能耗，确保景观照明设施安全运行。鼓励设置者使用节能环保的景观照明新技术、新材料、新工艺、新产品。

第四条 （职责分工）

本规定所称管理单位，包括区绿化市容部门和街道办事处、镇人民政府以及管理局（管委会）。

区绿化市容部门负责全区景观照明的指导、协调、监管以及区管景观照明设施的建设、管理工作。

街道办事处、镇人民政府以及管理局（管委会）在区绿化市容部门的指导下，按照各自职责承担辖区内景观照明的日常巡查、监督以及景观照明设施的建设、管理工作。

区发展改革、财政、规划资源、建设交通、市场监管、生态环境、商务、文体旅游、科技经济、公安、应急管理、城管执法等部门按照各自职责，协同实施本规定。

第五条 （规划实施方案）

区绿化市容部门应当会同规划资源、建设交通、商务、文体旅游等部门组织编制本辖区的景观照明重要区域、重要单体建（构）筑物的规划实施方案，经区人民政府批准后，报市绿化市容部门备案。

街道办事处、镇人民政府以及管理局（管委会）可以编制辖区内相关区域以及相关单体建（构）筑物景观照明设计方案，报区绿化市容部门备案。

The Pudong New Area shall implement low-carbon lighting practices pursuant to the Landscape Lighting plans and applicable rules, set energy conservation targets, strictly control the scope, brightness, and energy consumption of the lighting, and ensure the safe operation of the equipment. Installers are encouraged to adopt new, energy-efficient and environmentally friendly technologies, materials, processes, and products.

Section 4 [Assignment of Responsibilities]

"Administrative Parties" in these Provisions refer to the district landscaping and city appearance administration, sub-district offices, township people's governments, and administrative bureaus (or administration committees).

The district landscaping and city appearance administration is responsible for guiding, coordinating, and regulating Landscape Lighting throughout the district, as well as developing and managing the Landscape Lighting Equipment under the district.

Sub-district offices, township people's governments, and administrative bureaus (or administration committees), under the district landscaping and city appearance administration's guidance, are responsible for daily inspection, regulation, development, and administration of the Landscape Lighting Equipment within their jurisdictions, to the extent of their duties.

The district development and reform, finance, planning and resources, construction and transportation, market regulation, ecology and environment, commerce, culture, sports and tourism, technology and economy, public safety, emergency management, urban management and law enforcement departments shall cooperate to implement these Provisions to the extent of their duties.

Section 5 [Implementation Plan Development]

The district landscaping and city appearance administration shall develop the implementation plans for key Landscape Lighting areas and standalone buildings (or structures) in collaboration with the planning and resources, construction and transportation, commerce, and culture, sports and tourism departments to be filed with the municipal landscaping and city appearance administration upon the approval of the district people's government.

Sub-district offices, township people's governments, and administrative bureaus (or administration committees) may develop Landscape Lighting designs for specific areas or standalone buildings (or structures) for submission to the district landscaping and city appearance administration.

核心区域、重要区域、重要单体建（构）筑物的景观照明设施应当按照规划、规划实施方案和技术规范、标准设置。

第六条 （景观照明设施建设主体）

景观照明设施由下列单位或者个人设置：

（一）与载体配套建设的景观照明设施新建、改建、扩建的，由载体的建设单位设置，配套景观照明设施应当与主体工程同时设计、立项、施工、验收和投入使用；

（二）既有载体上景观照明设施新建、改建、扩建的，由既有载体的所有权人、使用权人或者经营管理单位设置；

（三）除上述情形外，管理单位认为确需设置景观照明设施的，经区人民政府批准后，由管理单位设置。

第七条 （土地供应要求）

按照规划和规划实施方案，核心区域、重要区域内应当设置照明的，区绿化市容部门应当在建设用地使用权出让征询时，明确景观照明设置要求、监管部门和违约责任，由区规划资源部门纳入建设用地使用权出让合同。

第八条 （景观照明设施新改扩建要求）

按照规划和规划实施方案，核心区域、重要区域内应当设置景观照明的建（构）筑物、公共场所，以及重要单体建（构）筑物进行新建、改建、扩建的，设置者应当按照景观照明设置要求，同步设计景观照明。区规划资源部门在审核建设工程设计方案时，应当就景观照明是否符合规定，征求区绿化市容部门的意见。

Landscape Lighting Equipment in key or important areas, or significant standalone buildings (or structures), shall be set up pursuant to planning, approved implementation plans, technical specifications, and required standards.

Section 6 [Parties Responsible for Landscape Lighting Equipment Development]

Landscape Lighting Equipment shall be set up by the following entities or individuals:

(1) the site developer may set up, refurbish, or expand Landscape Lighting Equipment to support the Installation Locations, coordinating design, approval, construction, and use concurrently with the main installation project;

(2) the owner, user, or operator of existing Installation Locations may set up, refurbish, or expand the Landscape Lighting Equipment; and

(3) in addition to the above circumstances, the Administrative Parties may install Landscape Lighting Equipment with the approval of the district people's government when deemed necessary.

Section 7 [Land Supply Requirements]

The district landscaping and city appearance administration shall determine the Landscape Lighting requirements, regulatory departments, and penalties for violations when negotiating leasehold assignments for construction land in key or important areas requiring Landscape Lighting Equipment based on overall planning or implementation plan requirements, which shall be recorded in the leasehold contract for the construction land by the district planning and resource department.

Section 8 [Requirements for Landscape Lighting Equipment Installation, Refurbishment, and Expansion]

Installers shall design Landscape Lighting for buildings (or structures), public places, and major standalone buildings (or structures) in key or important areas included in overall planning and approved implementation plans that require the installation, refurbishment, or expansion of Landscape Lighting Equipment, based on the applicable installation requirements. The district planning and resources department shall solicit the district landscaping and city appearance administration's opinions on compliance during reviews of installation plans.

按照规划和规划实施方案，核心区域、重要区域内既有建（构）筑物、公共场所，以及重要单体建（构）筑物的景观照明，设置者需要进行新建、改建、扩建的，应当按照景观照明设置要求形成景观照明设计方案，区绿化市容部门应当为设置者提供指导；管理单位认为应当进行新建、改建、扩建的，设置者予以配合，管理单位应当与设置者协商一致，形成符合条件的景观照明设计方案。

第九条　（设施建设监管要求）

景观照明设施应当根据以下情形办理手续和实施监管：

（一）景观照明设施的载体新建、改建、扩建的，配套景观照明设施纳入主体工程，办理施工许可或者开工备案手续，主体工程的质量安全监督机构应当对主体工程及配套景观照明设施的建设进行监督管理。

（二）既有载体上景观照明设施新建、改建、扩建的，设置者应当及时书面通知区绿化市容部门，区绿化市容部门应当对景观照明设施的建设进行监督管理。

设置者应当严格按照景观照明相关技术规范、标准组织施工，工程施工质量应当符合相关专业规范、标准。

第十条　（竣工验收要求）

景观照明设施应当根据以下情形开展竣工验收：

（一）景观照明设施的载体新建、改建、扩建的，由主体工程的行业监督管理部门牵头发起工程建设项目综合竣工验收，区绿化市容部门应当将景观照明设施是否符合设置要求和设计方案，纳入竣工验收内容；

（二）既有载体上景观照明设施新建、改建、扩建的，由区绿化市容部门牵头开展竣工验收。

Installers shall prepare a Landscape Lighting design in line with the installation requirements for existing buildings (or structures), public places, and major standalone buildings (or structures) that require the installation, refurbishment, or expansion of the Landscape Lighting Equipment in key or important areas, with assistance from the district landscaping and city appearance administration. Installers shall cooperate and reach an agreement with the Administrative Parties to ensure compliant Landscape Lighting designs for installations, refurbishments, or expansions deemed necessary by the Administrative Parties.

Section 9 [Equipment Installation Regulatory Requirements]

Procedures and regulatory enforcement of Landscape Lighting Equipment shall be subject to the following:

(1) When installing, renovating, or expanding a Landscape Lighting Equipment Installation Location, the supporting Landscape Lighting Equipment shall be included as part of the main project when requesting construction permits or completing filing procedures to commence construction; the main project's quality and safety inspectors shall also oversee the construction of the principal project and the supporting Landscape Lighting Equipment.

(2) Installers shall promptly inform the district landscaping and city appearance administration in writing before installing, renovating, or expanding Landscape Lighting Equipment at an existing Installation Location, and such administration shall oversee the installation of the Landscape Lighting Equipment.

Installers shall strictly comply with applicable technical standards during installation, and project quality shall meet the applicable specifications and standards.

Section 10 [Project Completion Acceptance Requirements]

Landscape Lighting Equipment installations shall be subject to acceptance as follows:

(1) The industry regulatory department overseeing the main project shall carry out an acceptance inspection in case of the installation, refurbishment, or expansion of Landscape Lighting Equipment. The district landscaping and city appearance administration shall assess whether the Landscape Lighting Equipment complies with the installation requirements and the design plans, and incorporate its findings into the overall acceptance inspection.

(2) The district landscaping and city appearance administration shall take charge of acceptance inspections for Landscape Lighting Equipment installed, refurbished, or expanded at existing Installation Locations.

第十一条 （维护管理要求）

景观照明设施由设置者负责日常运行和维护管理。设置者应当按照相关规定履行维护管理责任，保持景观照明设施安全、整洁、完好、美观。

设置者应当对景观照明设施进行安全检查，确保景观照明设施符合技术规范，安全运行。管理单位应当按照技术规范进行安全检测抽查，设置者应当予以配合。

区绿化市容部门会同区发展改革、财政等部门制定政策，对核心区域、重要区域内以及重要单体建（构）筑物的景观照明予以电费补贴。

第十二条 （集中控制分级管理及要求）

区绿化市容部门应当建立并完善区级景观照明集中控制系统。相关管理局（管委会）应当按照规划在区级城市副中心建立区域分控点，接入区级景观照明集中控制系统。

区级景观照明集中控制系统对所纳入的景观照明的开启关闭、照明模式、整体效果等实行统一控制。重大活动保障期间，区域分控点应当遵守区绿化市容部门的控制要求。

设置者应当按照规划和规划实施方案，在管理单位指导下，将景观照明设施分别纳入市级、区级景观照明集中控制系统以及区域分控点，并按照管理单位要求启闭景观照明设施。

如遇高温、暴雨、大风及冰雪严寒等极端天气或者重大活动保障期间，设置者应当遵守管理单位的控制要求。

Section 11 [Maintenance and Management Requirements]

Installers shall be responsible for the routine operation and maintenance of the Landscape Lighting Equipment. Installers shall perform maintenance duties in compliance with applicable provisions to ensure that the Landscape Lighting Equipment is safe, clean, intact, and visually appealing.

Installers shall perform safety inspections to ensure safe operation and compliance with technical standards, and cooperate with any safety sampling checks carried out by the Administrative Parties based on the technical standards.

The district landscaping and city appearance administration shall develop policies for electricity subsidies for Landscape Lighting in key or important areas or major standalone buildings (or structures) in cooperation with the district development and reform and finance departments.

Section 12 [Centralized Control System Administration and Requirements]

The district landscaping and city appearance administration shall develop and improve a centralized control system for Landscape Lighting for its jurisdiction. Appropriate administrative bureaus (or administration committees) shall establish branch control sites in district urban centers pursuant to the plan, to connect to the district's centralized Landscape Lighting control system.

The district centralized Landscape Lighting control system is to be used to centrally manage the activation, deactivation, lighting modes, and effects of all Landscape Lighting. During major events, the branch control sites shall operate in compliance with any control requirements mandated by the district landscaping and city appearance administration.

Installers shall be assisted by the Administrative Parties to ensure that the Landscape Lighting Equipment connects to both branch control site systems and municipal and district Landscape Lighting centralized control systems pursuant to the approved implementation plans. Landscape Lighting Equipment shall be turned on or off pursuant to the Administrative Parties' requirements.

Installers are required to comply with the Administrative Parties' control requirements in the event of extreme weather, such as high temperatures, rainstorms, gales, freezing weather, or other material events.

第十三条 （网络安全要求）

区绿化市容部门、相关管理局（管委会）应当加强对区级景观照明集中控制系统的网络安全管理，定期对集中控制系统的效能和安全性开展自查，提出安全管理结构、技术和网络的改进措施，防止集中控制系统被非法入侵、篡改数据或者非法利用。

区公安部门应当加强对管理单位网络安全工作的指导，定期开展督导检查，发现安全隐患的，通知相关单位及时整改。

第十四条 （临时迁移、拆除、占用要求）

因建设工程施工或者其他原因确需临时迁移、拆除、占用景观照明设施的，建设单位应当制定临时迁移、拆除、占用方案和恢复方案，并与设置者签订协议，明确双方权利义务后进行施工。

未经设置者同意擅自迁移、拆除、占用景观照明设施的，设置者有权依法要求建设单位承担相应法律责任。

第十五条 （施行日期）

本规定自 2023 年 12 月 1 日起施行，有效期至 2028 年 11 月 30 日。

Section 13 [Cybersecurity Requirements]

The district landscaping and city appearance administration and appropriate administrative bureaus (or administration committees) shall improve cybersecurity management for the centralized Landscape Lighting control system, carry out regular efficiency and safety reviews, recommend improvements for security management systems, technology, and networks, and prevent unauthorized access, data tampering, or non-compliant use of the centralized control system.

The district public security department shall improve guidance related to the Administrative Parties' cybersecurity work, carry out regular oversight and inspections, and promptly notify the appropriate departments of the need for corrective action due to a safety hazard.

Section 14 [Temporary Relocation, Removal, and Occupation Requirements]

The developer shall prepare temporary plans for the relocation, removal, occupation, and restoration of any Landscape Lighting Equipment that needs to be temporarily relocated, removed, or occupied due to construction projects or other reasons, and enter into an agreement with the installer to specify the rights and obligations of both parties before commencing any operations.

The installer is entitled to hold the developer liable for any relocation, removal, or occupation of the Landscape Lighting Equipment carried out without the consent of the installer.

Section 15 [Validity Period]

These Provisions shall take effect from December 1, 2023, and remain valid until November 30, 2028.

浦东新区促进法律服务业高质量发展若干规定

Several Provisions of the Pudong New Area on Facilitating the High-quality Development of the Legal Services Industry

浦东新区促进法律服务业高质量发展若干规定

（2023 年 11 月 14 日浦府管规〔2023〕4 号印发）

第一条 （目的和依据）

为了促进法律服务业高质量发展，加快构建适应开放型经济发展的法律服务体系，建设上海国际法律服务中心核心承载区，保障上海“五个中心”建设，根据《上海市人民代表大会常务委员会关于加强浦东新区高水平改革开放法治保障制定浦东新区法规的决定》以及相关规定，结合浦东新区（以下简称“新区”）实际，制定本规定。

第二条 （适用范围）

本规定适用于登记在新区的法律服务机构及其从业人员所开展的法律服务和相关促进活动。

本规定所称的法律服务，是指为满足各类主体维护合法权益、排除不法侵害、防范法律风险等需求而提供的专业服务，包括由律师、公证、仲裁、调解、司法鉴定、域外法查明等法律服务机构及其从业人员以法律知识和技能提供的服务。

第三条 （基本原则）

促进法律服务业高质量发展，应当坚持党建引领、市场主导、政府引导、开放创新、包容审慎的原则。

第四条 （部门职责）

区司法行政部门负责相关法律服务业的指导、管理、监督等工作，统筹推动法律服务业各项支持措施制定实施。

Several Provisions of the Pudong New Area on Facilitating the High-quality Development of the Legal Services Industry

(PGMM [2023] No.4, November 14, 2023)

Section 1 [Purpose and Basis]

The Several Provisions of the Pudong New Area on Facilitating the High-quality Development of the Legal Services Industry (these "Provisions") are formulated to facilitate the high-quality development of the legal services industry, accelerate the development of a legal services system suitable for an open economy, establish Shanghai's core area as an international legal services hub, and safeguard the development of the Shanghai Five-hub strategy, pursuant to the Decision of the Shanghai Municipal People's Congress Standing Committee on Formulating Regulations to Improve Law-based Safeguards for High-level Reform and Opening-up in the Pudong New Area, and other applicable provisions, and in light of the actual circumstances in the Pudong New Area.

Section 2 [Applicable Scope]

These Provisions shall apply to the provision of legal services and related supporting activities by legal service providers and their practitioners registered within the Pudong New Area.

"Legal services" in these Provisions refer to professional services aimed at protecting legal rights and interests, redressing unlawful torts, and mitigating potential legal risks. These services are provided by legal service providers and their practitioners, relying on their legal knowledge and expertise in areas such as law practice, notarization, arbitration, mediation, forensic identification, and foreign law ascertainment.

Section 3 [Basic Principles]

Support for the high-quality development of the legal services industry shall comply with principles of Party leadership, market orientation, government guidance, openness, innovation, prudence, and inclusivity.

Section 4 [Department Responsibilities]

The judicial administration of the Pudong New Area takes charge of the guidance, administration, and regulation of the legal services industry, as well as the development and implementation of support policies for the legal services industry.

区发展改革、商务、公安、财政、税务、金融、人力资源社会保障、市场监管等部门按照各自职责协同做好法律服务业的管理和服务工作。

第五条 （支持律师事务所发展）

吸引全国知名律师事务所在新区落户或者设立分所。

鼓励律师事务所通过在长三角以及全国设立分所等方式，推动专业化、规模化、品牌化发展。

鼓励律师事务所通过出资设立、并购、联营、合作、合同授权等方式在世界主要经济体和“一带一路”沿线国家、地区设立分支机构，或者与境外法律服务机构、从事外向型经济的中国企业开展相关业务合作。

第六条 （支持境外律师事务所开展业务）

支持符合条件的境外律师事务所通过以下方式提供法律服务：

（一）境外知名律师事务所在新区开设代表处；

（二）外国律师事务所与中国律师事务所在新区特定区域设立联营办公室；

（三）香港、澳门特别行政区律师事务所与内地律师事务所在新区开展合伙联营。

第七条 （探索律师特许创新）

建立境外法律服务人才引进机制，依据国家和市有关考核执业许可规定，吸引具有境外律师执业资质并具有较强实战能力的法律服务人才在新区从事律师职业。

鼓励律师事务所聘用符合条件的外籍律师担任外国法律顾问。

根据国家部署，依法、稳步、审慎探索符合条件的境内注册会计师、税务师、注册造价工程师、专利代理师等其他专业人员成为特殊的普通合伙律师事务所的合伙人。

District development and reform, commerce, public security, finance, taxation, finance, human resources and social security, and market regulation departments shall cooperate to effectively manage and support the legal services industry to the extent of their duties.

Section 5 [Facilitating Law Firm Development]

Efforts are to be made to attract nationally renowned law firms to set up their headquarters or branches in the Pudong New Area.

Law firms are encouraged to set up offices in the Yangtze River Delta and nationwide to advance their professional development, scale, and brand.

Law firms are encouraged to expand internationally into major economies and Belt and Road countries through investments, mergers, joint ventures, partnerships, contractual agreements, or by partnering with international legal services agencies or with Chinese organizations operating internationally.

Section 6 [Supporting International Law Firm Operations]

Eligible international law firms may offer legal services as follows:

(1) renowned international law firms may set up representative offices in the Pudong New Area;

(2) international law firms and local law firms may set up joint ventures in designated areas of the Pudong New Area; and

(3) law firms from the Hong Kong Special Administrative Region and Macao Special Administrative Region may form partnerships with law firms in the Chinese Mainland based in the Pudong New Area.

Section 7 [Pursuing Innovation in Access to Justice]

The Pudong New Area is to develop a process to attract specialized legal practitioners with international experience. International legal professionals with significant legal expertise and practice experience are encouraged to practice law in the Pudong New Area pursuant to national and municipal licensing regulations.

Law firms are encouraged to employ eligible foreign attorneys as legal consultants.

Lawful, steady, and prudent research shall be conducted to allow eligible professionals in the Chinese Mainland, such as certified public accountants, tax agents, certified cost engineers, and patent agents to become limited liability partners in law firms in line with the national plan.

第八条　（促进公证创新）

支持公证机构开展运营机制改革与探索，拓展更多公证事项实现“跨省通办”，打造集成式、一站式的标准化公证法律服务平台。

支持公证机构通过网络视频通话、生物识别、证件核验、电子签名等方式，开展海外远程公证事项和事务的办理。鼓励公证机构在人工智能、生物医药、集成电路等新型领域拓展业务，参与区块链存证等新兴公证领域的行业标准制定。

第九条　（支持仲裁发展）

支持本市仲裁机构落户新区，或者在新区设立专业性仲裁工作平台。支持境外知名仲裁机构在新区依法设立业务机构或者代表处。

根据国家授权，配合市司法行政部门探索在新区登记的涉外商事纠纷当事人自主约定在新区内，适用特定仲裁规则，由特定仲裁人员对有关争议进行仲裁。

第十条　（促进国际商事调解发展）

支持在新区建立国际商事调解组织，健全与国际调解规则相衔接的商事调解机制。鼓励法律服务机构及其从业人员参与国际商事调解，支持聘请律师、仲裁员、法学专家等专业人员担任国际商事调解机构的调解员。

支持境外知名调解机构在符合监管要求条件下，在新区依法设立业务机构。

第十一条　（推动司法鉴定规范发展）

区司法行政部门应当加强司法鉴定管理，支持声像资料和环境损害司法鉴定机构有序健康发展。鼓励司法鉴定行业优化基础资源配置，提升技术更新迭代能力，提高服务质量。

Section 8 [Supporting Notarial Innovation]

Notarial service providers are encouraged to reform their operational processes and expand cross-provincial resolution of notarial matters by developing integrated and standardized notarial legal service platforms.

Notarial service providers are also supported to engage in international notarization services through online video calls, biometric recognition, identity verification, or electronic signature, expanding their services into emerging fields such as artificial intelligence, biomedicine, and integrated circuits, and participating in setting industry standards for emerging notarial areas including blockchain notarization.

Section 9 [Supporting Arbitration Development]

Arbitration institutions in this Municipality are encouraged to register or set up specialized arbitration platforms in the Pudong New Area. Internationally renowned arbitration institutions are also encouraged to set up branches or representative offices within the Pudong New Area.

The Pudong New Area explores initiatives based on the national authorization and the collaboration of the municipal judicial administration to allow parties involved in international commercial disputes to select specific arbitration rules and designated arbitrators in the Pudong New Area.

Section 10 [Supporting the Development of International Commercial Mediation]

International commercial mediation organizations are encouraged to operate in the Pudong New Area. Efforts shall be made to enhance the commercial mediation system to align with international arbitration standards. Legal service providers and their practitioners are encouraged to participate in international commercial mediation, receiving support to allow lawyers, arbitrators, and legal experts to serve as mediators for these organizations.

Renowned mediation organizations outside the Chinese Mainland are permitted to set up offices in the Pudong New Area, subject to regulatory requirements.

Section 11 [Advancing the Well-regulated Development of Forensic Identification]

The judicial administration of the Pudong New Area shall improve the administration of forensic identification and facilitate its orderly and professional development in areas such as audio and visual data and environmental damage. The forensic identification sector is encouraged to improve resource allocation, technological upgrading, and service quality.

第十二条　（建设浦东国际法律服务集聚区）

支持构建全链条法治机构集聚、法律功能集约共享的国际法律服务集聚区，推动法律服务业全链条融合发展。

建设以法律科技为特色的国际法律服务集聚区，吸引境内外法律科技机构和专业服务机构集聚。鼓励法律服务机构与科技企业、高等院校合作共建、创新策源，孵化培育法律科技、法律智库等新业态。

第十三条　（支持举办高端法律论坛）

支持举办以“陆家嘴法治论坛”为代表的各类高端法律论坛、研讨会等交流对话活动，聚焦全球法律服务业发展热点和前沿问题，开展制度型开放创新探索，加强与境内外法律服务机构、行业组织的交流合作。

第十四条　（健全法律服务行业组织）

吸引各类法律服务行业组织向新区倾斜工作力量和资源供给。建立健全区律师行业自律组织，以党建为引领，发挥其在自律管理、人才培养、权利保障、对外交流中的作用。

支持法律服务行业组织和专业机构对标国际法律服务业发展水平，结合新区法律服务业发展状况，建立评价模型和评估体系，打造法律服务业的“浦东指数”。

第十五条　（倡导公益法律服务）

倡导法律服务机构及其从业人员发挥专业优势，开展公益法律服务，自觉承担社会责任。推动律师事务所按照相关规定规范会计核算，如实将律师参与公益法律服务的执业成本计入相应会计科目，规范申报成本抵扣。

Section 12 [Creating an International Legal Services Zone in the Pudong New Area]

An international legal services zone is to be established to consolidate comprehensive legal service providers and functions to facilitate the integrated development of the legal services industry.

This international legal services zone shall feature legal technologies to attract both international and domestic legal tech agencies and other professional services. Legal service providers are encouraged to collaborate with technology companies and universities to boost original innovation, including legal technology and think tanks.

Section 13 [Assisting Leading Law Forums]

The Pudong New Area supports leading law forums, seminars, and other discussion events, such as the Lujiazui Rule of Law Forum, to focus on and address development issues in the global legal services industry, explore openness and innovation at the institutional level, explore the openness and innovation in the system, and enhance collaborations with both domestic and international legal service providers and industry associations.

Section 14 [Improving Legal Services Industry Associations]

Efforts shall be made to attract various legal services industry associations to contribute their expertise and resources to the Pudong New Area. Self-regulated organizations shall be formed among attorneys, with Party development being a priority, to further develop their roles in self-regulation, professional training, rights protection, and international exchanges.

Legal services industry associations and professional organizations are encouraged to develop evaluation models and assessment systems to create the Pudong Index for the legal services industry, aligning with the development of the global legal services industry and considering the current state of the legal services industry in the Pudong New Area.

Section 15 [Encouraging *Pro Bono* Legal Services]

Legal service providers and their practitioners are encouraged to provide *pro bono* legal services, using their expertise to fulfill social responsibilities. Law firms are required to accurately record the costs of lawyers' *pro bono* services in their accounting records and regulate the reporting of cost deductions.

第十六条 （引进培养法律服务人才）

新区应当加大对境内外高层次法律服务人才的引进和培养力度，按照规定提供人才落户、安居等保障；推动为符合条件的外籍法律服务人才提供出入境和停居留等服务便利。

建立专业领域法律服务人才库，实行分类动态管理。探索建立青年法律服务人才在新区法治部门担任专职法务助理制度。探索在境外法律服务机构建立培训基地，定期组织涉外法律服务人才赴基地开展业务培训。

第十七条 （提供出入境便利）

对临时来新区参加仲裁、调解等法律活动的相关外籍人员，可由经备案的法律服务机构按照规定在浦东新区口岸代为申请口岸签证，享受口岸签证便利。

第十八条 （提供跨境收支便利）

支持符合条件的银行在“展业三原则”基础上，凭收付款指令直接为符合条件的法律服务机构办理其业务范围内的跨境贸易人民币结算业务以及资本项目跨境人民币收入、外汇收入及其结汇所得人民币在境内的支付使用。符合条件的法律服务机构外籍从业人员可开立多币种自由贸易账户。

对来新区参加仲裁、调解等法律活动的外籍仲裁员、调解员凭相关机构出具的文书，或者对法律服务机构长期聘任的外籍从业人员，凭外国人工作许可证明，由相关法律服务机构或者外籍从业人员本人按照有关外籍人才薪酬购付汇的规定办理外汇业务，享受购汇便利。

第十九条 （资金支持）

区人民政府相关职能部门应当对法律服务集聚区建设、符合条件的法律服务机构和人才发展给予支持。

Section 16 [Attracting and Developing Legal Service Professionals]

The Pudong New Area shall intensify efforts to attract and develop legal service professionals, ensuring support for household registration and housing as required. Eligible foreign legal professionals may benefit from preferential entry/exit, stay and residency policies.

A dynamic list of legal service professionals is to be created and managed through classification. Efforts shall be made for young legal service professionals to serve as full-time legal assistants in the legal departments within the Pudong New Area, establish a training center with international legal service providers, and regularly organize training at training bases for professionals specializing in international legal services.

Section 17 [Facilitating Exit and Entry]

Registered legal service providers may, on behalf of foreign nationals temporarily involved in arbitration, mediation, or other legal activities in the Pudong New Area, request port visas at the Pudong New Area port to facilitate their entry and exit.

Section 18 [Facilitating Cross-border Payments]

Eligible banks are to be supported to directly process cross-border Renminbi transactions, capital project Renminbi incomes, foreign exchange earnings, and the utilization of Renminbi from foreign exchange transactions, following the principles of Know Your Customer, Know Your Business and Due Diligence. Foreign practitioners working for eligible legal service agencies may open a free debit account in multiple currencies.

Foreign arbitrators and mediators involved in legal services such as arbitration and mediation in the Pudong New Area, or foreign practitioners employed by legal service providers long-term may perform currency exchanges with their work permits through the legal service providers or themselves based on regulations governing foreign national remittances to facilitate foreign exchange purchases.

Section 19 [Financial Support]

The appropriate functionaries of the Pudong New Area People's Government shall support the development of a legal services zone, eligible legal service providers, and professionals.

支持在新区设立法律服务业发展基金，接受社会捐赠，为推动新区法律服务业高质量发展提供资金支持。

第二十条 （施行日期）

本规定于 2023 年 12 月 15 日起施行，有效期至 2028 年 12 月 14 日。

Support shall be extended to set up a development fund for the legal services industry in the Pudong New Area, which accepts donations to provide financial support for the high-quality development of the legal services industry in the Pudong New Area.

Section 20 [Validity Period]

These Provisions shall take effect from December 15, 2023, and remain valid until December 14, 2028.

浦东新区小微企业法律帮扶若干规定（试行）

Several Provisions of the Pudong New Area on Legal Assistance for Small and Micro Enterprises (Trial)

浦东新区小微企业法律帮扶若干规定（试行）

（2023 年 12 月 21 日浦府管规〔2023〕5 号印发）

第一条 （目的依据）

为进一步加大法律帮扶供给，提高小型和微型企业（以下简称“小微企业”)合规经营能力,更好保障小微企业合法权益,优化法治化营商环境,根据《上海市人民代表大会常务委员会关于加强浦东新区高水平改革开放法治保障制定浦东新区法规的决定》以及相关规定,结合浦东新区实际,制定本规定。

第二条 （小微企业法律帮扶概念）

本规定所称小微企业法律帮扶，是指浦东新区探索建立的为符合条件的小微企业无偿提供法律咨询、代理等法律服务的制度，是公共法律服务体系的拓展和延伸。

小微企业的认定标准，按照《中小企业划型标准规定》执行。

个体工商户、农民专业合作社等组织的法律帮扶参照本规定执行。

第三条 （职责分工）

区人民政府加强对小微企业法律帮扶工作的领导，统筹推进小微企业法律服务创新和发展。

区司法行政部门负责指导、监督小微企业法律帮扶工作，制定相关措施。区相关公共法律服务机构负责受理、审查小微企业法律帮扶申请，选派律师等法律帮扶人员提供法律服务，向法律帮扶人员支付相关补贴。

Several Provisions of the Pudong New Area on Legal Assistance for Small and Micro Enterprises (Trial)

(PGMM [2023] No.5, December 21, 2023)

Section 1 [Purpose and Basis]

The Several Provisions of the Pudong New Area on Legal Assistance for Small and Micro Enterprises (Trial) (these "Provisions") are formulated to boost legal assistance, ensure small and micro enterprises ("SMEs") operate in compliance with applicable regulations, protect their lawful rights and interests, and create an optimal legal environment for business, pursuant to the Decision of the Shanghai Municipal People's Congress Standing Committee on Formulating Regulations to Improve Law-based Safeguards for High-level Reform and Opening-up in Pudong New Area and other applicable provisions, and in light of the actual circumstance in the Pudong New Area.

Section 2 [Definition of Legal Assistance for SMEs]

"Legal assistance for SMEs" in these Provisions refers to legal services, including free legal advice and representation, provided for eligible SMEs as part of the expanded public legal service system.

The criteria for determining SMEs follow the established guidelines from the Small and Medium Enterprises Classification.

Legal assistance shall be provided to entities, including sole proprietorships and farmers' professional cooperatives pursuant to these Provisions.

Section 3 [Assignment of Responsibilities]

The Pudong New Area People's Government shall lead and improve legal assistance services for SMEs and facilitate the development and innovation of these services.

The judicial administration of the Pudong New Area takes charge of guiding and overseeing SME legal assistance and developing the related policies. Public legal service providers in the Pudong New Area handle applications from SMEs, assign lawyers and legal assistance providers, and provide subsidies for their services.

区发展改革、财政、人力资源社会保障、市场监管、知识产权等部门以及有关单位，应当在各自职责范围内为小微企业法律帮扶工作提供便利。

区律师行业自律组织应当指导和支持律师事务所、律师参与小微企业法律帮扶工作。

第四条 （申请条件）

小微企业同时符合下列条件的，可以申请法律帮扶：

（一）在本区登记设立并经营的；

（二）小微企业及其法定代表人、实际控制人合规、诚信经营的；

（三）生产、经营过程中合法权益受到侵害，因经营困难不能承担市场化法律服务费用的；

（四）设立时间在三年以内的。

专精特新、区重点产业领域的小微企业申请法律帮扶的，可以不受前款第四项设立时间限制。

第五条 （帮扶形式）

区公共法律服务机构可以组织法律服务机构和人员提供下列形式的法律帮扶服务：

（一）合规经营、合同文本、纠纷解决等方面的法律咨询；

（二）法律知识讲座等法治培训；

（三）民商事纠纷调解；

（四）本市争议处理机关（机构）管辖的民商事诉讼、商事仲裁代理，知识产权类案件可以不受本市争议处理机关（机构）管辖的限制。

第六条 （申请和审查程序）

小微企业符合本规定第四条申请条件的，可以向区公共法律服务机构提出法律帮扶申请。

The Pudong New Area departments including but not limited to reform and development, finance, human resources and social security, market regulation, and intellectual property shall facilitate the legal assistance for SMEs to the extent of their duties.

The Pudong New Area legal professional organizations shall support and guide law firms and lawyers participating in this assistance program.

Section 4 [Application Requirements]

SMEs may apply for legal assistance if:

(1) they are registered and operate within this district;

(2) they and their representatives by operation of law and ultimate controllers operate lawfully and honestly;

(3) they face operational difficulties and cannot afford market-based legal service fees due to an infringement against their legitimate rights and interests during production and operations; and

(4) they have been formed within the last three years.

SMEs in specialized or key sectors may apply for legal assistance services regardless of their formation duration under Item (4).

Section 5 [Assistance Methods]

Public legal service providers in the Pudong New Area may employ legal service providers and practitioners to provide:

(1) legal advice on compliance, contracts, and dispute resolution;

(2) legal training sessions such as lectures;

(3) mediation for civil and commercial disputes; or

(4) agency in civil and commercial litigation and commercial arbitration, under the jurisdiction of dispute resolution authorities (or organizations) within this Municipality, and agency in intellectual property cases that may not be subject to the jurisdictional restrictions of such authorities (or organizations).

Section 6 [Application and Review Procedures]

SMEs may file assistance applications with the public legal service providers in the Pudong New Area if they meet the criteria in Section 4 of these Provisions.

区公共法律服务机构核查企业经营状况，可以通过信息共享查询，或者由企业进行诚信承诺。

区司法行政部门可以在管理局（管委会）、街道办事处、镇人民政府设立便企窗口，为小微企业申请法律帮扶提供咨询引导。

第七条 （法律帮扶人员和志愿者）

区司法行政部门组建法律帮扶律师库。律师库成员应当同时符合以下条件：

（一）在本区律师事务所执业；

（二）从事法律服务工作满三年；

（三）热心公益。

区公共法律服务机构从律师库中选派律师担任法律帮扶人员，为小微企业提供针对性法律帮扶服务。

支持符合条件的机构和个人作为志愿者，参与小微企业法律帮扶工作。

第八条 （履职要求）

法律帮扶人员应当及时为受助企业提供符合行业标准的法律服务，维护受助企业的合法权益。

法律帮扶人员应当恪守职业道德和执业纪律，不得在法律帮扶过程中向受助企业收取任何财物。

区公共法律服务机构、法律帮扶人员、志愿者对在法律服务过程中知悉的国家秘密、商业秘密和个人隐私应当予以保密。

第九条 （双方申请处理）

争议双方均符合法律帮扶条件的，区公共法律服务机构应当选派不同法律服务机构的法律帮扶人员办理，并优先引导双方进行调解。

The public legal service providers in the Pudong New Area shall verify the operational status of businesses via information exchanges or declarations from SMEs.

The judicial administration of the Pudong New Area shall set up a service counter for SMEs to facilitate access to legal advice and guidance services at administrative bureaus (or administration committees), sub-district offices, and township governments.

Section 7 [Legal Assistance Providers and Volunteers]

A directory of eligible lawyers is to be created by the judicial administration of the Pudong New Area. Eligible lawyers shall:

(1) practice within the Pudong New Area;

(2) have been engaged in legal services for no less than three years; and

(3) show a commitment to public welfare.

From this directory, the public legal service providers in the Pudong New Area shall select candidates to offer specialized legal assistance to SMEs.

Organizations and individuals meeting volunteer criteria are encouraged to participate in the legal assistance services for SMEs.

Section 8 [Performance Requirements]

Legal assistance providers shall deliver prompt and standard-compliant services and protect lawful rights and interests of the entities they assist.

Legal assistance providers shall maintain professional ethics and discipline and not accept any payment from the entities they assist.

The public legal service providers in the Pudong New Area, practitioners, and volunteers shall keep any national secrets, trade secrets, and personal privacy obtained while providing legal services confidential.

Section 9 [Application by Both Parties]

If both parties to a dispute are eligible for legal assistance, the public legal service provider in the Pudong New Area shall assign legal assistance providers from other legal service providers and prioritize mediation.

第十条 （帮扶费用）

区人民政府按照本规定为小微企业法律帮扶提供必要的经费支持。

鼓励相关单位和个人通过捐赠、设立基金等方式，对小微企业法律帮扶经费进行补充。

探索小微企业通过分担部分帮扶费用的方式维护自身合法权益。

鼓励公证机构、司法鉴定机构对受助企业减收部分公证费、鉴定费。

第十一条 （信息化保障）

区司法行政部门可以依托法律科技企业，建设信息化、智能化法律服务平台，提高小微企业法律帮扶的便利性和可及性。

第十二条 （表彰奖励）

区人民政府及其司法行政部门按照有关规定，对在小微企业法律帮扶工作中作出突出贡献的法律服务机构和人员进行表彰和奖励。

第十三条 （违规处理）

小微企业以欺骗或者其他不正当手段获得法律帮扶被查实的，不得再次申请法律帮扶。

法律服务机构及法律帮扶人员在提供小微企业法律帮扶过程中有不当行为的，由区司法行政部门按照有关规定处理。

第十四条 （实施细则）

本规定的具体实施细则，由区司法行政部门另行制定。

第十五条 （施行时间）

本规定自 2024 年 2 月 1 日起施行，有效期至 2026 年 1 月 31 日。

Section 10 [Assistance Expenses]

The Pudong New Area People's Government shall offer necessary financial support for SME legal services as prescribed by these Provisions.

Additional contributions through donations and funds from entities or individuals are encouraged.

The possibility of allowing SMEs to contribute to a portion of legal assistance expenses to safeguard their lawful rights and interests is to be explored.

Forensic identification and notary services are encouraged to reduce fees for entities they assist.

Section 11 [Information Technology Support]

The judicial administration of the Pudong New Area may collaborate with eligible technology enterprises to develop an IT-based and intelligent legal service platform and simplify access to legal support for SMEs.

Section 12 [Recognition and Rewards]

Legal service providers and practitioners that significantly contribute to SME support may be recognized and rewarded by the Pudong New Area People's Government and its judicial administration as required.

Section 13 [Enforcement Against Violations]

SMEs shall be barred from future assistance if they secure legal assistance through deceitful means or other improper methods and such instances are verified.

Misconduct by legal service providers or practitioners during the provision of legal services to SMEs shall be handled by the judicial administration of the Pudong New Area as required.

Section 14 [Implementation Guidelines]

The specific implementation guidelines are to be created separately by the judicial administration of the Pudong New Area.

Section 15 [Validity Period]

These Provisions shall take effect from February 1, 2024, and remain valid until January 31, 2026.

浦东新区人防工程管理若干规定

Several Provisions of the Pudong New Area on the Administration of Air Raid Shelter Projects

浦东新区人防工程管理若干规定

（2023 年 12 月 27 日浦府管规〔2023〕6 号印发）

第一条 （目的和依据）

为了加强本区人防工程建设和使用管理，提高城市整体防护能力，根据《上海市人民代表大会常务委员会关于加强浦东新区高水平改革开放法治保障制定浦东新区法规的决定》以及相关规定，结合浦东新区实际，制定本规定。

第二条 （工作原则）

人防工程的建设、使用、维护及其相关管理活动应当遵循确保安全、功能完备、责任明晰、属地管理的原则。

第三条 （主管部门职责）

浦东新区国防动员办公室（以下简称“区国动办”）负责本区人防工程的建设和使用管理以及综合协调工作，对街道办事处、镇人民政府以及具有相关管理职能的管理局（管委会）（以下简称“区域管理单位”）开展辖区内人防工程的管理工作进行指导、监督以及考核。

第四条 （区域管理单位职责）

区域管理单位根据国防动员工作要求履行以下职责：

（一）指定具体部门开展人防工程监督管理工作，建立巡查机制开展巡查检查、督促使用备案和隐患整改等工作；

Several Provisions of the Pudong New Area on the Administration of Air Raid Shelter Projects

(PGMM [2023] No.6, December 27, 2023)

Section 1 [Purpose and Basis]

The Several Provisions of the Pudong New Area on the Administration of Air Raid Shelter Projects (these "Provisions") are formulated to improve administration over the use and construction of air raid shelter projects in this district to improve urban defense capabilities, pursuant to the Decision of the Shanghai Municipal People's Congress Standing Committee on Formulating Regulations to Improve Law-based Safeguards for High-level Reform and Opening-up in the Pudong New Area, and other applicable provisions, and in light of the actual circumstance in the Pudong New Area.

Section 2 [Working Principles]

The construction, use, maintenance, and administration of air raid shelter projects shall comply with the principles of safety assurance, full functionality, clear responsibilities, and jurisdiction-based administration.

Section 3 [Competent Department Responsibilities]

The Pudong New Area National Defense Mobilization Office (the "District Defense Mobilization Office") takes charge of the administration of air raid shelter project construction and use, as well as the overall coordination of air raid shelter projects in the district. This Office takes charge of providing guidance and oversight for, and evaluating air raid shelter administration carried out by sub-district offices, township governments, and appropriate administrative bureaus (or administration committees) ("Regional Administrative Departments") concerning air raid shelter management within their jurisdictions.

Section 4 [Regional Administrative Department Responsibilities]

Regional Administrative Departments are required to fulfill the following obligations pursuant to national defense mobilization requirements:

(1) designate appropriate departments to oversee and manage air raid shelter projects, establish inspection systems, conduct inspections, oversee the documentation of usage records, and address potential hazards;

（二）指导辖区内建设工程企业、物业服务企业等单位以及个人做好人防工程的建设、使用和维护管理；

（三）发生突发事件时，按照有关要求及时处置并向区国动办报告；

（四）开展法治宣传，提高全社会人防工程使用安全意识和管理水平。

第五条　（管理责任人）

人防工程的管理责任人包括投资人、所有权人和使用人。

第六条　（日常指导和检查）

区域管理单位应当指导其他人防工程管理责任人建立人防工程安全使用管理制度、制定突发事件应急预案、开展日常自查和整改等工作。

区域管理单位应当开展人防工程日常检查，每季度至少一次；检查中发现问题的，督促相关责任主体及时整改。

区域管理单位应当在检查后填写人防工程安全使用日常检查单，做好信息核查和更新，并将检查情况及时报送区国动办。

第七条　（档案信息移交）

人防工程建设单位应当配合区国动办开展人防工程现场查验、核对工作，提供项目工程基础信息，向人防工程管理责任人提供一套满足平时维护管理、战时使用需要的人防工程档案。

人防工程管理责任人应当对建设单位移交的人防工程设施设备信息进行核对，经确认信息准确无误、土建结构以及防护设施设备效能完好后，接收人防工程并纳入日常管理。人防工程管理责任人应当自人防工程投入使用之日起10日内，向区国动办申请办理备案手续。

(2) provide guidance to organizations like construction companies, property management companies, and individuals within their jurisdictions to ensure proper construction, utilization, and maintenance for air raid shelter projects;

(3) respond to emergencies in accordance with the applicable requirements and report to the District Defense Mobilization Office; and

(4) implement public legal education initiatives to enhance safety awareness and management of air raid shelter projects.

Section 5 [Responsible Managers]

Investors, owners, and users shall take charge of managing air raid shelter projects.

Section 6 [Routine Guidance and Inspection]

Regional Administrative Departments shall provide ongoing guidance to managers responsible for air raid shelter projects to establish management systems that ensure the safe use of the projects, develop emergency response plans, and carry out routine internal assessments and improvements.

Regional Administrative Departments are required to carry out routine inspections at least once quarterly, directing the responsible parties to promptly address any issues found during routine inspections.

Following each inspection, Regional Administrative Departments shall complete a routine inspection form for the safe use of air raid shelter projects, verify and update the recorded information, and promptly submit the inspection results to the District Defense Mobilization Office.

Section 7 [Records Transfer]

Air raid shelter project construction entities are required to coordinate with the District Defense Mobilization Office for on-site inspections and reviews, provide the necessary project data, and deliver a complete set of records covering both routine maintenance and management, and wartime use requirements to the responsible project managers.

Responsible air raid shelter project managers shall review any information about the air raid shelter project equipment submitted by construction entities, as well as the functionality of any structural and protective equipment, before incorporating the air raid shelter project into routine management. They are then required to complete filing procedures with the District Defense Mobilization Office within ten days of the initial use of the air raid shelters

新建人防工程资料归档后，区国动办应当将人防工程信息和备案信息告知相关区域管理单位。区域管理单位应当会同区国动办进行现场查验、核对，及时更正工程基础信息，将新建人防工程纳入日常管理。

第八条 （人防工程使用和维护管理）

人防工程管理责任人可以采取多种形式使用人防工程，但不得影响人防工程的防护效能，并且应当符合国家和本市有关消防、治安、卫生、市场监督管理、物价等方面的规定。公用人防工程使用费的标准，按照本市国有资源（资产）有偿使用的相关规定执行。其他人防工程使用收益应当优先保障人防工程防护结构和专用设施设备的维护和更新，确保人防工程完好。

人防工程管理责任人应当贯彻执行市、区有关人防工程维护管理的要求，落实维护管理人员和经费，制定维修养护管理制度和计划。人防工程维护管理可以采取自行或者委托第三方的方式进行。

第九条 （平战转换）

人防工程管理责任人应当对人防工程平战转换设施设备进行检查、维修和保养，适时更新平战转换应急实施方案，在临战前按照国家和市、区要求做好平战转换工作，确保达到防护标准和要求。

第十条 （物联设施设备接入和信息推送）

新建人防工程按照要求设置或者已建人防工程设有物联设施设备的，区国动办和区域管理单位应当指导建设单位或者管理责任人将物联设施设备、视频监控接入区人防工程网格化平台，并及时推送相关数据和报警处置信息。

Following the completion of filing procedures for newly constructed air raid shelter projects, the District Defense Mobilization Office shall notify the appropriate Regional Administrative Departments of the project details and filing details for necessary follow-up actions. Regional Administrative Departments shall collaborate with the District Defense Mobilization Office to carry out on-site inspections and reviews, promptly correct any discrepancies in the basic project information, and incorporate the newly constructed air raid shelter projects into routine administration.

Section 8 [Use and Maintenance of Air Raid Shelter Projects]

Responsible air raid shelter project managers may utilize the projects in various ways, provided that such use does not compromise the project's protection effectiveness or violate national or municipal provisions on fire safety, public order, sanitation, market regulation, and pricing. The fee standards for using the public air raid shelter projects shall be subject to the relevant regulations on the paid use of state-owned resources (assets) of this Municipality. Any revenue generated from the use of the air raid shelter projects shall be prioritized for the maintenance and improvement of protective structures and equipment of such projects to ensure the integrity of the project.

Responsible air raid shelter project managers shall enforce local and district maintenance policies related to air raid shelter projects, provide the necessary management staffing and funding, and develop maintenance policies and schedules. Air raid shelter project maintenance may be performed internally or entrusted to third parties.

Section 9 [Transition from Peacetime to Wartime]

Responsible air raid shelter project managers shall inspect, repair, and maintain facilities and equipment to facilitate transitioning from peacetime operation to wartime readiness, regularly update emergency implementation plans for the transition, and carry out all transition work in compliance with defense standards and requirements in anticipation of imminent conflicts, as mandated by national, municipal, and district requirements.

Section 10 [Integration of IoT Devices and Information Relay]

The District Defense Mobilization Office and Regional Administrative Departments shall guide construction entities and responsible managers on connecting IoT devices and video monitoring systems for any new or existing air raid shelter projects equipped with IoT devices to the district's jurisdictional platform, ensuring prompt data communication and responses to alerts.

第十一条 （考核评价）

区国动办应当从日常检查、闭环处置、使用备案、台账资料、应急保障、法治宣传等方面对区域管理单位开展人防工程监督管理工作情况进行考核评价，并纳入年度绩效考核。

第十二条 （信用监管）

区域管理单位应当按照相关信用评价标准，对辖区内信用评价对象进行信用信息计分，并建立信用档案。相关信用信息报送区国动办汇总后上报市国防动员办公室，纳入信用管理系统。

区国动办应当按照信用管理相关规定，将人防工程相关责任单位或者个人在建设使用管理过程中的行政处罚信息，归集到公共信用信息服务平台，并依法对严重失信主体采取联合惩戒措施。

第十三条 （社会监督）

任何单位或者个人不得实施擅自拆除、破坏、占用人防工程等行为。

对破坏人防工程和影响人防工程防护效能的行为，任何单位或者个人都有权制止并向区国动办举报。

第十四条 （指引条款）

违反本规定的行为，法律、法规、规章有相应行政处罚规定的，依照有关法律、法规、规章处理。

区国动办在行政执法过程中发现违法行为涉嫌构成犯罪的，应当依法向公安机关移送涉嫌犯罪案件。

第十五条 （施行日期）

本规定自 2024 年 2 月 1 日起施行，有效期至 2029 年 1 月 31 日。

Section 11 [Evaluation and Assessment]

The District Defense Mobilization Office shall evaluate the performance of Regional Administrative Departments based on their administration of air raid shelter projects, including routine inspections, comprehensive management, usage documentation, work data, emergency preparedness, and public legal education, which are to be incorporated into annual performance reviews.

Section 12 [Credit Regulation]

Regional Administrative Departments shall assess and score evaluation entity credit within their jurisdictions pursuant to credit standards and create detailed credit profiles. The District Defense Mobilization Office will compile necessary data and report it to the municipal level, integrating it into the national credit management system.

The District Defense Mobilization Office shall compile administrative penalty data related to companies or individuals involved in the construction or use of air raid shelter projects and upload this information to public credit service information platforms pursuant to applicable credit administration regulations. Serious violators shall be subject to lawful disciplinary action.

Section 13 [Public Oversight]

No organization or individual may engage in unauthorized dismantling, destruction, or occupation of air raid shelter projects.

Organizations and individuals are encouraged to prevent and report any activities that affect the integrity or protective effectiveness of these projects to the District Defense Mobilization Office.

Section 14 [Governing Law]

Where applicable laws, regulations, or rules prescribe administrative penalties for violations of these Provisions, such violations shall be addressed in accordance with the governing legal provisions.

If the District Defense Mobilization Office discovers illegal activities during its enforcement that may constitute a criminal offense, it shall refer these matters to the public security department as required by law.

Section 15 [Validity Period]

These Provisions shall take effect from February 1, 2024, and remain valid until January 31, 2029.

浦东新区住宅小区房屋应急维修服务管理若干规定

Several Provisions of the Pudong New Area on the Management of Emergency Housing Repair Services in Residential Areas

浦东新区住宅小区房屋应急维修服务管理若干规定

（2023 年 12 月 29 日浦府管规〔2023〕7 号印发）

第一条 （目的和依据）

为了规范浦东新区住宅小区房屋应急维修服务，优化房屋应急维修服务体系，提升应急维修服务保障能级，根据《上海市人民代表大会常务委员会关于加强浦东新区高水平改革开放法治保障制定浦东新区法规的决定》以及相关规定，结合浦东新区实际，制定本规定。

第二条 （适用范围）

浦东新区行政区域内住宅小区房屋应急维修服务（以下简称“房屋应急维修服务”）及其监督管理，适用本规定。

本规定所称的房屋应急维修服务，是指区房屋应急维修指挥平台（以下简称“区应急维修平台”）、街镇房屋应急维修特约服务站（以下简称“街镇服务站”）以及物业服务企业对存在排水管道堵塞、屋顶外墙墙面渗漏等严重影响居民生活情况的住宅小区房屋及其配套设施设备提供的应急性维修服务。

第三条 （总体要求）

本区房屋应急维修服务应当坚持条块结合、属地管理、分级协同、有偿服务、政府补贴的原则，通过提升房屋应急维修协同服务能力和综合管理水平，不断增强群众的满意度、获得感。

Several Provisions of the Pudong New Area on the Management of Emergency Housing Repair Services in Residential Areas

(PGMM [2023] No.7, December 29, 2023)

Section 1 [Purpose and Basis]

The Several Provisions of the Pudong New Area on the Management of Emergency Housing Repair Services in Residential Areas (these "Provisions") are formulated to regulate emergency housing repair services in residential areas, improve the emergency housing repair services system, and improve safeguards for emergency housing repair services, pursuant to the Decision of the Shanghai Municipal People's Congress Standing Committee on Formulating Regulations to Improve Law-based Safeguards for High-level Reform and Opening-up in the Pudong New Area and other applicable provisions, and in light of the actual circumstances in the Pudong New Area.

Section 2 [Applicable Scope]

These Provisions shall apply to emergency housing repair services for residential communities in the Pudong New Area and their administration.

"Emergency housing repair services" in these Provisions refer to the emergency repair services provided by the District Housing Emergency Repair Guidance Platform (the "District Emergency Repair Platform"), sub-district and township housing emergency repair service centers ("Sub-district and Township Service Centers") and property management companies for residential areas and their supporting equipment and facilities impacted by issues such as blocked drains and leaks on the exterior walls of roofs that significantly affect residents' quality of life.

Section 3 [General Requirements]

Emergency housing repair services in this district shall follow the principles of comprehensive management, jurisdiction-based administration, hierarchical coordination, paid services, and government subsidies for the ongoing improvement of public satisfaction and accomplishments by improving emergency service coordination and integrated management capabilities.

第四条 （行业管理）

区建交委负责建立健全本区房屋应急维修服务体系，统筹协调房屋应急维修服务工作。

区物业管理事务中心设立区应急维修平台，并负责对区应急维修平台、街镇服务站进行指导、监督、考核，对物业服务企业提供房屋应急维修服务进行监督管理。

区应急维修平台具体承担以下职能：

（一）对街镇服务站、物业服务企业进行业务指导；

（二）承担房屋应急维修服务诉求的受理、交办和督办；

（三）协同街镇服务站和物业服务企业提供房屋应急维修服务；

（四）承担上级部门交办的其他房屋应急维修任务。

第五条 （属地责任）

街道办事处、镇人民政府负责辖区内房屋应急维修服务管理工作，设立街镇服务站，推进街镇服务站标准化建设，保障街镇服务站常态化运营，对街镇服务站、物业服务企业提供房屋应急维修服务进行指导和监督。

街镇服务站具体承担以下职能：

（一）受理处置辖区内房屋应急维修服务诉求，提供房屋应急维修服务；

（二）根据区应急维修平台统一调度，对辖区外房屋应急维修服务诉求提供支援；

（三）承担街道办事处、镇人民政府交办的其他房屋应急维修任务。

第六条 （物业服务企业职责）

住宅小区物业服务企业应当按照物业服务合同约定和物业管理服务规范对物业共用部位、共用设施设备提供房屋应急维修服务。

Section 4 [Industry Management]

The district construction and transportation committee takes charge of establishing and improving the emergency housing repair service system and coordinating emergency housing repair activities.

The district property management center creates the District Emergency Repair Platform and provide guidance, oversight, and assessment of the District Emergency Repair Platform and Sub-district and Township Service Centers, as well as regulate emergency housing repair services offered by the property management companies.

The District Emergency Repair Platform is assigned to:

(1) provide guidance for activities carried out by Sub-district and Township Service Centers and property service companies;

(2) manage the acceptance, processing, and oversight of emergency housing repair requests;

(3) coordinate with Sub-district and Township Service Centers and property management companies to ensure effective Emergency Housing Repair Service provision; and

(4) fulfill other emergency housing repair service tasks as directed by superior departments.

Section 5 [Jurisdiction-based Responsibilities]

Sub-district offices and township governments take charge of the administration of emergency repair services within their jurisdictions, establishing Sub-district and Township Service Centers and assisting in the centralized development of the Sub-district and Township Service Centers to ensure their effective operation, and regulating the emergency housing repair services offered by the Sub-district and Township Service Centers and property management companies.

Sub-district and Township Service Centers are assigned to :

(1) process and manage emergency repair requests within their jurisdictions and provide emergency housing repair services;

(2) assist with emergency housing repair requests outside their jurisdictions as directed by the District Emergency Repair Platform; and

(3) fulfill additional emergency repair tasks as required by sub-district offices and township governments.

Section 6 [Property Management Company Responsibilities]

Property management companies in residential areas shall provide emergency housing repair services for common areas, facilities, and equipment pursuant to their property service agreements and management standards.

鼓励有条件的物业服务企业对物业专有部分提供应急维修服务。

第七条 （房屋维修责任人）

住宅小区房屋所有权人为房屋维修责任人。房屋所有权人下落不明或者房屋权属不清的，房屋使用人为房屋维修责任人。房屋维修责任人应当依据《上海市住宅物业管理规定》《上海市房屋使用安全管理办法》以及《浦东新区住宅小区建筑物外墙墙面以及建筑附属构件脱落隐患治理办法》等规定，承担房屋应急维修服务费用。

第八条 （分级处置机制）

区应急维修平台、街镇服务站和物业服务企业自接到住宅小区房屋应急维修服务诉求后，原则上应当在30分钟内响应。

物业服务企业无法完成房屋应急维修服务的，可以由街镇服务站响应并提供应急维修服务；街镇服务站无法完成房屋应急维修服务的，可以由区应急维修平台响应并提供应急维修服务。

第九条 （紧急排险）

住宅小区房屋应急维修涉及危害公共安全情形的，物业服务企业应当立即向业主委员会、居（村）民委员会、街道办事处或者镇人民政府报告，并采取避险防范措施。

街道办事处、镇人民政府应当立即进行现场查看并视情采取紧急排险措施；无法完成紧急排险的，可以向区应急维修平台或者其他专业部门请求支援。

第十条 （服务公开）

区应急维修平台、街镇服务站应当公开房屋应急维修服务项目、服务流程、收费标准、报修渠道、监督方式等服务信息。

Eligible property management companies are encouraged to provide emergency repair services for specific parts of the property.

Section 7 [Housing Repair Responsible Parties]

Property owners in residential areas are responsible for repairs on their own properties. In instances where the owner is absent or property ownership is uncertain, the occupant shall be responsible for any necessary housing repairs. Those responsible for housing repairs shall bear the costs for emergency housing repair services pursuant to the Provisions of Shanghai Municipality on Residential Property Management, Procedures of Shanghai Municipality on the Administration of Residential Safety, and Procedures of the Pudong New Area on Addressing Potential Hazards from Falling Facades and Other Architectural Features of Residential Compound Buildings, and other applicable provisions.

Section 8 [Hierarchical Management Process]

The District Emergency Repair Platform, Sub-district and Township Service Centers, and property management companies shall respond to emergency housing repair service requests within thirty minutes.

If a property management company is unable to provide the necessary emergency housing repair services, a Sub-district and Township Service Center may take over and provide the emergency repair services; if a Sub-district and Township Service Center is unable to provide the emergency housing repair services, the District Emergency Repair Platform may intervene and provide emergency repair services.

Section 9 [Emergency Risk Mitigation]

If an emergency housing repair in a residential areas poses a public safety risk, property management companies shall immediately notify the appropriate residents' (or villagers') committees, sub-district offices, or township governments and take necessary actions to mitigate risks.

Sub-district offices and township governments are required to promptly inspect the site and take necessary actions to mitigate risks, and may seek assistance from the District Emergency Repair Platform or other professional agencies if they are unable to effectively mitigate risks.

Section 10 [Service Disclosure]

The District Emergency Repair Platform and Sub-district and Township Service Centers shall provide the public with information about emergency housing repair service availability, service procedures, charging standards, reporting channels, and oversight methods.

物业服务企业应当公开房屋维修服务办事制度、办事纪律、服务项目和收费标准等服务信息。

第十一条 （保障措施）

区应急维修平台、街镇服务站应当配备与房屋应急维修服务相适应的人员、设施设备和应急物资，按照规定对维修服务人员开展专业培训，定期对设施设备进行保养，根据实际情况及时调整应急物资储备。

鼓励区应急维修平台、街镇服务站和物业服务企业加强房屋应急维修信息化建设，健全房屋应急维修信息共享机制，推动房屋应急维修服务线上线下高效协同。

区物业管理事务中心和街道办事处、镇人民政府应当根据房屋应急维修情况分别为区应急维修平台、街镇服务站提供必要的补贴。

第十二条 （监督检查）

区建交委、区物业管理事务中心应当对区应急维修平台、街镇服务站和物业服务企业进行监督检查，发现存在问题的，督促及时整改落实。

第十三条 （考核评价）

区物业管理事务中心应当建立考核制度，制定房屋应急维修服务规范和考核标准，对区应急维修平台、街镇服务站的业务能力、服务水平以及机构建设等方面进行考核评价。

区应急维修平台、街镇服务站在应急维修服务过程中未按照协议约定提供应急维修服务的，相关部门、单位可以对其进行诫勉、约谈，督促及时整改。

物业服务企业存在失信行为的，按照信用管理有关规定记入信用档案。

Property management companies shall disclose their operational policies, rules of conduct, services, and charging standards for housing repairs.

Section 11 [Precautions]

The District Emergency Repair Platform and Sub-district and Township Service Centers shall employ the appropriate technicians, equipment, and emergency supplies to carry out emergency housing repair services. This includes providing ongoing professional training for the repair technicians, regularly maintaining equipment, and updating emergency supplies as needed.

District Emergency Repair Platform, Sub-district and Township Service Centers, and property management companies should improve the use of technologies for emergency housing repairs, optimize a data-sharing system for emergency housing repairs, and assist in the effective online and offline coordination of emergency housing repair services.

The district property management center, sub-district offices, and township governments are required to provide the necessary financial support for the District Emergency Repair Platform and Sub-district and Township Service Centers for the emergency housing repairs as necessary.

Section 12 [Oversight and Inspection]

The district construction and transportation committee and the district property management center shall oversee and inspect the District Emergency Repair Platform, Sub-district and Township Service Centers, and property management companies, and ensure the prompt correction of any issues identified.

Section 13 [Assessments and Evaluations]

The district property management center shall establish a system for emergency housing repair services, develop service standards and criteria, and evaluate the operational capabilities, service quality, and performance improvements of the District Emergency Repair Platforms and Sub-district and Township Service Centers.

District Emergency Repair Platform or Sub-district and Township Service Centers that fail to provide emergency repair services as agreed shall be subject to warnings or interviews to ensure prompt corrective action by the appropriate departments or parties.

Any deceptive acts by property management companies shall be recorded in their credit profile pursuant to applicable credit management provisions.

第十四条 （实施细则）

本规定的具体实施细则，由区建交委另行制定。

第十五条 （施行日期）

本规定自 2024 年 2 月 1 日起施行，有效期至 2029 年 1 月 31 日。

Section 14 [Implementation Guidelines]

The district construction and transportation committee takes charge of issuing the implementation guidelines for these Provisions.

Section 15 [Validity Period]

These Provisions shall take effect from February 1, 2024, and remain valid until January 31, 2029.